HISTORY AND LITERATURE IN CONTEMPORARY RUSSIA

History and Literature in Contemporary Russia

Rosalind Marsh
Professor of Russian Studies
University of Bath

NEW YORK UNIVERSITY PRESS
Washington Square, New York

First published in the U.S.A. in 1995 by
NEW YORK UNIVERSITY PRESS
Washington Square
New York, N.Y. 10003

Library of Congress Cataloging-in-Publication Data
Marsh, Rosalind J.
History and literature in contemporary Russia / Rosalind Marsh.
p.   cm.
Includes bibliographical references and index.
ISBN 0–8147–5527–5
1. Russian literature—20th century—History and criticism.
2. Literature and history—Russia (Federation)   3. Literature and
history—Soviet Union.   I. Title.
PG2975.M34   1995
891.7'09358—dc20   94–39054
                                                    CIP

Printed in Great Britain

Nothing is as unpredictable as the past.

Jean-Paul Sartre

Those who cannot remember the past are condemned to repeat it.

George Santayana

The literature-centredness of our society is an atavism, something like a tail which will fall off with the advent of civilization.

Alla Latynina, 1991

Contents

Acknowledgements

Research for this book has been conducted over six years, from 1987 to 1993, and has involved work in a number of libraries in Britain, Russia and the USA. I should like to thank the British Council for awarding me a three-month fellowship in Leningrad from February to April 1991, and the Kennan Institute for Advanced Russian Studies, Washington, DC, for a one-month fellowship in July 1991. I am also grateful to the Universities of Exeter and Bath for allowing me to take sabbatical terms, and to St Antony's College, Oxford, for making me a Senior Research Associate.

For useful references and assistance on a number of specific points I am grateful to Edwin Bacon, Archie Brown, Anne Davenport, R. W. Davies, David Gillespie, Robert Lewis, Michael Nicholson, Riitta Pittman, Robert Service, Gerald Smith, Arch Tait and Anne and Howard White. I have greatly benefited from conversations with Evgenii Anisimov, German Baluev, Mikhail Berg, Elena Chizhova, Natal'ya Ivanova, Nina Katerli, Alla Latynina, Aron Lur'e, Larisa Miller, Ol'ga Sedakova and Vitalii Shentalinskii. I also owe a general debt to a larger group of friends and colleagues, too numerous to mention individually, with whom I have discussed questions about literature, history and politics in Russia since the inception of *glasnost*.

I am particularly grateful for the help of Katy Jordan in the Bath University Library, David Howells, the Slavonic Librarian of the Taylorian Library, Oxford, and Jackie Willcox, Librarian of the Russian Library, St Antony's College, Oxford. Thanks are also due to the library staffs of the Saltykov–Shchedrin Public Library in St Petersburg, the Library of Congress in Washington, the Bodleian Library in Oxford and the Exeter University Library. I have also greatly benefited from the technical assistance of James Davenport, Robert Madden and Christopher Williams.

As always, special thanks are due to my parents, Ernest and Joyce Marsh, without whose unfailing help and support this book would never have been completed at a time of cataclysmic change in Russia and considerable upheaval in my own life.

Note on the Text

Translations are my own, unless otherwise stated. The transliteration system is a modified version of that used in *Europe–Asia Studies*. In the text, names such as Alexander and Pyotr and the surnames of prominent historical and political figures such as Trotsky, Zinoviev, Yeltsin and Zhirinovsky, and well-known Russian terms such as *glasnost*, are rendered in their more familiar, rather than their more strictly transliterated forms. Sources in the notes are cited in full on their first occurrence in each chapter, and thereafter in abbreviated form.

Fuller discussions of some of the issues treated in Chapter 12 and the Conclusion can be found in my articles: 'Reassessing the Past: Images of Stalin and Stalinism in Contemporary Russian Literature', in S. Duffin Graham (ed.), *New Directions in Soviet Literature* (Basingstoke and London: Macmillan, 1992), pp. 89–105; 'The Death of Soviet Literature: Can Russian Literature Survive?', *Europe-Asia Studies*, vol. 45, no. 1 (1993), pp. 115–39; and '*Glasnost* and Russian Literature', *Australian Slavonic and East European Studies*, vol. 6, no. 2 (1992), pp. 21–39.

List of Abbreviations

ASEES	*Australian Slavonic and East European Studies*
BASEES	British Association of Slavonic and East European Studies
CDSP	*Current Digest of the Soviet Press*
CDPSP	*Current Digest of the Post-Soviet Press*
CPSU	Communist Party of the Soviet Union
DN	*Druzhba narodov*
KGB	acronym for Soviet Secret Police after 1953; stands for State Security Committee
KO	*Knizhnoe obozrenie*
Komsomol	Young Communist League
KP	*Komsomol'skaya pravda*
KPSS	Communist Party of the Soviet Union
L.	Leningrad
LG	*Literaturnaya gazeta*
LO	*Literaturnoe obozrenie*
LR	*Literaturnaya Rossiya*
M.	Moscow
MG	*Molodaya gvardiya*
MGB	initials for Soviet Secret Police, 1946–53; acronym for Ministry of State Security; succeeded by KGB
MN	*Moskovskie novosti*
MSPS	International Community of Writers' Unions
NEP	acronym for New Economic Policy, a period of limited private enterprise, 1921–8
NG	*Nezavisimaya gazeta*
NKVD	designation of Soviet secret police, 1934–43; acronym for People's Commissariat of Internal Affairs
NM	*Novyi mir*
NS	*Nash sovremennik*
NY	New York
OGPU	designation of Soviet Secret Police, 1922–34; acronym for United State Political Administration
RFE	*Radio Free Europe*
RG	*Rossiiskaya gazeta*

RL	*Radio Liberty*
RM	*Russkaya mysl'*
RSFSR	Russian Soviet Federated Socialist Republic
SEER	*Slavonic and East European Review*
SK	*Sovetskaya kul'tura*
SR	*Sovetskaya Rossiya*
SR	Socialist Revolutionary
Sob. soch.	*Sobranie sochinenii*
SWB	*Summary of World Broadcasts*
THES	*Times Higher Education Supplement*
TLS	*Times Literary Supplement*
VI	*Voprosy istorii*
VL	*Voprosy literatury*
VRKhD	*Vestnik russkogo khristianskogo dvizheniya*

Introduction

The period since 1985 has been the most astonishing in the entire history of twentieth-century Russian culture. An unprecedented information explosion, and a flood of fiction by writers both living and dead which had never before been published in Russia has burst on the public. This amounted to far more than the 'thaw' which took place under Khrushchev; it was nothing less than a cultural and spiritual revolution. In recognition of this, Alec Nove characterized the period up to 1989 as one of 'cultural renaissance in Russia',[1] and Vitalii Shentalinskii, a member of the commission formed to investigate the cases of writers falsely condemned in Stalin's purges, spoke in 1990 of 'the formation of a new country and a new people'.[2] After the momentous events of 1991, when the Communist Party of the Soviet Union has been swept away after seventy-four years and the USSR has disintegrated, it would seem a suitable time to analyse one important aspect of the cultural revolution in the period since 1985: the relationship between history and literature, and the contribution which this relationship has made to the process of political change in Russia.

History and literature are closely related in every culture. A society's representation of its past is central to that society's understanding and definition of itself; and literature set in a historical context is one of the aesthetic forms best suited to an exploration of the complexities of past experience and to conveying these perceptions to a wide audience. In Russia the link between history and literature has always been particularly close. Nineteenth-century Russian writers regarded themselves as the chroniclers and conscience of their nation;[3] and this tradition has been inherited by many twentieth-century Russian writers. In Solzhenitsyn's *The First Circle*, for example, the writer Galakhov says, speaking for the author: 'For a country to have a great writer is like having a second government.'

Throughout most of the period 1917–85, and particularly since Stalin's rise to power in the late 1920s, the Soviet political leaders established control over all aspects of culture, including history and literature. They appropriated history and historical fiction, since they regarded control over the past as a key to their control over the present. History was to be used not merely to establish the truth about the past, but for the purpose of social engineering in the present. Together, history and

1

literature served the Communist Party, distorting the past and corrupting people's understanding of the present.

At no time has the relationship between history and literature in Russia been more significant than since Gorbachev's accession in 1985. Initially, the main focus of the Russian cultural revival was a widespread re-examination of Soviet and pre-revolutionary history, far surpassing the earlier reassessment which took place under Khrushchev. Literature played a very important part in this process, opening up new subjects for historical enquiry and challenging historians to produce a deeper analysis of their country's past. From 1987/8 millions of Soviet people became actively involved in studying their country's history, and this led to a far-reaching re-evaluation of the theoretical principles and the political practice of the Soviet state. Such a profound reassessment of the values officially propagated and privately cherished in the USSR since 1917 in turn radically altered Soviet people's understanding of their own history and paved the way for the dramatic political changes of the 1990s.

Studies of Gorbachev's USSR and the new post-communist era by political scientists and economists sometimes underestimate or even totally omit the cultural and spiritual factors which have transformed the consciousness of the Soviet people since 1985; but I would contend that literature and cultural debate played a more important role than either political science or historiography in 'preparing *perestroika* in the minds of the people'.[4] The aim of the present book is to rectify the omission, and thus to make a contribution to the social, intellectual and cultural history of Russia and the former USSR since 1985. It is important for historians to take account of literary works and public debates among the intelligentsia, since many Russian intellectuals, like their counterparts in Eastern Europe, are prominent public figures, and their ideas have exerted considerable influence on the political leaders and the population at large. Moreover, the changed climate of opinion among the Russian people which enabled them to resist the coup of August 1991 is to a significant extent attributable to the historical, political and cultural debates which took place in the media under *glasnost*.

The main subject of this book is a study of the reception of literary works newly published in Russia since 1985 which examine important aspects of twentieth-century Russian history. Historians such as Alec Nove and R. W. Davies have noted that historical fiction played a major part in reassessing the past and changing social attitudes in Gorbachev's Russia,[5] but no attempt has yet been made to provide an overview of this literary material, or to explore the role it played in transforming public opinion, and hence in promoting the gradual disintegration of communist values and the dismantling of the old political and social system.

This study will be concerned with the way in which literary works on historical themes were presented to the Russian public and the debates they engendered in the press. These include both discussions about the historical accuracy of the facts or interpretations presented in works of fiction, and the political debates they provoked among different sections of Russian society. Literary criticism has traditionally been an influential battleground for public ideological and social debate in Russia, and in the Gorbachev era history and historical fiction were used as political weapons in the bitter and continuing conflict between communists, nationalists, reformists and radical democrats. Although literary works reassessing Russian history have been used by Russian liberals to create a climate of opinion which has already helped to change the Soviet political system and which, many people hope, may eventually lead to the establishment of a genuinely democratic society and functioning market economy in Russia, conservative critics have interpreted the same literary works in a different way, using them to propound alternative, nationalist views which have also exerted considerable influence in Russia, leading to the failed coup of August 1991 and the armed rebellion of October 1993.

From late 1989, as political change began to gather speed, Russians became more interested in the present than the past, and, although analogies with the past were still regarded as instructive, the genre of historical fiction began to be less important than before. Whereas in 1987/8 commentators had welcomed an exhilarating new period in Soviet culture,[6] by 1989 critics were remarking on the 'chaos and uncertainty' of the Russian political and cultural scene;[7] and by 1991 it had become fashionable to speak of the 'death' of Soviet literature.[8] The last part of the book will therefore attempt to analyse why the condition of both history and literature in Russia has changed so radically since the euphoric early days of *glasnost*. The conclusion will investigate the achievements and limitations of the newly published historical fiction, then focus on the difficulties and challenges still facing Russian writers and historians under Yeltsin's presidency.

The mental revolution in the former USSR has created difficulties for western Slavists, who for a long time have seen themselves as high priests, privileged guardians of some arcane, though essentially static mystery. After Gorbachev's accession the USSR became a dynamically evolving society, and western Slavists too were forced to undergo their own personal *perestroika*, to rethink all their past views on Soviet history and literature. This book demonstrates how far my own thinking about the history of Soviet literature has changed since I painted a somewhat bleak picture of the Soviet literary scene in the pre-Gorbachev era in my book *Soviet Fiction since Stalin* (1986).[9] Moreover, this study, conceived in the heady early days of Gorbachev's *glasnost*, has itself had to be continually revised under the pressure of changing events. A comprehensive new history of twentieth-century Russian literature remains to be written; but I hope to demonstrate that many Russian writers died before their most outspoken works could be published in the USSR, or expressed ideas in literature written se-cretly 'for the drawer' which could only be hinted at in their works published before 1985. The differences of opinion which have surfaced in public debates about literature and history since 1985 also graphi-cally illustrate the submerged pluralism which existed in Soviet society before *perestroika*, and alter our conception of Soviet social history.

REVIEW OF PREVIOUS LITERATURE

In the years 1985–93 an enormous amount of new material on Soviet literature and history has appeared in Russia – far too much to be encompassed by any one person. The development of Soviet historical thought by journalists and historians in the years 1985–8 has been ably documented by R. W. Davies and Stephen Wheatcroft,[10] and later supplemented by Pierre Broué, Judith Shapiro and other scholars.[11] Some valuable surveys of *glasnost* literature have appeared, notably those by Alec Nove and Walter Laqueur which concentrate on publicistic writing;[12] but because of the need for haste and topical comment, such general works have been able to do little more than provide factual information about the wealth of materials that had recently appeared in print. Works by historians and political scientists draw on various salient or striking features of recently published fiction in order to illustrate specific points, but do not discuss the content or reception of literary works in detail. Julian Graffy's useful survey of literary jour-nals in the Gorbachev era simply enumerates the important fictional works published up to early 1989;[13] while studies of literature and cultural politics by N. N. Shneidman and Riitta Pittman,[14] as well as the valuable anthology of *glasnost* literature by Helena Goscilo and Byron Lindsey,[15] select certain works of literature for detailed comment, but are not primarily concerned with literature on historical themes. My own book *Images of Dictatorship* contains a section on literature of the early Gorbachev era, but focuses on the depiction of Stalin as an individual rather than on wider historical issues.[16] Deming Brown's survey of the last fifteen years of Soviet Russian prose includes one short chapter on the reassessment of Stalinism, but is primarily concerned with individual writers and literary trends, not the political context or reception of literature.[17] Many interesting responses to individual writers or works have also appeared; but while literary scholars generally avoid the political debates these works have engendered, historians and political scientists have concentrated on the political and historical aspects of literature, to the exclusion of aesthetic considerations. The time has come for a more systematic analysis of works of historical fiction published in Russia since 1985 and the debates they have inspired.

LIMITATIONS OF THE SUBJECT MATTER

Several restrictions have been placed on the scope of this study. Because of the sheer quantity of literary works on historical themes and the critical responses to them which have appeared in Russia since 1985, no hope can be entertained of encompassing all the available material. Inevitably, therefore, this book will be highly selective and may omit works which others consider of primary importance, although it is hoped that such omissions will not affect the general thrust of the argument. The main focus of attention will be literature dealing with aspects of Soviet history since 1917, concentrating on the Lenin and Stalin periods, but reference will also be made to works dealing with twentieth-century Russian history before the Revolution. Although the informational content of literature and the historical, political and moral debates it has provoked will be the main focus of this book, it will not totally eschew literary comment and judgement. In any case, the absence of detailed discussion of the literary merits of the works under consideration does not mean to imply that the literature is worthless from the aesthetic point of view, although, obviously, the literary qualities of the works vary considerably (and some, which have aroused heated debate, raise difficult questions of individual taste and literary judgement).

The book will attempt to establish a chronology of *glasnost* in relation to Russian historical fiction, and to provide a survey of some of the more important works on a variety of historical themes, demonstrating how the subject matter of fiction has gradually widened since

Gorbachev's accession, moving from an analysis of Stalin and the Stalin era to a reassessment of the New Economic Policy, the Civil War and the 1920s, a discussion of the role of Lenin, and ultimately to a reconsideration of the February and October revolutions and the fall of tsarism. An attempt will be made to examine the lively debates engendered by historical fiction, setting works of literary criticism in the context of other *glasnost* publications by publicists and historians, and, sometimes, of discussions among the Russian émigré community. Such an analysis will provide interesting insights into the relationship between history, literature and politics in the Gorbachev era and raise general questions about the role of both literature and history in post-communist Russia.

The main focus of the book will be prose fiction, since this is the literary genre best suited to the serious exploration of historical issues, and which has exerted the most impact on Russian society since 1985.[18] Nevertheless, particularly important plays, poems, literary memoirs and films will also be discussed;[19] and works of literary criticism, *publitsistika* (social and political journalism) in the press and literary journals, political memoirs and historical works will also be extensively drawn upon for background information. In particular, emphasis will be placed on literary works published in Russia since 1985 which are not already well known to a western audience, although salient points raised in discussions of the better known works will also be considered. For reasons of space, the book will be confined to a brief survey of the main historical subjects covered in literature and the press, and the most important debates which have accompanied the publication of significant works of historical fiction. The main focus will be on literature published in the 'Gorbachev era' – the years 1985–91 – although a tentative attempt will also be made to analyse the situation of history and culture in post-communist Russia until early 1994, encompassing the aftermath of the December 1993 elections.

The disintegration of the USSR has led to some problems of terminology: the terms 'Soviet' and 'Soviet Union' are used to refer to the period up to the end of 1991, while 'Russian' either refers specifically to the Russian Federation, or to the pre-revolutionary or post-communist eras. While the main focus of the book will be Russia and Soviet Russian literature, there will also be some reference to Ukraine, Georgia and the Baltic states; and many statements about the impact of Russian historical fiction and *publitsistika* and the re-examination of Soviet history are relevant to all the countries of the former USSR.

1 The Background: History and Literature in Contemporary Russia

Literature on historical themes and the debates it has engendered should be viewed against a background composed of the broad political issues, the changing approach to historical subjects and the condition of Russian literature. The political and historical aspects will be discussed later in connection with specific themes. In this chapter, however, it will be useful to give a brief survey of the condition of Soviet history before Gorbachev's accession, and of literary politics and the cultural scene in Russia since 1985, in order to understand the wider context in which historical fiction should be set.

THE CONDITION OF SOVIET HISTORY

The radical historian Yurii Afanas'ev, appointed director of the State Historical Archival Institute at the end of 1986, declared in 1987: 'There is no country in the world with a more falsified history than ours.'[1] At Gorbachev's accession, party history was still being taught as a quasi-religious dogma, and was perceived by many Soviet people as a tedious formality to which they were expected to conform. In the 'era of stagnation' a series of purges, campaigns of vilification and ostracism had been conducted against the historical profession, particularly during the period 1965–80 when Brezhnev's associate S.P. Trapeznikov, a conservative historian and ruthless opponent of unorthodox ideas, had been head of the Department of Science and Educational Establishments of the Party Central Committee.[2] Such repression had created a legacy of caution among Soviet historians and a fear of expressing individual opinions which was to persist well into the Gorbachev era.[3]

Yet, as Stephen Wheatcroft has argued,[4] a 'general mass or folk understanding of history' has always co-existed in the USSR alongside an official party understanding and an academic understanding of history, and may come into conflict with them. This approach to history

7

includes the folk memory of participants in historical events, first-hand accounts passed on from family members and friends, as well as accounts circulating in the media through literature, films, radio and television. Even in the most repressive years of the 'era of stagnation', the Soviet authorities could exert little control over personal reminiscences and private discussions about the past. Since Khrushchev's de-Stalinization campaign, many families had experienced the release or rehabilitation of their members, while some influential families of former party officials, such as Bukharin and Rykov, continued to campaign for their rehabilitation. Thus, long before Gorbachev's accession, discussions about the past continued to rage in private, away from the official world of party or academic history.

Control could only be exerted over the more indirect level of culture and the media, but such control was imperfect, and even in the repressive atmosphere of the Brezhnev era not all liberal cultural influences could be suppressed. Literature continued to act as a 'moral opposition', even after the dismissal in 1970 of Alexander Tvardovskii as editor of *Novyi mir*, which in the years 1958–70 had enjoyed a reputation as the most liberal literary journal.[5] Certain interesting works of historical fiction continued to appear, such as Yurii Trifonov's anti-Stalinist novel *The House on the Embankment* (1976);[6] although the historical establishment sometimes intervened to condemn liberal works of which they disapproved, as in the case of Mikhail Shatrov's play *This is How We Conquer* (1982), which praised the New Economic Policy of the 1920s.[7] The impact of certain liberal literary works was felt even at the highest levels of the party. Gorbachev, who had begun his party career in the Khrushchev era and had been a delegate at the reforming Twenty-Second Congress of 1961 when Khrushchev denounced Stalin in public, was on record as saying that the Kirghiz writer Chingiz Aitmatov was his favourite author.[8] He may well have been influenced by Aitmatov's novel *The Day Lasts Longer than a Hundred Years* (1980), which exposes the destruction of the past by the Soviet regime. Aitmatov depicts strange characters called 'mankurts' who, according to a Central Asian legend, were prisoners who had been turned into slaves by having their heads wrapped in camel skins which under the hot sun dried as tight as a steel band. A mankurt did not remember his tribe, his family, or even his own name; he 'did not recognize himself as a human being'.[9] Gorbachev's sympathy for Aitmatov's work was publicly acknowledged in 1990, when Aitmatov became a member of Gorbachev's presidential council.

During the Brezhnev era, many of the shades of opinion on historical topics which have been publicly expressed under *glasnost* already existed in embryo. Sometimes the differences of opinion between liberals and Russian nationalists surfaced in public, as in the debate of 1969–70 between the nationalist journal *Molodaya gvardiya* and the liberal *Novyi mir;* similarly, in 1982 the nationalist tendency of *Nash sovremennik*, associated with Suslov, came into conflict with the internationalist, technocratic tendency associated with Andropov.[10] However, it was in *samizdat* (uncensored materials in typescript) and *tamizdat* (literature published only in the West) that the great differences of opinion in the interpretation of Soviet history between neo-Stalinists, nationalists, democrats, liberals and dissident Communists came to the fore. Many dissident writers and popular guitar poets, such as Vysotskii and Galich, satirized the Stalin era and the Brezhnevite present.[11] Important tendencies within the dissident movement included the liberal Marxist viewpoint of the historian Roy Medvedev; Andrei Sakharov's advocacy of human rights, democracy and an eventual 'convergence' between the communist and western systems;[12] and the neo-Slavophile views of Solzhenitsyn and his supporters, who appealed to the traditions of Russian Orthodoxy and distinctively Russian forms of social organization.[13] Other more extreme nationalist, even fascist, views were expressed in *samizdat* journals such as *Veche* and *Slovo natsii*.

In the twenty years after Brezhnev's accession the most famous and vocal dissidents were imprisoned, sent to psychiatric hospitals, internally exiled, permitted or forced to emigrate. Yet persecution simply meant that the great variety of views on historical and political subjects which existed in the USSR was suppressed, not eliminated altogether. Historians and writers were silenced through terror and apathy, but, as became clear under *glasnost*, silence was far from meaning consent. Gorbachev thus inherited a somewhat paradoxical legacy in the field of history, which has coloured the period since 1985: repression and caution among academic historians coexisted with a longstanding tradition of treating historical subjects in fiction and literary criticism, and a wide range of views on historical subjects among writers, journalists and the population at large.

THE POLITICS OF LITERATURE, CULTURE AND THE MEDIA IN RUSSIA, 1985–93

This discussion of the impact of *glasnost* on culture and the media in Russia will to some extent follow the general periodization of the Gorbachev era proposed by political scientists such as Richard Sakwa and Archie Brown,[14] but the division into different phases of *glasnost* should be seen only as a helpful general guideline, as in the cultural field there are no sharp distinctions between different chronological periods. An attempt will be made to trace and analyse some of the patterns and processes which ran through the seeming chaos of this overwhelmingly diverse and contradictory period.

With hindsight, some observers have traced intimations of the forthcoming cultural liberalization to a speech made by Chernenko in September 1984, on the occasion of the fiftieth anniversary of the Soviet Writers' Union.[15] Gorbachev may have exerted some slight influence on the content of this speech, as at the time Chernenko was in poor health, and Gorbachev was in charge of ideology, acting effectively as second secretary of the party. Although the speech did contain one section which, taken out of context, could be interpreted as a promise of creative freedom, Chernenko decisively trampled on any hopes of greater artistic independence, and if any signs of Gorbachev's future policy of *glasnost* could be detected in this speech, they were at best embryonic and oblique. Clearer evidence of Gorbachev's liberal position was contained in a speech of December 1984, in which he praised *glasnost* as 'evidence of trust in people . . . of their ability to interpret one or other event for themselves'.[16]

When Mikhail Gorbachev was elected General Secretary of the Soviet Communist Party in March 1985, hopes for change were aroused by the appointment of a younger, healthier, more energetic leader. Gorbachev's very first speech as leader on 11 March 1985 sounded a new note, calling for more *glasnost* in the work of party and state organs,[17] but at first there were few signs that he would introduce a dramatically different cultural policy. Scholarly opinion has been divided on the question of whether *glasnost* in culture was imposed from above or emerged from below. In retrospect, it can be seen that both interpretations contain a measure of truth: the crucial factor was the alliance which arose between liberal party figures and members of the cultural intelligentsia, all of whom belonged to the generation which had risen to prominence under Khrushchev in the 1950s and 1960s (now known as the *shestidesyatniki*, or 'members of the sixties generation', and by their opponents as *proraby perestroiki*, or 'the clerks of perestroika'[18]), but whose influence had waned during the 'period of stagnation' under Brezhnev.

Gorbachev has always claimed that the policy of *glasnost* dated from the decisions of the April 1985 Plenum of the Party Central Committee, when the political leadership initiated the lengthy process of re-examining the purge trials of the 1930s.[19] However, the initiative in testing the limits of the permissible in cultural policy appears to have been taken by a prominent writer of the 'thaw' generation, Evgenii Evtushenko[20] and Vladimir Karpov, a former prison inmate who was then Editor-in-Chief of the journal *Novyi mir.*[21] Karpov helped Evtushenko to secure the publication of his outspoken anti-Stalin poem *Fuku!* in September 1985, but only by appealing directly to Gorbachev after it had initially been forbidden by the censorship.[22] The appearance of Evtushenko's poem was the first clear indication of a change of cultural policy;[23] subsequently, six months after its publication, Karpov was elected to the Central Committee. Gorbachev, himself a product of the Khrushchev 'thaw', was evidently aware of the degree of psychological and social power that creative writers can wield in Russia,[24] and recognized the importance of writers, the mass media and the intelligentsia as a whole for the success of his economic, social and cultural revolution.

Other cultural figures also took advantage of the changed political climate of 1985 in order to work in a new way. In July 1985, Mark Zakharov, director of the Lenin Komsomol Theatre, criticized the outdated economic and administrative structure of Soviet theatre and the large number of 'old-fashioned, boring, morally and materially out-of-date performances'.[25] This article, and others on the subject of the theatre repertoire published by *Literaturnaya gazeta* in 1986, may well have been organized by the Central Committee Cultural Department.

In early 1986 the burgeoning cultural liberalization was encouraged from above by Gorbachev. In a speech of 25 February 1986 at the Twenty-Seventh Party Congress, he publicly acknowledged the importance of *glasnost* in helping to change the ingrained conservatism of the Brezhnevite 'Old Guard'.[26] On 19 June 1986 Gorbachev met a delegation of writers who were deputies of the USSR Supreme Soviet and appealed to them for help in his *perestroika* campaign. He argued that the people and the leadership wanted change, but that both were being hindered by 'a managerial stratum, the ministerial and party apparatus, which does not . . . want to give up its . . . privileges'.[27] At the Eighth Writers' Congress of June 1986, Soviet writers, despite their differences, responded by sponsoring a public campaign against the diversion of the northern rivers and calling for the abolition of censorship.[28]

In the first phase of *glasnost* (March 1985 to mid-1986), Gorbachev made several new high-level appointments in the cultural field. The first and most significant was the elevation of his liberal party colleague

Alexander Yakovlev, former ambassador to Canada, who, as a cultured man and a trained historian, exerted a considerable influence on Gorbachev's policy towards both history and the arts.[29] The close association between Gorbachev and Yakovlev can be dated to Gorbachev's visit to Canada in May 1983; one month later Yakovlev was recalled to Moscow, and in July 1985 he returned to the Central Committee. Although it was not until the Twenty-Seventh Party Congress of March 1986 that Yakovlev was officially appointed director of the Propaganda Department of the Central Committee, which gave him overall responsibility for culture and academic affairs, he was probably exercizing a liberal influence on Gorbachev well before this date. Subsequently, on 28 January 1987, he was promoted to candidate member of the Politburo, and since then he continued to be close to Gorbachev, only dissociating himself from Gorbachev's anti-democratic stance in 1990 and his hostility to Yeltsin in the post-communist era.

Yakovlev has been widely credited by Soviet intellectuals with an important role in the liberalization of culture and the mass media in 1985–6.[30] Like Gorbachev himself, Yakovlev had a positive, well-informed attitude to literary culture, and was on record as condemning the 'aggressive and limited' pretensions to culture of 'the considerable stratum of fully literate, well-educated people who reject any kind of serious spiritual activity'.[31] Archie Brown has characterized Yakovlev's policy as one of 'benign non-intervention',[32] but it would also seem that Yakovlev actively supported a number of key appointments in the cultural field, and was instrumental in securing the release of many formerly banned documentary and feature films in 1986–7.[33]

The Chernobyl' disaster in April 1986 proved to be a watershed which tremendously speeded up Gorbachev's policy of *glasnost*. The magnitude of the catastrophe was at first covered up in the traditionally secretive Soviet manner,[34] but it soon became clear that concealment of vital information was sowing panic at home and harming the USSR's image abroad. It also brought home to Gorbachev the magnitude of the problems confronting him, and the need to break the power of the Brezhnevite 'Old Guard'. In the wake of Chernobyl, Gorbachev came to believe that freedom of speech and the rule of law were essential to any genuine change in society.[35] In order to endow his programme with ideological legitimacy, he began to advocate 'new thinking' – a philosophy supporting reform in Soviet economic, social, political and cultural life.

Since Gorbachev and Yakovlev recognized the need for an efficient machine to implement their reform programme, important personnel changes were made in the spring and summer of 1986 in the political and administrative sectors dealing with propaganda and culture. One significant change was the appointment in April 1986 of Yurii Voronov, a respected minor poet of the Leningrad blockade and that time chief editor of the journal *Znamya*, to head the Central Committee's Department of Culture. Subordinate to both Yakovlev and Voronov was the new Minister of Culture, Vasilii Zakharov, whose appointment to this post in September 1986 marked a promotion rather than a demotion for the first time since 1953.[36] This also marked the end of the influence of the Brezhnevite 'Old Guard' in culture, as Zakharov, who had a reputation as a liberal,[37] replaced the conservative P. Demichev, who had remained in power since 1974, blocking the publication of many good literary works, such as Alexander Bek's *The New Appointment*.[38] Zakharov ensured a certain continuity in cultural matters, as he remained in office until the summer of 1989, when he was replaced by another reformer, the film director Nikolai Gubenko.

With Yakovlev's support, in 1986 vital changes also took place in the editorial boards of journals and newspapers.[39] In April 1986 the arch-conservative Anatolii Sofronov was replaced by the liberal Ukrainian writer and journalist Vitalii Korotich as editor of the weekly colour magazine *Ogonek*, which became one of the most influential supporters of *glasnost*. In August 1986 Grigorii Baklanov, a writer of anti-war novels, became editor of the previously uninspiring journal *Znamya*, and co-opted to the editorial board the critic Vladimir Lakshin, who had worked with Tvardovskii on the liberal *Novyi mir* of the 1960s, and the unconventional writer Vladimir Makanin. At the same time the lack-lustre *Novyi mir* was revitalized by the appointment as Editor-in-Chief on 10 August 1986 of the veteran writer Sergei Zalygin, who at the beginning of 1987 brought on to the editorial board such radical figures as the journalist and short story writer Anatolii Strelyanyi and the poet Oleg Chukhontsev.[40] These new editors and their associates played a major part in extending the limits of the permissible, continually attempting to publish previously unpublished manuscripts by their friends and colleagues,[41] and major literary works which had previously been banned in the USSR.

For many Russian intellectuals, the publication of selected poems by Nikolai Gumilev in *Ogonek* in April 1986 seemed to be the first sign that *glasnost* meant a radical change in literary policy.[42] Gumilev's rehabilitation was particularly striking, because he had been executed by the Soviet regime in 1921 for alleged participation in a monarchist plot. The poet Larisa Miller wrote in an unpublished manuscript of

1990: 'I remember how *glasnost* began four years ago. A friend rang and asked in an excited voice: "Do you know that *Ogonek* has printed some of Gumilev's poems and an article about him?" "Gumilev? In *Ogonek*?" I thought I had misheard, then decided that it was a joke. But it turned out that poems by Gumilev, who had been shot by the Bolsheviks and whose work had been banned, had appeared in the Soviet press. And not just anywhere, but in *Ogonek,* which for many years had been the epitome of official, "varnished", false propaganda literature.'[43]

The operation of *glasnost* from below was also evident in the congresses of the creative unions. The most striking changes took place at the Congress of the Film Makers' Union of 13–15 May 1986, when two-thirds of the old board were dismissed, including the First Secretary, Lev Kulidzhanov, who was replaced by the talented liberal director Elem Klimov, whose nomination had been proposed by Yakovlev himself.[44] The Congress established a 'commission for the resolution of creative conflicts' chaired by Andrei Plakhov, the film critic of *Pravda,* to consider whether previously banned films could now be released.[45] The Eighth Writers' Congress of 24–8 June 1986 adopted a somewhat more cautious approach, but nevertheless Vladimir Karpov was appointed First Secretary of the Union, replacing the veteran conservative Georgii Markov; liberal writers, such as Evtushenko, Voznesenskii, Zalygin and Aitmatov, were elected to the Board; and pressure for reform led to the appointment of even more radical figures, such as Okudzhava, Akhmadulina and Chernichenko. A transcript of a Politburo meeting of 26 June 1986, recently released from the secret Kremlin archives, suggests that Gorbachev, Yakovlev and their colleagues had not bargained for such a radical outcome, and had hoped to influence the party group within the Writers' Union to elect the conservative Yurii Bondarev as First Secretary. Yet even if this document is to be believed, the changed approach of the new party leaders is still evident from the fact that they chose not to intervene when they did not get their way.[46] Although Karpov later came under attack for his caution and conservatism, and was eventually forced to resign in 1990, the importance of his election for the widening of the subject matter of literature and historical debate in 1986 should not be underestimated.

Another major achievement of the Congress was the abolition in June 1986 of the censorship functions of *Glavlit* (the Central Board for Literature and Press Affairs), the official Soviet censorship body which had existed since 1922. Materials for publication no longer had to be submitted for its approval; its functions were restricted to preventing the appearance in print of state and military secrets, pornography and overt racism. Editors and publishers were no longer directly answerable to the Propaganda Department of the Central Committee, although it has now become clear that writers and editors were still subject to various milder types of censorship and pressure throughout the Gorbachev era.[47]

During the exhilarating second phase of *glasnost* (mid-1986 to the beginning of 1988), Gorbachev's reform programme became more radical, as he came to believe that economic change could not be achieved without political democratization.[48] He sometimes went out of his way to appeal to the creative intelligentsia for help in his conflict with the administrative apparatus: at a closed meeting with writers in July 1986, after the Eighth Writers' Congress, he said: 'The Central Committee needs support. You cannot imagine how much we need the support of such a group as writers.'[49] In a speech broadcast shortly afterwards he argued that *glasnost* was an important instrument for promoting democratization in the absence of an opposition, although this point was so sensitive at the time that it was deleted from Soviet newspaper reports of the speech.[50] In September 1986 there was a promise of greater liberalization, when it was announced on Soviet television that hitherto forbidden literary works about the Stalin era by living writers, including Rybakov's *Children of the Arbat* and Dudintsev's *White Robes*, were to be published.[51]

After the reshuffle at the Central Committee Plenum of January 1987, Gorbachev felt sufficiently confident in his position to take a more prominent, and politically daring, part in the promotion of *glasnost*. At a meeting with media figures in February 1987 Gorbachev declared unequivocally: 'There should not be any blank pages in either our history or our literature', although he still made the proviso that 'criticism should always be from a party point of view'.[52]

In 1987–8 *glasnost* became more widespread and effective;[53] and many previously banned works, by writers living and dead, by Russian émigrés and dissidents still living in the USSR, achieved publication in their homeland for the first time. Literary works were published in an order commensurate with the amount of controversy they aroused which, to some extent, was a function of the generation to which their authors belonged and, in some cases, of how recently they had been persecuted by the regime.[54] The tremendous support for *glasnost* among Soviet readers was graphically demonstrated by the huge increases in the journal circulation figures for 1988: *Novyi mir*'s print-run rose from 500,000 when Zalygin took over in August 1986 to 1,150,000 in 1988;

Druzhba narodov's more than quintupled, from 150,000 in 1987 to 800,000 in 1988; *Ogonek*'s circulation rose above three million; while *Znamya* and *Neva* both doubled their print-runs for 1988.[55]

For all their excitement, the years 1987 and 1988 also demonstrated that the process of *glasnost* was still limited and precarious. In the first place, Gorbachev did not introduce *glasnost* for the love of Russian literature, but in order to contribute to his policy of *perestroika*. He wanted to release information about the legacy of the Stalinist and Brezhnevite past and the abuses and shortcomings in contemporary society, in order to promote his policies of economic and political reform. He thought that literature could be a particularly effective means of reassessing the past and helping to change ingrained attitudes of apathy and conservatism. Gorbachev hoped to gain the support of the intelligentsia and revitalize society by allowing more people to be involved in decision-making. His pragmatic approach to culture was made clear in an interview of May 1987, which formulated in a new guise the old socialist realist concept of the *partiinost'* (party-mindedness) of literature, and spoke of the duty of the creative artist to support the party's policy of *perestroika*: 'The interests of the intelligentsia and the aims of the development of Soviet society coincide. The artist and the party are moving towards a single aim – the renovation of society on socialist principles.'[56] So, once again, as under Stalin, literature was to be mobilized for social and political ends, even though these ends were more benign than they had been in the past.

It also became evident in 1987 that *glasnost* could have negative as well as positive consequences. Greater openness engendered not only liberal, democratic writings, but also reactionary writings by conservatives, nationalists and anti-Semites. The literary world, which had been divided into 'liberals' and 'conservatives' since the death of Stalin,[57] came to be split into two more openly warring camps, which have existed ever since. Angry conservatives were particularly vocal at the March 1987 meeting of the Secretariat of the Board of the RSFSR Writers' Union and at the April Plenum; and a collective appeal, signed by seventeen conservative writers, which attacked *Ogonek* and its chief editor Korotich for indulging in subversive activity and abusing *glasnost*, was sent to the Central Committee.[58] Literary journals and newspapers became increasingly polarized: *Molodaya gvardiya*, *Nash sovremennik* and *Moskva* represented the conservative, nationalist camp, while their opponents, in differing degrees, were represented by *Novyi mir*, *Znamya*, *Druzhba narodov*, *Ogonek*, *Literaturnaya gazeta*, *Moskovskie novosti*, *Oktyabr'*, *Neva*, *Sovetskaya kul'tura*, *Yunost'* and others.

Throughout 1987, as newspapers and journals became more and more outspoken, the danger that *glasnost* could be reversed still remained, as Gorbachev was attempting to steer a middle course between the radicalism of Yeltsin and his supporters and the conservatism of Ligachev. His speech on the seventieth anniversary of the Revolution to some extent endorsed the concerns of the conservatives;[59] and the summary dismissal of Yeltsin in November 1987 convinced them that the time had come to launch an attack. The conservative backlash took tangible form on 13 March 1988, when the 'Andreyeva affair' inspired the cultural intelligentsia with fear that the policy of *glasnost* might be reversed. Nina Andreyeva, a chemistry teacher from Leningrad, wrote a letter entitled 'I Cannot Give up my Principles', which voiced the fears of the neo-Stalinists and conservatives about the destabilizing effects of *glasnost* and *perestroika*, proposed a partial rehabilitation of Stalin, and attacked 'classless humanism' and 'left-liberal intellectual socialism'.[60] Ligachev later claimed that he had not commissioned Andreyeva's article, but he did admit that he had read it and sanctioned its publication.[61] After the publication of this letter, which was interpreted by many intellectuals as an officially approved 'manifesto against *perestroika*', the progressive press went very quiet for three weeks until 5 April, when Gorbachev sanctioned a rebuttal of Andreyeva's position in *Pravda*, whereupon a number of scathing attacks on her views were published.[62] As a consequence of the 'Andreyeva affair', part of Ligachev's portfolio was transferred to Yakovlev, thus helping to lessen the problems caused by the conflict of interests between the departments of ideology and propaganda, both of which had traditionally shared responsibility for Soviet culture.

From mid-1988 a new phase of *glasnost* began, as Gorbachev attempted to implement the democratic reforms he had promised. Until the end of 1988 the party leaders still tried to control the tide of *glasnost*, even though the emergence of a civil society in Russia made this increasingly difficult.[63] In a speech of 7 May 1988, Gorbachev once again confused the radicals by publicly acknowledging the possible negative consequences of his policies. He referred to the turmoil in Soviet society, and to people who were asking: 'Isn't *perestroika* coming to mean the wrecking and rejection of the values of socialism?'[64] Nevertheless, in 1988 party ideologists still attempted to limit the damage caused by *glasnost*, and persisted in adhering to a centrist, compromise position which was proving increasingly unworkable.

The divisions among the intelligentsia were graphically demonstrated at the Nineteenth Party Conference in June–July 1988.[65] Gorbachev himself made a welcome defence of artistic freedom: 'The administrative direction of culture and edifying lectures addressed to artists are things of the past'; and took a moderate, reformist line on the press: 'If we give up the further development of *glasnost*, criticism, self-criticism and democracy, it will be the end of *perestroika*.' However, he also felt the need to warn against radical domination of the media, declaring: 'We cannot permit the press to be turned into the domain of any particular group.'

In September 1988 Gorbachev introduced further personnel and organizational changes to enhance his own position and defeat his more conservative colleagues. The Central Committee's Propaganda Department became part of the Ideological Commission of the Central Committee and Ligachev was demoted by losing the deputy leadership and his responsibility for ideology. Although this pleased the cultural intelligentsia, the appointment of Vadim Medvedev as the new head of ideology gave them cause for concern, since he replaced the the architect of *glasnost*, Alexander Yakovlev, who was moved to head the international policy commission.[66]

The effect of this personnel change soon became evident in late 1988, when *glasnost* faced its ultimate test: the case of Solzhenitsyn. The October issue of *Novyi mir* contained an announcement that in 1989 the journal would publish several of Solzhenitsyn's works, including *Cancer Ward*, *The First Circle* and *The Gulag Archipelago*. However, under Vadim Medvedev's insistence, the cover was withdrawn and the announcement was cancelled. In October 1988 Zalygin, the editor of *Novyi mir*, met Gorbachev, who categorically refused to allow the publication of Solzhenitsyn's work.[67]

In two hard-line speeches of November 1988, Medvedev declared that Solzhenitsyn would not be published in the USSR because he was 'an opponent of all our ideology' and continued to be 'inimical to, and therefore unnecessary to Soviet society'.[68] Yet only a few days later, on 11 and 12 December, Solzhenitsyn's seventieth birthday was celebrated by large crowds in the House of Cinema and the House of Architects, suggesting that they must have had some official sanction.[69] The ensuing debate once again provided a graphic illustration of the divisions within the writers' community. Yurii Bondarev argued in late 1988 that the measures taken against Solzhenitsyn, including the decree of 1974 deporting him from the USSR, had been correct. Other liberal writers, such as Vladimir Lakshin, the deputy editor of *Znamya*, argued that, irrespective of his political views, Solzhenitsyn should be published. Lakshin's favourable comments were particularly significant, because he had previously launched an attack on Solzhenitsyn for his unflattering portrayal of Tvardovskii in his memoir *The Oak and the Calf*.[70]

By the end of 1988, *glasnost* had reached an impasse: Medvedev had prohibited the publication of *The Gulag Archipelago*, but *Novyi mir* had published Korolenko's *Letters to Lunacharsky*, which contained an outspoken attack on Lenin's Red Terror.[71] The winter of 1988–9 witnessed a battle for the future of *glasnost*, symbolized by the struggle for the repeal of the regulations of 29 December 1988 barring co-operatives from engaging in publishing. There was also a threat to limit journal subscriptions for 1989, blamed by some on the growing paper shortage caused by economic mismanagement,[72] and by others on political factors, particularly the desire to arrest the spread of subversive ideas, notably the dissemination of democratic nationalist tendencies in the Baltic states.[73] The dispute over *glasnost* also had wider political implications, since it involved the crucial struggle to extend democratization into democracy, embodied in 1989 by the elections and deliberations of the first Congress of People's Deputies. Gorbachev's concern to retain the support of the intelligentsia for his moderate line was demonstrated at a special meeting of the Politburo on 6 January 1989, when he told a range of intellectuals, including Andrei Sakharov, Sergei Zalygin and Yurii Bondarev, that they had a responsibility to promote a steady process of reform, avoiding, on the one hand, radical demands for a multi-party system and private ownership, and, on the other, conservative advocacy of a 'firm hand' in government.[74]

By April 1989 Zalygin had engaged in several other 'deep discussions' with Gorbachev,[75] who eventually changed his mind on the publication of Solzhenitsyn, probably because he could not afford to alienate further the liberals and liberal nationalists in his coalition, and because he was faced with the reality that some of Solzhenitsyn's writings were already slipping into print.[76] The Union of Writers, which had expelled Solzhenitsyn in 1970, readmitted him and called for the return of his Soviet citizenship. On 24 February 1989 the Board of the Union of Writers voted for the publication of *The Gulag Archipelago*, and from August extracts began to be published in *Novyi mir*.

The period from the end of 1988 to late 1990 witnessed a more mature phase of reform, as intellectuals began, tentatively, to believe that *glasnost* was more than a temporary campaign which could easily be stifled. An important political stimulus to the speeding up of *glasnost* was provided by the decision to disengage from the Soviet empire, which culminated in the final withdrawal from Afghanistan in February

1989, the revolutions in Eastern Europe and the fall of the Berlin Wall in November 1989. At the same time, the division of the cultural intelligentsia into two camps became more marked and virulent, turning into a permanent feature of Russian cultural and social life. While ideological differences played some part in Writers' Union disputes, the bureaucratic resistance to *glasnost*, and especially to translating *glasnost* into structural and institutional change, can to a great extent be attributed to the desire of conservative officials not to lose their power, privileges and perquisites.[77] The continuing conservative assault against liberal 'licence' led to the publication in *Pravda* in January 1989 of a letter highly critical of Korotich signed by six well-known cultural figures including the 'village prose' writers Vasilii Belov, Valentin Rasputin, Viktor Astaf'ev and the film director Sergei Bondarchuk, which accused *Ogonek* of 'distorting history, debasing cultural values and diminishing the social achievements of the people'.[78] In March 1989 liberal writers, disillusioned with the Union of Writers, began to band together in alternative professional associations, such as the reformist group 'Writers in Support of *Perestroika*', later called *Aprel'*.[79]

Another impetus was given to the development of *glasnost* by the elections to the Congress of People's Deputies in March 1989, which, despite the complicated, semi-free electoral system, demonstrated the new-found power of Russian democracy. Boris Yeltsin made an astonishing political comeback when he was elected to parliament with a huge popular vote, and the conservatives were heavily defeated. Although throughout 1989 conservative politicians and writers still continued their counter-attack against *perestroika* and the media,[80] by the autumn *glasnost* appeared irreversible under the pressure of public demands for the whole truth.[81]

Yet in the autumn of 1989 the authorities, alarmed by the public's profound pessimism about *perestroika*,[82] attempted to set limits to the new press freedoms. The editor of the radical newspaper *Argumenty i fakty*, Vladislav Starkov, was reprimanded by Gorbachev at a meeting on 13 October 1989 and by Medvedev on 16 October for publishing a survey of readers' letters which showed that Gorbachev was losing popularity, and that the radical deputies in the new parliament, including Sakharov, Yeltsin, Yurii Afanas'ev and the economist Gavriil Popov, were the most popular.[83] Afanas'ev himself and Ivan Laptev, the editor of *Izvestiya*, also came under attack; and the revitalized journal *Twentieth Century and Peace*, which had been the first, in early 1989, to publish a work by Solzhenitsyn – his article 'Live not by Lies' – prefaced by a comment by Igor' Vinogradov that his exile was 'shameful', was subjected to severe pressure in late 1989.

At the same time the polarization of the writers' community grew more intense, taking a particularly ugly form at the plenary meeting of the RSFSR Writers' Union in mid-November 1989, when the Union of Writers was accused of being a 'Zionist organization' (although at most a quarter of its members were Jewish, and all were writing in Russian). Another unpalatable incident occurred at an *Aprel'* meeting at the Central House of Writers in Moscow on 18 January 1990, when a gang of men from the reactionary organization *Pamyat'* penetrated the hall to break up the proceedings, led by Konstantin Smirnov-Ostashvili, who shouted into a megaphone such remarks as 'Judaeo-Masons' and 'Clear off to Israel'. Ostashvili was subsequently put on trial, and in October 1990 was sentenced to two years imprisonment; six months later he was found hanging dead in the prison.[84] Such conflicts demonstrate that politics, rather than literature, had become the dominant concern of many Russian writers by 1989–90.[85]

The second convocation of the Congress of People's Deputies in December 1989 abolished the quota system which had formerly guaranteed parliamentary seats for the Communist Party, meaning that even Gorbachev would in future have to put himself to the test of a popular vote. The year 1990, therefore, marked the end of *perestroika* and inaugurated a new phase of open multi-party politics. Freedom of the press and of culture was now officially codified in the Law on Press Freedoms of 12 June 1990,[86] which proved to be more liberal than its earlier draft of December 1989. The law consolidated the abolition of formal censorship and party control over the press (except for matters affecting national security), and regulated the conduct of the media under *glasnost*; a simple registration process allowed the formerly unofficial press to flourish. *Ogonek* divested itself of Communist Party tutelage and established itself as a self-financing independent journal after a management buy-out; while the newspaper *Literaturnaya gazeta* declared independence from the Writers' Union, leading to the resignation of Karpov from the leading post in the Writers' Union;[87] *Znamya* also won its independence from the Union; and many new papers and journals appeared, including a national daily, *Nezavisimaya gazeta* (*The Independent*), produced by the Moscow City Council.

In the 1990s, although the press and publishing have become much freer, the problems caused by commercialism and the growing economic crisis have come increasingly to be felt. Somewhat ironically, at a time when the publication of Solzhenitsyn and other controversial émigré writers suggested that there was almost nothing which could not be published and discussed in Russia, the Soviet public appeared to be losing interest in literature and the press, and the cultural intelligentsia even began to debate whether literature was necessary in Russia any more.[88] In 1990 there was an appreciable fall in the subscriptions to most major mass circulation papers,[89] and by 1991 the crisis had intensified. The consequences of the press law, along with the dictates of the market and the difficulty of obtaining paper and newsprint, all caused serious changes in the pricing of journals and their print-run figures for 1991. In 1990 *Novyi mir*, for example, had a circulation figure of 2,680,000 and a price of 1.20 roubles, whereas in 1991 these figures were 927,000 and 2.10 roubles respectively, and four issues did not appear until the following year.[90] The enthusiasm of the Russian people for the revelations of the media and 'returned literature', which had characterized the early years of *glasnost*, had by 1990–1 given way to exhaustion, indifference and a growing disillusionment with the literary and other press, as the price liberalization, increasing shortages, higher crime rate and generally deteriorating economic and social situation in the country lowered people's morale, reducing life to a mere struggle for survival.

A new setback to the development of press freedom occurred in the winter of 1990–1, when Gorbachev tried to preserve his power by making a deal with the conservatives. He called for a suspension of the press law because of the reporting of the 'Bloody Sunday' incident in Lithuania, but in the end agreed to a compromise solution: the establishment of a supervisory commission to monitor the reporting of such events.[91] Gorbachev was already rapidly losing the support of the cultural intelligentsia,[92] when in February 1991 it became known that Soviet television had again been subjected to severe censorship:[93] Leonid Kravchenko, the conservative head of Soviet television (*Gosteleradio*), caused consternation among Soviet intellectuals by banning such popular programmes as *Vzglyad* and *Do i posle polunochi*.[94] However, as distinct from the uncomfortable interval during the 'Andreyeva affair' of 1988, freedom of speech had by this time developed sufficiently for the press and literary journals to continue to speak out. In retrospect, this episode, which seemed ominous at the time, simply represented a last-ditch attempt on the part of the authorities to control the process of *glasnost*, which had by this stage become irreversible.

From April 1991, when Gorbachev reached a compromise with Yeltsin, *glasnost* continued unabated until the abortive coup of August 1991, which intensified the bitterness between 'democrats' and 'patriots'[95] in the writers' community.[96] Evtushenko, a Yeltsin supporter, demanded the closure of the conservative newspaper *Den'* and the journals *Nash sovremennik* and *Molodaya gvardiya*, and called for the resignation of the writers Bondarev, Rasputin and Prokhanov, who were accused of being 'ideological instigators of the putsch',[97] because they had signed the notorious letter of 23 July, 'A Word to the People', which had proposed an authoritarian solution to the country's problems, along with Tizyakov and Starodubtsev, members of the disbanded Emergency Committee.[98] The conservatives protested loudly that the 'democrats' were treating them in an undemocratic, even fascist manner.[99]

Since August 1991 the collapse of the Communist Party and the USSR itself has led to the disintegration of the organizations which formerly controlled Soviet culture.[100] In 1992, after prolonged wrangling, the old Soviet Writers' Union split into two factions. On the one hand, a conservative group led by Timur Pulatov held a depleted Ninth Writers' Congress on 2 June 1992, and formed itself into an 'International Community of Writers' Unions' (*Mezhdunarodnoe Soobshchestvo Pisatel'skikh Soyuzov*), which perceived itself as the natural heir of the old USSR Writers' Union.[101] On the other hand, a democratic group called the 'Commonwealth of Writers' Unions' (*Sodruzhestvo Soyuzov Pisatelei*) also emerged, which was open to all interested writers' unions in the Commonwealth of Independent States.[102] The democratic writers' organizations in the newly independent nations were envisaged as independent, non-political associations of professional people.[103] From 1992 the two warring factions both occupied offices in the building of the old Writers' Union, and parallel executive committees continued to compete for influence and funds.[104]

In 1991–2 the 'thick journals', which are such an institution in Russia, virtually a symbol of the Russian intelligentsia, fell into decline after the boom years of 1987–8, and critics began to predict their imminent demise.[105] However, by 1994 this crisis no longer appears so acute, even though many of the literary journals, which are currently the only publishers of serious contemporary literature, are still in financial crisis and are limping from one issue to another; and some good literary journals, such as *Literaturnoe obozrenie* and *Yunost'*, have been abandoned by some of their talented contributors, who have founded new journals.[106] The most famous journals, including *Novyi mir*, *Znamya* and their conservative competitor *Nash sovremennik*, now look as though they will be able to survive with the help of either government subsidies,[107] increased subscriptions, new commercial ventures[108] or foreign sponsorship. The most successful have been those which have carved out a special market niche for themselves, offering distinctive features such as Russian nationalist ideas or experimental literature. One new development in 1993 is that journals have experienced increased competition from newspapers, which are able to pay their contributors more than journals; some of the most interesting literary debates have moved to the broadsheet newspapers *Literaturnaya gazeta, Nezavisimaya gazeta, Obshchaya gazeta* and *Segodnya.*[109]

The 1990s have witnessed the emergence of a bewildering array of new journals, publishing ventures and writers' organizations. It is as yet too early to make definitive judgements about the literature and literary politics of the post-communist period, although institutional changes enshrining cultural freedom have been slow in coming. Some interest in serious contemporary fiction has been aroused by the establishment of the Booker Prize in Russia in 1992;[110] but the new market system in publishing has promoted kitsch and sensationalism, not good literature; fewer books than before are being published, and hardly any poetry.[111]

The greatest threat to Russian literature in the post-communist era initially appeared to be the 'economic censorship' imposed by the new market system;[112] but in 1991–2 fears of renewed political censorship were aroused by the authoritarian tendencies of Yeltsin and his government.[113] In early 1993 Yeltsin established control over the broadcasting media by appointing his supporter Vyacheslav Bragin as head of the Ostankino television station;[114] and in September–October 1993, during his conflict with the Congress of People's Deputies, he replaced the editor of the subsidized government newspaper *Rossiiskaya gazeta.* After the failed rebellion of 5 October he banned communist and nationalist papers such as *Pravda,*[115] *Sovetskaya Rossiya* and *Den',* and for two days even censored democratic papers such as *Nezavisimaya gazeta* and *Segodnya.*[116] In December 1993, after the poor showing of Yeltsin's supporters in the elections, Bragin was dismissed, reportedly for screening a film on Vladimir Zhirinovsky on the eve of the elections which increased support for him, rather than diminishing it. After the elections Yeltsin was again intent on establishing presidential control over the media; but, in an ironic twist, he appointed the seventy-year-old Alexander Yakovlev, the architect of Gorbachev's *glasnost,* as director of the Ostankino television station and the newly-created Federal Television and Radio service, in an attempt to restore faith in the electronic media, which had previously been perceived as dominated by Yeltsin's circle.[117]

At the beginning of 1994, notwithstanding Yakovlev's new appointment, freedom of the press, television and radio is still in a precarious position in Russia. It remains to be seen whether the literary journals will continue to avoid direct political control, and whether Yeltsin's authoritarian rule will be only a temporary phrase.

CONCLUSION

This brief analysis of Russian cultural politics since 1985 suggests that the intervention of Gorbachev and his party colleague Alexander Yakovlev was initially of paramount importance in promoting cultural liberalization in Russia. Gorbachev at first had an instrumental attitude to *glasnost*, encouraging the publication of outspoken works in the press and literary journals as 'constructive criticism' which might help him in his reform campaign. Subsequently, free speech was seized from below by writers and editors, who, encouraged by the abolition of censorship and the more liberal cultural climate, notwithstanding occasional setbacks and the inadequacy of laws on press freedom until 1990, continually breached the official bounds of *glasnost*. From 1988, party leaders and conservative cultural figures were engaged in an increasingly desperate attempt to control and limit the process of *glasnost*, which by 1990 had been transformed into a qualified freedom of speech.[118] Since 1991 'Soviet literature' has ceased to exist in its old form, but changed political circumstances and the transition to a market system have brought many new problems to Russian literature.[119]

2 The Years 1985–6: Reassessment of History Begins

The first major historical subject to be treated in literature published in Russia after Gorbachev's accession was a mild revisitation of the subject of Stalin and Stalinism which had been suppressed in Russia since 1966, and some of its first exponents were prominent 'men of the 1960s' who had played a major role in the 'thaw' period under Khrushchev or the late Brezhnev era.[1] Since Stalin's death, fiction on the theme of Stalinism had played a significant political role in promoting discussions about the legacy of the past and the possible future development of society, affording valuable insights into the persistent conflict between 'anti-Stalinists' and 'pro-Stalinists' in Soviet society.

From the perspective of the post-communist era, when far more controversial works have been published reappraising the entire history of the USSR since 1917, it is difficult to understand the impact which the early anti-Stalin products of *glasnost* had in the years 1985–7. In order to analyse their significance, they must be seen in the context of the political, historical and literary climate of the mid-1980s. At Gorbachev's accession, Soviet fiction was in the doldrums,[2] and historians were not allowed to provide a frank discussion of Stalinism,[3] although the system which existed in the USSR still contained many Stalinist features: a centralized power structure; the all-embracing influence of the Communist Party and KGB; a command economy; and the exercise of party control over all aspects of the individual's social and cultural life. After the limited revelations about Stalin permitted in the Khrushchev period,[4] under Brezhnev, Andropov and Chernenko Soviet writers had once again become more restricted in their choice of themes, and were expected to emphasize that Stalin, although occasionally fallible, had played a basically positive role in the development of the USSR.[5] Because of the official ban imposed on any discussion of questions of guilt and responsibility for past crimes, some Russian writers had been driven underground, feeling it their duty to return to the issue of Stalin and Stalinism in the name of historical justice. In the 'era of stagnation' under Brezhnev, some anti-

Stalin writers wrote manuscripts 'for the desk drawer', like Rybakov and Shatrov; others, including Bek, Dombrovskii and Shalamov, sent their works abroad, only to die long before their works could be published in the USSR; while the most controversial writers, such as Solzhenitsyn, Voinovich and Vladimov, were deported or forced to emigrate.

Since historians were bureaucratically controlled by the Soviet authorities, the role of writers in keeping anti-Stalinist sentiment alive during the post-Khrushchev period can hardly be overestimated, as literature, depending on highly individual skills, was one area in which the party had never been able to exert total control. Some Soviet intellectuals had long been familiar with manuscripts on Stalinism circulating in *samizdat* or *tamizdat* works which had become famous in the West in the 1960s and 1970s, such as Solzhenitsyn's *The Gulag Archipelago*, although they had not been available to a wide audience outside Moscow and Leningrad.[6] It has now become clear that the 'era of stagnation' was one of submerged pluralism, and that the dissidents were simply the tip of the oppositionist iceberg. For this reason, when after Gorbachev's accession anti-Stalin ideas were able to surface again publicly, they found a ready response and exerted a tremendous political impact.

RE-EVALUATION OF STALINISM BEGINS

For the first eighteen months after Gorbachev's appointment in May 1985, the public process of reassessing Stalinism proceeded in a cautious, even conservative manner.[7] One of the first decisions Gorbachev made was to release a film containing a favourable portrait of Stalin, which had been made in the years 1983–4, based on Alexander Chakovskii's novel *Victory* (1980–2), as a contribution to the fortieth anniversary celebrations of the end of the war (8 May 1985).[8] In his own anniversary speech, Gorbachev praised 'the gigantic work at the front and in the rear . . . led by the party . . . headed by Iosif Vissarionovich Stalin', and this statement was greeted with prolonged applause.[9] Evidently, Gorbachev did not at first wish to risk a period of upheaval by offending the military, the party or a large number of war veterans.

It has not always been acknowledged that, despite Gorbachev's conservative public statements, the question of Stalin and Stalinism was reopened as early as April 1985 by his decision to allow the Party

Control Commission to investigate the cases of some purged party members who had failed to achieve rehabilitation in the Khrushchev period.[10] In September 1985 the theme of Stalinism resurfaced in the literary journals as a result of the permission which Gorbachev gave Karpov, the editor of *Novyi mir*, to publish Evtushenko's poem *Fuku!*, a mixture of essay, poem, memoir and political polemic.[11] One controversial topic raised by Evtushenko's work was Stalin's police chief Beria, and his notorious habit of picking up teenage girls and forcing them into sex.[12] Evtushenko also referred to the prison camps in Kolyma and an argument with a lorry driver from Kolyma who kept a portrait of Stalin in his cab, and expressed disapproval of the assassination of Trotsky. In 1985 Stalin's complicity in Trotsky's murder could still not be officially admitted; the first serious public discussion of the issue did not take place until 1988.[13] Another attack on Stalinism which could not be fully reported in the USSR in 1985 was Evtushenko's outspoken speech at the December meeting of the RSFSR Writers' Union, which referred to the brutality of collectivization and the purges.[14]

STALINISM AND *PERESTROIKA*, 1986

In early 1986 Gorbachev still maintained his cautious approach, declaring in an interview with the French Communist paper *L'Humanité*: 'Stalinism as a concept is an invention of anti-Soviet forces in the West'.[15] But during the new phase of *glasnost* inaugurated by the appointment of Alexander Yakovlev as director of ideology in March 1986, a number of journal editors felt confident enough to press ahead with publishing more radical works of historical fiction. Joined by some courageous newspaper editors, historians and film directors, they opened up Soviet history again as a serious subject of enquiry. However, the limited nature of Gorbachev's support for an investigation of the past was still evident from his speech at an informal meeting with a group of Soviet writers on 19 July 1986: 'If we were to get too involved with the past, we would lose all our energy. It would be like hitting the people over the head. We have to go forward. We *will* sort out the past. Everything will be put in its place . . . It must be understood that for us everything lies in the future.'[16]

In the autumn of 1986 certain short stories were published which tentatively reopened the question of Stalin's terror. The first works to appear were similar to those which had been published in Khrushchev's 'thaw', telling individual tales of persecution, either from the point of view of relatives of victims or of the victims themselves. They did not dwell on the persecutions and camps or make political generalizations about the Stalin era, but generally implied that those who had suffered had been rehabilitated, and that the bad times had passed. One such story was Bulat Okudzhava's *The Girl of My Dreams*, written at the end of 1985 and published in October 1986, which depicts the author's meeting with his mother on her return from ten years of imprisonment in 1947, and the psychological difficulties she experienced in adjusting to her new-found freedom.[17]

If Okudzhava's story was a new work by a living writer, the appearance in December 1986 of Yurii Trifonov's autobiographical story *A Short Stay in the Torture Chamber* represented the posthumous publication of a work written earlier 'for the drawer'.[18] Trifonov was a relatively safe choice, as he was universally acknowledged as a major writer, who had been unusually successful in publishing relatively frank works on historical subjects even in the 'period of stagnation' under Brezhnev;[19] yet, in view of this, it was particularly significant for Soviet readers to discover that even he had formerly been unable to publish everything he wrote. Trifonov had intensely personal reasons for wishing to re-evaluate Stalinism, since his father, the Old Bolshevik Valentin Trifonov, had died in Stalin's purges, and his mother had spent eight years in camps and exile. Trifonov's works are subtle and allusive, eschewing direct political comment; because of the repressive censorship of the time in which they were written and in which he hoped to publish, they reveal merely 'half-truths' about the Stalin era.[20]

The author recalls a meeting in Innsbruck in 1964 with a certain person, designated only by the anonymous term 'N' (the Russian equivalent of 'X'), who had denounced him in 1950 when he was threatened with expulsion from the Komsomol at the Gor'kii Literary Institute on the grounds that he had concealed the fact that his father was an 'enemy of the people'. He was initially expelled – a dismissal which would have prevented Trifonov from joining the Writers' Union and pursuing a career as a professional writer – but subsequently reinstated by the City Committee 'with a severe reprimand and a warning'. The character of N could be based on either of the Stalinist writers Mikhail Bubennov or Leonid Sobolev (who died in 1983 and 1971 respectively), both of whom had demanded that Trifonov be disgraced and punished.[21] Since Trifonov and N meet in the torture chamber of a medieval castle outside Salzburg which they are visiting as tourists, Trifonov clearly intends to draw a parallel between this room and the torture chamber of Stalinism, where, fourteen years earlier, he had been publicly denounced, threatened with dismissal, ostracism and poverty.[22]

As in many other of his works, Trifonov suggests that subjective memory is unreliable. Whereas the author thinks that N's speech made a crucial contribution to his initial expulsion, N insists that his intervention had in fact been instrumental in saving him. The two men are ultimately reconciled; Trifonov implies that the individual's perception of the past is defective, and that it is important to forgive one's former enemies. Trifonov's message of reconciliation was highly relevant to the new era of *glasnost*, although his words appear to have been forgotten in the subsequent acrimonious literary disputes,[23] which have cast aspersions on Trifonov himself and all the 'men of the sixties generation' who published their works under Brezhnev.[24]

BEK'S *THE NEW APPOINTMENT*

One of the major literary events of 1986 was the first appearance in the USSR of Alexander Bek's novel *The New Appointment*, banned in 1964 and published abroad in 1971, which eventually achieved posthumous publication in October and November 1986.[25] The connection between anti-Stalin literature and Gorbachev's desire to enlist the support of the intelligentsia for his policy of *perestroika* and greater economic efficiency was made explicit in the introduction by Grigorii Baklanov, the editor of *Znamya*: 'In days when a revolutionary reorganization of the whole of society is occurring, when our society "is climbing in spirit out of those times", this novel sounds exceptionally contemporary.'[26]

Although Bek's novel is a talented artistic work far exceeding run-of-the-mill 'production novels' by hack writers,[27] it was the novel's historical and political significance which proved to be of most interest to Soviet critics and readers. *The New Appointment* contains an interesting psychological portrait of Stalin,[28] and a realistic depiction of a Stalinist official, Onisimov, President of the Committee for Metallurgy and Fuel of the Council of Ministers of the USSR, who in 1956–7 is demoted and appointed to the post of ambassador to a Northern European nation, where he is dying of cancer.

Perhaps the main reason for the novel's suppression in the Brezhnev era[29] was that it suggested that Stalin and the 'cult of personality' had not been solely responsible for past crimes, but that the dictator had been supported by the entire Stalinist system, based on the complicity of many individuals. Such a view would have been anathema to the Brezhnev–Kosygin regime, composed of party and state bureaucrats.[30] Baklanov later revealed that 'the same group of people, only twenty years older' tried to prevent the publication of Bek's novel in 1986.[31]

Bek, who specialized in documentary prose[32] about Soviet metallurgy and engineering,[33] raises important questions about the subordination to Stalin's whims of industrial managers and Soviet industry as a whole. He paints a relatively sympathetic portrait of his protagonist Onisimov, who embodies both the strengths and weaknesses of the typical Stalinist industrial executive. Ascetic, scrupulously honest, although leading a privileged life as a high party official, his dominant trait is obsession with his work and indifference to everything else, including his family. His fanatical devotion to his work is largely responsible for saving the Soviet steel industry from the depression caused by the purges of 1937–9, and for helping it to survive the war by supervizing its evacuation beyond the Urals.

Bek's portrait of Onisimov raises a number of questions which were still relevant in the Gorbachev era: the origins of the industrial manager's career; the reasons for his poor health; and the contradiction between his admirable qualities and his ultimate failure. Bek shows that Onisimov has maintained his position at the cost of a series of betrayals in the years 1937–40, accomplished because of his unthinking loyalty to Stalin: 'For him the expression "soldier of the party" was not just empty words. When the expression "soldier of Stalin" came into use, he proudly and doubtless rightfully considered himself to be such a soldier.'[34] However, Onisimov cannot entirely suppress his inner convictions; when ordered to implement a project of 1952 which he himself considers hopeless, but which is favoured by Stalin and Beria, Onisimov experiences for the first time a conflict between his devotion to carrying out orders and his own judgement. Bek implies that industrial officials' subservience to Stalin caused untold damage to the Soviet economy; and that Onisimov's inner conflict contributes to his subsequent fatal illness.

Soviet critics generally ignored the deeper resonances of *The New Appointment*, and, following the socio-political tradition of nineteenth- and twentieth-century Russian criticism, interpreted Bek's novel as a critical picture of Stalinist methods of running the economy and a contribution to Gorbachev's *perestroika*. The novel split critics into different camps: the conservative V. Kozlov attempted to defend Onisimov, protesting: 'It is very easy to condemn or justify. But Onisimov and his colleagues lived in bitterly difficult and heroic times.'[35] A more radical view was taken by A. Egorov, who claimed that Onisimov, despite his high rank, was a mere 'cog' in the Stalinist machine.[36] A cautious, centrist approach was adopted by F. Chapchakov, who contrasts Bek's novel favourably with 'sensational exposés' published in the early 1960s, in that it 'attempts to analyse all the contradictions of that heroic and tragic time thoroughly and in depth'.[37] This phrase closely resembles the new orthodoxy about Stalinism being promoted in the early years of *glasnost*, as reflected in the biography of Stalin by Colonel-General Dmitrii Volkogonov, Director of the Institute of Military History, entitled *Triumph and Tragedy*.[38]

The role of literature in initiating debates on topical contemporary issues in the early years of *glasnost* is graphically demonstrated by the influential review of Bek's novel by the economist and reformer Gavriil Popov,[39] who subsequently became a popular democratic deputy and was elected Mayor of Moscow in 1991. The contemporary significance accorded to this review written by a critic who himself admitted that he was 'far from literature' was reflected in the fact that the book version of the novel published in 1987 included Popov's article as a postscript. Popov's recourse to the genre of literary criticism can partly be attributed to its value as a means of making his views accessible to the general public but, more importantly, the greater freedom accorded to literature than to economic thought in the early Gorbachev years made it useful for Popov to disguise his economic analysis as a book review.

Popov's main point is that Onisimov's conduct was a direct result of the 'Administrative System' of the Stalinist economy, which he defines as 'the centralization of decisions and punctual, undeviating, wholehearted fulfilment of directives from Above, and particularly from Stalin – the Boss.' The main features of this system are intense workaholism on the part of Stalin and his officials, which keeps subordinates 'in a permanent state of tension'; formal relations between colleagues, based on 'ruthlessness, nothing personal, no compromises'; energy and willpower in executing decisions; constant suspiciousness, exemplified by endless checks, reports and denunciations; a rigid chain of command and unquestioning obedience to superiors, as in the army. In the postwar period the system was highly dependent on the 'sub-system of fear' represented by Beria's secret police empire, which gradually began to take over more and more construction, scientific and technological projects.

Popov acknowledges that in Onisimov Bek has depicted both 'an ideal of the Administrative System' and 'a typical image of the majority of leaders of those years'. The Stalinist totality of 'System, Style and Leader' enabled the USSR to achieve certain major technological successes: 'the best tanks of the Second World War, the first space rocket, nuclear liners and power stations in Siberia'; but this system contained the seeds of its own destruction, possessing certain major flaws which led to 'inner contradictions . . . or, in the author's words "*sshibki*"' ['collisions'].[40] According to Popov, the major weakness of the Administrative System was the deformation of the human personality and a lack of initiative, which caused many of the problems facing contemporary Soviet industry, as well as 'countless moral losses and nihilism among our young people'.

The most important contemporary conclusion drawn by Popov in the section 'What was Onisimov's Mistake?' is that the Administrative System outlived Stalin himself. In 1957 Onisimov (like his prototype Tevosyan), thinking that greater freedom of thought was now permitted, criticized Khrushchev's scheme to replace the industrial ministries by regional economic councils (*sovnarkhozy*), but was promptly dismissed and posted abroad.[41] Popov argues: 'Onisimov's mistake is undoubtedly the most valuable lesson for all of us from Alexander Bek's posthumous novel'; in his view, even in 1987 many conservatives still remain, who feel that strong methods are needed to improve works discipline, increase production and conquer dishonesty, greed and corruption, failing to see that 'the true roots of these phenomena lay in the Administrative System'. Although Popov's criticism of the Soviet economic system was outspoken for early 1987, he still had to be careful not to undermine the entire socialist system, and to link his review of Bek's novel with Gorbachev's speech at the January 1987 Plenum. He also relates his analysis to the entire fate of *perestroika*, arguing that contemporary Soviet people were in danger of repeating 'Onisimov's mistake', mistaking words for actions and the form of change for its substance. Ironically, the experience of the years 1987–91 suggests that Gorbachev and his followers did not heed this warning, and to some extent were guilty of repeating 'Onisimov's mistake'.

If Popov was influenced by Gorbachev, his analysis of the legacy of the Stalinist Administrative System influenced Gorbachev in turn;[42] and was subsequently echoed by many other Soviet economists, politicians and cultural figures. Baklanov said in an interview of 1988 that the publication of Bek's novel had marked an important stage in the *perestroika* of the journal *Znamya*;[43] and in 1989 the novel was still being referred to as *reportage*, rather than as fiction.[44]

ABULADZE'S *REPENTANCE*

Another important sign of liberalization occurred in September 1986, when Gorbachev instructed Yakovlev to investigate many previously banned films referred to the 'conflict commission' of the Film Makers' Union. After a concentrated two weeks in which Yakovlev watched a large number of controversial films, he reported to Gorbachev in October 1986.[45] As a result of this favourable report (and also, apparently, as a result of the influence of Raisa Gorbacheva and Eduard Shevardnadze[46]), the party's chief ideologue Egor Ligachev gave permission for the film *Repentance* by the Georgian director Tengiz Abuladze, banned on its completion in 1984, to be released in five hundred copies and shown to a limited audience in October 1986. It was eventually put on general release on 1 December,[47] first to audiences in Moscow, and then elsewhere.

The film depicts events surrounding the death of the mayor Varlam Aravidze, who is a composite dictator-figure, possessing Hitler's moustache, Beria's pince-nez, Mussolini's black shirt and many of Stalin's attributes. Varlam's body is mysteriously dug up several times; eventually the perpetrator of the outrage is exposed as Ketevan, the daughter of two of Varlam's victims, who declares: 'As long as I live, Varlam Aravidze will not lie in the earth, I will dig him up not three but three hundred times.'

Abuladze's film is a vivid allegorical representation of Stalin's repressions, which explores the nature of dictatorship, refers to Stalin's purges of the 1930s and the mass deportations of the post-war period, and dramatizes the need to confront the past in order to come to terms with it. The importance attached by Gorbachev to the message of this film is reflected in the fact that it was very widely shown (it was even given special showings at places of work, including research institutes, hotels and the Moscow circus[48]), widely discussed in the press,[49] and awarded one of only two Lenin Prizes for the arts in 1988.

Repentance evidently answered a need among the Soviet population: 700,000 people went to see it in the first ten days, and the total audience after ten months amounted to 10 million. One professor reportedly said that after seeing the film he was going to make major changes in his lectures on the 1930s.[50] However, reports of the audience's reaction are mixed: whereas many of the older generation came out weeping, feeling that the revelation of fifty-year-old crimes had enabled them to 'breathe again freely', and many young people too felt that the exorcizing of Stalin's ghost had been cathartic,[51] some other young people, especially in the provinces, reportedly greeted it with laughter and incomprehension. Reactions to the film varied from stunned revelation: 'How can one live in the old way after such a film?' and sceptical protest: 'Why remember?'.[52]

A spot survey conducted at Tbilisi cinemas established that, despite the complex form of *Repentance*, a majority of those surveyed clearly identified it as a political film that 'honestly and candidly reflects negative and alien elements that still exist in our life'. Older viewers, over sixty years of age, expressed misgivings: 'The film will have an adverse effect on young people';[53] whereas Abuladze himself claimed that he had made the film specifically for young people,[54] and that many young Georgians had understood of its themes, particularly the frank discussion about relations between generations, and the need to stop living by lies.[55]

Critical responses to the film concentrated on certain moving scenes which underline the message that the past should never be forgotten,[56] such as the episode reminiscent of the prologue of Akhmatova's *Requiem* depicting a 'mournful queue of women–future widows and children–future orphans that has formed at a prison window', which was recognized as a clear reference to the year 1937.[57] An anonymous voice from the window states baldly: 'Exiled without the right of correspondence', which was a euphemism for 'executed' (not all Soviet people knew this, even in Gorbachev's time).

Although Abuladze deliberately chose to avoid specificity in order to make a historical parable about tyranny in general, he nevertheless claimed that 'every episode in the film is based on an unfabricated fact, on a real person'. Although neither he personally nor his family suffered in Stalin's purges, he acknowledged that his 'friends and neighbours and all of Georgia – a small country – suffered. The intelligentsia suffered especially.'[58] But even in 1987, Abuladze felt unable to state explicitly that his main protagonist Ketevan is based on Ketevan Orakhelashvili, daughter of the old Georgian party leader who was shot together with his wife; Ketevan herself spent eighteen years in labour camps, and her husband, a leading musician, was tortured to death in prison.[59] He did, however, admit that he had made the film because 'even today truth cannot always make its own way'.[60]

Abuladze's film initiated a widespread discussion about the need to repent the crimes of the Stalin era so that they should never be repeated. The respected scholar Dmitrii Likhachev underlined the vital significance of Abuladze's theme for Soviet literature and society as a whole: 'The past does not die. It is necessary to publish in journals of mass circulation works which were not published in the past. The main theme in literature now is repentance.'[61] Less independent critics were, however, still careful to connect the director's advocacy of reassessment of the past with 'the truth that was taught by the Twenty-Seventh Congress'.[62] The most topical theme in Abuladze's film was the conduct of neo-Stalinists in the contemporary USSR, explored through the character of Varlam's son Avel', who incarcerates the awkward Ketevan in a psychiatric hospital. He has become successful and prosperous, resents any attack on his well-being, and tries to justify Varlam's conduct with such familar neo-Stalinist arguments as 'The times were difficult', 'We were surrounded by enemies', and 'I'm not saying that we didn't make mistakes. But what does the life of one or two people mean when it's a question of the happiness of millions?' It is only the death of his own son which brings him to his senses; eventually he digs up Varlam's body and flings it over a cliff. Abuladze drew a moral lesson for the present from his portrait of Avel': 'Avel' is concerned for nothing except his personal well-being. Even today, in the era of *perestroika* . . . it's people like Avel' who pull us backward. He is his father's son, and he feels more comfortable back there in the past. People like Avel' provide a nutrient broth for future Varlams.'[63]

One of the most interesting socio-political reviews of *Repentance* was an article by the sociologist Lev Ionin, which used the film to investigate the essence of the Stalinist system.[64] He interprets the story of Varlam as 'the story of a man who wanted to create heaven on earth'. For Varlam, every individual human being is an obstacle on the way to paradise, and can be ruthlessly sacrificed in the name of the masses. Ionin emphasizes the great danger of utopian thinking: 'Real Varlams destroyed whole nationalities, whole professional and social groups. If reality does not yield to their maniacal desire to achieve Utopia, they seek to destroy a whole people, like Pol Pot in Kampuchea.'

Ionin emphasizes the significance of Abuladze's image of the living corpse, suggesting that society is at fault for permitting Varlam's crimes to be concealed after his death. Ionin is one of the first writers published in Russia to draw an unfavourable contrast between the suppression of information about Stalinism in Russia and the public recognition of the guilt of the Nazi leaders in Germany. He argues that only through the collective repentance of the entire living nation can the guilt be assuaged; in a striking phrase, he declares: 'It is naive to think one can change the present wihout changing the past.'[65]

While all reviews of the film published in 1987 focused on its anti-Stalinist theme, its denouement raised wider questions about the whole direction of Soviet history. In a scene which became famous in the Soviet Union, an old woman asks Ketevan: 'Where does this street lead? Does it lead to the church?'[66] Ketevan answers: 'This is Varlam Street. It can't lead to a church.' The final words of the film are the old woman's indignant response: 'Who needs a road that doesn't lead to a church?' One critic drew the conventional conclusion that this metaphor is a 'socially significant idea: the only correct road is one that does not bypass the ideal of truth'.[67] Nevertheless, when viewed in conjunction with the artist Sandro's complaint that Varlam is conducting 'an experiment in the church', and Varlam's frequent references to his desire to build paradise on earth, this scene could be interpreted more boldly as a sceptical approach to the whole utopian socialist experiment. The old woman's words were subsequently used as the title of an influential article of 1987 by the publicist Igor' Klyamkin, which investigated the relationship between Stalinism and Leninism.[68]

A NEW APPROACH TO SOVIET HISTORY

In 1986 a play by Mikhail Shatrov, *The Dictatorship of Conscience*, went beyond Stalinism to initiate a deeper debate on Soviet history, and, in particular, to consider the question of Leninism and the socialist legacy. Shatrov's play, staged by Mark Zakharov at the Lenin Young Communist League Theatre, represented the boldest use of the device of the trial in order to subject injustice to the test of public opinion.[69] Its contemporary relevance was emphasized by its subtitle: 'Arguments and reflections in 1986'.

Mikhail Shatrov, one of the most influential playwrights of the early years of *glasnost*, chose to devote himself to the highly specialized genre of the 'play about Lenin' after the Twentieth Party Congress of 1956. Shatrov's own personal history had graphically demonstrated that love of Lenin could lead to persecution by Stalin: his father and uncle Aleksei Rykov, Soviet Premier in the years 1924–30, were shot, and his mother was arrested when he was seventeen.[70] Shatrov claimed in 1988: 'Every one of my plays was banned, and broke through [to publication and staging] with enormous difficulty.'[71] His problems were to some extent inherent in the genre he had chosen: the 'play about Lenin', initially commissioned by Stalin's Central Committee in 1936 in order to promote faith in the existing regime as the legitimate heir and continuer of the founder's sacred cause, had frequently been censored and redesigned at the highest level to suit the current party line.[72] Although the 'play about Lenin' would not seem a very promising vehicle for a critique of the basic values of the Communist regime, it was a potentially powerful medium, if party officials could be persuaded to listen. Shatrov's initial influence in the *glasnost* era can be partially attributed to the fact that his views coincided very closely with those of Gorbachev himself; his plays retained their influence as long as Gorbachev retained his, and as long as Lenin was held in general esteem.

The Dictatorship of Conscience evokes the attempts of a group of young journalists to produce and stage a 'trial of Lenin', a unique form of political debate used by theatre groups in the 1920s as a means of winning support for the Revolution. The young people summon to the stand serious witnesses against Lenin and his cause, then call for cross-examination and defence witnesses. The trial, like the original version in the 1920s, fully vindicates Lenin and the Party.

The Dictatorship of Conscience almost immediately elicited a mixed reaction from theatregoers. More conservative members of the audience were offended at the very idea of staging a dramatized 'trial of Lenin'. On the other hand, the play had a powerful impact, because it brought into the public domain complex aspects of Russian history which had hitherto been labelled taboo, and encouraged young people to think, argue and defend their points of view. Some critics who saw the play in 1986 commented that the reaction of the audience when faced with the 'negative characters', who included White Guards and foreign imperialists, as well as various opportunists and villains still prevalent in Russia, confirmed the topicality of the production. At the end of the first act an actor stepped out of his role to carry a microphone into the audience for a discussion – within circumscribed limits – of the issues which had been raised.[73]

For all its apparent boldness, Shatrov's play kept within the bounds of the permissible in 1986. His use of a 'play within a play' format acts as a means of distancing 'good' contemporary Russians from the evil people whom they represent on stage. Another device employed by Shatrov to help the audience get the point (and, perhaps, to insure him against criticism) is the character of the Outsider, who ensures that the production does not deviate from Leninist ideas, and makes one of the play's key statements: 'The truth should not depend on whomsoever it serves.'[74] At the end of the play the Outsider is revealed to be Engels,[75] thus emphasizing both Lenin's Marxist heritage and the impeccable Marxist–Leninist credentials of the current regime.

The most powerful witness for the prosecution in Shatrov's play is the revolutionary Pyotr Verkhovenskii, one of the main villains in Dostoevskii's novel *The Devils*, who declaims his famous monologue defining revolutionary socialism as equality for nine-tenths of the population achieved by enslaving them to an elite composed of the remaining one-tenth; the destruction of all genius and outstanding individual talents; the imposition of obedience through mutual suspicion, widespread denunciation and the removal of suspect individuals. Although some Soviet critics passed quickly over this scene, the American scholar David Joravsky, who saw the original production, pointed to the tremendous impact of Verkhovenskii's speech in 1986: 'For the intensely silent Soviet audience it is closer to lived experience than to literary fantasy.' Shatrov's aim, embodied in the title of the play, was to promote the somewhat sentimental view that conscience was supreme in Lenin's Russia, and that even in Stalin's time, when Verkhovenskii's values were dominant, the voice of conscience never faded in the hearts of good Soviet people. Even in 1988 Shatrov exclaimed: 'I really love Lenin without limit!';[76] he still believed that Leninist morality would ultimately triumph over Stalinist aberrations. Yet, as in Milton's *Paradise Lost*, evil in Shatrov's play proves more exciting and memorable than good. The relevance of Dostoevskii's prophetic interpretation of revolutionary socialism to the reassessment of history in the USSR since 1985 is attested by the fact that Shatrov's portrait of Verkhovenskii is only one early example of numerous references to Dostoevskii's *The Devils* in the Gorbachev era.

Shatrov emphasizes the hold which Stalinism still has over the contemporary Soviet population, presenting a caretaker who advocates a 'firm hand'; and his grandson, a lorry driver, who has a portrait of the chief exponent of 'firm authority' on his windscreen. The name of Stalin is not mentioned: the Outsider steps in and asks, 'Whose portrait is that?', whereupon the driver, embarrassed, whispers in his ear. After a slight pause, the Outsider asks: 'But why not Lenin?' This episode was singled out in a student discussion of the play at Moscow University as an excessively cautious, oblique reference to Stalin[77] – indeed, it simply repeats the episode mentioned a year earlier in Evtushenko's *Fuku!*

In *The Dictatorship of Conscience* the defence of Leninism is much weaker than the prosecution. The negative characters are presented in a manner consistent with the superficial view that oppositionist 'alien elements' have sometimes succeeded in infiltrating communist movements. Shatrov's shallow cross-examination of these characters fails to answer the difficult historical question: why did Lenin's party fall for so long under the influence of such 'alien elements' as Stalin? He also avoids a point sometimes raised by western historians: that the revolutionary extremist Sergei Nechaev, on whom Dostoevskii's Verkhovenskii is loosely based, exerted some influence on Lenin's thinking.[78]

The purity of the Leninist faith is affirmed by the positive characters, who simply ignore such typically Leninist concepts as democratic centralism, the one-party state and the use of terror. The fundamental Leninist tenet of the dictatorship of the proletariat is simply transformed into 'the dictatorship of conscience' without any explanation. Shatrov, who shared Gorbachev's faith in 'socialism with a human face', evades the question of whether this moral principle was indeed inherent in Marxist–Leninist thought, and if so, how and why it could have been distorted in the USSR so easily and for so long.

While by no means a totally satisfying theatrical experience, Shatrov's play was successful in its aim of provoking reflection and discussion, even though Soviet critics in 1986, not surprisingly, emphasized the positive Leninist aspects of the play rather than the unanswered questions it raises.[79]

3 The Second Phase of *Glasnost*: the Year 1987

While some of the major literary works of 1985–6 had been predominantly concerned with topical problems of the present, such as ecology and drug dealing,[1] in 1987 the focus moved very explicitly to an intense preoccupation with the past, and particularly with the Stalin era. The boldest works on an anti-Stalin theme to appear in early 1987 were by writers safely dead, who were less controversial than the living; but by the spring of 1987 previously censored works by writers living in the USSR, such as Rybakov, Dudintsev and Pristavkin, which were unknown even in the West, had begun to appear. It soon became obvious that writers and critics were taking their criticisms of the Stalin era much further than during the Khrushchev 'thaw', engaging in a more independent critique of history and society, with a less upbeat tone than during the thaw period. Works of historical fiction published in 1987 grew in frankness, moving gradually from an isolated view of the repressions of the year 1937 to a much broader perspective. Many new subjects were aired in literature almost simultaneously, suggesting that 'campaigns' may have been organized from above by the party, or initiated from below by new liberal editors. If in 1986 literary works had been of only limited influence, in 1987 works of historical fiction aroused tremendous excitement among the Soviet reading public, exerted a profound impact on Soviet historical consciousness, and provoked discussions which polarized the intellectual community.

It is unlikely that the fundamental reappraisal of Stalin in the years 1987–8 could have occurred without the approval, even encouragement, of the highest party leadership[2] (although Ligachev and Chebrikov expressed disapproval of this policy).[3] The publication of so many anti-Stalin works of fiction in 1987 was a direct result of Gorbachev's public reversal of his previous cautious position on Stalinism, and his frequent expression of more fundamental criticisms of the Stalin era.[4] By 1987 Gorbachev had come to believe that a re-examination of Stalinism was vital to his policy of *perestroika*, and that literature on this subject could help to change entrenched attitudes. He was correct in the sense that Stalin's totalitarian system, many aspects of which had survived throughout the 'era of stagnation' under Brezhnev, was the major reason for the low morale of the population, poor productivity in the economy, bureaucracy and corruption in society, and the poverty of intellectual and cultural life. Gorbachev now recognized that in order to repudiate the legacy of the past, it was first necessary to understand it. He hoped that opening up the past would help the USSR to build a better socialist future. What he did not foresee, however, was exactly where the limited reassessment of Stalinism permitted in 1987 would lead.

REHABILITATION OF CLASSIC WORKS

A changed attitude to classic works formerly deemed controversial in the USSR was evident at the very beginning of 1987, when on 6 January Boris Pasternak's Nobel Prize for literature, awarded in 1958 after the publication of *Doctor Zhivago* in Italy in 1957, was openly disclosed for the first time in the USSR.[5] In the spring of 1987, editors eagerly set about the task of publishing major works on Stalinism already well known to the Soviet intelligentsia through *samizdat*, simply in order to set the historical record straight and put an end to the hypocrisy which had suppressed these works for so long.

The most outstanding was Akhmatova's *Requiem*, a cycle of poems composed in the 1930s and published for the first time in the USSR in March 1987.[6] In this moving work Akhmatova's private grief at the arrest of her only son in 1937 merges with the wider grief she shares with the countless women whose loved ones had been arrested,[7] and with the tragedy of the entire Soviet people during the Stalin terror. In a sympathetic review the critic Adol'f Urban correctly remarked that the publication of Akhmatova's poem had 'righted a long-standing injustice' – Zhdanov's attack on Akhmatova in his decree of 14 August 1946 as 'half-nun, half-harlot', which led to her expulsion from the Writers' Union.[8] Although most references to Akhmatova's work in Gorbachev's USSR were laudatory, some dissenting voices were heard disputing the value of the new revelations about the past and claiming that Akhmatova's lyrical poetry expressed a solipsistic, egocentric view of the national tragedy – a milder, but nevertheless still repellent echo of Zhdanov's denunciation of Akhmatova's poetry.[9]

Another important poem published in early 1987 was *For the Right of Memory* (written in the years 1966–9) by Alexander Tvardovskii, the former liberal editor of *Novyi mir*, whose name had been invoked by a number of speakers at the Eighth Congress of the Soviet Writers' Union in June 1986. There was such competition to publish Tvardovskii's work that it appeared almost simultaneously in the journals *Znamya* and *Novyi mir*, whose joint print-run amounted to 680,000.[10] The poem is a memorial and act of repentance for Tvardovskii's father Trifon, who was exiled as a 'kulak' in 1931.[11]

Tvardovskii's poem, like Abuladze's film *Repentance*, suggests that it is essential to recall the past in order to expiate it. The poet tells of his own adulation of Stalin, and the guilt he felt at having a 'kulak' father, until he was relieved to hear the words 'A son does not answer for his father' from the lips of Stalin himself. With bitter irony, he recalls how young people in the 1930s expressed abject gratitude to 'the father of the peoples' for 'forgiving' their own fathers. His main theme is that all Soviet people are responsible for the Stalinist past, and that the judgement of history will continue.[12]

Tvardovskii's poem became one of the most influential literary works of early 1987. It was greeted by a huge post to the editors of the journal *Znamya*, which, unusually, continued seven months after its publication.[13] The poem was interpreted in different ways, dividing its readers into enthusiastic supporters of a re-examination of the Stalinist past, those who praised Tvardovskii's Leninist viewpoint, and neo-Stalinists who lambasted the journal for publishing a work which blackened Stalin's name. Those who welcomed Tvardovskii's poem far outnumbered the denouncers, whose letters were mostly sent anonymously, without a return address, suggesting that the neo-Stalinists felt themselves to be on the defensive.

Two words which constantly echo throughout these letters are 'truth' and 'need', reflecting the enormous need of the Soviet people for the return of their collective memory, for truthful information about the past, which they had been denied for so long. Some letters are moving appeals for the innocent victims of the purges not to be forgotten: 'This poem is a splash of the tormented soul and a muffled sob for what might not have been. It is like a gravestone, like a monument above the ashes of the innocent.'[14]

The publication of Tvardovskii's poem had great therapeutic value, as some correspondents were inspired to tell their own tragic life stories,[15] or to search for their 'innocently condemned, slandered, destroyed relatives'.[16] It is sometimes forgotten by sophisticated western critics how deeply such 'returned literature' of 1986–7 affected ordinary Soviet people, who, since the Khrushchev period, had not been able to express their grief publicly. This profound nationwide sorrow found expression in the desire for a memorial to the victims of Stalinism. One correspondent, inspired by Tvardovskii's poem, described his vision of the memorial: 'a grey, granite wall, very long – almost endless – and on the wall the contours of human faces protruding through the stone'.[17] In 1987 such sentiments were still considered controversial, as was demonstrated in November, when six people who began to collect signatures in favour of a monument were immediately arrrested by the police; but by August 1988 the movement received formal expression with the establishment of the *Memorial* society.[18] It was not until October 1990, however, that a publicly-funded monument 'to all the victims of the totalitarian regime' was eventually established in Moscow opposite KGB headquarters.[19]

THE EFFECT OF STALINISM ON SCIENCE

Some of the first aspects of Stalinism to be treated in literature in early 1987 continued the attempts in 1986 to analyse the reasons for the USSR's poor economic performance. One prominent theme was the repression of classical genetics and the domination of the charlatan T. D. Lysenko over Soviet biology and agricultural science, with the support of Stalin and Khrushchev, for several decades of Soviet history. This subject was perhaps less controversial than many others, because it had been opened up for discussion under Khrushchev, and Lysenko himself had fallen from grace in 1965.[20] However, the full extent of Lysenko's malign influence – the arrest of many prominent geneticists, including the world-famous Academician Nikolai Vavilov, who died in a death cell in Saratov prison in 1943, and the dismissal of three thousand biologists from their posts after the notorious 1948 Session of the Academy of Agricultural Sciences (VASKhNIL) – had never been made known in the USSR.[21] In the Brezhnev era Lysenko's harmful impact on Soviet biology had largely been passed over in silence, and Lysenko's disciples had been regaining in influence.[22]

After Gorbachev came to power Lysenko's teachings were immediately repudiated, and by the autumn of 1986 any censorship which had previously affected the treatment of Lysenkoism in literature must have been removed, as excerpts from Dudintsev's novel *White Robes*, which deals with the history of Soviet genetics, appeared in the journals *Ogonek* and *Nauka i zhizn'*. By the spring of 1987, when Dudintsev's work had been serialized in full, the subject of Lysenkoism had also been treated, almost simultaneously, in two other literary works by Vladimir Amlinskii and Daniil Granin.

The publication of these three works demonstrates the important role that Soviet literature could play as a witness to historical events, since few eye-witnesses of the period of Lysenko's ascendancy still remained, and such factual information on the subject as had appeared in the USSR had been strictly limited. These literary publications paved the way for numerous articles in the press about honest anti-Lysenkoite scientists who had preserved their integrity as far as possible;[23] two films and several articles about Nikolai Vavilov appeared in connection with the hundredth anniversary of his birth in November 1987.[24] Writers also played an important part in campaigning against the continuing abuses in Soviet science. Granin declared in 1987: 'Numerous Lysenkoites, incompetent and ignorant people, continue to work in science, holding important positions, heading laboratories and even institutes. This is the legacy of these gloomy years, and it is still making itself felt today.'[25]

Vladimir Amlinskii's *And Every Hour will be Justified* (1986–7) is a memoir about his father Professor I. E. Amlinskii, a historian of biology and head of a department at the Moscow Medical Institute, and the times in which he lived.[26] Amlinskii refers to the suppression of entire branches of biology, such as ecology and genetics, and gives a concise, but frank account of Nikolai Vavilov's persecution. He informs his readers about the troubled history of Soviet biology, reproducing long extracts from speeches made at the 1948 VASKhNIL session which give the flavour of Lysenko's aggressive, ignorant utterances, while also emphasizing the brave defiance of Lysenko by a handful of true scientists. Amlinskii explores the 'banality of evil' through his description of Lysenko as a 'polite, well-meaning, rather strange old man' who had 'nothing threatening, nothing repellent in his figure'.[27]

One topical issue raised by Amlinskii's memoir is the role of the intelligentsia formed by the Stalin era. He contrasts the integrity of his father, who was no hero, but a wise, gentle, gifted scientist who refused to surrender to obscurantism, with one of his father's pupils, an opportunist professor who moved into Lysenko's camp and attacked his former teacher for 'rejecting Darwinism', but subsequently became particularly assiduous in attacking Lysenko. In a review of Amlinskii's memoir, the liberal critic and professor Evgenii Sidorov (subsequently appointed Minister of Culture in Yeltsin's government) addressed the topical issue of the erstwhile conformist and turncoat among the Soviet intelligentsia: 'Some people who took an active part in shameful actions during that period and have survived quite successfully until the present day try both secretly and openly to justify themselves with references to the tragic nature of the times.'[28]

Perhaps the most controversial literary work on the history of Soviet science was Daniil Granin's *The Buffalo*, published in early 1987,[29] a semi-fictionalized biography of the famous geneticist Nikolai Timofeyev-Resovskii, who went to Berlin to work in 1925 and escaped the destruction of his science in the USSR by continuing to work in Germany in the 1930s and throughout the war. Granin's title *Zubr* has multiple resonances: it denotes a European bison, but also has connotations of a 'diehard' or 'dinosaur', evoking both a tough, outstanding specialist and one of the last examples of an endangered species. Granin does not idealize his subject, but presents Timofeyev-Resovskii as a complex man who 'did not know how to be great during his lifetime' and 'was constantly falling off his pedestal'. He emerges as a man of strong character, wide culture and selfless devotion to science, who steadfastly maintained his independence and honour, prizing them above a successful career.

In an interview of 1987, Granin revealed that there had been 'an open and fierce struggle' over the question of publishing *The Buffalo*, and that 'those who launched it used dirty, aggressive methods'.[30] As soon as they found out that *Novyi mir* wanted to publish the novella 'they began to assault S. Zalygin [the editor] with telephone calls and letters, and started to threaten the magazine'. The enemies of Granin's work fell into several categories: 'Lysenkoites, for whom Timofeyev-Resovskii was always one of the most serious adversaries; people who had achieved his expulsion from the Obninsk institute in more recent times; and those who were frightened that they might be recognized in the figures of the slanderers and informers who were Timofeyev-Resovskii's adversaries.'

The most controversial aspect of Granin's work was the fact that Timofeyev-Resovskii had stayed in Germany during the war, since at one time most Soviet people, including Granin himself, had taken a hard line against anyone suspected of collaboration with the Germans. In 1937 Timofeyev-Resovskii was ordered by an arrogant young diplomat in the Soviet embassy to return home urgently; but as the official swore at him, accusing him of praising 'alien science' and 'lousy liberalism', and geneticists were being arrested in the USSR, Timofeyev-Resovskii knew that it would be 'madness, pure suicide' to return. While acknowledging that some of Timofeyev's colleagues blamed him for not coming back, Granin suggests that people cannot be condemned for trying to stay alive. He does not pass judgement, but simply poses the moral dilemma: 'Was the Buffalo's decision not to return a heroic action? or self-preservation? Can one demand that a person should commit suicide? And if a person has refused to step into the abyss, is this a heroic action?'[31] Granin's evocation of the period of the Nazi–Soviet Pact diverges from the usual Soviet interpretation of the Pact as an enforced step, taken because the western Allies had broken faith with the USSR by making a deal with Hitler at Munich. He stresses the positive light in which Nazi Germany was presented in the Russian press during this period, implying that in these conditions Timofeyev's decision not to return to the USSR was even more justified.

After the Red Army's occupation of Germany in 1945, Timofeyev was sent to a Soviet labour camp, and did not return to Moscow from exile until 1956. Granin is not particularly frank in dealing with this episode in his protagonist's life: we learn only indirectly that he was rescued from a labour camp, half dead from pellagra, by Zavenyagin, the director of the Magnitogorsk steel works,[32] and, after a spell in hospital, was permitted to establish his own research institute in the Urals. Although Granin is less than candid in failing to admit that this research institute was a 'special prison', or *sharashka*, he does reveal that it was associated with the atomic programme, directed by Beria, and was concerned with studying the effects of nuclear radiation on human genes. Granin's reticence on this subject suggests that in early 1987 writers and editors still felt that they could not tell the whole truth about the repression of Soviet science under Stalin. Information about Stalin's 'special prisons' was not widely publicized in Russia until the appearance of Solzhenitsyn's *The First Circle* in 1990.[33]

Granin answers potential critics of his praise of a scientist who stayed in Germany during the war, emphasizing that Timofeyev for years maintained a stubborn silence about the fact that while in Germany he had constantly helped both his Jewish colleagues and prisoners of war of all nationalities, finding room for them in his own and other laboratories, and that his son, a member of the anti-fascist resistance, had died in the Nazi camp of Mauthausen. Timofeyev had remained silent even when slander accused him of being a 'defector' and 'Nazi accomplice', and he had been too proud to campaign for his own admission to the Academy of Sciences, even when his colleagues were exerting themselves on his behalf.

In the course of research on his book Granin met Timofeyev-Resovskii's enemy 'D', a former Lysenkoite and informer, who denounced Timofeyev for allegedly co-operating with Nazi science, and suggested that Lysenko was a sincere believer in his false ideas. Granin was startled to discover that 'not one person but several people recognized themselves in "D"', and he drew wider political implications from D's character, suggesting that Soviet society had a need for trials of those responsible for past denunciations and repressions, on the model of the Nuremberg trials in Germany.

Granin's work sparked off a great deal of discussion. Liberal Soviet critics regarded it as both a valuable contribution to the history of Soviet biology and as a work possessing considerable relevance for the present, because it revealed that many unworthy people had risen to positions of leadership in the USSR.[34] The economist Gavriil Popov used the novel to continue his exploration of the nature of Stalinism, launching a fiercer attack on Lysenkoism than Granin himself. He argued that the Stalin regime needed certain characters of the *Zubr* type, like the famous physicist Pyotr Kapitsa, who were prepared to accept the system in which they were working, while stoutly defending their independence and creativity in professional matters, because timid conformists were unable to carry out vital scientific tasks of benefit to industry and defence.[35] By contrast, Nikolai Vavilov was sacrificed because, unlike the charlatan Lysenko, he was unable to promise that his work would yield any immediate benefit to Soviet agriculture.

The conservative critic A. Kazintsev attacked Granin's admiration for a scientist who failed to return to his own country either in the 1930s or during the war, and contemplated permanent emigration in 1945, asking himself some 'strange questions': 'To stay or to go? America or Russia? West or East?'[36] A more dangerous distortion of Granin's ideas is contained in an article by the Russian nationalist critic Vadim Kozhinov, who claims that 'In *The Buffalo* D. Granin said with great conviction that Lysenko was, in essence, a blunt instrument in the hands of such "theoreticians" as Deborin and Prezent.'[37] Since Deborin and Prezent were Jewish, this is clearly an attempt by a chauvinist and anti-Semite to exonerate Russian scientists and blame Jews for the repressions in Soviet biology. Granin had angered conservatives by his comment on Timofeyev-Resovskii: 'Like all true Russian intellectuals, he hated anti-Semitism.'[38] Subsequently Kozhinov's interpretation was indignantly refuted by liberal critics, such as Stanislav Rassadin, who attacked his 'organized system of lying'.[39]

Criticism of a different kind was contained in an anonymous émigré article entitled 'Truth and half-truth in a new book about Soviet science'.[40] The critic ironically characterizes Granin, a deputy of the Supreme Soviet, as 'one of the most zealous supporters of Gorbachev's policy of "*glasnost*"', claiming that he was careful not to exceed the level of pessimism about Soviet science officially permitted in 1987. On the one hand, praise is accorded both to Granin's depiction of Timofeyev's life in Germany and the acceptance of his decision not to return, and his frank admission that Beria was in control of the Soviet atomic programme.[41] On the other hand, Granin is correctly reproached for giving the impression that Timofeyev was free after 1947, rather than working in a special prison, and for passing over in silence the persecution he suffered in the post-Stalin era, including his compulsory retirement and the disbandment of his laboratory in Obninsk, which he had directed since 1964.[42] Another justified criticism is that Granin bows to the prevailing orthodoxy by comparing Stalinism unfavourably with the alleged tolerance of Lenin's treatment of intellectuals, many of whom were arrested or forced to emigrate in the 1920s.[43] It is difficult to disagree with the critic's conclusion: that although Granin's work is 'a notable social and literary event which touches on complex and contradictory questions, it at the same time demonstrates to what extent taboos are still dominant in Soviet literature'.

If Granin's work had touched on subjects regarded as sensitive in Russia, it proved even more controversial in the GDR. In an article of 1993, Granin revealed that documents from Stasi files had shown that *The Buffalo* could not be published in the GDR until 1989, because until this time the KGB under Gorbachev had been involved in an exchange of information with the Stasi on whether Timofeyev had collaborated with the Nazis.[44] It had now also come to light that Timofeyev had been asked to work on the Nazi eugenics project, conducting experiments on gypsies, and that his refusal had been a direct cause of his son's death. This tragic dilemma helps to explain Timofeyev's persistent refusal to speak about his time in Germany. In 1991 the Procurator-General of the USSR asserted that there had been no legal basis for the original charge of treason issued against Timofeyev in 1946; but the controversy over his alleged collaboration with the Nazis still continues in the 1990s.[45]

The literary work which dealt most directly and comprehensively with Lysenkoism in Soviet biology is Vladimir Dudintsev's novel *White Robes* (1987).[46] Dudintsev spent twenty to thirty years collecting material on the subject, and it took over twenty years for the work to appear.[47] Dudintsev reproduces historical events with an almost documentary authenticity, while at the same time seeking to analyse the widespread bureaucracy and dogmatism which took root in Soviet science under Stalin (and by implication, in many other areas of Soviet scholarship and culture).

Dudintsev's novel is a very detailed – perhaps over-long – account of the activities of Fyodor Dezhkin, a candidate of biological sciences, who in September 1948, shortly after the VASKhNIL session, is sent by his patron, Academician Ryadno, to a research institute, with the task of identifying and eliminating the biologists who still remain faithful to classical genetics. Dezhkin is gradually revealed to be a complex character who is not Ryadno's loyal agent, but a philosophically-minded sceptic who becomes sympathetic to Strigalev, an outstanding scientist working to produce a new variety of disease- and pest-resistant potato, and falls in love with Elena Blazhko, an honest biologist who attends secret seminars on classical genetics. When Strigalev is arrested and dies in prison, Dezhkin battles to preserve his research. Dudintsev has stated that his novel was inspired by the examples of Vladimir Efroimson, the author of many works on genetics aimed against Lysenko, who had suffered for his scientific convictions, and Nina Lebedeva, who worked on the same problem as Strigalev does in the novel.[48]

Dudintsev provides some interesting new information about the genetics dispute: one particularly fascinating detail is a questionnaire issued to a secret police informer in order to tempt his interlocutor into anti-Soviet statements.[49] Dudintsev is not, however, primarily concerned with politics, but with a moral and psychological exploration of the effect of Stalinism on Soviet society. One of Dudintsev's finest achievements is the portrait of the chief villain, Academician Ryadno. Although Lysenko is also mentioned in the novel (possibly as a means of insuring against criticism), it is clear that the portrait of Kassian Damianovich Ryadno is based on Dudintsev's conception of Trofim Denisovich Lysenko, who, like his fictional prototype, bears the name and patronymic of a simple Russian peasant, and is also known as a 'people's academician'. Ryadno is a self-taught man, a clever political intriguer who manages to win Stalin's favour and frequently drinks tea with the Leader, a demagogue who always raises biological disputes to the 'ideological plane'. Dezhkin is aware of the charm Ryadno exerts over students and demobilized soldiers with his avuncular solicitude, simple clothes and assumed popular speech. It is not surprising that Ryadno, who becomes an 'idol' in science, is able to win the support of another 'sacred', 'godlike' personality who also prefers simple clothes and speech and claims to act in the name of the people. Dudintsev demonstrates Ryadno's remarkable tenacity in the post-Stalin period, but emphasizes that when he eventually dies in his bed, his ceremonial funeral cortège 'demonstrates artificial honours to someone whom no one honoured any more',[50] whereas the people who were now remembered with reverence, like Dudintsev's Strigalev and Academician Nikolai Vavilov, lay in unmarked graves.

Dudintsev's novel is disturbing to a Russian audience, since it points out the mass psychosis affecting Soviet society in Stalin's time, suggesting that not merely the scientific community, but also the Soviet population as a whole bear a collective guilt for the dominance of Lysenkoism.[51] Dudintsev attacks the distorted Stalinist morality which elevated into a hero the young Pioneer Pavlik Morozov who denounced his father as a 'kulak',[52] and emphasizes the importance of individual conscience and repentance. However, as in *Not by Bread Alone*, he is careful to present an optimistic message, suggesting that, although the Stalinist system was very powerful, a network of good individuals existed in different areas of Soviet life who opposed evil and upheld moral and intellectual ideals, including a member of Stalin's secret police.[53]

The aspect of Dudintsev's novel which caused most controversy in Russia was the moral issue of what methods it is permissible to use in the fight against evil. Dezhkin's observation of the apparent invincibility of evil leads him to formulate principles establishing his moral right to oppose evil using underhand methods like deceit, camouflage and double-dealing. Dudintsev has explained that this theme was first suggested to him by the conduct of Konstantin Simonov, editor of *Novyi mir* from 1954 to 1957, who first published his novel *Not by Bread Alone*, then repudiated it under pressure from literary bureaucrats.[54] At first Dudintsev was offended by Simonov's behaviour, but later came to understand its wisdom: 'It was then that I first understood that a good person who feels it is incumbent upon him to struggle for some higher truth must bid farewell to sentimentality. He must devise tactical principles of struggle and be prepared for grave moral losses.'[55] Dudintsev suggests that if good is too respectable, too constrained by morality, it will never triumph over evil, which has no such constraints. To the objection that someone who leads a double life will inevitably be drawn into betrayal, if he is not to give himself away completely, Dudintsev responds: 'Doubts as to the rightfulness of our actions impede the cause – they do not remove the evil itself, and they remove from the front one more soldier who could be fighting.' Dezhkin's behaviour was based on that of the geneticist Nina Lebedeva, who 'announced that she was a Lysenko supporter, and thanks to this, obtained access to a laboratory and a greenhouse. But every evening, on returning home, she shut everyone out and conducted experiments in classical genetics.'[56]

This theme in Dudintsev's novel was still being discussed by Russian intellectuals in the 1990s. The critic V. Kamyanov agreed with the iconoclastic young critic Igor' Zolotusskii that 'Dezhkin is a completely new type in our literature',[57] but complained that 'the situation is even newer when a humanitarian author advises us to arm ourselves with a progressive experience of counter-intrigue and lying in order to save . . . even a super-valuable sort of potato'.[58]

Although Dudintsev's novel comes to no overtly political conclusions, its moral and social analysis was regarded by influential commentators as an important contribution to the debate about Stalinism and its legacy which was raging in the Soviet press in the years 1987–8.[59] Dudintsev is fundamentally critical of the social culture which produced such charlatans as Lysenko and obtuse, ruthless officials like the secret police general Assikritov, arguing that they cannot be dismissed, as villains frequently were in Soviet literature before *glasnost*, as 'relics of capitalism'; they were not 'sent by the Tsar or America', but were products of the Soviet system.[60] Dudintsev suggests that a one-sided conception of socialism has prevailed ever since the Revolution; indeed, he subscribes to Dostoevskii's view that socialists are concerned only with social origin, failing to take human nature into account,[61] and considers that a fundamental reappraisal of values is necessary.[62]

For all their interest, the works of Amlinskii, Granin and Dudintsev are typical of the cautious *glasnost* of the early Gorbachev period, in that they do not provide a thorough analysis of the reasons for Lysenko's influence or the continued persecution of honest scientists after Stalin's death. They omit any direct reference to Khrushchev's support for Lysenko and the enduring problems of biologists in the Brezhnev era, merely stating that the Party reconsidered the position of biology in the late 1950s and early 1960s. It was not until May 1988 that Khrushchev's protection of Lysenko was openly discussed in the memoirs of Khrushchev's son-in-law Adzhubei.[63] By this time Amlinskii felt able to be more outspoken, arguing that the fundamental problem in the USSR was the lack of institutional limitations on dictatorial power.[64]

After the publication of these three works in 1987 the whole truth about the 'Lysenko affair' was still not made known in Russia, and articles on the subject in 1988 by Valerii Soifer, which described life during the genetics dispute as 'more complex and tragic than appears from the pages of the most public-spirited literary works' were denigrated by an anti-Semite at the Nineteenth Party Conference as the suspect work of an émigré.[65]

INDUSTRIALIZATION

One of the few newly published literary works to treat the theme of Stalin's industrialization policy, which had been brought to public attention in 1986 by Bek's *The New Appointment*, was Sergei Antonov's story *Vas'ka* (dated 1973, but published in 1987).[66] *Vas'ka* is unusual in that it concerns the working class, not the intelligentsia or the peasantry, the usual protagonists of Soviet literature: in particular, it depicts the new working class created by the dispossession of the 'kulaks' after collectivization. Antonov's story is a parody of conventional 'production literature', exploring such formerly taboo themes as the persecution of workers for their class origins; the defects involved in the construction of the Moscow metro (*Metrostroi*), one of the most prestigious projects of the 1930s; and, by implication, the problems attendant on Stalin's First Five Year Plan, as well as the general atmosphere of fear and repression prevalent during Stalin's Terror.

Antonov depicts Margarita Chugueva,[67] a shock worker (that is, a worker chosen or volunteering for some specially arduous task) employed on the *Metrostroi* in 1934, who is known by the male nickname 'Vas'ka' because of her strength and capacity for hard work. She is terrified of exposure as the daughter of a 'kulak', since she has escaped from exile in Siberia where she had been deported with her parents, and now hopes to conceal her social origins while working in Moscow. Such outlaws were quite common on construction sites in the 1930s; managers and foremen would willingly ignore their suspect backgrounds in order to recruit and retain labour which was vitally needed to fulfil the Five Year Plans. Antonov has related that Vas'ka's prototype was a striking photograph of a female shock worker in overalls in a memoir entitled *How We Built the Metro*, which contains interviews with young enthusiasts.[68]

Vas'ka becomes so terrified of exposure that she makes a clumsy attempt to kill her brigade leader, the enthusiastic Komsomol leader Mitya.[69] Mitya's first instinct is to cover up the incident, both because Vas'ka is a good worker and because he has human feelings for her, but, under pressure from his 'high-principled' girlfriend, he eventually decides to report it. As Mitya tries to enlist support for Vas'ka, he becomes aware of what Antonov described in an interview as the 'spiral of fear' engendered by Stalinism which grips all those whom he approaches.[70]

The conclusion of the novel is ambiguous: in a flush of adoration and enthusiasm Mitya writes directly to Stalin. However, we assume that Stalin will not help Vas'ka, and that she will be dismissed, because we subsequently learn that Kirov's murder in 1934 has ushered in an era of repression. The author himself confirmed this suspicion: 'In the middle of 1934 a campaign was carried out to purge *Metrostroi* of class-alien elements, and Vas'ka had to return to where she had fled from, and perhaps go further away.' Antonov also suggests a tragic ending by drawing a deliberate literary parallel with Chekhov's story *Van'ka*. Chekhov depicts an unhappy boy whose only hope of escaping from his situation is a letter which he addresses: 'To the country, to Uncle', after which: 'He scratched his head, thought and thought and added "Konstantin Makarych"'. At the end of *Vas'ka*, Antonov describes Mitya writing: 'To the Kremlin, to Comrade Stalin – he thought for a little and added: "Iosif Vissarionovich"'.[71]

Like Bek, Antonov provides a graphic illustration of the strengths and weaknesses of the Stalinist 'administrative-command economy'. On the one hand, he highlights the genuine enthusiasm of the young people who worked around the clock, against great obstacles, to complete the first underground line on time. When Vas'ka asks: 'Do you think we shall have communism in ten years?', the idealistic seventeen-year-old Mitya replies: 'No, earlier, first in Moscow, then in the rest of the country.' On the other hand, Antonov shows that the frenzied pace of construction, imposed by Stalin's insistence that the first line should open by the anniversary of the Revolution, 7 November 1934, was very wasteful, both of money and human lives. The only way of approaching Stalin's deadline was by seemingly impossible tempos leading to many accidents in which workers were killed or disabled; proper plans were ignored, and shortages were combated by hunting for timber and stealing marble from cemeteries. Although revolutionary enthusiasm eventually achieved the impossible, in that the first line opened on 15 May 1935, Antonov commented: 'This was a striking record, achieved contrary to engineering science. How many extra million roubles were spent to achieve this record is another matter.' The chief engineer in his story complains that the construction site was like a 'theatre of war', where victory had to be achieved 'at any price', and suggests that posterity will see only the 'confusion . . . chaos and senselessness' of it all.

THE TERROR

Some novels and stories newly published in 1987 transcended the more acceptable 'economic' themes, dealing with Stalin's Terror of the years 1936–9 more frankly than any works previously published in the USSR (with the possible exception of Solzhenitsyn's *One Day in the Life of Ivan Denisovich*). One of the first works on this theme to appear was Yurii Trifonov's posthumously published novel *Disappearance* (1987),[72] begun in the early 1960s and left unfinished at the time of his death, which investigates the psychological effect of the Terror on Soviet society and human relationships.

Disappearance was greeted by some Soviet critics with cautious disappointment, as it was felt not to contain any startling revelation, and to be little more than a 'paraphrase of a theme', a reworking of Trifonov's earlier novel *The House on the Embankment*. Indeed, there are striking similarities, as it is set in the same huge grey government house in Moscow where many members of the upper *nomenklatura* lived. It is also true that *Disappearance* is restrained, like most of Trifonov's works, and not particularly sensational, since it concentrates on the repression of party officials, and fails to depict interrogations or tortures. Nevertheless, the critic Yurii Gladil'shchikov comes closer to the truth when he calls *Disappearance* a 'sort of key to all of Trifonov's previous fiction', enabling us to see its 'essential unity'.[73]

Disappearance provides a vivid recreation of the atmosphere of the 1930s, a time of widespread arrests, fear of conspiracy and general depression. Trifonov tackles a theme which he treated obliquely in many of his other works: the destruction of family life, friendship and the human personality through the breakdown of mutual trust caused by the mass arrests and interrogations. In a series of understated scenes seen through the eyes of his young narrator Igor', Trifonov conveys the frightening nature of the process of adaptation whereby normal people accommodate themselves to an abnormal society. He describes an incident in a school at the time of the hundredth anniversary of Pushkin's death in 1937, when the first prize in a school competition is awarded to a boy who has made a statuette of 'Young Comrade Stalin reading Pushkin'. The boy, evidently encouraged by his parents, has adapted to the prevailing political climate, knowing that his teachers cannot possibly refuse him the prize for a work on such a theme.

Trifonov also explores the change which has taken place in the party and the security services since the early 1930s, suggesting that a new breed of greedy, cynical party official is replacing the old type of party idealist (like Trifonov's father Valentin) who made the October Revolution. Honourable men are being superseded by vindictive officials such as the notorious Vyshinskii and Ezhov's associate Artyusha Florinskii, whose main character traits are love of luxury, 'a rare capacity for bearing grudges' and 'a joyful feeling of power . . . a closeness to fate and divine providence'; while his subordinates in the OGPU are the sort of crude officials who will 'do anything they are ordered to do. The most terrible things.' Trifonov, like Arthur Koestler in *Darkness at Noon*,[74] evokes the tragedy of old party members who come to feel: 'We have made a mistake against the party, against the general line. We have made a mistake with the party, perhaps.' The only hope offered by Trifonov's work is that memory and art give the lie to Stalin's pretensions to 'immortality'; only the artist who remembers the past, provides a moral interpretation of it and traces the line of historical development can see which values are ephemeral and which are eternal.[75]

The deportation of nationalities

Another taboo subject opened up for discussion in literature in 1987 was Stalin's brutal deportation of whole nationalities in the years 1944–5 for alleged 'collaboration' with the Nazis. Anatolii Pristavkin's novel *A Golden Cloud Spent the Night* (the reference is to a poem by Lermontov), which was written in 1981, but published in the spring of 1987, once again illustrates the vital role of literature in bringing new topics to public attention, since it treats the theme of the 'punished peoples' of the north Caucasus, particularly the Chechens.[76]

Pristavkin's work tells the story of two war orphans, the eleven-year-old twins Sasha and Kolya Kuzmenysh, who are evacuated to the Caucasus in the summer of 1944 with a group consisting of five hundred other war orphans from Moscow children's homes and other settlers, after the area has been liberated from German occupation. The theme of the deportation of the Chechens is introduced subtly, from a child's point of view. The orphans' train pulls up alongside a train travelling in the opposite direction containing strange carriages out of which peer dark-eyed, starving adults and children, holding out their hands in entreaty and demanding 'Khi!' (we later learn that this means 'water' in the Chechens' language). Sasha knows that these carriages differ from those allocated both to convicts and prisoners of war, but, like prisoners, the strange people are guarded by soldiers who treat them insultingly and give them nothing to eat. In the Caucasus, the two boys are bewildered and frightened to encounter deserted villages and farms with traces of recent human habitation, but no living human beings. It turns out that the land to which they have been evacuated has been vacated by the recent deportation of the indigenous Chechens. Mysterious incidents of arson, theft and murder are the result of raids by a few survivors who live as outlaws in the mountains and return to attack, plunder and kill the settlers who have come to occupy their homes. Pristavkin's merit is that he does not simplify a complex issue, but shows how the unjust, arbitrary action of deportation leads to further injustices and arbitrary actions; the Chechens' understandable desire for revenge causes more innocent people to suffer.

In a tragic and horrifying denouement, Kolya Kuzmenysh narrowly escapes from a Chechen raid, but his brother Sasha is murdered, and, in a cruel parody of the Crucifixion, hung on a fence with ears of corn stuffed into his mouth and open stomach. In one of the best and most moving scenes of the book, Kolya drags his dead brother through the night, constantly talking to him, and, with his last strength, places him in an iron box under a railway carriage, sending him on a journey into the mountains where they had dreamed of going together. Kolya has turned into the lonely 'rock' in Lermontov's poem, whereas Sasha is the cloud which moves on, leaving an indelible trace on the rock.

It would, perhaps, have been better if Pristavkin had ended his work with this scene, but (perhaps because he was writing in the pre-*glasnost* era) he added an artificial, sentimental ending which clashes with the sombre tone of the rest of the novel. Kolya, severely ill and unconscious, is restored to life by the selfless care of an orphaned Chechen boy of his own age called Alkhuzur. In an obvious allusion to contemporary nationality problems in the USSR, Pristavkin draws a contrast between the two orphans and the adult world, with its senseless enmity and violence. Kolya saves Alkhuzur from the Russian soldiers; then Alkhuzur in his turn pleads with a Chechen tribesman to spare the life of his adopted brother. The boys wonder why Russians and Chechens are fighting, and Kolya remarks: 'I think that no one understands why.'

Pristavkin calls for friendship and reconciliation between peoples, although he does not underestimate the power of national enmity in the contemporary USSR. In the epilogue, Pristavkin relates how years later, in a Moscow bathhouse, he met a colonel who boasted of how he had rounded up the Chechens in three hours, following an 'order from Comrade Stalin personally!', and also denounced the Tartars, Kalmyks and Lithuanians as collaborators who should have been shot.

The narrator comments that many neo-Stalinists still exist in Soviet society: 'They are alive, somewhere the same people still exist who acted in His name and executed his will.' They are not tormented by nightmares, but play peacefully with their grandchildren, and recognize others like them: 'It seems that the stamp imprinted by their profession is tenacious.' Notwithstanding this realistic assessment of the contemporary problem, Pristavkin chooses to end his novel on a positive note, emphasizing the friendship between Kolya and Alkhuzur. Sasha's crucifixion can be interpreted as a kind of redemptive sacrifice that will enable the younger generation to break through the barriers of national enmity and vengeance, giving rise to love, self-sacrifice and brotherhood.

Another work which treated the problem of deportation more directly was Iosif Gerasimov's story *A Knock at the Door* (1987), published at about the same time as Pristavkin's novel, but written nearly twenty years earlier, in 1960.[77] Gerasimov focuses on the actual process of a later deportation – that of the Moldavians in July 1949. The protagonist Baulin, director of a school in the Moldavian town of Engeny, is urgently summoned at night by the district party committee and ordered to oversee the deportation 'of persons who collaborated with the German fascist occupiers, speculators and undesirable elements'. The actions taken against the Moldavians are milder than those taken against the Chechens and others in 1944: only selected individuals, not whole villages, are deported, and they are allowed to keep their passports and given an hour and a half to collect their belongings. At first, when Baulin is given his assignment, he does not doubt the justice of the resettlement decree, feeling that the 'bastards' ought to be rooted out, 'and it's actually lenient that they're only being taken and resettled'.

Gerasimov reveals that the deportation was carried out in a military-style operation in just twenty-four hours. Baulin's doubts first arise when he has to break down peasants' doors in the night, hear crying children and see the bewildered, terrified faces of people who do not understand why they must suddenly leave their homes and land. Gerasimov emphasizes the injustice of the deportations, and the unattractiveness of those who direct the operation. One woman screams: 'Where's the trial?', and a former resistance fighter earmarked for deportation ironically advises Baulin to 'think' while he is doing his 'dirty work': 'Hasn't it occurred to you that immediately following the war, fair trials were held of those who collaborated with the Germans?' Baulin himself feels a 'vague ambivalence' and sickness at the operation, but eventually writes the laconic report required by the authorities, because 'he has always been accustomed to living in this way, surrendering to the will of others above him, and because he had no other choice'.

In a careful 'Afterword' Gerasimov attempted to soften the force of his story, arguing that it had been written more than a quarter of a century earlier, and that almost forty years had passed since the events depicted in the story: 'Time has passed, and much, a very great deal has changed around them. Some of the deportees have returned home. They have children and grandchildren.' However, the author justifies the publication of his work by the need to tell the truth to young people, linking his story with 'the purifying work which has extended in all directions of our life after the Twenty-Seventh Congress of the CPSU'.

These works by Pristavkin and Gerasimov were welcomed by the liberal critic Alla Latynina, who admitted that Stalin's policy of deportation was a 'complex and painful subject that has hitherto been avoided on the grounds that there is no point in reopening painful wounds. After all, the reasoning has gone, the unjust decrees ordering the deportation of entire peoples have been revoked, and many families have returned to their homes.'[78] Latynina rejects such sophistry: 'We must know the past and draw lessons from it in order to avoid repeating its mistakes. There can be no events in history that are better forgotten than understood.' Latynina also addresses the wider question of Soviet people's guilt for alleged collaboration with the Nazis. While admitting that there were indeed some people in occupied territories who collaborated with the Germans, she emphasizes that the degree of guilt of different people varied, and that this was a matter for trials to determine. She correctly concludes: 'Certainly there could have been nothing done by individuals for which an entire people had to pay, as they had to in Pristavkin's novel.'

After the appearance of these two literary works, Stalin's treatment of other nationalities, such as the deportation of the Kalmyks in 1944, began to be discussed in the press in 1988–9;[79] although some files on the deportation of the Chechens and Ingush had to wait until 1992 to be released.[80] The case of the Crimean Tartars, who were not allowed to return to the Crimea, also surfaced in the press, but their grievances were only given limited publicity, as it was considered impossible to repatriate so many people. Unfortunately, although literature played a useful role in breaking taboos and bringing to public attention the issue of past injustices inflicted on non-Russian minorities, the scale of national conflict both before and after the break-up of the USSR demonstrated that in this sphere neither well-intentioned literary works nor political exhortations had any power to stem extreme nationalist feelings. Events in Nagorny-Karabakh, Tadzhikistan and Chechnya have been closer to the horrifying racial conflict depicted in *A Golden Cloud Spent the Night* than to the romantic reconciliation at the end of Pristavkin's novel. The disastrous long-term impact of Stalin's policies towards the non-Russian nationalities was publicly admitted in 1992, when, in the absence of Gorbachev, Alexander Yakovlev was asked by Sergei Shakhrai at the Constitutional Court's trial of the Communist Party: 'Isn't there a cause-and-effect relationship between Stalin's deportation of many peoples and today's ethnic tension?', and Yakovlev replied: 'Of course there is.'[81]

4 Two Key Writers: Shatrov and Rybakov

By the spring of 1987 the whole process of reassessing Stalinism was raised to a new plane by the publication of two formerly censored works by writers still living in the USSR – Anatolii Rybakov's novel *Children of the Arbat* and Mikhail Shatrov's play *The Peace of Brest-Litovsk*[1] – which ventured beyond the more limited anti-Stalin works which had already appeared. The publication of these two works in March and April 1987 graphically demonstrated how in the Gorbachev era literature could be used to signal a change of policy. Since Gorbachev's approval must have been required for the publication of these works, their appearance suggested that the new leadership was contemplating a more radical reappraisal of Soviet history than ever before, in order to prepare the way for far-reaching economic and political reforms.

RYBAKOV'S *CHILDREN OF THE ARBAT*

Rybakov's *Children of the Arbat*, which was completed in 1966 and twice announced for publication,[2] but suppressed by the censorship for twenty years,[3] was by far the boldest of the anti-Stalin works of prose fiction newly made available to the Soviet public in 1987. The enormous publicity with which Rybakov's critique of Stalin and Stalinism was surrounded was due to the fact that it was the first to be published in the USSR by a writer still living in his homeland, who could be interviewed and questioned about his work. It possessed novelty value, since it had not previously been published in the West and had only been known to a small circle of Soviet readers.[4]

Children of the Arbat presented the most extensive realistic depiction of Stalin and his entourage, and the first serious discussion of the mechanism and psychology of the purges to be published in the Soviet Union since the inception of *glasnost*.[5] The novel aroused such great interest that readers queued up to obtain it in bookshops and libraries,[6] and it was characterized as 'an event not only of literary, but also of public life'.[7] Whereas Bek's *The New Appointment* had been largely

concerned with Stalin's industrial policy, Rybakov's novel went straight
to the seat of political power, investigating the circumstances surrounding
the murder on 1 December 1934 of Sergei Kirov, head of the Leningrad
Party Organization, which sparked off the 'Great Terror' of the 1930s.
If Abuladze's film *Repentance* had treated the theme of dictatorship,
guilt and responsibility in an oblique, surrealistic way, Rybakov's approach was more direct, providing a realistic reconstruction of Stalin's
psychology and his 'philosophy of power'. Portrayals of Stalin by other
writers have aroused considerably less interest, because they were either
published posthumously (as in the case of Bek, Pil'nyak, Grossman
and Dombrovskii), written by authors currently living in the West (including Solzhenitsyn, Maksimov, Voinovich and Sinyavskii), or, if they
were by compatriots of Rybakov still living in the USSR (such as
Adamovich and Iskander), their works appeared later than his.

Children of the Arbat opened up many formerly sensitive historical
subjects for public discussion in the USSR. Rybakov hinted at Stalin's
complicity in Kirov's murder, (although he failed to make the charge
explicit), demonstrated that Stalin's terror began before the Seventeenth
Congress of January 1934, and reopened the question of whether NEP
should have lasted 'seriously and for a long time', as Lenin once maintained.[8] *Children of the Arbat* had tremendous educative value in the
USSR, because, as the Soviet historian Alexander Latsis affirmed, 'Having
taken into your hands the journal containing Rybakov's book, you lose
for ever the possibility of not knowing, not remembering, not compre-
hending.'[9] In a country where, as Alla Latynina remarked, the history
of Stalinism was less well known than the history of the Russian empire, this was a service indeed.[10]

Rybakov's novel was attacked for historical inaccuracy by Soviet,
western, and Russian émigré critics alike.[11] Latsis pointed out that
Rybakov invents certain episodes, such as the alleged meeting between
Kirov and Ordzhonikidze in Moscow in November 1934.[12] A stronger
criticism was made by the émigré Natal'ya Kuznetsova, who complained
that the novel fails to implicate Stalin directly in Kirov's murder.[13]
This stricture is, however, somewhat unfair, since Kirov's murder is
still a very controversial subject for historians,[14] and Rybakov did not
have sufficient evidence to do anything other than hint at Stalin's possible complicity.[15] Indeed, Stalin's guilt cannot be conclusively proved
without access to Soviet secret police files, and reliable reports suggest
that the relevant files were destroyed long ago. Nevertheless, Rybakov's
failure to implicate Stalin directly may represent a failure of nerve on
his part, as in 1987 such accusations had still not been voiced openly,

either in fiction or the press. Other serious criticisms levelled against Rybakov by western historians include the charges that Rybakov sometimes omits known facts, such as the opposition to Stalin among delegates to the Seventeenth Party Congress, and that all genuine differences over policy issues are simply reduced to Stalin's suspiciousness and megalomania.[16]

In the years 1987–8 Rybakov's novel became a major focus of the battle between the two hostile camps of 'democrats' and 'patriots' which was raging in Soviet society. Initially the Soviet liberal intelligentsia attempted to capitalize on the novel's publication by advancing the cause of de-Stalinization. The magazine *Ogonek* published a series of letters which Rybakov had received since 1966 from prominent literary and artistic figures who had read the novel in *samizdat*, demanding that the truth about Stalin be made public. Most writers were supportive, except for the Russian nationalist Valentin Rasputin, who rejected the author's alleged portrayal of the 'depravity' of the Siberian people, and claimed that it would have been more interesting if Rybakov had analysed the psychology of powerful, but shadowy figures such as Kaganovich rather than Stalin himself (no doubt Rasputin was influenced by the fact that Kaganovich was Jewish).[17]

The novel gave rise to an extensive correspondence, which provides a fascinating reflection of Soviet social attitudes in the years 1987–8.[18] In Rybakov's postbag the letters praising *Children of the Arbat* outnumbered the critical ones in the proportion of six to one; some twenty to twenty-five per cent of letters came from people who had themselves suffered repression, or whose relatives had. However, some readers clung to their old Stalinist principles, asking why it was necessary to 'muddy the waters', or even threatening to denounce Rybakov to the KGB;[19] while the fanatical student leader of a Stalin circle in Gori (Stalin's birthplace in Georgia) expressed a desire to burn the copy of *Druzhba narodov* containing Rybakov's novel.[20]

In 1987 and early 1988 democratic Soviet critics generally confined themselves to Rybakov's treatment of Stalin and Stalinism, since this was as far as the reassessment of history was officially allowed to go in 1987.[21] At that time it was only the émigré critic Kuznetsova who lambasted Rybakov for adopting a Leninist, pro-party position;[22] but by 1988, conservative, nationalist critics within Russia had also begun to attack the central conception of Rybakov's novel.[23] Sometimes, as Latynina later admitted, democratic critics, in their eagerness to counter criticism from neo-Stalinists, failed to see that the novel was equally vulnerable to attacks from radical right-wing quarters.[24]

Vadim Kozhinov's acrimonious criticism of Rybakov's novel was designed to minimize Stalin's own role in the terror, laying the blame on those around him, particularly Jews in his entourage such as Kaganovich. The nationalist critics' most serious stricture was that Rybakov's concentration on the privileged 'children of the Arbat' blinds him to the wider sufferings of the Russian people, especially during the collectivization campaign and the famine of 1932–3. Stanislav Kunyaev issued a challenge to the Soviet élite, who later became the victims of 1937: 'The children of the Arbat don't want to know that Russian priests and impoverished kulaks are dying of the cold in Narym ... the Arbat childhood happily continues.... Somewhere on the Volga there is cannibalism. The Gulag is flourishing in Solovki.'[25] The implication is that Rybakov is only interested in Stalin's repressions against the Communist Party and the intelligentsia after 1934, not the persecution of the peasantry and non-party intellectuals before that date – that is, he goes no further than Khrushchev in his 'Secret Speech' of 1956. This criticism is unfair, since Rybakov does go further than Khrushchev by praising NEP and referring to oppositionist communists whom Stalin defeated before 1934, such as Ryutin; in any case, Rybakov could not have ventured any further in 1987, since writers who wished to attack Stalin still had to elevate a Leninist ideal worthy of emulation.

By August 1989, when criticism of Lenin was permitted in the USSR, the magazine *Ogonek,* which had previously been among Rybakov's strongest supporters, changed its tune and admitted: 'The thoughtful reader will of course already have realized that the publicistic "Staliniana" which has bored him was enforced ... it was essentially imposed on *publitsistika* by the lack of *glasnost,* by the censorship restrictions: criticism of Stalin was already permitted, but there was a veto, as before, on attempts at a deeper causal analysis ... at serious conceptual criticism.' *Ogonek*'s admission seems to be a tacit acknowledgement of the fact that in 1987–8 democratic critics had been restrained in their criticism of Rybakov's views, since an analysis of Stalinism which laid any blame on Lenin and Leninism was still taboo.

In retrospect, the enthusiastic, perhaps disproportionate praise lavished on *Children of the Arbat* immediately after its publication may have been due in part to the Soviet intelligentsia's delight that a serious analysis of Stalinism had now become possible, and to their desire 'not to harm it with a careless word'.[26] This was not an idle threat in 1987, as was demonstrated by the 'Andreyeva affair' of early 1988. In 1987 the political significance of Rybakov's novel was so great that it was only western critics who were at all concerned with the artistic shortcomings of *Children of the Arbat.*

In retrospect, it could be argued that the polemics about the novel were more important than the novel itself, and that one of the main achievements of *Children of the Arbat* was to initiate a serious discussion of Stalin and Stalinism in historical journals and the media.[27] Critics and publicists advanced widely differing interpretations of Stalinism, demonstrating how far Soviet 'pluralism' had advanced by 1988.[28] From 1988, serious historical and biographical works about Stalinism began to be published in the USSR.[29]

SHATROV'S *THE PEACE OF BREST-LITOVSK*

The publication in April 1987 after a twenty-year delay of Shatrov's play *The Peace of Brest-Litovsk* (begun in 1962),[30] provided another illustration of Gorbachev's policy of reinterpreting Soviet history in order to shed light on the problems of the present. The play is an orthodox demonstration of the correctness of Lenin's decision to sign the Treaty of Brest-Litovsk in 1918; its most sensational aspect was that it put on stage not only Lenin and Stalin, but also other Old Bolsheviks condemned by Stalin, such as Trotsky, Bukharin and Zinoviev. This suggests that the activation of the Control Commission to investigate the purge trials had at last made it possible to re-evaluate the contribution to Soviet history of Stalin's opponents and victims. The closeness of Shatrov's viewpoint to that of the party leaders was demonstrated by the fact that Gorbachev and other members of the Politburo were present at the first performance at Moscow's Vakhtangov Theatre in December 1987; later Shatrov travelled with Gorbachev and became a member of his presidential council. The play was subsequently shown on television, to an audience of millions.

One of Shatrov's main aims is to debunk the myth that Stalin was Lenin's best disciple and natural successor. In the original production Stalin was depicted as a fanatic, totally devoted to his leader, who followed Lenin's movements closely and persistently, acquiring the skill of posing as Lenin. However, Shatrov emphasizes the great difference between Stalin's approach to the party and that of Lenin: Stalin is accused by the Soviet President, Yakov Sverdlov, of regarding the party as a 'closed order of crusaders with its hierarchy, discipline, morality and philosophy', while Lenin has a more tolerant approach to intra-party disputes: 'Leaving the Central Committee does not mean leaving the party.' The implication of publishing Shatrov's play in 1987 is that Gorbachev's democratic approach to the Party is closer to that of Lenin than Stalin. The denouement, when Stalin moves at the last minute to side with Lenin, is richly suggestive of Stalin's later malign role in Soviet history.[31]

Notwithstanding its overt Lenin worship, to a thoughtful reader or spectator Shatrov's play implicitly raises questions about legitimacy in Soviet history. If most of Lenin's disciples had been condemned by Stalin in the 1930s and Stalin himself had been reviled in the 1950s, how could intelligent Soviet people maintain faith in the continuity of Lenin's cause? Indeed, what exactly did the Leninist cause amount to if it had to be continually protected from successive errors and distortions?

The aspect of Shatrov's play which aroused most interest among Soviet critics and scholars was the portrayal of Trotsky and Bukharin, which was generally regarded as completely plausible, the incarnation of Lenin's views in his recently-published *Letter to the Congress* (1923).[32] To a western spectator, however, although Shatrov allows Lenin's opponents to put their case, he underlines the wisdom of Lenin's policy and does not present either Trotsky or Bukharin as worthy comrades of Lenin who might deserve 'political rehabilitation' – the restoration of party membership, and therefore the legitimation of the dead men's political views and activities – rather than merely 'civil rehabilitation' – the rejection of the criminal charges against them. The Trotsky and Bukharin depicted by Shatrov are misguided rather than criminal, but, as Shatrov himself admitted, still 'caricatures'.[33] Shatrov's depiction of Trotsky as a conceited theatrical poseur, never a serious revolutionary leader because he lacked Lenin's 'correct' strategic vision, was a simplistic image reminiscent of Stalinist propaganda of the 1920s, which was beginning to become popular again in the Gorbachev era.[34]

Although Shatrov's *The Peace of Brest-Litovsk* performed the useful function of encouraging the Soviet press to discuss Trotsky, Bukharin and alternatives to Stalinism,[35] this discussion was not particularly profound. Shatrov does not express the slightest doubt that Lenin was absolutely right, and Trotsky and Bukharin absolutely wrong, and avoids any deeper discussion of the way in which the Treaty of Brest-Litovsk forced the Bolsheviks inwards, creating a climate of opinion conducive to the acceptance of Stalin's 'socialism in one country'. There is no recognition that all these problems stemmed from the 'premature revolution' – the seizure of power in a backward peasant country.

SHATROV'S *ONWARD . . . ONWARD . . . ONWARD!*

Shatrov's new play *Onward . . . onward . . . onward!*, published in January 1988,[36] also became a *cause célèbre* in the Soviet press even before it was performed on stage, provoking a bitter dispute among writers, readers, historians and political activists. The debate about Shatrov's play both reflected and contributed to the wider struggle for the future of *perestroika* which was taking place in the difficult period between the Plenary Session of the Central Committee in February 1988 and the opening of the Nineteenth Party Conference in June. The relationship between art and politics proved to be so close in this case that the views held by Soviet readers on Shatrov's play became a reliable indicator of their general standpoint on Gorbachev and his reform programme.

Shatrov's *Onward . . . onward . . . onward!* has the subtitle 'The author's version of events which occurred on 24 October 1917 and significantly later', reflecting the play's complex structure. At the simplest level, it moves through the events of twenty-four hours in Petrograd on the day before the Bolshevik Revolution, demonstrating that when Lenin takes command, the date of the revolution is brought forward and its success assured. However, the main aim of Shatrov's play – as the title suggests – is to analyse the forward movement of the Russian revolution after 1917, and to investigate how and why the Bolshevik revolution, with its high ideals, degenerated into Stalinism. The fundamental question which Shatrov addresses is: would Lenin have seized power if he had known what was going to follow his death in 1924? Shatrov explores this question with the help of two dramatic techniques which are highly unusual in a Soviet context. His play opens with twenty-two major historical characters of the revolutionary period introducing themselves in turn, many of whom were former 'unpersons', and little known to a Soviet audience.[37] The second dramatic device is that the characters are released from 'real time' and, in full knowledge of their own and the country's future, conduct an otherworldly conversation with one another across the decades, explaining their views and actions with the advantage of hindsight. The characters' lines sometimes form part of the historical record, sometimes contain a measure of poetic licence, and sometimes represent the author's own invention. Shatrov's concentration on the individuals who made choices in history brings the revolution alive as a process depending on human relationships, and, by implication, opens up the Russian past once again to individual judgement and analysis.

It should be remembered that, whereas western readers have a variety of histories of the USSR to consult, with diverse interpretations drawing on commonly available sources, Soviet readers had, by the late 1980s, been subjected for fifty years to an official interpretation which required the suppression of vital sources and facts. Shatrov's play fulfilled a valuable function by considerably extending Soviet people's knowledge of their past. The novelty of many of his themes for a Soviet readership is demonstrated by the fact that the play's first director claimed that it had taken his actors a month of historical study even to read the play properly.[38] Shatrov's sharp posing of historical questions never discussed so openly in literature before is more important than the unoriginal answers he gives, which frequently run counter to informed western interpretations.

One striking aspect of Shatrov's play was that it included a reading of Bukharin's last letter to 'a future generation of Party leaders', dictated to his wife on the eve of his arrest.[39] Another sensational revelation was Trotsky's accusation that Stalin murdered him 'without the semblance of a trial' – an issue still so sensitive in 1988 that no Soviet critic felt bold enough even to mention it.[40] Other new issues explored by Shatrov included the debate on the end of NEP; the reasons why the accused in the Moscow trials confessed,[41] and a challenge to the commonly accepted Soviet view that Trotsky played only a minor part in the revolution and the consolidation of Soviet power (although Shatrov still underestimates Trotsky's role in 1917). Some of the arguments Shatrov uses to distance Stalin from Lenin are highly debatable: for example, the claim that Stalin, like Trotsky, was opposed to Lenin's plan to stage the uprising in 1917 before the meeting of the Congress of Soviets could give it legitimacy. Shatrov's insistence on the vital importance of Lenin's last-minute presence, which received support from radical historians like Yurii Afanas'ev,[42] was attacked by conservative critics who charged him with 'oversimplification' and 'historical inaccuracy'.[43] In view of the uncertainty which still surrounds this question,[44] it is incumbent on Russian writers and historians to treat the subject with a certain caution.

One of the reasons for Shatrov's controversial interpretation is his desire to draw a direct comparison between Stalin and Trotsky – a view which by 1988 was gaining currency in the USSR.[45] He presents the two chief contenders for leadership after Lenin's death as morally corrupt, concerned only with their own power.[46] Another important reason for Shatrov's emphasis on the importance of timing in a revolution is that he wishes to draw a parallel between the Bolshevik

Revolution of 1917 and Gorbachev's 'revolutionary' policy of *perestroika.*

Shatrov's play, for all its apparent boldness, conformed perfectly to the controlled *glasnost* which Gorbachev initially wished to introduce. It simultaneously offered the Soviet reader the excitement of previously forbidden debate and the reassurance of the familiar version of Soviet history. In Shatrov's play the October Revolution, the founding act of the Soviet state, is still elevated as a supremely important, positive event in Russian history, and Lenin himself, virtually unaided, is presented as leading the people to liberation. None of the arguments of Lenin's opponents are examined seriously, and the only plausible alternative which Shatrov offers is a different kind of Bolshevik revolution which might have avoided the pitfalls which culminated in Stalinism. Any unfortunate consequences of the revolution are blamed on Lenin's unreliable disciples who almost succeeded in obstructing him in 1917 and actually succeeded in 1922, when Lenin's first stroke effectively removed him from political control. Thus to a considerable degree the message of *Onward . . . onward . . . onward!* hardly differs from that of Shatrov's earlier plays. The main conflict is between the ideal Leninist revolution of Shatrov's imagination, which might have led to a moral, democratic socialist society, and the reality of the Stalinist tyranny. It is possible, however, that Shatrov's play might have led some more enquiring readers to investigate alternative philosophies for themselves.

For all its shortcomings, Shatrov's analysis of Stalinism and its origins is more profound than the view of some Soviet historians in 1987–8, such as Volkogonov, who, while acknowledging Stalin's crimes, continued to emphasize the benefits of Stalin's industrialization policy and the victory over Nazi Germany, which transformed the USSR into a super-power.[47] Certain aspects of the play suggest alternative, more complex readings of Soviet history than simply a struggle between Lenin and Stalin. One major reason for Stalin's success is seen as the collective conduct of the Old Bolsheviks after Lenin's death – their suppression of his *Testament,* their refusal to allow debate outside the inner ruling circle and, particularly, their complicity in Stalin's crimes. They are shown to have subordinated the interests of the revolution and the party to their own 'behind-the-scenes bureaucratic struggle'. Shatrov does not fully explain why the Bolsheviks behave in this way, although Bukharin is allowed to attribute it to their devotion to party unity. Other interpretations are advanced by Maria Spiridonova, the Left Socialist Revolutionary, who blames the rival socialist parties for failing to accept the Soviet structure of the new state; by the right-wing generals and Stalin, who seek the source of tyranny deeper, in

Russians' age-old inability to govern themselves and their need for a despot; and by Plekhanov, the founder of Russian Marxism, who attributes Russian submissiveness not to national character, but 'the absence of Marxist culture'.

The cumulative effect of such views is to reinforce the portrait of Stalin as a product and an exploiter of Russia's backward political culture, and to emphasize that, whereas Stalin wished to keep Russia in slavery, Lenin believed in a new, free socialist way of life. As in *The Dictatorship of Conscience*, Shatrov implies that Leninism has lived on in the hearts of good Soviet people and can still triumph, if everyone joins in to support a revival of 'the revolution as a network of political and moral coordinates'. This somewhat vague concept is all that Shatrov has to offer, except his usual emphasis on a sense of moral worth and conscience (*chest'* and *sovest'*). Shatrov's Lenin argues that the past is only prologue, and the beneficence of the revolution can only be discovered by pushing it 'onward ... onward ... onward'.

Shatrov's play aroused considerable excitement and controversy in Soviet society in 1988. Like the official critics, his correspondents were sharply divided about the merits of the play and its author, but his postbag displayed a heavy preponderance of positive responses: in the spring of 1988 his letters were running six to one in favour of the play.[48]

Press coverage of the play began almost the moment it was published, leading hostile commentators to question the 'forcing of society's attention upon it'.[49] The editor of *Pravda*, Viktor Afanas'ev, condemned it as 'irresponsible' at a meeting with Gorbachev in January 1988, and when the party leader did not respond, published two articles critical of it in his paper.[50] In the second of these, two obscure professors and doctors of science complained that 'Shatrov presents Stalin not as the antipodes of Lenin, but merely as another hypostasis', and cast doubt on the authenticity of 'the so-called eve-of-death Bukharin last letter'.[51] This superficial attack seems simply to have whetted readers' appetite for deeper analysis of the play, judging by the large number of letters the paper received.[52]

A more serious assessment, couched in an authoritative, denunciatory style, was made by two historians in the main party research institute, including V. Zhuravlev, who had helped to initiate the reform of the history profession in 1987.[53] They objected to the whole line of Shatrov's play, interpreting Lenin's remark: 'I understood too late ... the system which allowed one man to concentrate unlimited power in his hands ought to have been changed' as implying that Shatrov was himself blaming Lenin for 'the decisive mistake which influenced the whole course of the future development of events'. In fact, the sentiment which Shatrov attributes to Lenin is very close to some of his last words, dictated on his deathbed: 'I am deeply culpable before the workers of Russia. I put too much hope in my recovery.'[54]

The play proved so controversial that for some time permission was not given for it to be performed on the stage, except in Tomsk, and then only in a fringe theatre. Shatrov's opponents condemned the fact that he had 'given the stage to our enemies', whereas his supporters congratulated him for presenting an array of previously forbidden views of Soviet history. Although Shatrov's clear intention was to praise Lenin and Leninism, the suggestiveness and ambiguity of the play hinted at more profound causes of Stalinism than were proposed in Shatrov's public statements.

Although Shatrov's research over many years had earned him the right for his historical analysis to be taken seriously, one favourable reviewer, Dmitrii Kazutin, correctly pointed out that it can be a mistake for drama to overtake history, but asked: 'What is to be done when our historians have remained silent for so long?'[55] Another sympathetic critic, the Doctor of Philosophy A. Butenko, claimed that many historians who were being called upon to attack Shatrov were simply engaged in a demarcation dispute, trying to avoid controversial issues and protect their own discipline from the incursions of fiction writers.[56]

Shatrov's work was used as a weapon in the concentrated attack on the reappraisal of history and Gorbachev's policy of *perestroika* which occurred in the spring of 1988. The most notorious article was by the chemistry teacher Nina Andreyeva in March 1988,[57] who denounced Shatrov for his alien political views and defamation of Soviet achievements. Andreyeva admitted that she had not yet read Shatrov's offending new play, but, in the spirit of Sydney Smith's dictum: 'I never read a book before reviewing it; it prejudices a man so',[58] launched into a fierce critique of it based on the favourable and unfavourable reviews she had read. Unconfused by the text, she was convinced that 'Shatrov deviates substantially from the accepted principles of socialist realism', and that Shatrov 'puts into his characters' mouths what was asserted by enemies of Leninism concerning the course of the Revolution, Lenin's role in it, relations among members of the Central Committee at different stages of the inner-party struggle'.[59]

Andreyeva was particularly incensed at the 'haste' with which liberal critics in 1988 were trying to get Shatrov's play staged. This was a reference to a letter to *Pravda* on 29 February from a number of famous theatre directors and playwrights complaining about old-fashioned ideological objections to Shatrov's play, which had been denounced simultaneously as 'Menshevik' and ultra-revolutionary, and publicizing 'warning signals to the effect that a number of cities are already prohibiting the production of the new play about Lenin'.[60] They found it disturbing that censorship was being carried out in a 'new style – not by order or peremptory shout but by strong, friendly admonition', which was no less effective, threatening to return Russian theatre to 'administrative-command methods of managing culture'. Referring to the stage directions at the end of Shatrov's play: 'We wish very much that Stalin would leave, but he's still on the scene' (a comment relevant to the USSR of the 1980s, as well as the 1920s), the liberal theatrical figures declared: 'Yes, we would very much like Stalin to leave not only the stage but our lives as well; we would like to see the end of his methods, his "morality" and his ways of resolving disputes, in art too.'

CONCLUSION

The experience of Rybakov and Shatrov demonstrates the significant role which historical fiction played in the general political debate of 1987–8. As the critic A. Turkov pointed out, the appearance of *Children of the Arbat* was an important event in the USSR, since this was one occasion when literature was able to make invaluable use of its own resources in order to overtake its 'neighbours', history and biography.[61] In July 1987 the senior historian Yurii Polyakov had been forced to admit: 'The writers have long since overtaken the historians in posing sharp questions';[62] but by late 1988 Soviet society had begun to 'grow out of' Rybakov's novels,[63] and historians at last began to rise to the challenge. As the press became freer and historians took a more prominent role in investigating the archives, historical fiction was never again to assume such great significance in Russian society.

The works of Rybakov and Shatrov, however daring they seemed on first publication, simply represented the new orthodoxy which was emerging in the USSR in 1987 and early 1988. Soviet history was yet again being presented by writers and journalists in a biased way, although the bias was less extreme and more acceptable to the West than formerly. Most works of fiction either stated or implied that Stalin and a few of his closest associates had been personally responsible for the tragedy of the 1930s; no reference was made to internal conflict (for example, the presence of a militant faction within the leadership, or active collaborators) or other wider factors such as external threat, Soviet ideology or political culture. There were no works of fiction published in 1987 which explicitly stated that the oppositionists of the 1920s, whether Trotsky or Bukharin, might have had a valid case. Lenin was still placed on a pedestal, and there was no hint that he might have bequeathed ideas and institutions to Stalin which had enabled him to carry out the purges. In the works of Rybakov and Shatrov, Lenin is seen as a wise leader, not as Stalin's mentor. In particular, his democratic tendencies are over-accentuated and his New Economic Policy over-praised as the most suitable model for the future development of the economy; there is no discussion of the tightening of political control during the 1920s, or of whether Lenin intended the NEP as merely a temporary measure.

The works of Rybakov and Shatrov played a significant part in preparing the climate of opinion which led to the rehabilitation of Bukharin and Rykov in February 1988,[64] and of Zinoviev and Kamenev in June 1988;[65] and to the non-rehabilitation of Trotsky.[66] Their influence, however, proved to be short-lived, as such 'rehabilitations' were irrelevant after 1991, when the whole communist enterprise collapsed.

The further fate of the works by Rybakov and Shatrov in 1987–8 reflects that of all highly politicized 'liberal' works of historical fiction published in Russia since the inception of *glasnost*. By 1990–1 *Children of the Arbat* already appeared old-fashioned because of its overly respectful attitude towards Lenin and Kirov,[67] and in 1993 a group of Russian historians argued that there was no longer any point in reading Rybakov, as he was simply a time-server who had seized an 'opportune moment' in 1987.[68] Similarly, Mikhail Shatrov's series of plays demythologizing Lenin, when televised in 1991 to mark the anniversary of Lenin's birthday, felt like a desperate attempt on the part of Leonid Kravchenko, the conservative head of Soviet television, to rekindle people's fading enthusiasm for Lenin. A rather different view was expressed in 1993 by the critic Mikhail Zolotonosov, who regarded Rybakov's novel with ironic nostalgia as one of the last examples of a truly popular literary work published at a time when it was still possible to harbour 'socialist illusions'.[69]

5 Collectivization and the Repression of the Peasantry

The vital role of literature in bringing new subjects to public attention was again demonstrated by fiction on the subject of collectivation and the repression of the peasantry published in the years 1987–8.[1] Some outspoken works on this theme had appeared before Gorbachev's accession,[2] but since 1982 there had been a clampdown on further works on collectivization until early 1987, when the publication of Part Two of Boris Mozhaev's *Peasant Men and Women* again brought this subject before the reading public.[3] The aim of Mozhaev's novel, set in two fictional villages in Mozhaev's native Ryazan province, is to register 'the last months in the life of the peasant community, and the destruction of its thousand-year-old way of life'.[4] The controversial nature of Mozhaev's work, completed in 1980,[5] is demonstrated by the fact that even when it finally achieved publication in the USSR, it appeared only in the provincial journal *Don*, which had a relatively small circulation and was not easily available in the country at large, except in public libraries.[6] Moreover, the journal also felt the need to include an introduction by Academician Tikhonov of the Lenin Agricultural Academy, who endorsed Mozhaev's novel as 'valuable' and 'useful', confirming that the events depicted are based on fact, and that Mozhaev does not exaggerate the extent of the tragedy.[7]

In the spring and summer of 1987, the direct encouragement given to discussion of collectivization by Gorbachev and Yakovlev[8] led to the appearance of a series of memoirs, literary works and articles on collectivization and the fate of the peasantry in the 1930s, sometimes containing completely new material.[9] It became known that some prominent writers had opposed collectivization: revelations included a forceful letter of 18 June 1929 from Sholokhov protesting about the condition of the peasantry in the Don region, and Pasternak's description of the 'inhuman, unimaginable woe' of the peasantry in 1930.[10] The publication of fiction and *publitsistika* on the subject of collectivization was initially designed to arouse support for the introduction of Gorbachev's economic reforms at the June 1987 Plenum.

A major literary work touching on this theme to be published in the summer of 1987 was Andrei Platonov's surreal anti-utopian novel *The Foundation Pit*, written at the height of the collectivization drive in the years 1929–30 and never previously published in the USSR.[11] Platonov is a complex, but hitherto unjustly neglected writer whom Brodskii has characterized as 'one of the greatest Russian novelists of the twentieth century'.[12] In *The Foundation Pit* Platonov satirizes a self-confident village activist who slavishly follows higher authority in his attempt to drag the masses into the 'fixed and immutable happiness-to-be in the future'. The frantic digging of a foundation pit in order to build a many-storeyed building called 'socialism' takes place against the background of 'the universal decrepitude of poverty' in a neighbouring village. Platonov mocks official jargon by interpreting it literally and thus reducing it to absurdity: for example, he depicts the 'liquidation' of the kulak sector as the kulaks floating away *en masse* on a raft down the river.[13] He also casts doubt on the whole concept of a 'kulak', referring only to the 'less unprosperous' peasants', and asking sadly: 'Where is the collective farm wealth?' In a satirical reference to the Leninist concept of *smychka* (the alliance between the proletariat and the peasantry), it is suggested that the foundation pit must be built wider and deeper so that the peasants can join the proletariat, whereupon the collective farm peasantry dig the ground 'to save themselves in the abyss of the foundation pit'. The publicist Igor' Klyamkin commented on this scene: 'in view of what happened afterwards, they were dancing on their own graves'.[14] Platonov's allegory suggests that collectivization, introduced with triumphant fanfares and promises of a rapid leap into communism, ended in destruction. The tragic death of young Katya may symbolize the death of the peasantry, or even of the socialist ideal itself. It recalls the words of Dostoevskii's Ivan Karamazov that the aim of paradise on earth is not worth the tears of a single child, and that if children suffer he will respectfully 'return his ticket' to paradise.[15] Platonov's novel was published in *Novyi mir* (with a print run of 600,000) and therefore may have reached a wider audience than some other fictional works on collectivization. It had a great impact on Soviet readers: one party historian stated: 'It is necessary to recognize that A. Platonov's *The Foundation Pit* has to a considerable extent entered the consciousness of people, especially of young people';[16] and the radical historian Yurii Afanas'ev spoke of a time when 'digging a pit meant storming heaven'.[17] For the critic Natal'ya Ivanova, poetry editor of *Druzhba narodov* and a significant force in the democratic camp, Platonov's work demonstrated that 'to build socialism by serf labour is not only impossible but monstrous'.[18]

The serialization of Mozhaev's *Peasant Men and Women* paved the way for the publication of two other important novels of 1987–8 – Part Three of Belov's *Eves*, and Sergei Antonov's *The Ravines* – which also represented a significant contribution to the reinterpretation of collectivization in the USSR.[19] All three novels contain many similar scenes and characters, but whereas Belov's novel takes the story up to 1929, stopping on the eve of de-kulakization and collectivization in the winter of 1929, Mozhaev and Antonov depict the far more sensitive subject of the 'great turning point' of the years 1929–30. All three writers treat such themes as the bitter hostility of the peasants to grain requisitioning and forcible collectivization; the cruel and unjust 'dekulakization' of the more efficient farmers, the labelling of any opponents of party policy, even poor peasants as 'sub-kulaks' (*podkulachniki*), and the cycle of violence and injustice unleashed by the collectivization policy which sometimes culminated in full-scale peasant revolts that had to be suppressed by the Red Army. Notwithstanding their similarities, the novels have differences in style: Belov's is more poetic and apocalyptic than Mozhaev's, and permeated with a sense of supernatural foreboding, while Antonov's contains elements of humour and the detective story. Most importantly, they represent three distinctive points of view on collectivization: Mozhaev's stance is a moderate nationalist view similar to that of Solzhenitsyn; Belov's is a more extreme nationalist, anti-Semitic viewpoint; and Antonov's is a reformist socialist position similar to that of Gorbachev. This divergence of viewpoint reflects the pluralism in the analysis of collectivization among historians and politicians which had emerged in the USSR by 1988.[20] Although these novels all possess certain limitations if they are to be considered purely as historical interpretations of collectivization, they nevertheless present a radical re-evaluation of a subject formerly treated only in euphemisms, and are bolder than most 'village prose' in their explicit criticism of the party's collectivization policy itself, not merely of the individuals responsible for implementing it.[21]

One of the central questions raised in these novels was one which agitated historians and publicists in the Gorbachev era: whether or not the peasants resisted collectivization.[22] In many previous Soviet publications, notably the first part of Sholokhov's *Virgin Soil Upturned* (1932),[23] the peasantry had been depicted as basically passive, and any resistance during the collectivization drive had been presented as anti-Soviet in inspiration.[24] In *Peasant Men and Women*, however, Mozhaev takes an opposing view, praising the resistance of the majority of the peasantry and implying that the true patriots were not those who collaborated with the unjust Stalinist regime, but those who rioted in defence of their way of life, fled to the towns to avoid compulsory collectivization, or worked badly in the new kolkhozes.[25]

Mozhaev, Belov and Antonov provide a radical reinterpretation of the whole notion of the 'kulak class', suggesting that the richer peasants, with their capacity for hard work and enterprise, were highly respected in the community, representing a dynamic force in the Russian countryside. Mozhaev demonstrates that the authorities were foolish to destroy the very people who could have made the greatest contribution to Soviet agriculture. Lenin's land distribution in 1917–8, he implies, gave peasants roughly equal amounts of land; so by the late 1920s those who had grown poor, on whom the party relied to implement its collectivization policy, were, for the most part, lazy and drunken, while many of the richer peasants were not exploiters and speculators, but those who had succeeded through their own hard work.[26] Similarly, in *Eves* Belov points out that the peasants labelled 'kulaks' in the village are simply efficient farmers, unlike those who support the kolkhoz, who include an epileptic (Sopronov), a drunkard (Erokhin), an irresponsible womanizer (the old chairman Mikulen′ka), as well as Jewish ideologues, such as Meerson and Zhuk ('Beetle').

Mozhaev undermines the whole social basis of the mass collectivization policy, making the point that it is not only so-called 'kulaks', but many honest and sensible 'middle peasants' who slaughter their animals and burn their own homes rather than submit to political coercion. The 'middle peasant' Zinovii Borodin speaks for the whole of the rural community when he complains of the demoralization of the peasantry 'driven into collective farms like a herd of cattle'.[27] Similarly, Zinovii's brother Andrei, whose honesty and integrity are emphasized throughout the novel, and who refuses to join the dekulakization brigades, voices concern that collectivization has deprived the peasant of his two most vital qualities: his independence (*samostoyatel′nost′*) and sense of being the master (*khozyain*) of the land.[28] Andrei's words reflect the view of Mozhaev himself, in his afterword to the novel and in other public pronouncements about Soviet agriculture.[29]

Since these novels were all written before the *glasnost* era, their authors were less frank than in their interviews or later fiction, and sometimes gave an over-favourable interpretation of Lenin's policy towards the peasantry. However, the views of Mozhaev cannot entirely be attributed to the desire to insure against criticism in the pre-*glasnost* era, since he has not revised his opinions in the book version of his novel, or in his later works.[30] In the works of all three writers the policy of forced collectivization is contrasted with the more gradualist view of Lenin, whose name is either linked directly with that of Bukharin, or sometimes invoked as a cover for Bukharin's views.[31] Mozhaev and Belov refer to Lenin's article 'On Co-operation', which favoured a continuation of NEP and free trade, culminating in a gradual transition to collectivization.[32] Through his depiction of the 'positive' party official Ozimov, whose views are very similar to those of Bukharin, Mozhaev implicitly succeeds in rehabilitating Bukharin a year before the Central Committee did so officially in February 1988. However, his view of Bukharin is highly ambiguous, possibly because of Bukharin's radical intelligentsia background: Mozhaev sometimes cites his radical works of the 1920s out of context, and associates him with Trotsky, thus contrasting his ideas with the wise opinions in Lenin's late articles. At a meeting called to discuss the novel in a Rostov collective farm in April 1988, Mozhaev expressed greater support for Bukharin's views, especially those in Bukharin's article 'Lenin's Political Testament' (1929), recently republished in the USSR.[33] He condemned the argument frequently voiced in the press that there was no alternative to the 'great breakthrough', expressed support for 'Lenin's co-operation and NEP, adopted "seriously and for a long time"', but also added:

> We are well aware that Bukharin did not have his own line; he defended the policy of Leninist co-operation and NEP jointly with Rykov, Tomsky, Dzerzhinsky, Frunze and others. Bukharin justified this policy for the last time in January 1929 as the political testament of Lenin. Then Bukharin and the remaining supporters of the Leninist policy were thrown out of the political arena, and many were physically exterminated.[34]

Mozhaev's statement is highly debatable, both because of his simplistic interpretation of Lenin's economic ideas, and his anachronistic references to Bukharin's alleged supporters Dzerzhinsky and Frunze, who died some time before the conflict between Bukharin and Stalin in 1928.

The most controversial aspect of the novels of Mozhaev and Belov was their distinctive philosophical vision of the history and destiny of Russia, which is fundamentally opposed to Marxism. Indeed, the Leninist sentiments they espouse (no doubt for reasons of 'camouflage') are difficult to reconcile with their deeper attack on Marxist ideology. Although these novels create a powerful impression, their somewhat disingenuous, nationalistic interpretations of collectivization are highly controversial. They have serious shortcomings if they are to be considered as history, demonstrating little knowledge of western scholarly disputes about the causes of the grain crisis of 1927–8 and the viability, or otherwise, of NEP. The subtext of the works of Mozhaev and Belov is an elegiac, nationalistic lament for the Russian Orthodox Church and a naïve idealization of the village before collectivization.

If Mozhaev, through the character of the school teacher Uspenskii, makes a strong philosophical case for considering collectivization as a manifestation of the destructive, utopian trend in westernist Russian thought,[35] his political views are more controversial. Uspensky explicitly blames the leftist deviation of the 1920s, and specifically the Jews Trotsky, Zinoviev, Kamenev and Yakovlev, for the policy of forcible collectivization.[36] This view was contested by Academician Danilov, who pointed out that after 1927 neither Zinoviev nor Kamenev was in a position to implement policy, and Trotsky had already been deported to Central Asia. Danilov also castigated Mozhaev for 'shifting the responsibility for the violence' of collectivization from the 'real culprits', Stalin and his immediate entourage in 1929–30, especially Molotov and Kaganovich.[37] David Gillespie has countered Danilov's criticism by claiming that 'Mozhaev does not shift any blame from Stalin and his henchmen: he merely shows that Stalin used the ideas of the "Left Opposition" once he had defeated them'.[38] This argument cannot be substantiated, however, as Mozhaev does not specifically refer to Stalin's defeat of the 'Left Opposition'; indeed, although Kaganovich receives a negative mention, Stalin's name is conspicuous by its absence throughout much of the novel, and Stalin is favourably mentioned in the conclusion as the author of the moderate article 'Dizzy with Success' (1930), which puts an end to the ruthless activities of over-zealous local officials. Gillespie sees this conclusion as 'ironic', but it can be read in this way only in the light of later articles by Mozhaev. It seems more likely that Mozhaev, writing before Gorbachev's accession, was 'insuring' against criticism. Certainly, the difficulties which Mozhaev experienced in securing the publication of his novel show that even in early 1987, his work was testing the limits of *glasnost*. Whatever Mozhaev's reasons for letting Stalin off lightly, Danilov was right to argue in connection with Mozhaev's novel that 'Trotsky and his supporters must finally be freed from the attribution to them of the variant carried out by Stalin.'[39]

The nationalist bias of Mozhaev's novel is reflected in the fact that the collectivization drive is carried out largely by non-Russians: the Ukrainian Vozvyshaev and the Tartars Radimov and Ashikhmin. The elements of anti-Semitism in his novel, although not as extreme as in

Belov's *Eves*, are also distasteful: for example, the opprobrious references to 'Judas' and 'belated followers of Yudushka, Trotsky's penpusher'. Although Mozhaev may have intended an allusion to Yudushka ('Little Judas'), the nickname of Porfirii Golovlev, the unctuous hypocrite in Saltykov-Shchedrin's satire *The Golovlev Family* (1872–6), an epithet used by Lenin to denigrate Trotsky in the years 1912–13,[40] this would not have been the primary interpretation of these epithets to suggest itself to a contemporary Soviet audience. Mozhaev himself is not an extreme nationalist, but some of the sentiments he attributes to his hero Uspenskii – the allegation that the Russian radical intelligentsia had nothing but contempt for the national historical experience, or that the suffering of the Russian peasantry was primarily a result of harmful foreign influences, both in the realm of theory, through alien Western European ideas, and on the practical level, through Jewish associates of Stalin – have later been developed in a less acceptable form by radical Slavophiles writing in the journal *Nash sovremennik* and by supporters of *Pamyat'*.

Belov's interpretation of collectivization is even more controversial.[41] He goes further than Mozhaev in implying that nearly all those who impose collectivization on the village are Jewish. In discussing the co-operative movement, he claims that Otto Schmidt, another Jewish Bolshevik, was responsible for undermining Lenin's promising initiative.[42] Belov refers more directly to Stalin and Molotov than Mozhaev does, but the implication of his novel is that Jewish Bolsheviks, particularly Stalin's Commissar of Agriculture Yakovlev and the exiled Trotsky, were primarily to blame for the crimes committed against the Russian peasantry.[43] Belov expressed this belief more explicitly in an interview of 1988,[44] in which he argued that the collectivization policy involving 'excessive taxes, loans, the dispersal of the co-operatives, the depletion of their resources, and, ultimately, repressions, executions, trials, deportations . . . was what Trotskyism turned into for millions of peasant families'. Using a somewhat convoluted argument, Belov asserted: 'In my opinion, the main Trotskyite was Stalin, although some scholars pretend that he was an anti-Trotskyite. Stalin defeated Trotsky by organizational means – removed him as a rival for personal power. But Stalin and his entourage took the essence of Trotskyism into their armoury.' Belov argues that Stalin himself had no original ideas on agriculture, and that he appointed as Commissar of Agriculture the Jew Yakov Yakovlev – 'a man far from agriculture, who understood little about it'. Although some historians would agree that Stalin, having defeated Trotsky, took over some of his ideas in order to defeat the Right Opposition, few would deny that the responsibility for collectivization ultimately lies with Stalin and his associates who remained in power in the years 1928–30, and that Stalin, having adopted some of Trotsky's ideas, took them to an extreme which even Trotsky and his supporters had not envisaged.

The liberal critic Andrei Turkov provided a convincing response to the works of both Mozhaev and Belov.[45] While appreciating the value and artistry of their novels, Turkov attacks the historical inaccuracy of their association of collectivization with Trotsky, commenting ironically: 'Stalin was a strange kind of Trotskyite'. He finds it somewhat strange that both Belov and Mozhaev, writers who differ considerably from each other, succumb to familiar, stereotyped views about Trotsky. Somewhat charitably, he ascribes their failure to launch an outright attack on Stalin to the re-Stalinization of the Brezhnev years when Mozhaev and Belov were writing. However, with hindsight, particularly in the case of Belov, who made nationalistic pronouncements as a Congress deputy and produced a highly provocative anti-Semitic novel, *All is Ahead* (1986),[46] the attack on Trotsky and Yakovlev as the main villains cannot be seen as entirely an unwitting product of the 'era of stagnation', but as a deliberate misinterpretation and underestimation of Stalin's responsibility. This assumption was borne out by the serial publication in 1989 and 1991 of his sequel to *Eves*, *A Year of Great Change*, which while condemning Stalin more explicitly, is also more obviously anti-Semitic.[47] Belov's literary works, for all their strengths, have helped to perpetuate the myth that the blameless Russian people have, since 1917, been mercilessly crushed by a savage regime of Jews and non-Russians – the same myth propagated in such suspect propagandistic works as Igor' Shafarevich's *Russophobia*.[48]

THE FAMINE OF 1932–3

The first literary work since Gorbachev's accession to raise another highly sensitive subject – the famine in Ukraine in 1932–3[49] – was *Bread for the Dog*, a previously unknown autobiographical story written in the years 1969–71 by Vladimir Tendryakov, posthumously published in August 1988. Tendryakov himself had touched upon this subject in a novel of 1968, *The Death of the Boss*,[50] and it had already been raised in the Gorbachev era by Yurii Afanas'ev in a powerful article of June 1988: 'The organized hunger of 1932–3 carried away millions of lives.'[51] Tendryakov's story depicts huge numbers of dekulakized peasants from Voronezh, Kursk and Oryol who 'no longer looked like people', lying on the roads like skeletons, slowly dying of starvation.[52] The young narrator cannot bear to watch people dying in front of him, so he begins to feed a few beggars. At first he tries to feed them all, but there are far too many of them, and they eventually crowd around his house, harassing him. Tendryakov points to the contrast between ideological slogans and universal human values of kindness and compassion: grown-ups tell the boy that the starving peasants are nothing but 'bloodsuckers' and 'enemies'.[53]

Eventually the young Vladimir stops feeding people, but shares his bread with a starving dog in order to assuage his guilt: 'It wasn't a dog grown mangy from hunger which I fed with scraps of bread, but my own conscience.' In a documentary note appended to his story, Tendryakov cites Roy Medvedev's figure that approximately 3–4 million people died in the famine – a figure which corresponds to Danilov's estimates of 1988 – avoiding the extreme view of Robert Conquest, who refers to a possible 6 million dead.[54] Tendryakov also mentions the astonishing fact that in 1933, the worst year of the famine, the USSR continued to export ten times as much grain as from the harvest of 1928.[55] These stories, and his other posthumously published works, completely alter our view of Tendryakov as a writer and citizen,[56] showing him to be a much more outspoken critic of the Soviet regime than his previous interesting, but limited works had led his readers to believe.[57]

The publication of Tendryakov's story, and further information about the famine in the press in 1988–9, paved the way for the posthumous publication in 1989 of Vasilii Grossman's *Everything Flows . . .*, which contains the most frank and harrowing depiction of the famine in the whole of Soviet literature, drawing a direct comparison between the Nazi destruction of the Jews and Stalin's destruction of the peasantry. It can be assumed that by 1989 the Soviet public already knew about, and had come to accept this terrible historical tragedy, as criticism of Grossman's work focused on other issues, largely ignoring his powerful depiction of the famine.[58]

CONCLUSION

If in 1987 the theme of collectivization had been treated with some caution in literature and the press, by 1988–9 numerous literary works and articles expressing alternative views on the subject had been published,[59] and a new, honourable tradition of truthful literature about collectivization and the famine had been established in Russia. In contrast with the old stereotypes of the 'positive' party official and the greedy 'kulaks' depicted in classic socialist realist novels like Sholokhov's *Virgin Soil Upturned,* new 'reverse' stereotypes were beginning to emerge in Russian literature: the efficient peasant unjustly 'dekulakized' and the disorganized, envious poor peasant.[60] Fiction on this theme published in the Gorbachev era helped to provide a more accurate picture of the years 1929–34, challenging journalists and historians to investigate this tragic period more thoroughly.[61] At the same time, literary works possessed great relevance for the present, leading Russians to discuss the contemporary problems of Soviet agriculture, with the hope that they could learn from their past mistakes. Writers of collectivization novels were regarded as experts on agricultural questions, frequently being interviewed in the press and participating in discussions about the current state of Soviet agriculture. Antonov made more modest claims than Mozhaev and Belov, suggesting that it is not the function of the novelist to 'issue instructions to agricultural workers'.[62]

By mid-1988, what R. W. Davies has called a 'new radical consensus' had emerged in liberal journals and newspapers committed to Gorbachev's *perestroika.*[63] This viewpoint went beyond Gorbachev's cautious report on the anniversary of the Revolution in November 1987, totally rejecting the collectivization of agriculture at the end of the 1920s, arguing that Lenin's strategy of voluntary peasant co-operation should have continued, and that the mixed market system of NEP should not have been replaced by administrative planning. By the end of 1988 Bukharin had been rehabilitated, many of his writings had been published, and his view of Soviet economic development was increasingly being accepted as a feasible alternative to Stalin's policy of forcible collectivization, both in literary works and many works of non-fiction.[64] Indeed, praise of Bukharin had become so extravagant that Soviet intellectuals on both sides of the political divide now found it necessary to counter his new elevation to privileged status.[65]

6 The Stalin Terror: Prisons and Camps

If 'returned literature' of 1987 had opened up the subject of Stalin's repressive regime, the year 1988 marked a new phase in which Stalin's terror could be depicted with much greater frankness in the USSR.[1] One new development was that by 1988 it became possible to admit that torture, both physical and mental, had been used in interrogations by Stalin's secret police. Harrowing descriptions were permitted to appear in the press and literary journals: for example, the horrific torture of the famous theatre director Meyerhol'd and his wife, which could not be revealed in the Soviet press in 1987,[2] was publicly disclosed in May 1988.[3] Another taboo broken in 1988 was the depiction of the worst prison camps in Stalin's system, the camps of Vorkuta, Taishet and Kolyma in Eastern Siberia, which do not even figure in Solzhenitsyn's *The Gulag Archipelago*.[4] Whereas in the autumn of 1987, the American scholar John Glad had told Sergei Zalygin that the value of *glasnost* was questionable if Varlam Shalamov's *Kolyma Tales* still could not be published,[5] the change which had occurred by June 1988 was evident when Zalygin published a selection of Shalamov's stories in *Novyi mir*.[6]

Conditions in Stalin's prisons and camps have long been familiar to western readers; but in Gorbachev's USSR they were described in great detail and on an unprecedented scale in the popular press and the broadcasting media.[7] In Khrushchev's time such accounts had been far more limited, confined mainly to literary journals, particularly Tvardovskii's *Novyi mir*; and for over twenty years since Khrushchev's fall the Soviet press had kept silent about the labour camps. By contrast, in the literary journals of the Gorbachev era, documentary prose, memoirs and autobiographical fiction by survivors of Stalin's purges, which drew readers right into prisons and camps, began to enjoy more popularity than historical novels, and no Soviet citizens who read the press, listened to the radio or watched the television could fail to be informed about the cruelty, suffering and death which the deliberate policy of Stalin and his government had inflicted on countless numbers of their fellow countrymen. The enormous flood of memoir literature by survivors of Stalin's terror which began to be published in the USSR in the years

1988–9 included powerful works already known in the West, such as the memoirs of Nadezhda Mandel'shtam and Evgeniya Ginzburg,[8] as well as previously unknown memoirs by writers still living in Russia, such as Lev Razgon and Anatolii Zhigulin.[9] It became clear that, like the dissident and émigré writers who had become well known in the West, writers who were still living in the USSR had also tried to keep the memory of Stalin's terror alive during the 'era of stagnation' through private readings and correspondence.[10]

Prison and camp memoirs of the Stalin period published since the inception of *glasnost* are too numerous to analyse in detail here,[11] but their interest and variety stem from three main factors: the type of reality they depict, which is a function of when and where the author was imprisoned; the point of view from which the prison or camp is perceived, which depends partly on the political viewpoint of the author, and partly on whether the main emphasis is placed on survival, opposition or demoralization; and the extent to which experiences are presented realistically or filtered selectively through art and memory.

INTERPRETATIONS OF THE TERROR

The most fundamental question of concern to Soviet people in 1988 which arose from the memoirs was: why did it happen? Many memoirs attest to the feelings of bewilderment experienced by innocent people unjustly imprisoned.[12] Evgeniya Ginzburg, in *Into the Whirlwind*, discloses: 'Many different feelings tormented me in those years. But the dominant feeling was a sense of amazement.'[13] The liberal critic Andrei Vasilevskii refers to many explanations of the purges current in the Gorbachev era:

> We too ask: what *was* this? Stalin? Stalinism? The Administrative System? The administrative-command mechanism? Beria? Barracks socialism? . . . Retribution for the attempt at a 'proletarian revolution' in a peasant country? A collapse of the attempt to build a society with features laid down in advance? The fruits of leftist adventurism? 'Devils'? Divine wrath?

Vasilevskii speaks for many of his contemporaries when he argues that all these 'explanations' are totally inadequate to interpret 'the irrational abyss of what happened', and that 'in reality *no one* knows, and anyone who says he knows is deceiving himself and others'.[14]

Another issue which divided the Soviet intelligentsia in the Gorbachev era was a discussion of when Stalin's terror began. Many authors of memoirs published in 1988 regarded 1937 as the true beginning of the terror,[15] or implied that it was an intensification of a trend set in motion by the murder of Kirov in 1934.[16] This common interpretation can be ascribed to the fact that the late 1930s was the time when party members began to be arrested in large numbers; there is a shortage of memoirs about the repressions of 1929–34, because ordinary peasants who suffered during collectivization were often illiterate, and certainly not as articulate as the party intellectuals who were later condemned.[17]

By 1988 many Soviet intellectuals had come to feel that the narrow party interpretation of the national tragedy current in Khrushchev's time was no longer adequate. Yet even in 1988, democratic critics, intent to refute the arguments of Kunyaev, Kozhinov and other nationalist critics who dated the beginning of the terror before 1934, still continued to assert that the year when repressions began was 1929, rather than earlier, under Lenin.

In 1988, nationalist opponents of the long-established version of the Khrushchev era, which had focused exclusively on the repressions against party members after 1934, began to propagate an equally false conception: that 1937 was nothing more than a year of 'local' repressions focused only on the upper echelons of Soviet society. Some even went so far as to regard it as 'revenge' for the former sufferings of the Russian people. The critic Vasilevskii aptly characterizes such views: 'One extreme gives rise to another, one narrowness of vision to another, one falsehood to another, suspiciously similar.'[18]

Contemporary responses to memoirs of the Stalin period varied according to whether writers regarded the Stalinist prison system as a deformation of their own, fundamentally sound system, or as a reflection of an alien ideology. If before 1988 it had been almost obligatory to express faith in the party and the basic tenets of Marxism–Leninism, in 1988 far more hard-hitting critiques of Stalinism were published by writers formerly considered 'anti-Soviet'. Nadezhda Mandel'shtam's memoirs, for example, characterized Stalinism as an absolute evil: 'We never asked when we heard about some arrest: "Why has he been taken?" But there were not many like us . . . "What for?" shouted Anna Andreyeva [Akhmatova] in fury. – "What do you mean, what for? It's time to understand that people are taken for no reason . . .".'

However, many memoirs by former party members published in 1988, such as those of Evgeniya Ginzburg and Sof'ya Shved, still attested to their continuing belief that although they themselves were innocent, there were some real 'enemies' and 'wreckers' who did deserve imprisonment, and they therefore found it difficult to blame Stalin and the party for what was happening. In 1988–9 democratic critics such as Vasilevskii and Ivanova were intent on refuting the naïve version of events propagated by former communists. Vasilevskii points to the experience of those victims who 'saw the light' after a long psychological struggle, such as Evgenii Gnedin, the former head of an NKVD department, who only came to distinguish right from wrong after he had been tortured, and even in prison in 1939 found it difficult to compare Nazi villains with NKVD men like his torturers Beria and Kobulov, whom he saw as 'ugly exceptions'. Other writers of 1988, however, were prepared to make a direct comparison between the Hitler and Stalin regimes.[19]

In contrast to the majority of works published in the Khrushchev era, which had attempted to demonstrate how party members remained true to their principles even in camp,[20] some works published in 1988 ventured much further, pouring scorn on party loyalists who tried to justify the repressions. Likewise, the horrific accounts of camp life by Zhigulin and Shalamov highlight the relative mildness of the description of the camp in Solzhenitsyn's *One Day in the Life of Ivan Denisovich*. The passions to which accounts of camp life could still give rise in the Gorbachev era were demonstrated by the reaction to Zhigulin's account by another camp survivor, G. Gorchakov, who takes issue with many details of Zhigulin's description of Kolyma, unfairly blames him for allegedly collaborating with 'thieves' in order to survive, and, along with another former camp inmate, M. Korallov, casts doubt on the veracity of Zhigulin's account of his escape attempt.[21] Gorchakov's reaction also highlights the great diversity of experience of Stalin's camps revealed in the Gorbachev era. Even when writers describe the same camps, some seem to have lived in different worlds. The German Communist Trude Rikhter, for example, refers to privileged women in Kolyma who worked in 'hothouses' and lived in 'cleanly whitewashed barracks';[22] whereas for Il'ya Taratin, Kolyma is a murderous place where prisoners are shot in the back of the head by the camp authorities, or taken by escaping criminals as 'deer' to be killed for meat.[23]

PASSIVITY

Many different views were expressed in the 1980s on the question of why so few people resisted arrest or tried to escape.[24] This was particularly difficult to understand in the case of the military men arrested in 1937.[25] Boris Yampol'skii's posthumously published novel *Moscow Street* suggests that few Soviet people opposed arrest or imprisonment, because they were psychologically unprepared to escape and hide in their own country.[26] Many memoirs claim that it was difficult to know whom to resist, because simply shooting one camp guard would not have destroyed the whole system, which to many appeared a supernatural incarnation of evil. As Nadezhda Mandel'shtam has explained: 'The clash with an irrational force, irrational inevitability, irrational terror sharply changed our psyche. Many of us believed in the inevitability, others in the expediency of what was happening.'[27] Some writers suggest that many Soviet people genuinely believed in Stalin and thought the purges must have some rational explanation.[28] Shalamov argues that the intellectuals imprisoned in the 1930s were not enemies of the regime, and hence had no inner resources to combat the camp system.[29] The critic Vasilevskii suggests that even if many people did know or suspect the truth, Soviet society was too atomized for this knowledge to become more widely accepted until Khrushchev's denunciation of Stalin at the Twentieth Congress of 1956.[30]

RESISTANCE

In 1988 it also began to be widely revealed in the Soviet press that, notwithstanding the general conformism in Stalin's time, a brave minority who actively resisted Stalin and Stalinism had existed at different levels of Soviet society throughout the Stalin period,[31] and that in 1954–5 uprisings took place in the camps of Norilsk, Vorkuta and Karaganda, which were 'horrifically pacified' by mass executions.[32]

Shalamov's moving tale *Major Pugachev's Last Battle* demonstrated that resistance had begun earlier in the 1940s, when a new breed of repatriated prisoners of war had been sent to the camps after the war: 'They were very different men, formed by war, bold and willing to take risks . . . Officers and soldiers, airmen and commanders.' Shalamov shows that, although the escape attempt was unsuccessful, it gave the men back their sense of human dignity.[33]

One of the most interesting accounts of resistance to Stalin was Zhigulin's discussion of the activities and arrest of members of a small oppositionist political group, the Communist Party of Youth (KPM) in the provincial Russian town of Voronezh in the years 1948–9.[34] Zhigulin's memoir provided new information for both Russian and western readers, since it had previously been assumed that there had been almost no overt resistance to Stalinism in the post-war period, apart from the concealed resistance of writers such as Akhmatova and Pasternak, who were writing 'for the drawer'.[35]

Zhigulin provides a detailed analysis of the genesis and administrative structure of the KPM, 'an illegal youth organization with a Marxist-Leninist platform',[36] founded in Voronezh in 1947 by pupils of the ninth form in a boys' secondary school, Boris Batuev, Yurii Kiselev and 'Igor' Zlotnikov', because he is aware that many of his readers will find it difficult to believe that seventeen-year-old students could set up such an organization in Stalin's time. He claims that ill-informed questions of the type: what did the KPM achieve in the ten months between October 1948 and August 1949? are usually asked by people who do not understand the all-embracing atmosphere of terror and mutual suspicion which existed in Stalin's time. The group's main achievement was to create, in incredibly difficult circumstances, a conspiratorial organization consisting of about fifty people prepared to take Leninist ideas to the masses. As Zhigulin remarks, 'Is all this so little?'

Zhigulin relates that when in March 1963 he offered Tvardovskii his poem *Guilt*, which he had written about his case in the Stalin era, Tvardovskii could not believe that lines such as

> That they bow down in vain
> To a living god on the earth.

had been written in the 1940s and not with hindsight. Although Zhigulin told Tvardovskii about the KPM, such cases could not be publicly admitted in Khrushchev's time. Zhigulin agreed to Tvardovskii's suggestion that the poem should be published without its ten middle lines, and it was set up in type, only to be forbidden by the censorship. It is not surprising that the poem was banned at that time, as it suggested that Zhigulin had been involved in a real opposition movement, not simply one invented by the secret police:[37]

> Guilt! Of course there was
> We were so strong in our guilt.
> It was easier for us, the guilty ones
> Than those taken with no guilt at all.

Zhigulin contrasts his experience with Tvardovskii's own lines, first published in the Khrushchev period:

> Who in his time did not praise him [Stalin],
> Did not eulogize him – find such a one![38]

While conceding that Tvardovskii was correct in saying that there were not many 'such ones', Zhigulin nevertheless considers it important to emphasize that some pockets of resistance did exist under Stalin. The KPM was not the only illegal youth organization in the post-war period: in other towns the secret police exposed 'The Circle of Marxist Thought' and 'The Lenin Union of Students.' In prison camp Zhigulin claims to have met members of other illegal anti-Stalin Marxist organizations – Pyotr Khodov from Novosibirsk, Vladimir Filin from Astrakhan and Slavka Yankovskii from Kiev – although these groups were much smaller and less well organized than the KPM, consisting of only three to five members. Doubt has, however, been cast on the extent of resistance in the late 1940s by a camp survivor, S. Lominadze, who is not entirely convinced that the other small resistance circles Zhigulin mentions were not simply invented by Stalin's security organs in the wave of repressions of 1948–9.[39] This subject is still highly topical in 1994, when support is coming from the newly-opened archives for the existence of social protest and resistance groups in Stalin's time, but counter-arguments like Lominadze's are still being used.[40]

Zhigulin's tense account of the betrayal of the KPM in 1949 and the reactions to it provide a graphic illustration of the passions which still raged about cases which had occurred in Stalin's time.[41] Although Zhigulin himself wished to name names in order to settle old scores, his editors made him change the names of the alleged traitors twice, 'in case, God forbid, somebody recognized them from my story'.[42] Zhigulin's harshest censure is reserved for the chief traitor, 'Arkadii Chizhov', who was initially arrested only because he was known to be one of Zhigulin's friends, but subsequently betrayed the whole of the organization. Zhigulin alleges that when the case was reviewed in 1953–4 the informer may have removed documents pertaining to his own interrogation, since he later claimed that the confession had been 'beaten out of him'.

Doubt has been shed on the veracity of Zhigulin's account of the KPM by M. Korallov, whose meticulous dissection of Zhigulin's narrative demonstrates that this story, particularly the allegations of treachery, could still provoke controversy in the contemporary USSR.[43] The de-

bate about Zhigulin's work is instructive, as it suggests what bitter
and widespread recriminations could be unleashed if all former Soviet
citizens took advantage of the new law permitting them access to their
own secret police files, as many people have done in Germany.[44]

Zhigulin's memoir aroused considerable hostility in the Soviet press.[45]
One of the loudest protests came from a certain Leonid Korobkov,
writing in a local Voronezh paper,[46] who, as a former insider in the
KPM, dubbed Zhigulin's story 'falsehood, slander, juggling with facts',
claimed that 'Arkadii Chizhov' did not betray anyone, and that the
game of shooting at Stalin's portrait never took place. The vehemence
of this attack suggests that Korobkov may have had a personal interest
in the story of 'Chizhov's' treachery; in the polemics that ensued critics
maintained that Korobkov was 'trying to justify the sentence conferred
by Beria's investigators'.[47]

While making the interesting admission that the theme of betrayal is
'historically and socially very important' in contemporary Russian society,[48] Korallov takes issue with Zhigulin's narrative about the alleged traitors to the KPM. He even expresses some sympathy for 'Igor'
Zlotnikov's' complaint that the organization was fascist, and hints that
its leaders could be regarded as precursors of the young fascists who
met in Pushkin Square in Moscow in the Gorbachev era. He also argues that Zhigulin is too prone to posturing when he continues to utter
threats against the alleged chief traitor 'Arkadii Chizhov', claiming
that after Batuev had pardoned him in 1950 Zhigulin had originally
accepted his leader's verdict and actually worked alongside Chizhov
for a while before his release. In Korallov's opinion, the acceptance of
a statute of limitations which allows even clearly proven crimes to be
forgiven is the hallmark of a civilized society. This is an argument
which still rages in Russia in 1994, after the release of the coup leaders
of 1991 and 1993.

Another powerful literary work published in 1988, Dombrovskii's
The Faculty of Unnecessary Things,[49] portrayed a non-communist hero,
the archaeologist Georgii Zybin,[50] who opposed Stalinist tyranny through
the power of thought and moral courage. Among the democratic Russian intelligentsia, Dombrovskii's novel became one of the most influential works on Stalinism published under *glasnost*.[51] It had not
been well known in Russia before, and possessed both great moral
force and higher literary quality than many other fictional works published in 1987–8. In prison the autobiographical hero Zybin comes to
understand not only that he, with his 'classless humanism', is intolerable
to the Stalinist world, but also that the Stalinist world is intolerable to

him, since all human values – law, morality, truth, beauty, honour, culture, love, compassion, honest work, national traditions – have been ascribed to 'the faculty of unnecessary things'.[52] This realization liberates him, and he is free to adopt the only rational position in relation to this world: compassion and scorn. Zybin is a historian of early Christianity who is able to hate sin and evil, while pitying the perpetrators of the evil;[53] and the novel is permeated by a Dostoevskian contrast between life, morality, vitality, and the non-existence of the world based on Stalinist values. Dombrovskii's emphasis on 'the great power of liberating scorn' towards Stalinist oppressors created a great impression on liberal critics in the 1980s.[54]

Prison fiction and memoirs and the responses they provoked in 1988 suggest that a new myth had emerged in Soviet society of the Gorbachev era: the desire to discover resistance to Stalinism in the past. The criticism of dissidence characteristic of the Brezhnev era was turned on its head, and conformism now came under attack. The critic S. Lominadze commented ironically that it had reached the level of a new 'social command: to find "resistance", "protest" in the past'.[55]

A genuine history of resistance to Stalinism in Russia, which in the 1990s is the subject of archival research by the Petersburg historian Boris Starkov, would be a valuable contribution to twentieth-century Russian history; but it would be quite wrong to imply that resistance was widespread in Stalin's time. Not surprisingly, most Soviet people were outwardly conformist, even if they opposed Stalinism in the privacy of their homes or secretly in their hearts, and such resistance as there was usually took the form of spontaneous protest against economic crisis, or a desire to return to Leninism. An acknowledgement of these truths entails no slur on the people of the former Soviet Union; it is simply a timely reminder of the widespread fear, deformation of character and mass hypnosis created by a totalitarian system. By the 1990s, however, such considerations had become irrelevant in Russia, since the cultural intelligentsia had become so polarized that some radicals (rather ahistorically) now evinced little sympathy for party members such as Bukharin and Ryutin who had offered resistance to Stalin, or for those opponents of Stalinism who believed in true Marxism–Leninism.

IMPACT ON HUMAN BEINGS

For readers in Gorbachev's Russia, one of the most important issues raised by the newly-published fiction and memoirs was the long-term effect of Stalin's prisons and camps on the psychology of the Soviet people. If works on this subject published in Khrushchev's time generally had to sound an optimistic note, some works published in 1988 were far more pessimistic in tone. Whereas Solzhenitsyn suggests in *One Day in the Life of Ivan Denisovich* that people were able to preserve their human dignity even in prison camp, Shalamov asserts: 'The author of *Kolyma Tales* considers camp a negative experience for a human being – from the first to the final hour . . . Camp is a negative experience, a negative school, corruption for everyone – for the warders and prisoners, convoy guards and spectators, passers by and readers of fiction.'[56] He regards the fate of the characters in *Kolyma Tales* as 'the fate of martyrs, who were not, could not be, and did not become heroes', and does not wish the suffering of the Stalin era to be justified, romanticized or sentimentalized.[57]

Another prominent theme in memoirs and documentary prose published in 1988 was an analysis of the psychology of the camp warders and torturers as well as their victims. Razgon relates that he eventually came to understand 'immediately and for ever, that they are not like us. . . . You should not enter into human relations with them.'[58] He provides a fascinating insight into the different characters of the warders and secret police officials whom he has met, including men who were 'clever and stupid, good and evil'.[59] His most revealing encounter is with the Siberian Tartar Niyazov, who speaks in a very matter-of-fact way about his duties at the *spetsob"ekt* (special point) fifty kilometres from the station of Bikin on the railway line between Khabarovsk and Vladivostok.[60] The 'special points', which had not previously been depicted in Soviet literature, were small camps where those sentenced to death were brought for execution from the prisons and camps in the neighbouring region. When Razgon questions Niyazov about his feelings after the shootings, he claims that he lost no sleep and felt no remorse. His main complaint was boredom, as there were no women at the *spetsob"ekt*; married men were not hired to do this particular job. Even later, when he was told that the people whom he had shot were innocent, and that there had been 'excesses', he accepted the official view that he and his colleagues were not guilty, as they had just been obeying orders. Even then he felt no pangs of conscience: 'I'm not sorry for them, it's as if they didn't exist.'

According to Razgon's calculations, the *spetsob"ekt* at Bikin exterminated between fifteen and eighteen thousand people during the two and a half years of its existence; and Bikin itself was only one of the many 'special points' which worked 'precisely and regularly' throughout Siberia. Razgon's revelations complement the discoveries of mass graves in Siberia, Belorussia and the Baltic states reported in the Soviet press from 1988 onwards.[61] In the spirit of the organization *Memorial*, Razgon declares: 'They were everywhere, these "points", and nothing remains of them: neither terrible museums like those in Auschwitz or Mauthausen, nor ceremonial memorials of mourning, as in Katyn.' In a striking phrase, Razgon claims: 'We live among murderers.' He has in mind not only the actual executioners like Niyazov (although many of them are still alive), but the bureaucrats 'who wrote papers, signed their names under the words "I would suggest", "agreed", "I confirm", "to sentence".' Many of these Stalinist officials survive, and even flourish, in the post-Stalin era.

Yurii Dombrovskii also pays particular attention to the members of Stalin's security services as well as their victims, seeing in their psychology a key to modern Soviet history.[62] This theme in Dombrovskii's novel proved to be very topical in 1988, when many other articles were published discussing the mechanism of Stalin's terror and asking why members of the NKVD had obeyed orders, when so many of them also perished.[63] Dombrovskii presents a series of varied types, but, unlike Razgon, portrays most of them as normal people, not pathological sadists. Dombrovskii implies that it is such intelligent people, and not the brutal Khripushins, subordinates only capable of executing other people's orders, who have the real power to send people to camps, prisons, exile and execution, and arrange the scenarios of show trials. Dombrovskii suggests that the key to their behaviour is that they have no moral absolutes, which form the basis of all other values of human culture, including law. He demonstrates logically that if class interest, not morality, rules conduct in Stalin's USSR, there is nothing to stop the interrogators becoming the next victims of the punitive machine. Dombrovskii also provides interesting insights into the pressures on the members of Stalin's security services, showing that procurators were forbidden to inquire into the details of the cases, even when called upon to 'sanction' arrest and sentence, and that interrogators were under great pressure to condemn innocent people. The interrogators receive instructions from Moscow informing them that their work will be judged according to the number of satisfactory cases they bring to court, and that reference to the infamous 'special councils' of the NKVD may be seen as demonstrating their failure to secure (or beat out) incriminating 'evidence'. Although Dombrovskii's Christian values enabled him to express compassion for his persecutors, some democratic critics in the Gorbachev era expressed indignation at what they saw as the current vogue for urging people to 'take pity on the guards'.[64]

WAS STALIN ALONE RESPONSIBLE?

One of the main questions raised by the memoirs of Stalin's prisons and camps in 1988 was whether Stalin alone should be seen as the 'reason for our misfortunes', as the poet Yulian Tarnovskii called him.[65] Natal'ya Ivanova took the view that the Russian people were also responsible for Stalinism: 'To see Stalin as the main culprit of our ills is just as short-sighted as a stubborn reluctance to acknowledge that he was a criminal.'[66] Dombrovskii's *The Faculty of Unnecessary Things* differs from many other works on an anti-Stalin theme by illustrating not merely the 'evil will' of Stalin and his henchmen, but also the whole environment of Stalinist Russia. Dombrovskii attempts to explore the underlying mechanism of repression, asking how ordinary people could have been drawn in to co-operate with such a monstrous system.

The last scene of the novel sets Stalinism in the wider context of Russian and world history. Zybin, who has just come out of prison, sits on a park bench, where he is joined first by the interrogator Neiman, then by the informer Kornilov. All three sit together, and are by chance captured on canvas by an artist who happens to be working nearby. The implication is that these three types – idealistic victim, persecutor and traitor – are universal in Russian history (and perhaps in history as a whole, as the parallels which Dombrovskii draws with the story of Christ, Pilate and Judas are designed to illustrate).[67]

CONCLUSION

The many terrible individual experiences evoked in works on Stalinism, prisons and camps published in the years 1987–8 mounted up to a monstrous collective picture. Literary critics and publicists emphasized the great value of the writings about the Stalin Terror, which, in the words of Natal'ya Ivanova, 'return to society a living, direct, concrete historical experience'.[68] The newly published writings of Varlam Shalamov provide the most profound analysis of the significance of the camp theme for Russian society: 'The need for documents of this sort is extremely great. After all, in every family, in both countryside and city, among the intelligentsia, workers and peasants, there were people, either relatives or acquaintances, who died in prison. That is the Russian reader – and not just Russian – who is waiting for an answer from us.' Shalamov's central theme of 'the individual's struggle against the state machine' has become a crucial moral and political question in contemporary Russia.[69]

The most moving aspect of responses to the newly published prison fiction and memoirs was the overwhelming desire of contemporary Russian people to learn from the mistakes of the past. The critic Vasilevskii, however, sadly maintained that even though so much information had now been made available, 'Sometimes it seems that the terrible experience is disappearing without trace, like light into a black hole.'[70] Many of those who understood the essence of Stalinism correctly may well have died without producing memoirs; while many of those who survived 'understood little and learned nothing'.

In the Gorbachev era, Russian readers were no longer satisfied by the simplistic conclusions of Evgeniya Ginzburg, who had claimed in the early 1960s that 'The great Leninist truth again rules our party and our country';[71] or by Rikhter's offensive view that the gold mined at Kolyma had been 'a significant achievement of the Second Five Year Plan'. By 1988, cultural debate could no longer be confined to an analysis of the nature of Stalinism, but naturally led on to a more profound historical analysis of its origins. By 1988 some of the most radical criticisms of the limited process of *glasnost* in history came from conservative, nationalist writers and critics. The Russian Orthodox writer Vladimir Soloukhin refused to sign a letter calling for a memorial to Stalin's victims, explaining that the motive for his refusal was not sympathy for Stalin, but the absence of any answer from *Memorial* to his question: 'From which year must we consider repressions illegal and unjustified, and up to which year should we consider them legal and justified?'[72] A similar point was made by Vadim Kozhinov, who went beyond the repressions of the late 1930s to speak of the enormous population losses of the period 1917–35, particularly the sufferings of the peasantry.[73]

Kozhinov's work provoked bitter polemics, during which, as Alla Latynina ironically remarked, 'The Christian Igor' Shafarevich reminds us that it is naïve to explain a national catastrophe by the sinister role of one man, and the Marxist Roy Medvedev obstinately insists that historical necessity bent before one criminal personality.'[74] By 1988 many intellectuals, both 'democrats' and 'patriots', had come to believe that people other than Stalin shared some responsibility for the terror. While still not mentioning Lenin by name, commentators suggested that the instigators of repression should not be forgiven simply because they later perished,[75] although they should be blamed for their real crimes, not for the fictitious ones which Stalin ascribed to them. In 1988 it was no longer sufficient to contrast an innocent Central Committee with an uncontrollable NKVD, as Bukharin had done in the final letter dictated to his wife.

In 1989 the so-called 'prose of historical experience' written in earlier historical periods continued to be extremely popular;[76] and the cumulative effect of memoirs by intellectuals far from sympathetic to the party, along with the many revelations in the press, meant that little of the general information contained in Solzhenitsyn's *The Gulag Archipelago* was new to the Soviet public. However, the main omission in the memoirs published in 1988 had been a systematic analysis of the prison and camp system, which Solzhenitsyn's *The Gulag Archipelago* was able to contribute in 1989. In the critic Vasilevskii's opinion, Solzhenitsyn's work represented an incomparably higher 'level of comprehension of evil'.[77]

One of the main achievements of fiction and memoirs on Stalin's terror was to discredit Stalin so completely that it became increasingly difficult for people to surround his name with any honour.[78] By 1988–9 the publication of literature about Stalin's crimes had exposed the limitations of *glasnost* in history, and many critics and historians asserted the need to take de-Stalinization to its logical conclusion.[79] Since democratic and nationalist critics both agreed about the need to expose Stalin's crimes, the main issue in the late 1980s and 1990s was not Stalin himself, but the lingering neo-Stalinism in Soviet society. A film by Tofik Shakhverdiev, *Is Stalin with Us?* (1989), contained interviews with many contemporary Stalinists, including a taxi driver from Tbilisi and an NKVD man who had guarded Bukharin. Some democratic commentators, anxious that anti-Stalin writings had become repetitive and reached a dead end, demanded a trial of Stalin and Stalinism in open court.[80]

Journalists and writers were becoming increasingly frustrated that they could not overtly challenge the current manifestation of the totalitarian Stalinist legacy, feeling that the excessive concentration on the crimes of Stalin was actually hindering an investigation of the fundamental source of the USSR's current problems: the monopoly of power by a single party. From 1988 until the end of his period in power, Gorbachev himself remained hesitant and indecisive, sometimes leaning to one side, sometimes to the other.

7 The Second World War

Another important issue subject to a major reassessment after Gorbachev's accession was Soviet participation in the Second World War, and Stalin's record as a war leader.[1] The subject of the Second World War has been, and still is, a very emotive one in Russia, as, according to one Soviet estimate, deaths directly resulting from the war amounted to 26–7 million,[2] while nearly six million prisoners of war were held in Nazi prison camps.[3] But, quite apart from the unimaginable losses which affected almost every Soviet family, since the inception of *glasnost* passions have been aroused by revelations about aspects of the war which had not previously been discussed in public in the USSR. Disputes have arisen between war veterans, military men and patriotic Soviet citizens, for whom great pride in the victory over Nazi Germany takes precedence over the tragedy, and more radical historians, political commentators and critics who wish to confront harsher realities about the USSR's conduct of the war. It should also be remembered that such a reinterpretation of the Second World War in the press and literature was also relevant to the reassessment of the war in Afghanistan which was proceeding at the same time, leading to the withdrawal of Soviet troops in 1989.[4]

Before 1985, the most sensitive issues connected with the war had been raised in the USSR in works of fiction, by such writers as Vasil' Bykau, Grigorii Baklanov and Bulat Okudzhava.[5] The official assessment of the war did not immediately change after Gorbachev's accession; indeed, the importance of Marxism-Leninism in the interpretation of the war was reaffirmed by a senior army officer, Lieutenant-Colonel Repin, in May 1985.[6] However, even as early as 1985 it was evident that there was a disparity between official perceptions and those of some talented Soviet writers, who sought the truth about the war and wanted its significance for contemporary society to be recognized.

During the years 1986–8, radical changes took place in the assessment of the war in the USSR, but until the spring of 1987 the public debates which surfaced in the press did not always reflect the full extent of the Russian public's knowledge or desire for greater truth on this subject.[7] An official change of heart occurred in April 1987, when the General Staff and Chief Political Administration of the Red Army recommended the publication of Konstantin Simonov's interviews with

Marshal Zhukov.[8] From this time onwards the press was able to discuss with much greater frankness such fundamental questions as Stalin's role as a war leader, the making of military policy, and the conduct of the war. In the years 1987–8 controversial issues debated in the press included: Stalin's unpreparedness for war in 1941;[9] the initial disasters, which Stalin covered up by executing the generals responsible for the frontier defences and other senior officers;[10] the purges of the higher echelons of the army and navy on the eve of war;[11] the Nazi–Soviet Pact;[12] and the imprisonment in Stalin's Gulag of Soviet prisoners of war, even those who had escaped from Nazi concentration camps.[13] By June 1988 the commentator Viktor Shaposhnikov noted the 'vast distance' that had been covered, the huge extent 'to which we have all moved forward in mastering the subject of the Great Patriotic War'.[14]

Well-known writers of different political persuasions contributed to the reinterpretation of the war through their speeches, journalism and memoirs.[15] One of the first issues they raised in the *glasnost* era was the need to accord respect to former Soviet prisoners of war.[16] Other writers condemned the outdated strategy of some Russian commanders: for example, Lev Razgon revealed that a cavalry charge against tanks had been sanctioned during the battle for the Crimea, allowing the 'overjoyed Germans' to mow their enemy down.[17]

One of the most incisive critics of officialdom was the Russian nationalist author Viktor Astaf'ev, who attempted to express the viewpoint of the ordinary Russian soldier, presenting officers in a critical light[18] – an approach which aroused considerable resentment from senior military men.[19] At a 1988 conference on 'Topical Questions of Historical Science and Literature',[20] Astaf'ev made an outspoken speech attacking the twelve-volume official history of the war for being completely unrealistic from the viewpoint of an ordinary soldier. He declared: 'I was in a completely different war', and complained that the history had been falsified and cooked up by 'very highly-paid people, who knew perfectly well what they were doing'. He disputed the official figure for Soviet losses in men, claiming that the USSR still did not know the exact number of its war dead. Although he acknowledged Stalin's mistakes, he deplored the modern tendency to use Stalin as the latest scapegoat to whom all the nation's problems could be attributed. Alluding to Evtushenko's poem 'Do the Russians Want War?', widely used as propaganda in the Brezhnev era, which contains the line: 'Yes, we knew how to fight', Astaf'ev said bitterly: 'We simply did not know how to fight. We even finished the war without knowing how to fight. We shed our blood, overwhelmed our enemies with our corpses'. He admitted that the number of men fighting in the Soviet armies and the losses they incurred hugely outnumbered those of the enemy, indicating a massive lack of military expertise among the Russian commanders. He reached the sad conclusion: 'I understand that it is very hard to write about this. Of course, it's better to proclaim that we were victorious to the sound of drums.'

Although *publitsistika* by journalists, writers and historians was in the forefront of the campaign to reassess the war, by 1988 few new scholarly interpretations of the war by historians had as yet appeared. V. Shaposhnikov argued that until historians could give satisfactory answers to all the questions troubling people, literature would have to fulfil this need as best it could. Historians had still not responded to Astaf'ev's question about why the Russians had lost twice as many men as the Germans, and 'in the meantime, as often happens, and, in essence, has already become a tradition, writers take upon themselves the mission of truth-seekers and truth-disseminators'.[21] However, Shaposhnikov and other commentators felt that it was first necessary to contest the false image of the war presented in many literary works of the Brezhnev era, which had suggested that the Russian victory had been achieved through a combination of national heroism and the wise strategy of Stalin and the Soviet leadership. Particularly harsh criticism was reserved for Ivan Stadnyuk's multi-volume novel *War* (1971–4), written after close consultation with Molotov.[22] At the 1988 conference on history and literature, Stadnyuk's attempted defence against the accusation that he was an apologist for Stalin sounded shallow and unconvincing, suggesting that the image of the war presented in literature of the Brezhnev era had, thankfully, become a thing of the past.[23]

Several works of fiction published in 1987–8 provided a more realistic picture of the war, exploring the effect of Stalin's harsh policies on ordinary soldiers, the suffering inflicted on the men at the front by the incompetence and ignorance of the politicians and commanders, and the different reactions of individuals to the strains of war.[24]

Dmitrii Gusarov's fictionalized account of the partisan movement in Karelia, *The Lost Detachment*,[25] is designed to counter the usual Soviet myth about 'the partisan movement, the people's avengers',[26] and to raise the issue of the pointless losses and sacrifices which occurred in the rear of the Soviet army. Gusarov demonstrates that the partisans suffered tremendous losses because of their lack of professional training and leadership, which resulted from Stalin's mistaken decision to liquidate the partisan bases earlier set up on the initiative of Yakir and Uborevich, because he refused to believe that war would

take place on Russian soil. Gusarov stresses that enthusiasm is no substitute for professionalism: as soon as war breaks out, Finnish scouts
track the Russian partisans down and kill nearly all of them. Six of
the handful of partisans who survive their disastrous engagement with
the enemy escape from a Finnish concentration camp, and, with great
difficulty, make their way back behind the Soviet lines, whereupon
they are treated with great suspicion: three are shot as alleged spies,
and the others are imprisoned and sent to Siberia. Gusarov attributes
their sad fate to the fact that the SMERSH system needed to find live
spies, and notes with tragic irony that it was often the most courageous, effective partisans who deserved the highest awards who were
labelled traitors and wreckers. Gusarov suggests that the Eternal Flame
at the grave of the Unknown Soldier should inspire not only sorrow,
but also guilt for all those who were lost without trace, and for the
'insulting suspicion ... even of those who managed at mortal risk to
break out of enemy barbed wire'.

Some literary works transcended their immediate war theme, raising
wider questions about Stalinism and the effects of ideology on individual human beings. A posthumously published story by Tendryakov,
Donna Anna (written in 1969–70 but not published until 1988), explores the severe, shifting definitions of treason during the war, and
the impact of Stalinist ideology on soldiers of the narrator's generation who experienced war and Stalinism at first hand.[27] The title alludes to a poem by Alexander Blok, *The Commendatore's Footsteps*
(1912),[28] which uses the figure of the Commendatore in Mozart's *Don
Giovanni* to treat the theme of betrayal and retribution.[29] A significant
motif in the poem is the black car whose horn signals the arrival of
the Commendatore, the agent of retribution. In Tendryakov's story this
image is transmuted into the black vehicle which transports a military
execution squad at the beginning and end of the story. *Donna Anna* is
set in the summer of 1942, when the Soviet armies are in retreat, trying to hold the Germans off before moving on to defend Stalingrad.
The first execution is carried out to make an 'example' of Ivan Kislov,
a young soldier who mutilates himself to try to avoid the fighting. In
the first two days the narrator's regiment has lost half its men, but
succeeded in halting the Germans, and the other soldiers cannot understand the need for yet another death. This episode provides a background against which to judge the second execution, of the idealistic
junior lieutenant Galchevskii, who shares with the narrator a love of
Blok's poetry, but, unlike him, harbours an exalted, romantic attitude to
war based on Stalinist novels and films. He despises the down-to-earth

commanders whom he sees as cowards because they spare their soldiers, avoiding enemy fire. Inspired by jingoistic platitudes, he shoots his commanding officer and urges his squadron on to a senseless attack, in which they are all killed. When Galchevskii is shot for infringing military discipline, he shouts in bewilderment: 'I am not an enemy! I was lied to! I believed! I'm not an enemy! Long live . . .'

Tendryakov's story emphasizes the disparity between the futile romanticism of Stalinist ideology, with its pompous phrases about 'dying well', and the hard, everyday experience of war for ordinary soldiers,[30] which Tendryakov describes as 'the comfortless eternity of the expanse of the steppe'. Whereas Galchevskii is inspired by the ideology of sacrifice and heroism which spares neither himself nor others, and loves reading Blok's poems about Donna Anna and the Beautiful Stranger, the other soldiers 'talked about women. About women and food – eternal, inexhaustible themes.' Although Galchevskii 'raved about the scene of the shooting of the soldiers in the film *We from Kronstadt*', feeling that the best way to die would be to 'look into the eyes of the enemy and laugh at him', his own death is an ignominious one. When Galchevskii finally realizes the difference between the reality of war and the heroic rhetoric of Stalinist propaganda, he utters the despairing cry: 'Kill me! Kill him!. . . Who produced the play *If War Comes Tomorrow*?? Kill him!' Tendryakov's story ends with a realistic depiction of the ragged remnants of the Soviet army retreating across the Don, which contrasts the wretched state of the soldiers with heroic propaganda about the justice of their cause: '"Our cause is righteous. . . ." The monstrously unrighteous enemy was approaching close to the quiet Don. And how pitiful we looked, the righteous ones. The naked truth, arrayed in its underpants?'[31]

Tendryakov's story reveals the humiliating reality of the Soviet army's initial failures and retreats, and its depiction of the unnecessarily severe military discipline imposed on the troops complements the impression already created by the publication in February 1988 of the text of Stalin's notorious Order No. 227 of 28 July 1942, issued when the enemy were on the outskirts of Stalingrad. This previously unpublished order abused the troops who had surrendered Rostov, Novocherkassk and other places 'without putting up serious resistance and without an order from Moscow, thereby covering our flag in shame' and demanded 'not a step backwards without an order from the superior Command'.[32]

In an article of 1989 the critic Natal'ya Ivanova drew deeper implications from the figure of Galchevskii, characterizing him as 'a continuation of the type of Russian "ideologue"' who is ready to 'provoke himself and the people around him to heroic acts of sacrifice which go to the extreme, to the stake'.[33] Ivanova attributes the origin of Galchevskii's character not only to military and revolutionary films about the 1920s such as *Chapaev*, but also to the values of the Russian intelligentsia of an earlier period who welcomed the Bolshevik Revolution. Galchevskii likes Blok's poetry, Ivanova implies, because of Blok's 'ideological romanticization of violence' and his sense of the 'collapse of humanism, the shaking of thousand-year values and ideals'.[34] Ivanova is correct in suggesting that one of the purposes of Tendryakov's story is to question whether the Soviet cultural intelligentsia bears some blame for fostering a romantic belief in heroism and self-sacrifice, which in wartime could lead to such crimes as Galchevskii's sacrifice of the lives of his men. This questioning of the role of the Soviet writer in promoting a false ideology springs from the ambiguity of Tendryakov's own position, as a writer who produced interesting, but limited works acceptable for publication in the USSR, while keeping silent about other taboo subjects which concerned him. His self-doubt eventually led to pitiless self-analysis. 'I became a writer and did not consider myself to be a time-server, but every time I thought about the plot of a new story, I weighed up whether it would get by or not get by; I didn't lie directly, but only kept silent about what was forbidden ... and I felt that lack of self-respect was beginning to build up.'[35]

The most profound literary work to be published in the Gorbachev era on the theme of the Soviet Union's involvement in the Second World War was Vasilii Grossman's great and multi-faceted novel *Life and Fate*, an extract from which appeared in the journal *Ogonek* in 1987 before it was eventually published (with some omissions) in *Oktyabr'* in 1988.[36] The publication of Grossman's novel was a great surprise to many western observers, since other controversial novels, such as *Children of the Arbat* and *Doctor Zhivago*, were politically harmless in comparison with a work which perceives no basic difference between fascism and communism, and provides a passionate defence of the freedom of the individual. The editor of *Oktyabr'*, Anatolii Anan'ev, was fully aware of the significance of *Life and Fate*, which he saw as one of the ten best novels of the Soviet period: 'When I read it, I was literally stunned by its significance, the topics it raises, and the truly Tolstoyan scale of its novelistic thinking.'[37]

Before its publication, *Life and Fate* was introduced to Soviet readers in 1987 by Grossman's friend Semyon Lipkin, who had been one of the first people to read the novel in the winter of 1960.[38] Lipkin confirms the legendary story of Grossman's attempt to publish *Life and Fate* in the Soviet Union, the 'arrest' of the novel in 1961, and the smuggling of a microfilm of the manuscript to the West by Vladimir Voinovich.[39] The extract from *Life and Fate* chosen for publication in *Ogonek* in 1987 contrasted the competence of the professional military commanders and the heroism of the ordinary soldiers at Stalingrad with the cunning and ideological orthodoxy of the political commissars. The selection of this particular episode complemented the reappraisal of the political conduct of the war that was proceeding in the Soviet press at that time, and was also designed to reinforce Gorbachev's policy of *perestroika*, which advocated the superiority of initiative, responsibility and flexibility over dogmatic adherence to rules and blind submission to political authority.[40]

An awareness of the controversial nature of Grossman's novel inspired the journal *Oktyabr'* to commission an afterword to each instalment of *Life and Fate* from the critic A. Bocharov, the author of a conventional study of Grossman published in 1970.[41] Although some aspects of Bocharov's commentary are reasonably fair, others are misleading or overly critical of Grossman. Bocharov strives too hard to make Grossman's views appear compatible with Leninist socialism and Gorbachev's *perestroika*, and seeks to ignore or minimize the powerful parallels drawn between Nazism and Stalinism in the novel, finding some of the author's views 'excessive and unacceptable'.[42] In particular, he does not accept Grossman's comparison between the anti-Semitism of Nazi Germany and Stalinist Russia. This is partly due to the decision of the journal *Oktyabr'* to omit two pages devoted to the analysis and critique of anti-Semitism, which are clearly meant to apply to the USSR.[43] While attacking former Soviet attempts to diminish the seriousness of Hitler's liquidation of the Jews by stating that Hitler killed people of other nations too, Bocharov nevertheless finds that Grossman sometimes 'forces the tone' when he discusses Soviet anti-Semitism. In his view, Grossman's disgust at the 'anti-cosmopolitan campaign' of the late 1940s and the anti-Semitic case of the 'Doctors' Plot' led him to over-emphasize the anti-Semitism of the war years in Russia. However, the experience of post-war Russia suggests that it is Bocharov, rather than Grossman, who underestimates the power of Russian anti-Semitism.

Bocharov's analysis of the war theme in Grossman's novel is fairly accurate, although he concentrates on Grossman's assessment of the positive reasons for the USSR's success, rather than his exposure of the ambiguous nature of Stalin's victory. The critic over-emphasizes

Grossman's alleged revolutionary sympathies and faith in 'the people'; Grossman's concentration on the value of individual freedom actually casts doubt on the concept of nationalism and the whole revolutionary enterprise in Russia. Bocharov largely omits certain controversial aspects of Grossman's evaluation of the Soviet war effort, such as the obstructive attitude of political commissars in the army, and the hardships of civilian life in wartime, which sometimes engendered rudeness and insensitivity.

In June 1988 an article by the liberal critic Igor' Zolotusskii came much closer to the essence of Grossman's work, and, even for Russians who had not read the novel, made a valuable contribution to the general reappraisal of Stalinism and the Second World War which was taking place in Soviet society.[44] Zolotusskii's article demonstrates how a democratic intellectual could make skilful use of literary criticism to push back the boundaries of historical and political analysis. He sees the main conflict in the novel as the conflict between the totalitarian regimes of Stalin's Russia and Nazi Germany on the one hand, and the spirit of human freedom on the other.

In contrast to Bocharov, Zolotusskii lays emphasis on Grossman's evocation of the tragic and contradictory nature of the war for the Soviet people: 'while waging a war of liberation and realizing that the goals of the war on our side are just, they are waging a war on two fronts (while they do not yet realize this, historically it is the case). The liberator-people is led by a tyrant and a criminal who sees in the people's triumph his own triumph, the triumph of his personal power.' Here the critic's interpretation, which seizes the essence of Grossman's view of the war, resembles that of western historians who have analysed the USSR's war as a threefold conflict: for the survival of the Soviet state, the Soviet system and Stalin's personal power.

Zolotusskii points out that Grossman's novel 'is probably one of the first to depict the conflicts within the liberating army as conflicts that were just as strong as the conflict with the enemy'. Unlike Bocharov, who tried to sanitize Grossman's ideas and reduce them to the level of criticism expressed in Gorbachev's speeches of 1987–8, Zolotusskii confronts Grossman's boldest ideas and uses them to expand the boundaries of the permissible, questioning the value of Marxism–Leninism itself. He lays particular emphasis on the affinity between the Communist Mostovskoi and the Nazi Obersturmbannfuehrer Liss, whose meeting resembles 'not an interrogation but rather a debate between one party member and another party member'.

The liberal critic draws from Grossman's work explicit historical and moral lessons for his contemporaries. The victory at Stalingrad determined the outcome of the war, but the 'spiritual movement of the war' was ambiguous. On the one hand, the war helped to strengthen Stalin's dictatorship and reinforce his personal power; on the other hand, it rapidly liberated the spirit of the people, thus sowing the seeds of the system's destruction. Although the Soviet people still had to live for some time under Stalin's totalitarian system, a 'silent argument' was taking place between the state and its people, which was to determine the fate and freedom of human beings. Zolotusskii emphasizes the importance of Grossman for people in the contemporary USSR: 'It's as if he is looking at our day, and, seeing our agonies of liberation, our agonies of emerging from a condition of mass submission and hypnosis, is saying: life is stronger than fate, man is more than his fear.'

Although the publication of Grossman's novel vastly increased the frankness with which the subject of the war could be discussed, this issue, like other aspects of Stalinism, became a battleground on which defenders and opponents of reform attempted to secure the ascendancy for their point of view. Since 1988 marked the seventieth anniversary of the Red Army's creation, it was not surprising that military and party men wished to reassert the role of the army in the victory over Germany. The plurality of viewpoints became evident in the second edition of the journal *Oktyabr'* for 1988, which, alongside Grossman's *Life and Fate*, published a neo-Stalinist article by M. Gareyev which ignored Stalin's incompetence, reaffirmed the importance of Marxism–Leninism, warned supporters of *glasnost* not to be carried away with the wholesale disparagement of the past and defended the need to maintain the reputation of the armed forces.[45]

From mid-1988 the limitations on aspects of the war that it was permissible to debate in print became eroded, and by 1989 there were almost no questions which could not be raised and discussed.[46] Indeed, by the time that Solzhenitsyn's *The Gulag Archipelago* was published in 1989, many important issues which he explores, such as the purges in the Red Army and Navy, Stalin's unpreparedness for war, the motivation of General Andrei Vlasov and his Russian Liberation Army which fought against Stalin on the side of Nazi Germany,[47] and the imprisonment in the Gulag of Soviet prisoners of war, no longer had any novelty value. In the 1990s, literary works on the war theme continued to appear, such as the third part of Rybakov's trilogy, *Fear* (1990), which deals with the purges of military officers; but by this time such historical fiction aroused less interest than memoirs and the opinions of journalists and historians.[48]

Although by 1989 numerous frank investigations of the war had appeared in the press, literary works on this theme could still cause controversy. One such work was the satirical novel by the émigré writer Vladimir Voinovich, *The Life and Extraordinary Adventures of Private Ivan Chonkin*, which first achieved publication in the USSR in 1989, although it had appeared in the West in 1976.[49] Voinovich depicts the innocent soldier, Chonkin, whose war experience consists of an inexplicable mission to guard a German aeroplane shot down in a remote country area. Voinovich pokes fun at Stalin's role as a war leader, the inefficiency of the commanders and the ignorance of the ordinary soldiers. Although this novel has been regarded by western critics as a delightful, good-humoured critique of Stalinism,[50] it provoked opposition in the USSR from Stalinists, war veterans and some critics who considered that it had overstepped the line between humour and 'outrageous boorishness'.[51] The critic A. Vasilevskii felt that the Soviet experience of war was too tragic to be treated in a humorous manner, and that Voinovich is too dispassionate: 'In my opinion, it is possible to write *Chonkin* in the way that it is written only by feeling total lack of involvement in the fate of our people.' Vasilevskii claims that Voinovich has no sense of measure, no compassion for the Russian people, and holds nothing sacred. In his view, the whole genre of satire is destructive and inappropriate in the current national crisis.

Fortunately, not all Russian critics shared Vasilevskii's objections to *Chonkin*.[52] G. Gordeyeva felt that Russians should be able to take jokes against themselves, and that Voinovich's humour is honest and cheerful; whereas many 'just' and 'laudatory' works about the war would disappear from readers' memories, Voinovich's novel, with its 'blasphemous jokes', would remain.[53] A more extreme view was taken by the young critic Alexander Arkhangel'skii, who claimed that the trouble with *Chonkin* and another recently published work which had aroused the wrath of conservative critics – Sinyavskii's *Walks with Pushkin* – is that they are written too seriously, in a manner which suggests that the authors feared they might be misunderstood. The critic is obliged to point out to his audience that one of the signs of free works of art created by a free people is that 'to laugh at or even be angry with one's native land certainly does not mean that one does not love it'. Arkhangel'skii correctly argues that both Voinovich's novel and Sinyavskii's essay demonstrate the authors' love of their subject matter, while also suggesting that the topics of the war and Pushkin 'are sacred, but not sacred cows'.[54]

The controversy aroused by Voinovich's novel indicates that even in 1989 the war was still regarded by some Russians as a subject too serious for humorous treatment. Moreover, the sensitivities exposed in this debate help to explain why satirical works by Voinovich, Iskander and Venedikt Erofeyev, whether they were mocking Stalinism, the conduct of the war or the Russian character, were some of the last works to be published in the era of *glasnost*. As the critic A. Nemzer correctly observed: 'In order to interpret Voinovich's novel about Chonkin adequately, it is necessary to liberate ourselves not only from official stereotypes, but also from our inner "priestly" seriousness. And this is difficult.'[55]

CONCLUSION

The interpretation of the Second World War which has emerged in the press and literature of the *glasnost* era totally contradicts the notion prevalent in the Brezhnev period, that the Soviet Union's victory over Nazi Germany represented the greatest justification of Stalin and his policies. By the 1990s it was pointed out that victory had been achieved in spite of Stalinism, rather than because of it, and that the Soviet people did not gain much from their victory. The dark sides of the war continued to be emphasized;[56] but Russian historians have still proved unable to tell the full truth (a revised edition of the history of the war has been withdrawn by professional historians). Granin complained in June 1993 that 'There is still no honest history of the beginning of the war', although the work of Volkogonov and Astaf'ev had aroused 'lively interest' in Russia.[57] Astaf'ev's novel *The Accursed and the Dead* (1992), short-listed for the Booker Prize in 1993, adopts a new approach to the war, ignoring the front-line conflict with the Germans. Astaf'ev's depiction of a barracks in the shadow of the Gulag where young Siberians wait to be sent to the front, and the execution for desertion of twin brothers who go back to their mother in the village, once again issues a challenge to Russian historians by suggesting that the seeds of Russia's destruction came from within, not from the Nazi invader.[58]

In the 1990s, although the war has been subject to widespread reassessment in Russia,[59] some war veterans still cling to their old certainties. Many had genuinely felt comfort and inspiration at the idea that they were fighting for Stalin and the Soviet system, as well as for their fatherland. They and their younger conservative allies demonstrated against the break-up of the Soviet Union, which they saw as a betrayal of everything for which they and their dead comrades had fought.[60] In 1991 Alexander Nevzorov, the presenter of the sensationalist Leningrad television programme *600 Seconds*, encouraged viewers to support the Union treaty by presenting a lurid image of blood spurting from the ground, suggesting that the break-up of the Soviet Union would mean a desecration of Soviet war dead. The resurgence of Russian nationalism in the post-communist period, and the amnesty for the coup leaders of August 1991 and October 1993 suggest that such sentiments are still very much alive in contemporary Russia.

8 Lenin and Leninism

In the early years of *glasnost*, the subject of Lenin and his years in power after the Bolshevik Revolution remained a most sensitive issue which hardly received any public discussion until the end of 1987.[1] Although Gorbachev had condemned both Stalin personally and various aspects of the Stalinist system, Lenin's theory and practice were still regarded as the essence of true socialism, subsequently distorted by Stalin; and Lenin as a human being was held up as a model to emulate. Gorbachev was fully aware that a Soviet Communist leadership professing Marxism-Leninism would lose all legitimacy if faith in Lenin and the October Revolution were undermined. In his book *Perestroika* (1987) Gorbachev presented his own philosophy as a return to true Leninism.[2]

However, it was not long before historians and writers engaged in a fundamental reappraisal of the Soviet past felt the need to examine the roots of Stalinism, and in the years 1987–8 some came to the conclusion that the unjustified repression of the 1930s could not be entirely explained away by 'the cult of personality', but that many aspects of the Stalinist dictatorship had been present, at least in embryo, since shortly after the October Revolution.[3] It is in the context of contemporary discussions about the Marxist–Leninist approach to socialism[4] and the legacy of the Civil War period[5] that literature dealing with Lenin should be seen.

DEMYTHOLOGIZING LENIN

In the years 1986–7 criticism of Lenin was still taboo, but, as we have seen, some literary works appeared, such as the plays of Mikhail Shatrov, which attempted to portray Lenin as a human being rather than as an icon. When accused of deifying Lenin, Shatrov claimed that he presented Lenin as a human being with faults, quoting as an example the intimation in *The Peace of Brest-Litovsk* that Lenin may have had a love affair with the revolutionary Inessa Armand.[6]

A significant advance occurred in 1988, with the publication of Shatrov's *Onward ... onward ... onward!*, which ventured further than any previously published work in demythologizing Lenin and re-examining his role in October 1917. One series of scenes which may have shocked some Soviet readers dealt with Lenin's last illness, notably the circumstances surrounding the creation of his *Testament*, which called for the removal of Stalin as General Secretary of the Party, and his note to Stalin demanding an apology for insulting his wife Krupskaya,[7] which the Bolsheviks decided to suppress, thus helping Stalin to consolidate his position as Lenin's heir. Shatrov shows that Stalin played a malign role in controlling the sick Lenin's activities, limiting access to him and subverting his dying wishes. Stalin shouts at Krupskaya: 'Sleeping with the leader does not mean knowing the leader', whereupon she is shocked, regarding his words as deeply 'foul'. For many Soviet readers convinced of Lenin's divinity, the implication that Lenin may have had a sex life would have been even more shocking than Shatrov's political revelations.

Shatrov's Lenin emerges as a multi-faceted character, or perhaps, as several different characters whose contradictions are difficult to reconcile. There appears to be a dichotomy between the Lenin of 1917, who is eager to make the Revolution and confront the Congress of Soviets with a *fait accompli*, and the imaginary liberal Lenin, who, with the wisdom of hindsight, sees the dangers of one-party rule and the advantage of constraining those in power by rival parties, free discussion and elections. Another, more plausible Lenin whom Shatrov portrays is a wise, self-questioning statesman who admits that he bears some responsibility for the emergence of Stalin's tyranny, and for failing to distance himself from him.

For supporters of Lenin, the most unacceptable aspect of Shatrov's play was that Lenin is forced to confront the issue of democracy again and again; he rejects Stalin's rule by terror and idolatry as 'pseudo-Marxism', but is less convincing in his lame defence of his own suppression of dissent within the party as 'essential at critical moments'. Perhaps the most controversial moment in Shatrov's play is Rosa Luxemburg's quotation from a letter written in a German prison in 1918, which predicted that the Soviet regime would turn into 'the dictatorship of a handful of politicians . . . without general elections, without unrestricted freedom of the press and assembly, without a free struggle of opinions'.[8] To this Shatrov's Lenin of 1988 shouts 'Bravo!' – in direct contrast to the Lenin of 1918, who denounced such talk as counter-revolutionary, while being actively engaged in building the kind of system that Rosa Luxemburg was warning against.

Although *Onward . . . onward . . . onward!* was heavily criticized by conservatives, this play, like Shatrov's other 'Lenin plays', simply represented another attempt to present Lenin in a good light, albeit in a rather more complex guise than before. Lenin was seen by Shatrov, as by other publicists in favour of *perestroika*, as a precursor of Gorbachev, a leader who wished to establish a democratic socialist system based on strong economic incentives.[9] The insistence on a worthy Leninist ideal was essential to Gorbachev's *perestroika* campaign, since it offered people a model to emulate and an inspiration to press forward with reform.[10] Indeed, at that time deeper thinking about the past would probably have been disruptive of Gorbachev's reforms, which required co-operation among diverse interest groups and political constituencies.[11] This view was borne out by events; the superficial Lenin of *Onward . . . onward . . . onward!* soon became outdated. Nevertheless, in the post-communist era, when Lenin is out of favour and the play is unlikely to be performed, it can still be read as an analysis of the multiple possibilities of Leninism for good or ill, or, more generally, as a warning that historical personalities can never know the long-term consequences of their actions, and that every revolution carries the risk of doing more harm than good.

Other publicists of the years 1987–8 emphasized Lenin's tolerance to his opponent Kamenev, who in October 1917 revealed in *Pravda* the decision of the Bolshevik Central Committee, in his opinion mistaken, to launch an insurrection;[12] and his willingness to allow critics at party congresses and within the Young Communist League.[13] Such writers confined themselves to Lenin's last two years as an active politician, in which he had the prescience to introduce the New Economic Policy, and the period of his illness, when he displayed remarkable foresight in his writings about bureaucracy, Russian nationalism and the threat posed by Stalin. The Lenin portrayed by Shatrov and other supporters of Gorbachev was only a mythical image designed for the new era of *perestroika* which bore little relation to the real Lenin. One conservative critic put his finger on the problem when he complained: 'In my opinion Lenin's viewpoint is blatantly liberalized nowadays. The person bearing Lenin's name is a kind of Chekhovian intellectual.'[14]

CRITICISM OF LENIN

Although conservative responses to *Onward . . . onward . . . onward!* demonstrated that in 1987 and early 1988 it was still difficult for writers to point out Lenin's limitations and mistakes, by mid-1988 Lenin's views and actions were beginning to be considered more honestly.[15] In November 1987, when the historian Yurii Polyakov had been asked at a press conference: 'Will Lenin ever be portrayed as a multi-dimensional figure who also made definite mistakes?', he had replied: 'For the time being we are ashamed to speak about this, and, I think, wrongly so', although Polyakov merely cited a mistake which Lenin himself had freely admitted – his overestimation of the revolutionary potential of the western working class in 1920.[16] In May 1988 the Ukrainian poet Boris Oleinik admitted that he had received a letter from a reader maintaining that 'It is wrong to make Jesus Christ out of Lenin, raising him up to heaven as if he were watching life on earth'[17] A consultant to the Institute of Marxism–Leninism subsequently claimed that 'attempts to canonize Lenin, to make him into something like a "Bolshevik Christ" are still found today'.[18] Eventually Boris Yeltsin too contributed to this discussion, arguing 'We have for much too long idealized and deified Lenin. Although he also made mistakes and changed decisions according to the situation. It is impossible to live by quotations alone.'[19] It was in this changing climate that tentative plans were first broached in 1988 to make public unexpurgated versions of Lenin's previously censored writings contained in closed archives.

The first direct criticism of Lenin in a work published in the USSR was contained in the well-known article entitled 'Origins' by the economist Vasilii Selyunin, a supporter of the market system.[20] Selyunin refers to Lenin's decree of 10 November 1917 on 'petty-bourgeois speculators' who need to be 'shot on the spot' to suppress the peasant counter-revolution, and quotes some of Lenin's other abusive statements of the Civil War period. Selyunin emphasizes the ruthless methods Lenin used to suppress opposition: his closure of the opposition press and establishment of the Cheka (the secret police) within weeks of his accession to power. Selyunin frankly states that the system of forced labour and the first concentration camps were established by Lenin and Trotsky in the period of War Communism. Subsequently, explicit criticisms were expressed of the ban on factions within the party, introduced by Lenin at the Tenth Party Congress of March 1921, and of Lenin's failure to control bureaucracy.[21]

The sharpest criticism of Lenin and Leninism to appear in the USSR in 1988 was a consequence of the decision to publish the Nobel Prize Lecture by the famous émigré poet Iosif Brodskii.[22] This development can perhaps be attributed to the fierce competition between journals, and the nationalistic desire to gain credit for the first publication of a

Russian Nobel Prize winner, who had previously been unrecognized in his homeland. However, émigré writers still had to be treated with caution: the Soviet version of the speech printed a section critical of the October Revolution, but omitted the sentence: 'Lenin was literate, Stalin was literate, so were Hitler and Mao-Tse-Tung, who even wrote poetry.' Yet by 1988 *glasnost* and media rivalry had developed sufficiently for *Moscow News* to point out the omission and publish it under the title 'Absurd!'[23]

The dominant view of Lenin in the Soviet media in 1988 was still the idealistic interpretation associated with Gorbachev and pro-*perestroika* reformers. This became clear in the debate about whether Solzhenitsyn's work should be published in the USSR. The anti-Stalinist group *Memorial* had invited Solzhenitsyn to become a member, but, according to one report, he had refused to join because of the group's failure to consider the true origins of Soviet terror, which had begun in 1918 and not under Stalin.[24] Perhaps because of this incident, the different views on Soviet history held by Solzhenitsyn and another prominent member of *Memorial*, the historian Roy Medvedev, came to public attention. Medvedev lambasted *The Gulag Archipelago* as 'full of slander and fabrications', and disputed Solzhenitsyn's thesis that the seeds of Stalin's terror had been sown by Lenin.[25] However, after arguing initially that 'the notorious slander' of *The Gulag Archipelago* should not be published, Medvedev then softened his stance to concede that it might be publishable if accompanied by a commentary. A similar view was expressed by Mikhail Shatrov, who stated that he considered himself an enemy of Solzhenitsyn, although he respected his contribution to the battle against Stalinism. Shatrov claimed to find it incomprehensible that someone could accept Stalin's culpability but fail to concede that Lenin made a positive contribution to Soviet history.[26] Nevertheless, although he regarded Solzhenitsyn's role in Soviet society as complex, Shatrov had no wish to see the publication of his work prohibited, and suggested that the pen was the only acceptable instrument to use in combating his ideas.

One of the official reasons given by Vadim Medvedev, Gorbachev's chief ideological spokesman in 1988, for prohibiting Solzhenitsyn's work was that he was 'an opponent of Lenin'.[27] In October 1988 Gorbachev met Zalygin, who was distressed that a last-minute call from the government directly to the printers had blocked the publication of Solzhenitsyn's writings in *Novyi mir*,[28] and told him that he was unable to forgive Solzhenitsyn for his view on Lenin, the founder of the Soviet state.[29]

By the end of 1988, however, the 'neo-Leninist tendency' represented by Medvedev and Shatrov, while enjoying strong support from Gorbachev and his followers in the party *apparat*, had relatively few adherents among Soviet intellectuals, who wished to read more profound analyses of Lenin and Leninism. One influential work of 1988 was a documentary film, *Solovetskii Power* (its Russian title is a pun on 'Soviet Power'), which presented Lenin as the founder of the first concentration camp in Solovki, formerly a monastery on an island in the White Sea, where Academician Dmitrii Likhachev had been imprisoned in the 1920s. Another seminal work analysing the roots of Stalinism which ventured beyond Stalin to Lenin and Marx was a series of four major articles published in 1988–9 by the philosopher A. Tsipko, who criticized the Bolshevik Old Guard which 'already in Lenin's lifetime, voluntarily handed over to Stalin the vast power created by the revolution'. Tsipko laid considerable blame on the messianic, maximalist and anti-market strands in Marxism and the ideas of the Russian radical intelligentsia for the mistaken policies of Lenin and the Bolsheviks, and argued that Marxist–Leninist ideology itself was now outdated.[30]

By 1989, when the 'revolution from below' was beginning to gather pace, criticism of Lenin became much more vocal and hostile. This sometimes took the form of a direct attack on Lenin's character: some Soviet intellectuals, for example, began to discuss references in memoirs to the pleasure Lenin had taken in hunting hares. Environmentally-conscious Russians disliked the idea of Lenin's malign glee at destroying nature, and his attitude to hares, which often figure as the heroes of Russian folk tales, was seen as symbolic of his callous attitude to people. Such tales helped to undermine people's faith in Lenin because, as a Russian historian explained to me,'a cult must be destroyed by emotion, not reason'.[31]

The event which probably did most to speed up the process of Lenin's dethronement was the elections to the Congress of People's Deputies in March–April 1989, when the Communists suffered heavy losses. This was the sign that doubts about Lenin which intellectuals had harboured for a long time could at last be expressed in public. On the eve of Lenin's birthday, on 18 April 1989, the director Mark Zakharov appealed on the popular current affairs programme *Vzglyad* (Viewpoint) for an end to the 'religious cult of Lenin', and suggested: 'It is time to take Lenin's remains from their case in the Red Square Mausoleum and bury them like those of other mortals.'[32] However, the extreme sensitivity of this issue was demonstrated by the fact that after the programme an emergency meeting of Central Television officials was held, and Alexander Aksyonov, a member of the Communist Party Central Committee and Chairman of the USSR State Committee for Television and Radio, issued a statement taking 'full responsibility' for Zakharov's 'shocking statement', even though he himself had been in hospital at the time. Aksyonov claimed that this incident, which had arisen because the programme was being broadcast live, had been given a 'very severe appraisal', leading to the drawing of 'proper conclusions', and that *Vzglyad* as a whole had repeatedly been subjected to 'severe critical analysis'.[33]

Nevertheless, after this incident the floodgates were opened, and severe criticisms of Lenin were voiced a few weeks later by Zakharov and other delegates to the newly elected Congress, watched by millions on television. The historian and philosopher Yurii Karyakin suggested that Lenin should be buried in the Volkov cemetery in Leningrad alongside his mother, as Lenin had requested in his will, and his wife Krupskaya had wished.[34] Speculation continued about the possibly imminent removal of Lenin's body from the Mausoleum; and the embalmer responsible for Lenin's body, Sergei Sedov, shrewdly acknowledged in the autumn of 1989: 'People who want to bury Lenin today want to bury Leninism.'[35]

The first publication in the USSR of some outspoken, formerly censored literary works also played a major part in dethroning Lenin in 1989. The most famous was Solzhenitsyn's *The Gulag Archipelago*, which finally achieved publication in August 1989.[36] The main theme of Solzhenitsyn's work is that Stalin's huge concentration camp empire was simply a continuation of the tradition established by Lenin, who was responsible for introducing secret police, purges and concentration camps to Soviet Russia. Solzhenitsyn argues: 'It is just to doubt whether there is any separate Stalinism. Did it ever exist? Stalin himself never affirmed either his own separate doctrine (with his low intellectual development he could not have constructed one) or his own separate political system. . . . Stalin was a very untalented, but a very consistent and true continuer of the spirit of Lenin's teaching.' Elsewhere Solzhenitsyn declares: 'Stalin had given a fateful direction to the course of the Soviet state . . . He did add a personal note of stupidity, petty despotism and self-adulation. But otherwise he simply followed in the path that had been already marked out'.

At the same time, in 1989 support for Lenin could still be forcibly expressed. One of the first responses to Solzhenitsyn's *The Gulag Archipelago* to appear in Russia was an article by Roy Medvedev, first published in the West in 1974, which was reprinted in *Pravda* in order to provide a Marxist refutation of Solzhenitsyn's ideas.[37] Medvedev rejects Solzhenitsyn's view of the role of Lenin and the October Revolution; for him Lenin's mistakes, which he does not deny, were a result of the 'step into the unknown', and he claims that 'It is easy to analyse revolutionaries' mistakes 50 years after the revolution.' Medvedev admits that 'a reasonable measure in the use of force was already exceeded many times in the first years of Soviet power', that from the summer of 1918 the country was 'overwhelmed by a wave of White, as well as Red Terror', and that 'Lenin used the word "execution" more often than the situation warranted'. However, for Medvedev this abuse of power does not mean that 'the armed uprising of 24 October was premature' or that the evils of Stalin's regime 'followed on from this fateful mistake of Lenin's'. He also contests Solzhenitsyn's view that Stalin simply continued Leninism; for him, 'Stalinism in many respects is a denial and a bloody destruction of Bolshevism and all revolutionary forces.' Yet, despite all his disagreements with Solzhenitsyn, Medvedev feels that Marxism can only gain from 'polemics with such an opponent as Solzhenitsyn'.

Vasilii Grossman's *Everything Flows* . . . contains the most complex and extensive reappraisal of the Soviet myth about Lenin to appear in the USSR in 1989.[38] The publication of this work provides a measure of how the attitude to Lenin in the USSR had changed by 1989, since a reference to Lenin as the architect of Soviet slavery had been omitted from both the Soviet journal and book versions of Grossman's *Life and Fate*, published in 1988. *Everything Flows* . . ., composed in the years 1955–63, was hastily rewritten shortly before Grossman's death in 1964, after his other manuscripts had been confiscated by the KGB. It falls into two distinct parts: the first part is a powerful examination of Stalinism; the second is a highly original meditation by Grossman's protagonist, Ivan Grigor'evich, who has returned to Moscow after nearly thirty years in camps, on Lenin and his place in Russian history. Grossman is careful to emphasize that the two parts of the work are indivisible, just as Leninism and Stalinism are indivisible.

Grossman attacks Lenin from three main angles, criticizing his character, his role in Russian history and his political philosophy. Although his portrait of Lenin is very critical in a Soviet context, Grossman himself takes pains to emphasize that he is trying to counter the two extreme views of Lenin, both the 'familiar deified image' and the equally crude version created by his enemies, 'the monolithic simpleton, combining the cruel characteristics of the leader of a new world order with equally primitive, crude traits in his everyday life'.

In his jottings on Lenin's character, Ivan Grigor'evich remarks on the fact that 'October selected those traits of Vladimir Il'ich that it required, and October cast out those it did not need.' It was not Lenin's more endearing, human qualities, such as his rapt listening to Beethoven's Apassionata sonata, his love of Tolstoi's *War and Peace*, his democratic modesty, attentiveness to ordinary people or kindness to pets, which were chosen by the history of the Russian state, but his harsher traits, particularly his 'absolute intolerance towards political democracy'. Grossman alludes to one occasion when, sitting on a mountain top in Switzerland with a young woman companion, Lenin expressed no interest in the beauty of his surroundings, but complained: 'How those Mensheviks are pouring filth on us!' For Grossman this 'tender episode' shed a revealing light on Lenin's character and nature: 'On one side of the scales was God's good world, and on the other – the Party.' This incident apparently made a strong impact on some members of the Russian intelligentsia in the 1980s.[39]

Grossman characterizes the main traits of the historical leader as 'intolerance, Lenin's implacable drive to achieve his purpose, his contempt for freedom, his cruelty toward those who held different opinions, and his capacity to wipe off the face of the earth, without trembling, not only fortresses, but entire counties, districts and provinces that questioned his orthodox truth'. All his talents, energies and 'unbending, unyielding, iron, frenzied will' were devoted towards one purpose – to seize power – and for him the end justified the means. In Grossman's view Lenin sacrificed to this end 'what was most sacred in Russia: Russia's freedom'.

Grossman contests the myth of Lenin's uniqueness, suggesting that many of his character traits have been shared by other political and religious fanatics. Such qualities as Lenin's abstract love of humanity in general coupled with his contempt for the individual human being in particular; and his determination to destroy not only enemies but also comrades who deviated even slightly from his revolutionary theory were also characteristic of many nineteenth-century Russian revolutionaries, such as Pestel', Bakunin, Nechaev, and some of the *Narodnaya volya* terrorists of the 1880s. Grossman's identification of Lenin's character and values with those of the Russian revolutionary tradition, which has also been pointed out by many western historians, contradicts the conventional Soviet view that Lenin was influenced solely by Marxist theory.

Grossman's work also counters the view current in the first years of *glasnost* that Lenin was a tolerant adversary who respected his opponents' point of view. In Grossman's opinion, Lenin was not an intellectual trying to convince his opponents in reasoned debate, but a demagogue striving to appeal to his audience's emotions: 'In a dispute Lenin was not trying to arrive at the truth. He wanted to win!' Using a forceful image similar to that employed by Pasternak in *Doctor Zhivago*, Grossman sees Lenin as a surgeon whose 'soul is really in his knife'. Lenin has a fanatical faith in the therapeutic value of revolution, just as the surgeon has faith in his knife.

The most controversial aspect of Grossman's interpretation of Lenin was the discussion of his role in Russian history and, particularly, his refutation of the myth of the 'Russian soul'. Grossman diverges from many Russian thinkers of the nineteenth century, such as Chaadaev, Gogol', Belinskii and Dostoevskii, who looked for an explanation of Russia's historical path in the special traits of the Russian national character, in Russian religious fervour. He rejects as a 'fatal fallacy' their view that Russia was destined to lead the spiritual development not only of Europe but of the entire world, since 'all failed to see that the particular qualities of the Russian soul did not derive from freedom, and that the Russian soul had been a slave for a thousand years. What could the slave of a thousand years give the world, even a slave become omnipotent?' For Grossman, Russia's thousand-year history is a history of 'implacable suppression of the individual' by the prince, the estate and serf owner, the sovereign and the state.

Grossman's fundamental belief is that 'The history of humanity is the history of human freedom', and that Russia's development was particularly distinctive, since 'it became the development of nonfreedom'. Even when Russia began to industrialize and modernize in the nineteenth century, creating a superficial impression of growing enlightenment and rapprochement with the West, there was nevertheless a widening gap between the essence of Russian life and that of Europe: 'This chasm lay in the fact that Western development was based on a growth in freedom, while Russia's was based on the intensification of slavery.' The Russian Revolution was based on ideas of freedom and the individual's human dignity evolved by Western philosophers, but 'Lenin himself was the slave of Russian history, and he preserved that link between progress and slavery which has historically been Russia's curse.' Grossman contests the usual Soviet view that the Bolshevik Revolution was a liberation from the slavery of the old order, arguing that Lenin replaced serfdom by a new enslavement of peasants and workers to collective farms and factories, substituting a new socialist dictatorship for the old tsarist autocracy.

Grossman's attack on Lenin's political philosophy would not have aroused so much criticism from Russian nationalists if he had confined his strictures to Marx, Lenin and Stalin. However, he places Lenin in a long line of Russian autocrats, starting with Peter the Great, who laid the foundations of Russian scientific and military progress, while intensifying the severity of serfdom. Perhaps Grossman's most provocative point is to compare the philosophies of Lenin and Dostoevskii, who has traditionally been regarded as a great enemy of the revolutionaries, a religious thinker hostile to materialism. Grossman claims that Dostoevskii's mysticism and messianic fervour are as much of a manifestation of Russian slavery as Lenin's fanatical materialism. He makes a devastating critique of the historical achievements of the so-called Russian soul, which has materialized in the 'identical creaking of the barbed wire stretched around the Siberian *taiga* and around Auschwitz'.

The aspect of Grossman's analysis which caused most dispute in Russia is his emphasis on the 'Russianness' of Lenin's ideas. Whereas most Russian nationalists prefer to see Leninism as an alien excrescence on the basically healthy body of Russian history, Grossman regards domination and submission as two sides of the same coin of the Russian 'slave-soul'. He asks: 'What hope is there for Russia if even her greatest prophets cannot tell freedom from slavery? . . . What hope is there for Russia if Lenin, who transformed her most, did not destroy but strengthened the tie between Russian progress and Russian slavery?' Grossman would not have endeared himself either to the democrats of the Gorbachev era with his pessimistic conclusion, which is still relevant in the post-communist era:

> When will Russia ever be free?
> Perhaps never.

Even in 1989 *Everything Flows* . . . was deemed to be so controversial that the journal *Oktyabr'* prefaced its publication by a long article by Professor Vodolazov, a member of the Academy of Social Sciences attached to the Central Committee of the CPSU, whose brief was to refute Grossman's view of Lenin.[40] Vodolazov expresses agreement with 'all the fundamental artistic ideas' of Grossman's story and defends the author's right to say what he thinks, but totally rejects Grossman's view of 'the reasons, roots, origins of Stalinism, the identification of Lenin with Stalin and of Leninism with Stalinism'. Vodolazov claims that Grossman's essay on Lenin does not stand up to serious scholarly

analysis, since Grossman sometimes includes distorted interpretations
or mistaken facts, such as the claim that Lenin ordered a search of the
dying Plekhanov's flat. To Vodolazov, Lenin's preference for attacking his political enemies rather than enjoying the scenery on top of a
Swiss mountain is not, as Grossman suggests, a sign of 'narrowness of
mind, poverty of feeling', but a result of Lenin's conscience, which
will not allow him to gaze at beauty when 'Russia lives as it does,
with Rasputins and Romanovs, throwing millions of people to their
death in a senseless world war.' Vodolazov's argument might be more
convincing if Lenin's words on top of the mountain had been a lament
for Russia's suffering rather than an imprecation against the Mensheviks.
Moreover, his allegation that Grossman's protagonist Ivan Grigor'evich
is 'gloomy, "one-sided", always thinking about the same thing' is in-
sensitive in view of the fact that Ivan has spent most of his life in
concentration camps and quite naturally wishes to investigate the nature
of the system which has imprisoned him. His complaint that Ivan's
life 'took place far away from archives and special collections in libraries' is also unfair, as Ivan's bitter personal experience has taught
him truths not available in books; and in the 1950s and early 1960s
Grossman himself would have been unable to gain access to the special
collections, memoirs and western accounts of Lenin available in the
USSR in the late 1980s.

There is some truth in Vodolazov's argument that Grossman is too
categorical in his claim that Lenin never respected his opponents' views
and never discussed them in private, preferring to appeal to a wider
audience. Yet although Vodolazov correctly cites individual instances
when Lenin consulted with his colleagues, they do not invalidate
Grossman's general interpretation of Lenin's narrow-mindedness and
ruthlessness towards his opponents; moreover, they refer only to Lenin's
opponents within the party. Vodolazov is also right to point out that
Lenin was not the only revolutionary to use intemperate language in
debate; Plekhanov did not mince his words either when attacking Lenin.
However, the critic fails to draw the obvious conclusion: that intolerance in political debate is a general characteristic of the Russian radical intelligentsia.

The main interest of Vodolazov's article is his acknowledgement
that Grossman reflects one of the major tendencies in the intellectual
life of contemporary Soviet society: agonizing questioning of 'the original
project of the construction of a new society ... the project created by
Marx, Engels and Lenin, ... the programmes and plans of October'.
For Vodolazov, Grossman's story is remarkable in that it raised these

issues in the late 1950s and early 1960s, when this phenomenon was very new and weak in Soviet society; whereas in the 1980s a 'dramatic intellectual break', akin to a believer's loss of faith in God, has become a 'clearly defined major phenomenon in people's spiritual life'. It is a measure of Grossman's achievement that the publication of *Everything Flows*... in the USSR was able to make party loyalists reconsider the basic tenets of their faith and adopt a new approach to Lenin. Vodolazov's countervailing attempt to present Lenin not as an infallible authority, but, as in Shatrov's plays, as a democrat whose humane methods were distorted by Stalin; and the Communist Party not as a 'closed, medieval "order", a privileged caste, ruling the people and secretly resolving all the questions of its fate', but an 'open, democratic organization voluntarily taking upon itself the obligation to fulfil the will of the people', is, to say the least, highly unconvincing.

Vodolazov's article, the most authoritative attempt to refute Grossman's position to appear in the USSR in 1989, devoted far more attention to Grossman's analysis of Stalinism than to his reinterpretation of Lenin. Even in 1989, scholars and commentators did not have complete freedom to discuss Lenin, who was, according to Natal'ya Ivanova, still regarded as a ' "taboo", sacred personality'.[41] However, as Geoffrey Hosking has argued, the fact that most attacks on Grossman's work were ethnic suggests that Russian democrats did not object to his analysis.[42]

By 1990, articles adopting a more favourable approach to *Everything Flows*... and a more hostile view of Lenin had begun to appear. The radical critic Mikhail Zolotonosov, for example, explicitly characterized Grossman's view of Lenin and Leninism as 'intolerance to dissidents, fanaticism, cruelty to opponents... a tragedy, the culmination of which was Stalinism'.[43] Zolotonosov correctly points out that Grossman's attempt to prove the truth of the slogan 'Stalin is the Lenin of today' took place in the period of the denunciation of the 'cult of personality', when an attack on Stalin's 'personal' evil-doing was still enough to save the system in the eyes of many scholars. The implication is that in 1990 this is no longer true, and that such articles as Vodolazov's are powerless to refute Grossman's deeper analysis of historical processes, which will now be taken to their logical conclusion. Zolotonosov interprets the three dots in the title *Everything Flows*... as a 'hope for the evolution of society, a hope that a time will come when taboos will be removed, and not only party activists can think about Lenin, and even a Jewish writer can reflect on Russia'.

Zolotonosov's reference to Grossman's Jewishness highlights one of the most controversial aspects of Grossman's work for contemporary Russian society. Anan'ev's journal *Oktyabr'* was greeted by anti-Semitic denunciations for publishing *Everything Flows . . .*; indeed, the three 'patriots' Igor' Shafarevich, V. Klykov and Mikhail Antonov demanded that administrative curbs should be placed on the 'Russo-phobic policy of the journal'.[44] Zolotonosov countered such views by envisaging an imaginary time when a Jew's meditations on Lenin 'would not evoke either orthodox or chauvinist hysterics, justified by some-one's imagined hatred towards Russia (erroneously named "Russo-phobia", but "phobia" is not hatred, but fear).There is no hatred in Grossman.'[45] Yet despite Zolotonosov's best endeavours, in 1989 or-thodox Communists and 'Russophile' patriots combined forces to defend Lenin, either on the grounds of his revolutionary past or his creden-tials as a great Russian leader.[46]

Another work which may have exerted more influence on Soviet public opinion than Grossman's *Everything Flows . . .*, because of its conciseness, greater simplicity and Russian nationalist orientation, was Vladimir Soloukhin's *On Reading Lenin*, a short article first published in the émigré journal *Posev* which was sold in mimeographed form in Moscow on the Arbat and Pushkin Square until it finally achieved publication in 1989.[47] Soloukhin simply collects and juxtaposes a series of little-known extracts from Lenin's collected works, presenting Lenin as a narrow-minded dictator hostile to democracy, a ruthless instigator of the Red Terror. Soloukhin's work is very effective in destroying the myth of the humane, tolerant Lenin, as Lenin condemns himself through his own mouth. Soloukhin's work, like Grossman's, was so controversial that when it did achieve publication it appeared alongside critical as-sessments by supporters of Lenin.[48] However, by 1989 even Lenin's protagonists had become willing to acknowledge that his policies from mid-1918 had been authoritarian, although they attributed this mainly to circumstances which allegedly could have been neither predicted nor prevented by the Bolsheviks.[49]

DETHRONEMENT OF LENIN IN THE 1990s

In 1990 the formerly idealized image of Lenin was further undermined by the release from the archives of Lenin's letter of 19 May 1922 which advocated the mass shooting of 'the reactionary clergy and the reactionary bourgeoisie',[50] and fundamental questions about Lenin and the Revolution could at last be raised in the USSR. Stanislav Govorukhin's influential film of 1990, *This is No Way to Live*, made frequent strategic cuts to monuments and portraits of Lenin to suggest that the founder of the Soviet state had been the author of Russia's ills in the twentieth century, the first 'faulty gene' which had produced a new human type: *Homo sovieticus.*[51] The democratic critic Alla Latynina cited some of Solzhenitsyn's anti-Lenin statements in *The Gulag Archipelago*, depicting Solzhenitsyn as a defender of human freedom, a religious believer and a moderate nationalist, and using his ideas to refute both Marxism–Leninism and the distorted views of radical slavophiles in contemporary Russia. In her view, Solzhenitsyn attributes the mechanism of repression to 'the party, which was seduced by the possibility of establishing an earthly paradise by means of violence'. Even in 1990, however, Latynina still had to be cautious in her conclusion, suggesting that it was not yet clear whether Marxism would gain from the existence of such an opponent as Solzhenitsyn, as Medvedev believed, or whether it would lose out, but that 'time would tell'.[52]

In another article of 1990, Latynina expressed agreement with Solzhenitsyn's view that 'no matter how criminal Stalin was, the Stalin phenomenon was a natural development of the Revolution', and his attempt to show 'the costs that our unprecedented social experiment has exacted from the people' by starting his count of victims in the year 1918.[53] Although Latynina's interpretation of Solzhenitsyn is largely valid, her article represents just one example of a general phenomenon observable in the USSR since 1989: the attempt by all the emerging political and ideological factions to adopt the aspect of Solzhenitsyn that best suits their philosophy and political aims.[54]

By 1990, the rise in general cultural freedom meant that professional historians could no longer automatically dominate informed public discussion of Soviet history. It was unfortunate that some of the novelists and non-professional historians who published influential works hostile to Lenin were zealots (although hardly surprising, since they had been raised on a surfeit of tracts by Lenin), as to a considerable degree they merely turned the older Soviet dogmatism on its head. It has often been acknowledged that much dissident and émigré Russian literature is socialist realism upside-down,[55] and nowhere is this more true than of dissident portraits of Lenin.

The most famous anti-Soviet portrayal of Lenin is contained in Solzhenitsyn's epic *The Red Wheel*, which began to be published in Russia in 1990.[56] Russians were obliged to read the Lenin chapters of Solzhenitsyn's novel in the context of the whole work, as they were not published in a separate volume, as they had been in the West. Some Russian intellectuals, however, would no doubt already have been familiar with Solzhenitsyn's interpretation of Lenin through reading *Lenin in Zurich* in *samizdat* or listening to the author's readings from *The Red Wheel* on the *Voice of America*.[57] Solzhenitsyn's portrait of Lenin has already been analysed in the West,[58] but it will be useful here to recapitulate the main points of his interpretation in order to understand its reception in Russia.

Solzhenitsyn's intends his depiction of Lenin to be treated as an accurate historical account which employs some of the devices of fiction to enhance its impact. In the original version of *Lenin in Zurich*, Solzhenitsyn had referred readers to certain pages in Lenin's collected works, to three western books on Lenin and one memoir printed in a periodical, and included a note suggesting that 'Those who are shocked by Lenin's words, his manner of thinking or acting, may wish to read more closely those of his works that were consulted here.'[59] The unfortunate omission of historical references in the Soviet journal version can, perhaps, be attributed to the fact that even in the 1990s a reappraisal of Lenin was still such a controversial subject that the editors did not wish to draw attention to it.

The distinctive feature of Solzhenitsyn's portayal of Lenin is that he is a demonic figure driven by an inner compulsion. In contrast to the traditional Soviet view of Lenin, which has emphasized his patriotism and love of humanity, Solzhenitsyn is intent to demonstrate that Lenin's main motivating forces are anger and hatred towards all enemies, suspicion of most other human beings, and, most of all, hatred of Russia as a nation (not merely hatred of capitalism or the tsarist system of government). Solzhenitsyn reproduces the invective Lenin used in his own writings in order to demonstrate that, unlike the tolerant, friendly Lenin depicted in Shatrov's plays, Lenin despised moderate Marxists, liberals and reformers, both in Russia and abroad, and had little respect for his own comrades. The only people whom Lenin ever trusted were his mother, his unattractive but devoted wife Krupskaya, and the beautiful revolutionary Inessa Armand, who, Solzhenitsyn implies, without adequate evidence, was his mistress.

Whereas most commentators agree that Lenin was an impressive thinker, Solzhenitsyn portrays him as basically unintelligent, although he concedes that he is a shrewd political operator. Solzhenitsyn also attempts to discredit Lenin by emphasizing that he was not in control of events: he is surprised by the February Revolution, which he has to learn about from foreign newspapers (he had predicted that the revolution would break out in Switzerland). Lenin's successes are not analysed as a result of his own efforts or the inevitable consequence of scientific historical processes, but rather as the fortuitous outcome of a series of accidents.

Solzhenitsyn also diminishes Lenin by implying that he was a mere tool in the hands of the main villain, the Social Democrat Alexander Gel'fand (nicknamed 'Parvus'), who arranges for him to travel through Germany in a sealed train, using money from the Kaiser's Germany. Solzhenitsyn underlines Parvus's gleeful willingness to abandon his Russian nationality and co-operate with Russia's traditional enemies in order to turn Russia into the first victim of the Revolution. This emphasis on Parvus's important role has not been substantiated by the historical evidence, and the image of Lenin as a German spy relies heavily on George Katkov's controversial book *The February Revolution*. Parvus is presented as a 'Satan', and the parallels which Solzhenitsyn draws with Dostoevskii's *The Devils* become particularly clear in the scenes between Lenin, Parvus and Radek. Although critics have generally agreed that Solzhenitsyn's satanic Parvus is a more satisfactory artistic creation than Lenin, his larger-than-life portrait lends ammunition to those who emphasize the anti-Semitic elements in Solzhenitsyn's art.[60]

Solzhenitsyn's Lenin is driven to a frenzy by the prospect of the disintegration of the Russian empire: 'Amputate Russia all around! To Poland and Finland – separation! To the Ukraine – separation! To the Caucasus – separation! May you drop dead!' This alleged sentiment of Lenin's would naturally have had considerable resonance in the USSR of 1990, threatened by separatist movements. Solzhenitsyn also maintains that Lenin was only one-quarter Russian (his Kalmyk and Jewish origins are emphasized), but feels trapped by his nationality, which he despises: 'Why was he born in that backward, peasant country? Just because one-quarter of his blood was Russian, fate had roped him to the wretched Russian oxcart! One-quarter of his blood, yes: but neither his character, nor his will, nor his inclinations showed any kinship with this clumsy, alcohol-ridden country. . . . Socialism has no nationality.'

Although Solzhenitsyn's 'Lenin chapters' became available to Russian readers in the years 1990–1,[61] and aroused some objections from Communist critics, including the Politburo member Vadim Medvedev,[62] particularly because of the insinuation that Lenin used money from the German secret police,[63] they have as yet elicited relatively few informed critical responses within Russia; the best assessments are those of western critics which have been reproduced in the Russian press.[64] This may be due to the fact that Solzhenitsyn's *The Red Wheel* is so long – and, in the opinion of some readers, so tedious – that not many people have read it.[65] Another possible reason for this lack of interest could be that by 1990–1 Lenin's place in Soviet history had already been irrevocably compromised, and that Russians were now preoccupied by the problems of the present. By this time too, historians were free to investigate Lenin, so literary portraits were of less significance than in the years 1987–9. However, it is also possible that up to 1991– 2 Russian commentators were still restrained because they remained subject to an old Central Committee decree prohibiting sacrilegious allusions to Lenin.[66]

Of the few critics who make direct references to the 'Lenin chapters' in the Soviet press, some merely set themselves the task of acquainting Solzhenitsyn's new Russian readers with the author's intentions and the historical characters he depicts. Pyotr Palamarchuk, for example, emphasizes that Solzhenitsyn regarded his portrait of Lenin as one of the most important aspects of *The Red Wheel*,[67] citing his aim 'to create the living Lenin as he was, rejecting all official haloes and official legends', and his assertion that he writes about Lenin 'from his own viewpoint (from himself)'. Palamarchuk ventures very few comments of his own about Solzhenitsyn's portrait of Lenin, describing Solzhenitsyn's artistic method entirely through an extensive quotation from the western critic Nikita Struve.[68]

One of the advantages of reading Solzhenitsyn's 'Lenin chapters' in the context of the whole of *The Red Wheel* cycle is that a sharp contrast emerges between Lenin, the émigré theoretician who was isolated from events in Russia, and Alexander Shlyapnikov, the leader of the Bolsheviks in Russia before Lenin's return in April 1917, subsequently a leader of the Workers' Opposition, who was executed in prison in the 1930s. Palamarchuk highlights the contrast Solzhenitsyn draws between Shlyapnikov, a genuine workers' leader, and Lenin, who claimed to operate in the name of the proletariat, but actually suppressed the real interests of the working class.[69] The critic also introduces to his readers 'the fairy-tale figure' of Gel'fand-Parvus, who 'in his time had been extremely widely known in international social democracy, but since the years of Stalin had been almost crossed out of the annals of the revolution'.[70] Palamarchuk refers to Parvus by his full name, Izrail' Lazarevich Gel'fand, but otherwise does not comment on his Jewish origin. He simply characterizes him as 'an inhabitant of Odessa, a socialist and millionaire', and claims that Parvus was the founder of the theory of 'permanent revolution', later adopted by Trotsky, with whom he led the Petrograd Soviet of 1905.

The democratic critic Andrei Nemzer also provides a mainly favourable, if somewhat cautious evaluation of Solzhenitsyn's Lenin, analysing the reasons for his success. He argues that Lenin is presented as a 'politician "of a new type"' who is prepared to act decisively, in contrast to all the other participants in the February Revolution. The most controversial point in Nemzer's commentary is his assertion that 'there is no special "Russophobia" in Solzhenitsyn's Lenin (to use a fashionable term)'. In Nemzer's opinion, Lenin hates bourgeois Switzerland as much as autocratic Russia, and is prepared to start a revolution there too; the Paris Commune is no less dear to him than the 1905 revolution in Russia. However, Nemzer protests rather too much; Solzhenitsyn undoubtedly devotes special attention to Lenin's obsessive hatred of Russia. Nemzer's attack on 'Russophobia' is another example of the way in which Solzhenitsyn's work was used to bolster up different political and ideological tendencies in Russia.

In an article of 1990 Alla Latynina analysed the significance of Solzhenitsyn's view of Lenin for the contemporary political scene in Russia. While expressing agreement with Solzhenitsyn's interpretation of Lenin and the Revolution, she implied that it was very difficult for neo-Leninists of the Khrushchev era, the so-called 'children of the Twentieth Congress', who had supported Solzhenitsyn's anti-Stalin stance in the 1960s, to sympathize with Solzhenitsyn's developing views.[71] Many critics and publicists continued 'to insist that Stalin bears the principal blame for all of our woes, and to reject any criticism of the Revolution's ideological foundations or any questioning of Lenin's exceptional sagacity'. Latynina argued that it was not necessary to number oneself among the 'children of Solzhenitsyn' to agree with his interpretation of the underlying causes of Stalinism, and that those intellectuals of the 1960s who had developed sufficiently to reappraise Marxism–Leninism and the legacy of the Revolution would gain more from reading Solzhenitsyn than those who clung to their old faith.

Although few serious assessments of Solzhenitsyn's Lenin appeared in the Soviet press in 1990–4, not all Russian intellectuals were in agreement with Solzhenitsyn's approach. The radical critic Aron Lur'e, in a lecture in Leningrad in March 1991, provided an interesting analysis of Solzhenitsyn's biased portrayal which concurs with the views of some western historians. Lur'e argued that Solzhenitsyn relies too heavily on the views of George Katkov and some of his pupils who did research into Parvus. In Lur'e's view, Lenin's interior monologue contains a number of dubious points: the implication that Lenin was only one-quarter Russian and hated the Russian people; the alleged affair with Inessa Armand, which is presented as established fact; the unrealistic notion that Lenin was considering a revolution in Switzerland at the time of the outbreak of the February Revolution; and the far-fetched account of Lenin's acceptance of Parvus's satanic plan to destroy Russia. Some of Lur'e's points concur with the criticisms of Solzhenitsyn's historical accuracy voiced by Boris Souvarine, which Solzhenitsyn has somewhat unconvincingly attempted to refute.[72] Lur'e was also correct to note the similarity between Solzhenitsyn's Parvus and Lenin and Dostoevskii's 'devils' Pyotr Verkhovenskii and Stavrogin, who hated Russia. As a Jew himself, Lur'e could not avoid feeling the impact of Solzhenitsyn's demonic picture of the Jew Parvus; in his opinion, a reassessment of Lenin was opportune and necessary, but Solzhenitsyn's approach had gone to the other extreme and totally lacked objectivity. Lur'e's view that Solzhenitsyn's portrait of Lenin is 'low farce' (*balagan*) from a historical point of view has also been expressed by historians, both Russian and western.[73] In view of this, it is regrettable that professional historians in Russia have been slow to produce serious new works reassessing Lenin.[74] Initially, the most valuable historical works on Lenin and Leninism newly made available to Russian readers were those by western and émigré Russian historians.

In 1991 an alternative view of Lenin to that of Solzhenitsyn was made available to the Soviet public with the appearance of *Suicide* by the émigré writer Mark Aldanov, (first published in New York in 1958), the only other major work by an émigré Russian author to contain an extended portrait of Lenin.[75] Although Aldanov felt repelled by Lenin's fanaticism, he recognized the power of his personality, acknowledging his combination of intellect and strength of will. Aldanov's depiction of Lenin is more rounded and dispassionate than Solzhenitsyn's. Although his Lenin aspires to become the absolute dictator of his party, 'many party comrades worshipped him, and in all honesty considered him kind, pleasant and thoughtful'.[76] Although, like Solzhenitsyn's Lenin, he is profoundly ashamed of Russia, his feeling is less obsessive and more rational.

Aldanov does not disguise Lenin's propensity for performing despicable acts, and his Lenin is full of as much hatred as Solzhenitsyn's; he is, however, also prepared to acknowledge Lenin's talents and even virtues. In direct contrast to Solzhenitsyn, he claims that Lenin was not vengeful towards defeated enemies, and even had time for cultural activities. Aldanov stresses that even a man from the opposite camp, the tsarist minister Naumov who was for several years a classmate of Lenin's in a Simbirsk gymnasium, considered him to be a genius. Aldanov also lays more emphasis than Solzhenitsyn on Lenin's life-long relationship with Inessa Armand, emphasizing Lenin's capacity for love.[77] Although Aldanov's portrait of Lenin also contains some dubious historical points, Adamovich's judgement of 1958 still remains valid: 'It is possible that Aldanov's portrait of Lenin will be supplemented. Yet it is not likely to be viewed as flawed by malicious distortion or an apologist's myopia.'[78]

It is to be hoped that a more moderate view such as that of Aldanov, along with objective works by historians, will come to dominate Russian attitudes towards Lenin in the post-communist period, although the Russian public's love of sensation is likely to make the more vicious views of Solzhenitsyn and nationalist publicists more widely known. This analysis is confirmed by Astaf'ev's novel *The Accursed and the Dead* (1992), which refers to Lenin as 'a degenerate of degenerates who hatched out of a family of foreign hatters and tsar-murderers . . . and was punished by God with infertility for his grave sins'.[79]

CONCLUSION

The significant role played by Russian writers in undermining support for Lenin was evident from library lists and public opinion surveys which showed that *The Gulag Archipelago*, *Everything Flows* . . . and *On Reading Lenin* were the most frequently requested and influential publications of 1989.[80] By 1990, both unreconstructed Communists and serious 'democratic Leninist' historians from the Institute of Marxism–Leninism were becoming uneasy about the dethronement of Lenin in literature and the media, and an editorial in the journal *Kommunist* spoke of the need to fight against this nihilistic approach.[81] Yet even Lenin's erstwhile defenders had now ceased to claim that his authoritarianism had been forced on him by external pressures; they expressed regret that Lenin had not tried harder to become reconciled with Martov and the Left Wing Mensheviks at the Second Congress of Soviets,[82] and that he had sought to increase people's enthusiasm for the Cheka and its Terror in the winter of 1917–18.[83] At the Twenty-Eighth Party Congress of July 1990 Gorbachev still expressed support for Lenin and the 'socialist choice',[84] and the delegates, led by Gorbachev, placed a wreath on Lenin's Mausoleum;[85] but in the wake of the Congress public monuments to Lenin were removed by the local authorities in the Baltic states, Georgia, Moldavia and Western Ukraine. Despite vigorous protests from Communist officials,[86] and a presidential decree from Gorbachev designed to protect statues of Lenin,[87] the dethronement of Lenin continued unabated, reaching a climax in 1991, when the inhabitants of Leningrad voted for the city to revert to its original name, St Petersburg.

After the fall of the Communist Party in 1991, Lenin was no longer held up as an ideal, and the process of reappraisal continued: in 1992, for example, the Lenin Library in Moscow was renamed the Russian State Library. Nevertheless, interest in Lenin's personality and role in history still persisted: émigré memoirs of Lenin continued to appear;[88] and Yeltsin's adviser Dmitrii Volkogonov was given access to 3,700 formerly secret documents in order to produce an authorized biography.[89]

In the post-communist period Lenin's body remained in the Mausoleum, even though far fewer people visited it. There were too many sensitive former Communists in Russia for Yeltsin to risk offending them, and the Mausoleum could still be seen as a valuable tourist attraction. However, after the armed rebellion of October 1993, the guard of honour at Lenin's tomb was symbolically removed, and Yurii Luzhkov, the Mayor of Moscow, once again broached the question of reburial, although he subsequently passed the decision on to Yeltsin.[90] As one commentator sensibly argued, it would be a mistake to move Lenin's body unless it could be done in such a way as to promote reconciliation, rather than to inflame passions further.[91]

9 The Civil War and the Revolutionary Period, 1917–22

In the early years of *glasnost*, there was no explicit questioning of official interpretations of the February and October revolutions of 1917, or of Bolshevik theory and practice in the early years of Soviet power. Gorbachev and his supporters viewed the revolutionary period, from the turn of the century to the 1920s, as all of a piece. The vital role of Lenin and the Bolshevik Party continued to be emphasized; it was repeatedly claimed that Bolshevism had brought down the Russian monarchy, turned the workers and peasants against the Provisional Government, and formulated admirable decrees after the Revolution. The period 1917–22 continued to be seen as a period of heroic revolutionary struggle, when, despite bitter resistance by the old ruling classes and the whole capitalist world, the Bolsheviks had emerged victorious and started to construct a humane socialist society. Gorbachev's speech in 1987 on the seventieth anniversary of the Bolshevik Revolution made no reference to the negative side of Bolshevism: the creation of the Cheka, the dispersal of the Constituent Assembly in 1918, the Red Terror, the curbing of the power of the soviets and trade unions, the banning of factions within the party or the suppression of the Kronstadt Revolt in 1921. Gorbachev passed cursorily over the period of the Civil War and said nothing about the ruthlessness of the Bolsheviks either before or after the Revolution.[1]

Although after Gorbachev's accession historians and political commentators continued to be more inhibited in their study of the Revolution and Civil War than of NEP and the Stalin period, they all realized the vital significance of the early years of Bolshevism for the legitimacy of Gorbachev and the Communist Party. Soviet historians were no longer obliged to adhere to the viewpoint expressed by the General Secretary,[2] and those scholars who had for some time disputed the interpretation of the Russian Revolution laid down by the Brezhnevite scholarly establishment were given licence to attack their former bosses.[3] Gradually discussions on the revolutionary period became more acrimonious, and all participants in the debate were fully aware that controversies about the causes, nature and results of the Revolution were intimately connected with contemporary disputes about Gorbachev and *perestroika*.

THE CIVIL WAR

In the years 1987–8 commentators began to discuss, guardedly, the cruelties and intolerance of the Civil War period, touching on the persecution of the old ruling classes,[4] the harsh methods of the grain requisitioning squads,[5] and the policy of ruthless de-Cossackization.[6] Another previously taboo subject newly brought to public attention was the insurrection at the Kronstadt naval base in 1921, truthfully depicted for the first time in Mikhail Kuraev's fantastic novella *Captain Dikshtein* (1987) as an outbreak of popular discontent with Communist rule followed by indiscriminate executions.[7] The progressively franker revelations about the unjustified execution of the poet Nikolai Gumilev for alleged participation in a counter-revolutionary monarchist conspiracy provide an interesting barometer of changing attitudes to the Civil War and Red Terror throughout the Gorbachev era.[8]

By the autumn of 1987, even though there had been no official re-evaluation of the Revolution and Civil War, the publication or planned publication of some works by writers of the first wave of emigration after the Revolution had forced even conservative critics and historians to make some modification to their ideological position. Feliks Kuznetsov, an authoritative party-line critic in the Brezhnev era, had come round to the view that 'Today our view of the Revolution is more comprehensive, complete, realistic and wise', although he still referred to canonical works of Soviet literature which presented the Revolution and Civil War from a viewpoint favourable to the Bolsheviks: 'the prose of Gor'kii, Sholokhov and Leonov, the poetry of Mayakovskii and Blok, Fadeyev's *Rout* and A. Tolstoi's *Road to Calvary*'.[9] A rather different view was expressed in 1987 by the literary scholar V. Baranov, who advocated the study of all twentieth-century Russian literature, including émigré literature, while stressing the distinctiveness and independence of specifically Soviet literature.[10]

Kuznetsov expressed indignation at what he saw as the attempt of liberal writers such as Evtushenko to 'varnish' or 'embellish' the reputations of writers of the Silver Age and émigrés who had been implacable ideological opponents of Soviet power.[11] In his view, critics should acknowledge that Nabokov and other well known first-wave émigrés such as Zinaida Gippius and Dmitrii Merezhkovskii had combined literary talent with 'a rejection of the Revolution and the social system that was established in our country after 1917'.[12] The historian Yurii Polyakov was prepared to admit in 1987 that 'Quite a few excesses were committed with respect to the intelligentsia', and that many intellectuals had been alienated from the Revolution, although he also claimed that 'broad sectors of the intelligentsia' had accepted the Revolution.[13] Although such commentators still laid emphasis on orthodox interpretations of the Revolution, and the epithet 'White Guardist' was still used in a pejorative manner, the vehemence of their response suggests that they were on the defensive, and that a very different view was beginning to be expressed by the liberal intelligentsia in 1987. The extent of this feeling can be gauged from Polyakov's complaints that some formerly censored works were being greeted with 'immoderate enthusiasm'.

In 1987–8 some liberal writers were beginning to contest the official view of the Civil War as a heroic and necessary manifestation of the class struggle. O. Chaikovskaya denounced 'a certain cult of the Civil War . . . which threatens and undermines the idea of the unity of the country and the solidarity of the people'.[14] However, Chaikovskaya's view was fiercely attacked by an orthodox historian, V. Mel'nichenko, in the party history journal: 'As for "the unity of the country and the solidarity of the people", these supreme socialist values were in fact established in the course of a deadly struggle imposed on the people . . . The barrier of fire of the Civil War went through the whole country, and through every family. Those are the objective laws of the class struggle. They cannot be abolished.'[15] In 1988 even some historians engaged in a radical reappraisal of Stalinism and Russian twentieth-century history, such as Igor' Klyamkin, still accepted the view that the Bolshevik Revolution represented the only possible path of Soviet development, and that the cruelties of the Civil War could be explained away as grim necessities arising from a situation of national emergency.[16] Klyamkin quotes approvingly from *Change of Landmarks* (1921),[17] a pamphlet by a group of pro-Bolshevik émigré intellectuals written as a reply to the famous anti-revolutionary collection of 1909, *Landmarks*, which was exerting considerable influence in the contemporary USSR.[18] Klyamkin asserts: 'Soviet power was opposed by a world-wide coalition, by White armies which occupied three-quarters of Russian territory, by internal destruction, famine, cold and the power of a centrifugal tendency hurling Russia into anarchy. Only Soviet power was able to achieve victory over all these difficulties, which were historically without precedent.'

Nevertheless, by 1987–8 some works newly published in literary journals began to depict the complexities and cruelties of the Civil War period more frankly, to shed new light on their their causes, and to present the Whites in a more objective manner. Memoirs of the revolutionary period, 'returned literature' and the rehabilitation of people unjustly repressed in the early years of Soviet power all contributed to this process of reassessment. Previously censored works by and about Bulgakov, who figured in opinion polls as the most popular twentieth-century Russian writer, were now able to mention his association with the Whites in the Civil War.[19]

The publication in early 1988 of Shatrov's play *Onward . . . onward . . . onward!* represented a significant advance on the usual stereotyped portrayal of Lenin's opponents of the revolutionary period. Some scenes take place in a prison cell where four rightist offiicers, Kornilov, Denikin and the lesser known Lukomskii and Markov, arrested in connection with the abortive 'Kornilov affair' of August 1917, are planning a new coup. The generals are portrayed with a certain dignity, and with distinctive political views, not as the usual caricatured, undifferentiated 'Whites' who had previously appeared in Soviet literature (although with much less sympathy than in works published a mere two years later).[20] A close parallel is drawn between the proposed tactics of the right wing – the elimination of rival parties, the closure of the opposition press and the dispersal of the Constituent Assembly – and the actual tactics of the Bolsheviks in power. Although Stalin, rather than Lenin, is presented as the main supporter of strong-arm tactics in 1917, the main difference between Denikin's views and those of Stalin are that Denikin insists that a Russian, not a Georgian, must 'sit on the . . . throne'.

The most important work dealing with the Civil War to be published in 1988 was Pasternak's *Doctor Zhivago*, which at last appeared in the USSR twenty-eight years after the death of its author.[21] Many Soviet intellectuals were already familiar with *Doctor Zhivago* through *samizdat* or *tamizdat*, and were conscious that a large body of scholarship on the novel already existed in the West;[22] but many of those who read it for the first time in 1988 must have wondered why it had caused such a controversy in 1958.[23] According to the conservative critic Kozhinov, 'They [magazines] give people the impression that what is now being published is unusually critical, interesting, and fascinating', but Pasternak's novel appealed only to a minority readership; many readers were indignant that they had subscribed to *Novyi mir*, and some even demanded their money back.[24] Similarly, the national-ist critic Vladimir Bondarenko claimed that readers were dissatisfied with the lack of explicit anti-Soviet content in the novel: 'We have all been inculcated with the belief that this is an anti-Soviet work. Those reading it for the first time thought that there was something terrible in it, but by today's standards they were late in publishing *Doctor Zhivago* . . . people read it and think: "What is anti-Soviet here?".'[25] Despite such comments, opinion polls suggested that *Doctor Zhivago* was one of the most widely read novels newly published in the USSR, and therefore can be assumed to have exerted considerable influence on people's thinking in contemporary Russian society. There is, how-ever, some truth in the critics' remarks, in the sense that *Doctor Zhivago* contains little obvious anti-Soviet rhetoric, and is not primarily a his-torical or political novel; it concerns the attempt of one individual, a poet, to remain true to himself and his art in a time of historical cata-clysm. A detailed analysis of the reception of *Doctor Zhivago* in Rus-sia is beyond the scope of this study;[26] the present discussion will focus on new attitudes towards the Civil War and Red Terror, albeit still cautious and limited, which emerged in the ensuing debate.

Academician Dmitrii Likhachev, who introduced *Doctor Zhivago* to its new Soviet audience, returned to some of the points raised in the notorious 1956 letter to Pasternak from the editors of *Novyi mir* ex-plaining why his novel could not be published, which was reprinted in the USSR under Gorbachev.[27] In contrast with the *Novyi mir* editors, who claim that the novel is permeated by 'a spirit of non-acceptance of the socialist revolution', Likhachev argues that Pasternak empha-sizes Zhivago's initial enthusiasm for the October Revolution, citing his exclamation: '"What magnificent surgery!" (It's necessary to re-member that Doctor Zhivago is a surgeon, and for him this is high praise).' Likhachev suggests that this euphoric sense that the Revolu-tion represented a stroke of genius, the beginning of a new world, or 'a revelation bang in the very thick of daily life' was characteristic of the initial reaction not only of Pasternak himself, but also of a consid-erable proportion of the progressive intelligentsia to the news of the October Revolution. Likhachev goes on to highlight Zhivago's later disillusionment with the Bolshevik regime, quoting lines which, although Likhachev could not have foretold it in 1988, still possess a consider-able resonance after the 'Second Russian Revolution' of 1991: 'Revol-utions are made by activists, limited fanatics, short-sighted geniuses. In a few hours or days they overthrow the existing authority, the old regime. And then for decades people bow before the short-sighted spirit that had made the revolution'. The contemporary message Likhachev derives from the novel is that, for Pasternak, the Revolution was an absolute given, whose legitimacy could not be questioned;[28] his philosophy of history enables people to analyse events, or, rather, to reject all analysis.

Likhachev regards Doctor Zhivago's doubts and hesitations during the Civil War as a sign of his poetic approach to life and his intellectual and moral strength: 'He has no will, if you mean by will the ability to accept simple decisions, but he has the resoluteness of spirit not to succumb to the temptation of simple decisions freeing him from doubts.' Likhachev emphasizes that Pasternak's hero regards historical events as independent of man's will, like elemental forces of nature. Although Zhivago is contrasted with Strel'nikov, an incarnation of will power who actively intervenes in the Revolution on the side of the Reds, Pasternak eventually highlights their similarity when Strel'nikov too becomes powerless to control the course of history, and is driven to suicide. Likhachev's response to criticisms of Zhivago's conduct during the Civil War is a terse legalistic point: 'Yurii Zhivago's neutrality in the Civil War is determined by his profession: he is a military doctor, that is, a person who is officially neutral according to international conventions.' Although Likhachev's view is undoubtedly correct, it begs the question of why Pasternak took a conscious decision to portray a neutral hero in the first place, and of why Zhivago abandons his medical profession during the Civil War.

Not all critics took such a positive view of Zhivago's character and conduct. The die-hard party-line critic Dmitrii Urnov echoed the views of the *Novyi mir* editors in 1956 when he denounced Zhivago's alleged 'intellectual individualism', self-importance, exaggerated view of his own talent and self-pity.[29] As for the disputed scene among the partisans when Zhivago tries to avoid shooting the White cadets, which the *Novyi mir* editors saw as a 'triple, if not quadruple betrayal', Urnov maintains, 'in the context of the whole narrative it is hardly noticeable on account of the inner flabbiness and spiritual non-participation of the main character in what is happening'. The partisans can be forgiven, Urnov argues, because they, at least, know why they are killing each other, but Zhivago displays greater cruelty in killing 'by accident, out of the best motives, trying "not to hit anyone"'.

However, by 1988, as distinct from 1958, Urnov's old-fashioned views were the exception rather than the rule. Most critics attacked Urnov's evaluation, and some adopted a more radical interpretation of Pasternak's depiction of the Civil War. In a 'round table' discussion of *Doctor*

Zhivago, the philosopher A. Gulyga spoke of the importance of the 'new thinking' in contemporary Russian society which arose from the understanding that 'universal human interests are above any personal ones, that violence in high politics is inadmissible'.[30] Gulyga proceeds from this assumption, maintaining: 'I agree with those who consider that Stalin and the year 1937 are only the consequence of deeper circumstances which had arisen earlier, with those who see the causes of our troubles in the Civil War. It was then that the great tragedy of our people began, its self-destruction.' Gulyga characterizes the Civil War as a 'human meat-grinder', which Zhivago is right to oppose on Christian grounds.

The response to *Doctor Zhivago* provides an effective illustration of how critics were able to use one newly published work to promote the publication of other important literature on a similar theme, or to disseminate the ideas in other recently published works. The critics Andrei Turkov and Natal'ya Ivanova, for example, related Zhivago's ideas on the Revolution and Civil War to those of Pasternak's contemporaries Korolenko, Gor'kii, and Voloshin, whose doubts about the Revolution were only gradually returning into print in the USSR.[31] Natal'ya Ivanova did not share Likhachev's view that Zhivago's neutrality was simply a natural consequence of his profession as a doctor; in her opinion it also sprang from a general human compassion for both sides in the Civil War. Ivanova observes that Zhivago is repelled by 'the cruelty unleashed by the Red partisans; he is repelled by the cruelty of the Whites. He is also repelled by the new power's indifference towards culture.'

After the publication of *Doctor Zhivago*, *Novyi mir* continued to play a prominent part in the reappraisal of the Civil War and Red Terror in 1988 by publishing other formerly banned works which evoked the horror of war and the atrocities committed by the Bolsheviks. One newly published writer was Maksimilian Voloshin, who had died in 1932, virtually unknown to the Soviet reader.[32] His historical cycle *Intestine Strife* (subtitled 'Poems about the Terror') vividly evokes the executions, violence and famine experienced by both sides in the Civil War, and sets Bolshevik violence in the context of Russian history as a whole, proclaiming: 'Peter the Great was the first Bolshevik.' Like Pasternak, Voloshin takes a neutral position in the fratricidal struggle:

> And I stand alone between them
> In roaring flame and smoke
> And with all my strength
> Pray for the one and the other.[33]

However, even in 1988 Voloshin's poetry and ideas were still deemed too controversial for *Novyi mir* to publish more than a selection of his 'poems about the terror'; it was not until 1990 that the full cycle appeared, with his essay *Russia Crucified*.[34]

Another interesting development was the publication of some new material written in 1928 by the Bolshevik writer Artem Veselyi (the pseudonym of Nikolai Kochkurov, 1899–1939), which was to have formed part of his unfinished epic novel *Russia Washed in Blood*, but had been censored by *Novyi mir* in the years 1928–31.[35] The fragments published in *Novyi mir* in 1988[36] were juxtaposed with notes by Veselyi's daughter Zayara, which contain new information about her father.[37] Veselyi was arrested in 1937, but his daughter disputes the official date of death (February 1939), because a fellow prisoner, Emel'yanov, who shared a cell with Veselyi in Lefortovo prison in March 1938, recalls: 'Artem was taken to interrogation every night, and in the morning he was carried back.'[38] Shortly before Veselyi's arrest, *Komsomol'skaya pravda* had published a vicious article attributing his fame to the 'Trotskyist Voronskii' and denouncing his allegedly mistaken view of the Civil War: 'His entire book is a slander on our heroic battle with our enemies, a libel on the fighters and builders of the young Soviet republic.'[39] Veselyi was rehabilitated in 1956, and some of his selected works were published in 1958, exerting considerable influence, among others, on the 'village prose' writer Valentin Rasputin.

Veselyi's *Russia Washed in Blood* aroused so much controversy because it was one of the first Soviet novels not to depict any specific Bolshevik hero, but to concentrate on the activities of the masses in the 1920s. Veselyi, like Isaac Babel', another prominent victim of Stalin's purges, came under attack for painting an allegedly over-pessimistic picture of the Civil War. In a letter to a censor in 1925 Veselyi had complained: 'Dark colours?! What can I do, in the years 1918–19 alongside brightness there was also a lot of difficulty and confusion.'[40] The fragments newly published in 1988 highlight the chaos and cruelty of the Civil War, drawing no distinction between Red and White terror: 'In the Kuban, Terek and Stavropol' regions fluttered the fiery flags of conflagrations: the Reds burned the villages of rebellious Cossacks, the Whites destroyed peasant villages and workers' settlements.'[41] While not attempting to disguise the extortion, arson and executions perpetrated by the Whites, he also makes no secret of the atrocities committed against the peasantry by Lenin's secret police: 'In the villages the Chekists raged . . . and their evil fame spread. From

Firsanovka the priest was deported. There was no one who could christen or bury. . . . In a Tartar village they rode around drunk, shooting many dogs and wounding a woman. Tax-avoiders were bathed in icy water and made to stand barefoot for hours in the snow. . . . They ate six geese without paying. Requisitions and confiscations right and left, with beatings in the place of a receipt. . . . They beat the chairman of the district soviet half to death for "carrying on in the old ways".[42] After numerous complaints, a certain Fil'ka and his two fellow Chekists were removed, whereupon Fil'ka became 'grave commander': his job was to ensure that a large pit was dug, to accompany the condemned on their last journey and shoot them in the back of the head.[43] Zayara Veselaya points out that such men as Fil'ka existed in real life; Veselyi, who was chairman of a local soviet in Samara province and editor of a local newspaper in 1920, denounced 'disgraceful and illegal' acts by the local Cheka, which led to an inquiry and the dismissal of the 'adventurers who had infiltrated the Cheka'. The extracts from Veselyi's novel were also of interest because they depicted episodes which had previously been taboo, such as the retreat of the Eleventh Red Army over the Astrakhan sands in 1919. It also emerged that Veselyi intended to recount the history of the Tambov uprising of 1920–1 led by the peasant Antonov, an episode mentioned in Solzhenitsyn's *The Gulag Archipelago*.[44]

Another attempt in 1988 to stimulate debate about the Civil War period was the decision to reprint in *Novyi mir* letters protesting against certain instances of Red Terror, written by the famous Ukrainian writer Vladimir Korolenko to the Commissar for Education and Enlightenment, Lunacharsky (originally published abroad in 1922).[45] In his first letter, for example, Korolenko speaks of the 'nightmarish episode . . . of five executions without trial' carried out in 'administrative order' which Lunacharsky had failed to prevent. Korolenko relates that in Tsarist times he had protested against the death penalty, and had occasionally even succeeded in saving the lives of prospective victims by proving their innocence; the implication is that tsarist justice was more lenient than that of the Bolsheviks: 'Executions without trial, executions in administrative order were a great rarity even then.'[46] By contrast, 'the activity of the Bolshevik Extraordinary Commissions provides an example which is, perhaps, unique in the history of cultured peoples'. He views the terror as systematic, like the terror of the French Revolution, and totally rejects the view that such harsh methods are applied 'for the good of the people'. Although, like Pasternak, he acknowledges the 'mutual brutalization' which characterized the Civil

War, Korolenko feels that the Bolsheviks' systematic use of administrative executions cannot either provide bread or act as a force for good.

In his introduction to Korolenko's letters, the editor of *Novyi mir*, Sergei Zalygin, frankly admitted that the Red Terror had been simply the beginning of many waves of terror which occurred in peacetime too 'in 1929–31, 1937–8 and 1948–9'.[47] However, Zalygin is less than frank in speaking of the Red Terror itself, suggesting that this was still a highly sensitive subject in 1988. Zalygin interprets the Bolshevik terror as a drama typical of all civil wars, and cites with approbation Lenin's view that the initial period after the Bolshevik Revolution was the most peaceful and bloodless, until 'the Civil War broke out, provoked to a significant degree by the interventionists in the north, west, south and east of Russia'. Zalygin admits that this led to 'mutual terror', against which Korolenko's civic conscience was bound to protest. The critic links Korolenko with other resistance heroes of Soviet history, from the victims of Stalinism to the dissidents of the Brezhnev era, who were by 1988 being hailed as the true heroes of twentieth-century Russian history. Nevertheless, Zalygin was still trying to hedge his bets, claiming that such defenders of justice as Korolenko were 'perhaps, historically not correct in everything', but that despite this they 'do not cease to be heroes and should live in the people's memory for an extremely long time'.

By the end of 1988 the climate of opinion had changed sufficently for the philosopher A. Tsipko to provide a profound analysis of the harmful psychological effect of the Revolution and Civil War on generations of Soviet people. In complete contrast to the emphasis on revolution and class struggle which had always been an integral part of the Leninist mythology of the Soviet state, he warned of the darker side of revolution and civil war, which can cripple human beings spiritually: 'In and of itself a revolution creates nothing, of course.... Undoubtedly it was not easy to restore, in a few years, the human values overturned by the Civil War, the notions of good and evil, life and death. People who have lived for a time with corpses lying about in the streets and who have grown accustomed to the sight of death can hardly be considered spiritually whole.' In his view, Stalinism could not have been prevented without a fundamental transformation in the entire political system formed during the Civil War; and he drew a lesson for his contemporaries: 'The attitude to the tragedy of the Civil War is a measure of the extent to which a person is a true member of the intelligentsia.'[48]

In 1988–9 the publication of Solzhenitsyn's *The Gulag Archipelago* and some eye-witness accounts of the revolutionary period, which had long been known in the West but never before published in the USSR, helped to counter the distortions of Soviet propaganda and restore to the Russian public a more realistic picture of these events. One newly published work was Gor'kii's *Untimely Thoughts*, which reveals a very different Gor'kii from the uncritical Bolshevik supporter hitherto portrayed in the USSR.[49] *Untimely Thoughts* is a collection of essays which originally appeared in Gor'kii's paper *Novaya zhizn'* in the years 1917–8, until the paper was permanently suppressed, on Lenin's orders, on 16 July 1918. The essays were subsequently published as a collection in 1918 by Gor'kii's society 'Culture and Freedom', and exerted considerable influence on people's thinking in the years 1917–22, but had not been reprinted in the USSR since 1918. For Gor'kii, the Bolshevik coup and the dispersal of the Constituent Assembly meant the end of democracy in Russia and the unleashing of a fratricidal civil war which, he feared, might lead to the extermination of the finest section of the working class. He did not believe that Russia, composed of eighty-five per cent individual peasant farmers, was ready for socialism; the events of 1917 had not been a socialist revolution, only an explosion of 'zoological anarchism' aroused by Lenin's slogan 'Rob the robbers!' Gor'kii expressed his revulsion at the power-hungry, anti-democratic conduct of Lenin, Trotsky and their companions, and their methods of government: the use of executions, arrests of 'completely innocent people', slander, demagoguery and the suppression of free speech, elections and demonstrations. Gor'kii's comparison of Bolshevik methods to those of the tsarist regime under Pleve and Stolypin was one of the worst insults which one socialist could level against another. Gor'kii also equates the Red Terror with the criminal methods of the nineteenth-century terrorist Nechaev, declaring: stating that 'Vladimir Lenin is introducing a socialist order in Russia by Nechaev's method – "full steam ahead through the swamp"'.

Gor'kii's powerful comparison of the October Revolution to a ruthless experiment performed on the skin and blood of the people has become an image widely used in contemporary Russia to characterize the seventy years of communist rule. Another theme in Gor'kii's memoirs which has particular significance for contemporary Russia is his fierce attack on anti-Semitism: 'equating Jews and Bolsheviks is stupid and is a product of the animal instincts of enraged Russians'.[50] Gor'kii also asks the pertinent question: 'Should all the inhabitants of Simbirsk answer for Lenin, a pure-blooded Russian?' (this is a telling comment, in the light of recent attempts by Solzhenitsyn and others to prove that Lenin was not really Russian).

Another important work first published in Russia in 1989 was *Accursed Days*, the fascinating eye-witness account by the Nobel Laureate Ivan Bunin of his last three years in Russia (he emigrated on 26 January 1920).[51] Bunin, as an aristocratic émigré who retained an implacable hatred of Bolshevism all his life, had been totally unacceptable in the USSR until 1988. Bunin's diary, set in Moscow in the winter of 1917–18 and thereafter in Odessa, is a loose, fragmentary narrative evoking the general chaos and instability which accompanied the Revolution and Civil War. Throughout *Accursed Days* Bunin expresses hatred for revolutionary anarchy and mob rule, and suggests that Bolshevik officials committed innumerable murders with impunity, inspiring the people with a total disregard for human life. Bunin hates all revolutions, whose common denominator is to change the form of government without benefit for the majority of the people, and considers the October Revolution to be the end of historic Russia, Russian culture and spirituality established through centuries of tradition. His tone is very pessimistic at times: he suggests that 'We Russians have peculiar psyches',[52] and that his fellow countrymen actually enjoy the troubled times of revolution because they give people an occasion for idleness, supposedly the typical desire of the Russian peasant, and accentuate other negative aspects of the Russian character: bloodthirstiness, drunkenness and anarchic tendencies.

Bunin supports his view by reporting an incident in Odessa when the mob tore two thieves to pieces, and repeating rumours of other atrocities: 'People say that there is indescribable horror in Simferopol': soldiers and workers simply walk up to their knees in blood. Some old colonel was fried alive in the ship's stove.' There is a modern ring to the following exchange between an old man and a Bolshevik who has just conducted an execution:

– Have you just been executing the fifth of those peaceful men?
– What business is it of yours? And what about the executions you carried out for three hundred years?[53]

Bunin ironically demolishes all the arguments used by the Bolsheviks to justify their use of terror. To the suggestion that 'The revolution is an elemental force', he retorts: 'An earthquake, a plague and cholera are also elemental. But nobody praises them, nobody canonizes them, people fight against them. But people always make the revolution more

"profound".' He also claims that people forgive the Reds for everything, using the phrase: 'All those are only excesses.' Unlike Gor'kii,
who criticises the Bolsheviks from a socialist perspective, Bunin's work
expresses support for the educated classes who had been robbed of
their possessions. Although he expresses no explicit political views,
his sympathies appear to be on the side of the Whites, since he detests
the mass of the people, who seem to have changed for the worse:
'Above all, there is no ordinariness or simplicity on their faces. They
are all sharply repellent virtually through and through, frightening in
their evil dullness, their morose, brazen challenge to everyone and
everything.'[54]

In the years 1989–90 Soviet people were exposed to much more
truthful information about the Civil War, and, although no scholarly
accounts by western historians had yet been published,[55] the Bolshevik
Terror began to be treated in greater detail. The book by S. P. Mel'gunov,
Red Terror in Russia, first published in the 1920s, was republished in
1990;[56] and Lenin's excessive reliance on the Cheka in 1917–8 also
came under attack.[57] Some professional historians traced the authoritarianism of Bolshevism in the Civil War back to the October Revolution, suggesting that an excessively regimented attitude to politics and
the economy had persisted among party officials until the height of
the NEP period.[58] In the non-Russian republics, especially Georgia and
Ukraine, it was frequently asserted that local wishes had been suppressed during the Civil War.[59]

Literary journals continued to disseminate revised views of the Civil
War period to a wider audience. Numerous literary and historical works
by émigré writers, including the memoirs of writers as hostile to Bolshevism as Gippius and Khodasevich, posed fundamental questions about
Marxism and the whole Soviet experience since 1917.[60] At the same
time, newly published works by Russian political scientists, written
both within the USSR and in emigration, were openly undermining
the whole basis of Soviet ideology. A. Avtorkhanov, for example, suggested that the purges of party dissidents dated back to Lenin's resolution of 1921 'On Party Unity': 'All the standards of intra-party life
were laid down by Lenin. The only difference is that in Lenin's time
the purges were periodic, while under Stalin they became permanent.'[61]

In October 1990 a whole issue of the young people's journal *Yunost'*
was devoted to the Civil War, illustrating the range of views now available
to the Soviet reader.[62] The editorial introduction explained that seven
decades after the Civil War the Soviet people were only just beginning to understand 'what a misfortune this had been for the whole of

Russia'; the previous approach had been to portray the heroism of the Civil War from the viewpoint of 'Glory to the victors, shame to the vanquished!' The editors of *Yunost'* regarded the Civil War as a nationwide tragedy, and related it to the contemporary troubled political situation in Russia: 'It is time to understand and bow our heads in sorrow before the millions who perished in this fratricidal war. It is time to repudiate hatred (in a tragedy there is always something fateful which is above all partisanship), to eliminate it, so that the bloody madness of division should never be repeated in the future.' This new emphasis on 'the pity of war'[63] was supported by an article citing the historian Danilov's calculations of the 'huge, terrible sacrifices' of the Civil War, which amounted to the death of sixteen million people.[64] By 1990 many nationalities of the USSR were already at war, and dire warnings about the possibility of a new civil war between different political factions within Russia itself had rendered such works of a more than academic interest.[65]

Yunost' published previously unknown or little known works from both sides of the Red/White divide, laying emphasis not on the correctness of one side rather than the other, but on the fratricidal nature of the conflict and the confused motives of its participants. Perhaps the most powerful document published by *Yunost'* was a 'Dialogue in Quotations' which juxtaposed critical comments on the Civil War and Red Terror by members of the intelligentsia who witnessed the events, such as Korolenko, Bunin, Gor'kii and the scientist and philosopher V. Vernadskii, with extracts from historical documents and remarks by Lenin, Trotsky and other Bolsheviks justifying the terror. This brief selection of telling quotations may well have had more impact on young Soviet readers' attitudes to the Civil War than any number of academic articles.[66]

Another result of the Soviet public's growing interest in the historical facts about the Civil War by the years 1989–90 was the desire to know more about the commanders of the White armies, who had hitherto only been mentioned in passing or presented in a negative, caricatured fashion in official Soviet literature and historiography. In 1990 *History of Russian Discord*, the memoirs of the White general Denikin (1872–1947), were published for the first time in the USSR.[67] Denikin's work was introduced to its Soviet readership by the historian L. M. Spirin, in an article entitled 'Unknown pages of known historical events.' Spirin acknowledged that even in 1990 it was still unusual to publish a White general's ideas in the USSR, but offered a convincing justification of 'the need to understand the history of Russia as it was in reality, with all its complexity and contradictions'. Spirin argued, quite correctly, that hitherto the Soviet people had been subjected to a one-sided, distorted view of the intellectual and spiritual life of Russian people in the era of the October Revolution and Civil War, since the only version of history available to them had been the one propagated by the Bolsheviks in official history books. Moreover, Spirin, along with other contemporary historians,[68] deemed the history of the October Revolution and Civil War to be particularly important to an analysis of 'the crisis phenomena of the present day'.

Both Spirin's introduction and the note by Denikin's daughter Marina paint a sympathetic picture of the White general, who emerges as a man who loved his country deeply, and wanted, through his memoirs, to 'tell the TRUTH about the White movement'.[69] Denikin is realistically presented by Spirin as a 'nobleman with a half-Kadet, half-monarchist cast of mind'. He was not a Kadet (Constitutional Democrat), although he was close to them and shared their aspiration of creating a strong state power; but, unlike them, did not advocate a bourgeois republic, but a military dictatorship. He was in favour of a 'single and indivisible' Russia, and had sympathy for monarchism, although he was not a monarchist himself. He was the only White general who realized the need to consolidate control over the areas which the Whites occupied, advocating land reform for the peasantry. Denikin never became reconciled with the Communists or Soviet power, but 'to the end of his life remained a Russian patriot. He even loved Russia "crucified" – as, in his words, she became after two revolutions.[70] He frequently repeated: "I am fighting for Russia, not for the Revolution".' As Solzhenitsyn states in *The Gulag Archipelago*, Denikin's patriotism became evident during the Second World War, when he refused to collaborate with Hitler,[71] and even sent a trainload of medicine for the Red Army in 1943, which Stalin accepted, while concealing the source of the aid. Although even in 1990 Spirin still felt the need to approach his subject with caution, pointing out that Denikin's memoirs contain 'much that is debatable and contradictory', it is clear that Denikin's work would have had considerable appeal for conservative, nationalist thinkers in contemporary Russia. The 'national Bolsheviks' of the Gorbachev era, and conservative politicians like Rutskoi and Zhirinovsky in the post-communist era could regard themselves as inheritors of the tradition upheld by Denikin and other White generals.

The most important aspect of Denikin's memoirs for the contemporary Russian reader was that they posed many topical questions which were exercising people's minds in 1990. Was there an alternative route for Russia apart from the two revolutions of 1917? In what conditions do dictatorial regimes occur, and what is the relationship between dictatorship and democracy? Why did a multi-party system exist after the February Revolution, while the October Revolution inaugurated a one-party state? Was the Civil War in Russia inevitable, who began it, and why did it prove to be so long and cruel? Why do civil wars arise, and is it possible to avoid them? How is it possible to minimize the mental costs of such upheavals, and what lessons could be learnt from the civil strife? Spirin admits that Denikin's memoirs cannot provide all the answers, but that it is now necessary 'to sit down at the same table with our enemy of yesterday and talk'. Lenin's simplistic, offensive dismissal of Denikin's work – 'The author "approaches" the class struggle like a blind puppy' – was no longer sufficient for Russian readers in the 1990s.

Both Denikin's memoirs and Spirin's illuminating introduction made an important contribution to the frank reassessment of the Revolution and Civil War which was taking place in the 1990s. The picture which emerged was a complex one, which drew a distinction between the views of different personalities and political forces involved in the conflict, and provided an analysis of the failure of the White movement which bore a resemblance to the dispassionate accounts of western historians. Yet if Spirin's view of Denikin and his ideas was objective, albeit sympathetic, some writers, newly published, in the USSR used their depiction of White leaders to advance their own nationalistic, conservative interpretations of Russian history.

One work which contributed to the new interest in forgotten or previously distorted aspects of the Civil War was Vladimir Maksimov's *Looking into the Abyss*.[72] Maksimov's novel contains a fascinating portrait of Admiral Kolchak, the Commander-in-Chief of the White forces and the head of the Siberian government in 1919. Maksimov, a conservative, Russian Orthodox thinker and until 1992 editor of the Paris émigré journal *Kontinent*, was a controversial figure in Soviet terms who had made no secret of his total rejection of the Bolshevik Revolution, and hence had been one of the last major émigré writers to be published in the USSR. In the 1990s Maksimov's views were still regarded as provocative by some Soviet critics: Igor' Vinogradov, for example, argued that Maksimov had often been 'too harsh' in his statements both within the USSR and in emigration.[73]

Maksimov's sympathy for the Russian nationalist Kolchak is obvious. He humanizes his hero by depicting Kolchak's romantic love affair with a married woman, Anna Timireva, who eventually leaves her husband to spend the last few months with Kolchak after they have been parted by the 'fateful catastrophe' of revolution and civil war. Whereas Kolchak has usually been presented as a supporter of the old regime, Maksimov emphasizes his difference from the die-hard conservative General Khorvath, the commander of the Czech Legion.

Maksimov does not, however, concentrate entirely on the positive side of the White commander and his forces. He treats his protagonist objectively, emphasizing his contradictory nature: 'responsive kindness was combined with assumed severity, childish obstinacy with weak-willed compliance and a rare magnanimity with extreme cruelty'. When the White armies are in retreat, the Admiral becomes more irritable and despotic, speaking to ministers as if they were 'servants who had annoyed him', and setting more store by the use of force. Kolchak also orders that all Communist prisoners should be shot, justifying his strong-arm tactics by the argument that 'A civil war must be ruth-less . . . either we shoot them, or they shoot us. That was the way it was in England during the Wars of the Roses, and this is the way it must inevitably be with us, and in every civil war.' Although it is certainly true that civil wars are among the cruellest, the Wars of the Roses, which occurred long ago, in the Middle Ages, can hardly be used as a model for civilized warfare in the twentieth century. Nevertheless, the discussion of the cruelty of civil war sounded topical in 1990, and the remarks which Maksimov attributes to Kolchak about the primacy of tanks over meetings bear a striking similarity to the views of some of the hard-liners in the Communist Party responsible for the coup of August 1991. Maksimov's account takes on a particularly contemporary resonance when he depicts Kolchak meditating on Pushkin's words from *The Captain's Daughter*: 'God save us from a Russian rebellion, so senseless and merciless', a phrase which was much quoted in the USSR in the early 1990s.

Maksimov's sympathetic account of Kolchak's downfall contains information previously not known to the Soviet public. First, he de-scribes how Kolchak was entrusted to the care of the Czech Legion, who betrayed him to the Bolsheviks. Subsequently, in one of the parts of the novel which may have aroused most interest in Russia, Maksimov includes the transcript of Kolchak's interrogation, held on 21 January 1920, which traced his whole biography. Whereas to a Soviet audience Kolchak had usually been portrayed as a die-hard monarchist and conservative, the document reveals Kolchak's claim not to have been interested in politics: 'My point of view was the point of view of a serving officer, who was not concerned with these questions.' Kolchak's monarchist views appear not as an ideological principle, but merely as a recognition of the *status quo*. When asked whether his political views changed after the February Revolution, Kolchak replied that he welcomed the revolution whole-heartedly, since: 'It was clear to me, as before, that the government which had existed for the preceding months, Protopopov, etc., was not capable of coping with the task of waging war.' Kolchak's position appears similar to that of other military leaders, such as General Alekseyev, who urged the Tsar to abdicate in order to save the war effort, and swore an oath of loyalty to the new Provisional Government.

Maksimov's work presents a sympathetic image of Admiral Kolchak, restoring him to a more honourable place in Russian history, and tempering the extreme monarchist and conservative views which are usually attributed to him. His analysis of Kolchak's defeat concentrates more on military mistakes, the half-heartedness and treachery of the Allies and the personal shortcomings of the White commanders than on the political failures of the Whites which are admitted in Denikin's memoirs, such as the fact that they had little to offer the people except a return to the hated old regime. However, as always in Maksimov's works, politics are secondary; he sees the Civil War as just one episode in the metaphysical struggle between God and the Devil for the soul of Russia.

Maksimov's own views about the contemporary lessons to be drawn from the Civil War period were made clear in 1990, in an interesting introduction to extracts from *I Will Repay*, a novel on the fate of Russian Cossacks in the Civil War.[74] Maksimov's religious faith leads him to the view that every evil has its consequences, and that history brings its own reckoning. He observes that the representatives of many classes and groupings in Russia – Leninists, democrats, nobles, intellectuals, peasants, workers, national minorities and Cossacks – all experienced tragedies, then blamed their sufferings on everything and everyone, except themselves. Guilt has been pinned on the Jews, the Russians, the Allies, foreigners in general, or all of these together. Yet after studying the revolutionary period 'attentively, without preconceptions', Maksimov has come to the conclusion that 'Everybody and nobody is guilty.' He claims, with considerable justification, that no one emerged victorious 'from that political discord which was unprecedented in human history; all turned out to be defeated by it, even the victors themselves, who as a result became weak-willed prisoners of the system they had created'. In his view, it is impossible to separate the tragedy of the true Leninists, who ended up in the Lubyanka in Stalin's time, from the tragedy of those whom they themselves had previously imprisoned.

Similarly, the tragedy of the noblemen, intelligentsia, peasantry, working class and national minorities cannot be looked at 'without considering their own collaboration in the crimes of Bolshevism'. By this he means either the decision to emigrate, leaving the country to its fate, or 'the bloody brutalities of these classes against people guilty of nothing but their origin, the nightmarish kangaroo courts, arson attacks and sadism shown by them in the years of the Civil War'. Maksimov expresses a tolerant view designed to defuse contemporary passions in Russia, when many different groups were trying to find a convenient scapegoat for the tragedies of Russian history. He argues that it is necessary for all Russians to accept their own responsibility and not blame others: 'If each of us does not take his part of the blame for what has happened to Russia, but continues to attach blame to others, then I am profoundly convinced that there will be no end to the blood, and the world will be doomed to totalitarian tyranny.' In a recent interview, Maksimov has explained how Solzhenitsyn's view of Russian history differs from his own: 'Solzhenitsyn believes that the Russian people are victims. I do not. I love them. I am Russian. Russians are both executioners and victims, just as all peoples are.'[75]

Solzhenitsyn's *The Red Wheel* is another major work newly published in the USSR which attempts to reassess the whole period of the Revolution and Civil War. Since 1990 Russians have been able to read Solzhenitsyn's statement that he wished to overturn the legend that the Civil War was merely 'a war between the Whites and the Reds'; in his view 'the most important thing was the people's resistance to the Reds, from 1918 to 1922. And in this war the losses amounted to several million!'[76] The liberal critic Andrei Nemzer revealed in 1990 that a topical question in contemporary Russia was: when did the Civil War begin in Russia? and referred to various possible dates: the revolt of the Left SRs in July 1918, the spring of 1918, the dispersal of the Constituent Assembly, the day of the Revolution, 25 October 1917, and the arrest of the Tsar. Nemzer contrasts this question with the preoccupation of many characters in Solzhenitsyn's *March 1917*: when will civil war begin? He correctly observes that although politicians of many different political views thought they were doing everything in their power to prevent civil war, in fact the hostility and intolerance between supporters of different political groupings, even between members of the same family, was so extreme that war was bound to break out.[77] In the context of the passionate antagonisms in the USSR in the 1990s, Nemzer's review of Solzhenitsyn's work can be interpreted as a warning to his contemporaries.[78]

CONCLUSION

The new prominence accorded to the Whites in the Gorbachev era was a necessary corrective to the pro-Red bias of the previous seventy years, but to some extent gave a false impression of their importance and the value of their ideas. Some myths have been corrected: for example, Kornilov is no longer presented as a monarchist, and the variety of opinions on the White side has now been admitted. Unfortunately, however, some critics of literature about the Civil War have taken sides, supporting White writers (who were mainly Russian) against Reds (who were mainly Jewish), thus exacerbating the divisions in contemporary Russian society.[79] Democratic commentators have recognized that there is now a need to correct the current bias in favour of the Whites, which reflects a new form of Great Russian chauvinism, and some works have been published which demonstrate that the Whites wished to return to the old system, which the people did not want. The terror on both sides has been acknowledged, and it has been admitted that the main loser in the struggle was Russia herself.

In retrospect, the hidden agenda behind the publication of so much literature about the Civil War in the years 1990–1 was to issue a warning about the possibility of a new civil war in the present and future. The phrase 'civil war' has been used by many Russians in private conversations during the years 1990–4, and was pronounced in public by Eduard Shevardnadze, Yurii Afanas'ev and others on the first day of the coup, 19 August 1991. With hindsight, the experiences of White leaders like Denikin and Kolchak could have been of interest in the early 1990s not merely to Russian liberals seeking a deeper knowledge of their own history, but also to hard-line party and state bureaucrats and military patriots such as those responsible for the failed coups of August 1991 and October 1993. The leaders of the White armies, like the plotters of 1991 and 1993, epitomized a tradition of law and order and a 'single and indivisible' Russian Empire, as opposed to the chaotic democracy represented by Kerensky, Gorbachev and Yeltsin prior to his disbandment of the Congress of People's Deputies in September 1993.[80] Like the Whites in the Civil War, such hard-liners had little to offer the people except a return to an authoritarian regime. However, such discredited values have not prevented Vladimir Zhirinovsky and his Liberal Democratic Party from achieving considerable success in the elections of December 1993.

10 The February Revolution and the Provisional Government

The subjects of the October Revolution and Civil War could not be investigated adequately without some analysis of the activities and failure of the democratic political forces which took power after the revolution of February 1917. Before Gorbachev's accession the activities of Lenin and the October Revolution had been the main focus of academic study; very little had been known about the personalities involved in the February Revolution and Provisional Government, and the reasons for their failure. The fact that the Provisional Government was one of the last historical subjects to receive attention after the introduction of *glasnost* suggests that it was one of the most sensitive issues, not only for the Communists, who were not particularly eager for Russians to become aware of the plurality of views represented in their political heritage, but also, when by 1990 the Communist Party began to lose its grip on power, for the new democratic political leaders, who did not wish to confront the reasons for the failure of democracy in 1917. This subject has been touched upon in fiction and press debates, and is beginning to be investigated by historians in the 1990s, but has still not been fully or objectively researched in Russia. There is still a significant degree of public ignorance about these events.

Soviet historiography had always passed rapidly over the eight months when the Provisional Government was in power, regarding it as merely a chaotic and insignificant prelude to the inevitable Bolshevik Revolution. All the opponents of tsarism who were not associated with Lenin and the Bolsheviks had either been ignored or crudely caricatured;[1] their opinions had not been analysed, and they had certainly not been given credit for any positive achievements. However, by 1987 *glasnost* permitted a more accurate picture of Lenin's opponents: *Moscow News* presented biographical sketches of leading opponents of the October revolution.[2] Milyukov, the leader of the liberal Constitutional Democratic (Kadet) party, was presented as a cultured man who played the violin, and 'a major historian, whose works have not lost scholarly significance', but was criticized for having 'ruled the party in a dictatorial manner, while paying lip service to democracy'. This characterization may have been partially designed to issue a veiled warning to Gorbachev and other Communists who at that time were using the word 'democratization', while still supporting a one-party dictatorship. However, it also bears a strong resemblance to the criticisms levelled against Milyukov in Solzhenitsyn's *The Red Wheel*, suggesting that this image may have been familiar to the journalist. This article did not go very deeply into the political views of Lenin's opponents, but a major development occurred in 1987–8 when the state censorship organization Glavlit moved many books in 'special reserves' (*spetsfondy*), including the writings of Kerensky and Milyukov, the SR Boris Savinkov and the Anarchist Pyotr Kropotkin, into general library stores.[3]

In the Gorbachev era rather more attention was paid to the Mensheviks than to other anti-Lenin parties, since official attitudes to Menshevism were becoming more sympathetic, especially to the left-wing Mensheviks Martov and Dan, who had come round to Lenin's programme on the eve of the Revolution. In 1987 the rehabilitation of fifteen prominent Soviet economists who had been accused of membership of an alleged 'Toiling Peasant Party' in 1930–1,[4] also implied the innocence of those falsely condemned in the public trial of the 'Menshevik Union Bureau' in March 1931.[5] Henceforth a positive reference to the Mensheviks could be presented as part of the acceptable process of examining alternative models of socialism.

This new approach was reflected in Rybakov's *Children of the Arbat*, which provided one of the first sympathetic pictures in Soviet fiction of the conditions experienced in the 1930s by Mensheviks, SRs and Anarchists exiled to Siberia. Shatrov's *Onward . . . onward . . . onward!* explored the limits of the permissible in 1988, suggesting that Lenin in his last years even contemplated the legalization of the Mensheviks. This episode was just one example of a liberal trend in 1988 of using the figure of Lenin to advocate democracy and tolerance towards political opponents.[6] However, Shatrov's sympathetic reference to Menshevism was still sufficiently controversial in 1988 to provoke attacks both on political grounds and on grounds of historical accuracy. When challenged, Shatrov stated that Lenin's jottings for his *Notes of a Publicist* included the brief comment: 'On relationship with Mensheviks. Their legalization'; but his critic Yurii Aksyutin refuted this argument by pointing out that a later note by Lenin justified the suppression of the Mensheviks.[7] Shatrov was reviled for being a 'Menshevik' himself;[8] the most virulent criticism was contained in the notorious letter by Nina Andreyeva, which suggested that Shatrov's arguments and evaluations were close to the line of argument of the émigré Menshevik historian Boris Souvarine[9] (this is tantamount to an anti-Semitic accusation of 'cosmopolitanism'). Andreyeva suggested that the current attacks on the dictatorship of the proletariat were motivated by professional anti-communists in the West and 'the remnants of the defeated classes within the USSR', including the spiritual successors of such Mensheviks as Dan and Martov. (In context, it is significant that Dan, Martov and Shatrov are all Jewish.)

Shatrov brings to life many of the important theoretical disputes from the time of the revolution. Plekhanov, the 'father of Russian Marxism', argues that Russia is not ready for socialism, and the Menshevik Martov predicts that Lenin will have to resort to terror to carry out his programme. Shatrov also presents a sympathetic portrait of another previously taboo figure, the Left SR leader Maria Spiridonova, whose historical role had not been objectively analysed in the USSR because she had led her party in and out of alliance with the Bolsheviks and in 1918 had sanctioned a rebellion against them. She makes a confused but sincere speech reflecting her dilemma as a libertarian revolutionary, and eventually reveals that she was shot on Soviet orders in 1941.

By contrast, Shatrov's depiction of the 'bourgeois' members of the Provisional Government is still highly tendentious. Shatrov's Kerensky never rises above the usual Soviet caricature: he is an unreliable, egoistic windbag, although his longevity enables him to make some perceptive comments on the subsequent course of Soviet history. In general, Kerensky has received a bad press in Soviet literature, both in the works of reformist communists like Shatrov and Russian nationalists such as Solzhenitsyn. Polemics have become so polarized in contemporary Russia that the democracy he represented has never been seen as offering a serious alternative in 1917.

Shatrov presents Lenin's opinion of Kerensky and the procrastinating tactics of the Provisional Government as a thinly veiled reflection of Gorbachev's attitude to the conservatives hindering his reform programme: 'A gigantic fossilized army of office-holders who will introduce reforms that undermine their domination? . . . Whom are you laughing at, gentlemen? . . . To try to carry out a revolutionary transformation through such an apparatus is . . . the greatest self-deception and deception of the people.' Here Shatrov's publicist passion comes into conflict with his objectivity as a historian. Although Shatrov's play was fiercely denounced, suggesting that even in 1988 it remained difficult to present Lenin's opponents in a fairer light, *Onward . . . onward . . . onward!* is, as we have seen, a conventional pro-Lenin work which sheds little new light on the Provisional Government, merely implying that in 1917 the only alternative to Bolshevism was a right-wing military dictatorship.

Gradually the publication of memoirs and 'returned literature', including émigré works, began to paint a more sympathetic picture of Silver Age intellectuals who originally welcomed the February Revolution, but were later disillusioned by Bolshevism. Pasternak's *Doctor Zhivago* (1988) evokes the rapture experienced by many Russian intellectuals at the news of the February Revolution,[10] and a similar view emerges from Pasternak's poem of 1918, *Russian Revolution*, previously unknown in the USSR, which was published in 1989.[11] The poet evokes the excitement and ferment of the February revolution, welcoming it as 'the brightest of all the great revolutions', which, it seemed 'would not shed blood'. However, the evocation of the post-February interval is by no means entirely positive in Pasternak's work. In an image reminiscent of the famous winged troika symbolizing Russia at the end of Gogol's *Dead Souls*, Pasternak suggests that in April 1917 Lenin's armoured train was gathering speed in the distance. The last verse points to the gulf between the promise of the Revolution and the horror of the Civil War, a 'rebellion' which spreads 'blood, brains and the vomit of drunken sailors'. Similarly, the vivid scene of the murder of Commissar Gintz in Pasternak's *Doctor Zhivago* graphically demonstrates the cruel forms of retaliation which long-suppressed resentment led rank-and-file soldiers to wreak on their officers after the Tsar's abdication.[12]

The rapid growth of 'informal associations' in the years 1988–9 suggested that Russians were rediscovering their long-buried political traditions, as (among many others), a Constitutional Democratic Party and an Anarchist party were formed. Yet it was not until 1989–90, with the introduction of greater democratic freedoms, that the ideas and actions of the Provisional Government began to come under increasing scrutiny in Russia. The eight months between February and October 1917 represented the only previous experience of genuine democracy in Russia (as opposed to the 'semi-constitutional politics' of the Duma period, 1906–17), and it began to be recognized that a study of this period might yield valuable lessons for the embryonic Russian democracy of the 1990s.[13] However, the February Revolution is yet another historical topic which has created divided responses among the intelligentsia. Right-wing, nationalist writers generally take a pessimistic view of that period; whereas democrats and radicals look to it as a short-lived interval of freedom between the tsarist autocracy and the Bolshevik dictatorship, the only eight months of democracy which

Russia had experienced in the entire twentieth century until the advent of Gorbachev. (Ironically, the democrats' viewpoint was shared by Lenin himself, who on his return to Russia in April 1917 called it 'the freest country in the world'.) Contemporary Russian democrats recognize the failures and limitations of the Provisional Government, but, rather than jettisoning the whole concept of democracy, seek to learn from past mistakes in order to safeguard their fledgling democracy and ensure its continuation in the future.

One of the most positive references to the democratic traditions in Russian history was contained in Grossman's controversial work *Everything Flows . . .* (1989). Grossman takes the iconoclastic view that the most significant revolution occurred not in 1917, but in 1861, when the serfs were liberated, since this broke the 'thousand-year-old link between progress and slavery' in Russian history. The true revolutionaries were the democrats who after the emancipation of the serfs struggled for human dignity and progress without slavery until the February Revolution. Grossman comments ruefully: 'In February 1917 the path of freedom lay straight ahead for Russia. And Russia chose Lenin.'

A more critical view of the February Revolution was contained in the memoirs of the White general Denikin (1990).[14] On the one hand, Denikin admits that the revolution was rapturously received by the whole people, because it granted freedom and sowed bright hopes in the 'intoxicated crowd'. On the other hand, like Pasternak, he points to the bloody reprisals taken against officers, and warns against an excessively optimistic interpretation of the February Revolution, since he considers that it was at this time that moral degeneration began in the army and the population at large. Denikin, like Solzhenitsyn after him, is a resolute opponent of all revolutions. The ambiguity of his newly published memoirs corresponds well to the mood of 1990, when the first euphoria of *glasnost* was past, and Russians were beginning to feel disillusioned with the chaotic democracy they were witnessing in the Congress of People's Deputies. However, Denikin's analysis does not add much to the interpretation of the February revolution presented in Shatrov's play, since he also discounted the democrats and pinned his hopes on a military dictatorship (if a more benign one than has sometimes been assumed).

Another sceptical view of the February Revolution was expressed in a novel by the Russian nationalist and religious believer Vladimir Maksimov, *Looking into the Abyss*, first published in Russia in 1990,[15] which suggests that the events of 1917 encouraged the Russian people's innate anarchic tendencies. Like Voloshin in his lecture 'Russia Crucified', Maksimov regards anarchy as the inevitable consequence of the end of despotism in Russia. He suggests that the 'general madness' unleashed after the February Revolution led to anarchy and self-will, underpinning his interpretation with the Dostoevskian idea that 'When God is dead, everything is lawful.' It is interesting that Maksimov, like Solzhenitsyn in *The Red Wheel*, sees the root cause of Russia's problems as the February, rather than the October Revolution.

Solzhenitsyn is, of course, the writer who has devoted most attention to the February Revolution and the political and intellectual forces opposed to Bolshevism. Although not many Russian readers have read all his historical novels dealing with this subject which began to be published in the USSR in 1990 – *The First Circle* and *The Red Wheel*[16] – certain of his ideas have been popularized in the press and given rise to some, if hitherto only limited, discussion. In March 1991 the literary critic Aron Lur'e expressed regret that Solzhenitsyn's work had, as yet, received little critical analysis by historians. In the early 1990s Russian historians, for the most part, devoted their attention only to certain discrete episodes of the tsarist and revolutionary period, like the activities of the Social Democratic double agent Malinovsky;[17] while journals and newspapers made a useful contribution to the study of non-Bolshevik leaders by publishing memoirs, such as those of Kerensky and Guchkov.[18] However, hitherto no historian living in Russia has seriously engaged with Solzhenitsyn's interpretation of the February Revolution. In the West too, *The Red Wheel* as a whole still awaits thorough historical evaluation, although historians have provided interesting assessments of individual aspects of Solzhenitsyn's epic, such as his portraits of Stolypin and Lenin. Some western historians consider that a historical novel is not worth serious comment; but in the case of Solzhenitsyn's epic such analysis would be a worthwhile endeavour, as in his homeland Solzhenitsyn's passionate work combining fact and fiction is liable to exert considerable influence on popular thinking.

The critic Alla Latynina, speaking for those members of the intelligentsia who, by 1990, were prepared to admit that the Soviet experiment had failed, and no longer cared 'to think in the categories of the Civil War era and to date their intellectual genealogy from 1917', selected from Solzhenitsyn's definitive version of *The First Circle* the sections on pre-revolutionary culture, which she regarded as the most relevant to her contemporaries.[19] She refers to the chapter in which Innokentii Volodin sorts out the papers of his mother, a member of the pre-revolutionary intelligentsia, and is astonished at the freedom and variety of ideas he finds in the old letters, diary entries and magazine supplements. When Latynina reports that Innokentii's Soviet upbringing had previously taught him to regard this as a 'disgraceful' period that was 'devoid of talent', the implication is that this reflects the experience of many Soviet intellectuals. Latynina repeats, without comment, the author's own observation on this period: 'Granted, it was too talkative, that decade, in part too self-assured and in part too powerless. But what a sprouting of possibilities! What a diversity of ideas! Innokentii realised that until now he had been robbed.' Solzhenitsyn's analysis of the ferment of the immediate pre-revolutionary era can, perhaps, be assumed to bear some resemblance to Latynina's view of contemporary Russian society.

The critic also devotes particular attention to the chapter 'An Uncle from Tver'', which was omitted from the version of *The First Circle* that circulated in *samizdat* in the 1960s, and which, in her opinion, is one of the most important in the novel. Innokentii's Uncle Avenir, who lives in poverty, is portrayed, in Latynina's words, as 'the custodian of intellectual and cultural riches that have been squandered by the Russian intelligentsia's illegitimate heirs'. Solzhenitsyn's Uncle Avenir is an attractive portrait of a Russian intellectual whose loyalty was not to the monarchy, but to the democratic values dashed when the Constituent Assembly was dispersed in January 1918. Latynina accepts Solzhenitsyn's rejection of the official Soviet version of history, which claimed that unarmed demonstrators had gathered outside the Tauride Palace on 5 January 1918 to protest against the closure of the Constituent Assembly simply in order to protect their own privileges. Latynina stresses that they gathered 'in the name of freedom.... The peaceful demonstrators carrying the red flags of revolution were fired on by the same people who had driven away the deputies gathered from all over Russia to express the people's will.' Uncle Avenir makes it clear to Innokentii that even people who had actively opposed the tsarist regime found themselves in opposition to the October coup, which they interpreted as anti-democratic and anti-popular. Latynina implicitly accepts Avenir's view that the peasants had been promised land, but had obtained serfdom instead; the workers had been promised control over production, but had been crushed by the central state authority; the people had been promised freedom, but had been given concentration camps. Solzhenitsyn does not portray Uncle Avenir as a member of any particular party; he is clearly meant to represent the entire anti-Bolshevik intelligentsia, and symbolize the hope for a future democratic regeneration of Russia ('Avenir' is the French word for 'future').

The third and fourth volumes (known as 'knots') of Solzhenitsyn's *The Red Wheel, March 1917* and *April 1917*, represent the most detailed historical and artistic investigation yet published in Russia of the failure of the February Revolution and the non-Bolshevik forces in 1917. The journal *Neva* introduced its publication of *March 1917* by quoting an interview of 1989, in which Solzhenitsyn himself outlined his intellectual reassessment of the February Revolution, the chief motivation behind his work: 'Initially I started from the conception that most people in the West and the East today share: that the so-called October Revolution and its consequences were the main, decisive event. But gradually it became clear to me that the main and decisive event was not the October Revolution, and that this was not a revolution at all. . . . The genuine revolution was the February Revolution, October does not even deserve the name of revolution. It was a state coup, and until the 1920s everyone including the Bolsheviks called it "the October coup".'[20] The editors of *Neva* admitted that at one time not only supporters of the October Revolution, but also many of its opponents, would not have accepted such an untraditional view. However, they expressed the belief that 'all who love their native land and feel its pain will agree with the great Russian humanist that "We must think about the dangers of the future transition. In the ensuing historical transition a new trial threatens us – and this is what we are completely unprepared for. These are a completely new type of danger for us, and in order to withstand them, we must at least have a good knowledge of our Russian past".' Thus the liberal journal presented Solzhenitsyn's analysis of the February Revolution not only as a historical reappraisal, but also as an important guide to contemporary action.

By contrast, conservative critics seized on the view of the February Revolution and the Soviet intelligentsia's indifference to it expressed in Solzhenitsyn's notorious article of 1982, 'Our Pluralists', which had been aimed against the liberal and dissident intelligentsia of the Brezhnev era.[21] Solzhenitsyn attributes neglect of the February Revolution to two main factors: ignorance, and the difficulty of explaining it 'in a manner favourable to liberals, radicals and the intelligentsia'. Solzhenitsyn's observations, though excessively harsh, are correct in the sense that Russians had previously been allowed almost no access to works by western historians or archival materials which might have helped them understand the February Revolution and the Provisional Government. And although, in Solzhenitsyn's interpretation, the historical record presents liberals and intellectuals in a bad light, this is not the only possible assessment of the events of 1917. Some of the participants in these events and some western historians, perhaps going too far to the opposite extreme from Solzhenitsyn, have interpreted the members of the Provisional Government as weak, tragic idealists overwhelmed by the magnitude of the problems which they had inherited from the tsarist regime, who were inevitably defeated by the intrigues of extremists on the right and the left. Other contemporary western historians have painted a more complex picture, pointing to both the achievements and failures of the Provisional government, and to events which were outside their control.[22]

The critic Palamarchuk also makes it clear that Solzhenitsyn's aim in *The Red Wheel* is to warn his countrymen against any repetition of the events of 1917. He points to the enormous amount of research which Solzhenitsyn has done on the causes and consequences of the February Revolution, and supports Solzhenitsyn's contention that his work has been unjustly neglected by his opponents. The critic quotes with approbation Solzhenitsyn's comment that: 'February will be all the more dangerous for us in the future if we don't remember it in the past. And it will be all the easier to deluge Russia in its new fateful hour – with idle chatter. You don't need to remember? But we must! for we don't want a repetition in Russia of that boisterous bar-rooom talk which ruined the country in eight months.' Solzhenitsyn considers that the February Revolution incited 'the people's dissipation', not, as in the conventional Soviet view, 'a grass-roots outbreak of age-old class anger, for which the Bolsheviks proved to be obedient, convenient spokesmen'.[23] Palamarchuk emphasizes the topical nature of Solzhenitsyn's statement of 1979: 'The unfortunate experience of February, the consciousness of it, is the most necessary thing now for our people.'[24]

If Palamarchuk's quotations from Solzhenitsyn's articles hostile to the liberal intelligentsia can be justified by the critic's aim of introducing Solzhenitsyn's ideas and literary works to the Russian public, some conservative Russian nationalists used the same works in a more explicit manner, in order to attack their democratic opponents who had risen to prominence under Gorbachev. In a number of speeches made in December 1988, which remained unpublished until 1990, Russian nationalists began to claim Solzhenitsyn as their ally.[25] Vladimir Krupin, for example, argued that in the essay 'Our Pluralists' Solzhenitsyn 'predicted precisely what we now see: this frenzied clamour, a kind of endless dissection of problems'. Valentin Rasputin, once regarded as a good 'village prose' writer, but by 1990 reviled by the liberal intelligentsia,[26] expressed the hope that the publication of Solzhenitsyn's work might provide an 'authoritative voice' to calm contemporary passions about the future of Russia, and supported Solzhenitsyn's anti-western stance, claiming that Russia has its own traditions which foreigners cannot fathom, and that western researchers are wrong to demand that Russia should follow the same path of development as the West. While regretting the necessity for the simultaneous publication of the different 'knots' of *The Red Wheel*, which for many readers will 'break the sequence of events, thoughts, causes and effects of the ever increasing destructive tendencies at the end of the last and the beginning of the present century', Rasputin realises that such haste is inevitable, as the work is too important to be spread over many years. He sees Solzhenitsyn's epic as vital for contemporary Russian society, because history is repeating itself: 'It is necessary now, necessary as quickly as possible, since much of what happened then is repeating itself now, both in its aims and methods. It is being repeated to the extent of a striking similarity of figures and events, presaging a repetition of the outcome, if we are to remain observers on the sidelines.' Rasputin claims that Russian readers 'will read it, with surprise, ecstasy and concern, and draw conclusions'.

Palamarchuk emphasizes that, apart from issuing prophetic warnings about the future of Russian democracy, Solzhenitsyn's *The Red Wheel* is designed to overturn certain myths which had surrounded the February revolution in Soviet historiography.[27] In the first place, he shows that the legend which maintained that the Tsar had engaged in negotiations with Germany about a separate peace were completely untrue. In Solzhenitsyn's view, Nicholas II lost his throne because he was too loyal to England and France, too loyal to 'that senseless war which was not necessary to Russia in the slightest'. Palamarchuk cites with approbation Solzhenitsyn's opinion that the Tsar 'allowed himself to be carried away by that militant madness which possessed liberal circles'. Solzhenitsyn's view that the First World War was not necessary to Russia accords with the views of some western historians.[28] However, the blame he attributes to the liberal circles overlooks the fact that Russia's involvement in wars with Japan in 1904–5 and with Germany in 1914 was, to a great extent, due to Nicholas II's adventurist foreign policy and his desire for Russia to retain 'Great Power' status, and that it was the Tsar, not the liberals, who was responsible for declaring war against Germany. Once war had broken out, the liberal circles regarded it as their patriotic duty to support the war effort. Palamarchuk also quotes Solzhenitsyn's opinion that 'The liberal circles strove to rescue their western allies with the lives of Russian peasants. They were afraid of receiving a bad mark from the Allies.' Once again, this is a simplistic view: the members of the Provisional Government continued the war partly because they were afraid that victory and occupation by the Kaiser's Germany might destroy the gains of the Revolution; they did have a sense of duty (and financial obligation) to the Allies, but were also blocked by them when they urged a general peace.

Solzhenitsyn is also concerned to counter the myth about the important role played by the Soviet of Workers' Deputies, elected in February 1917. He is correct to point out that the Petrograd Soviet, which contained more than a thousand members, was of little significance; the practical decisions were taken by a self-selecting Executive Committee of political activists, mainly from the Menshevik and SR parties. However, one of the weaknesses of *The Red Wheel*, if it is to be considered a polyphonic narrative evoking the different views of all the forces involved in the February Revolution, is Solzhenitsyn's extremely hostile, caricatured portrayal of the moderate socialists, such as the Menshevik Chkheidze and the SR Chernov, who were involved in the Petrograd Soviet, and later in the coalition government established in May 1917.

Solzhenitsyn's failure to provide an adequate analysis of the dilemma of such socialist leaders as Chernov, who wished to give land to the peasants, but found himself unable to carry out the SR policy adequately amid war and peasant uprisings, and of Tseretelli, the only Menshevik to advocate the use of force against the Bolsheviks, is a missed opportunity. His attitude to the Soviet leaders is as schematic as his observation, quoted by Palamarchuk: 'The second-rate trashy party socialists selected themselves and led Russia to the abyss.'[29]

Solzhenitsyn also pours scorn on the Provisional Government, presenting its members as 'the same liberal activists who had been shouting for years that they were men empowered to act for Russia, who were incomparably clever, and knew everything about how to rule Russia, and would naturally be better than the tsarist ministers – but turned out to be a panopticon of weak-willed mediocrities, and rapidly let everything go'. Solzhenitsyn is correct in the sense that the politicians who rose to prominence after the February Revolution were mediocre statesmen with no experience of government, only of opposition, as Russia had little tradition of democracy. They were not prepared to take power, and were hamstrung by their own liberal principles, refusing to use force against their enemies, and attempting to form a coalition, which is the most difficult form of government, even in peacetime. Solzhenitsyn's criticisms also overlook the desperate situation of war and economic collapse which the Provisional Government had inherited from the tsarist regime. Even if the Provisional Government was weak, Solzhenitsyn's strong bias in favour of Stolypin and against liberals and socialists, rendered it unlikely that his research into the Provisional Government would be fairly conducted.

Another charge which Solzhenitsyn levels against the Provisional Government is not only that they relinquished power, but that they were unable to take power in the first place. Palamarchuk reports to Russian readers Solzhenitsyn's view that 'The Provisional Government existed, mathematically speaking, for minus two days: that is, it was completely deprived of power two days before its creation.' Solzhenitsyn is correct in the sense that the Provisional Government's position was weak from the start, as they lacked all legitimacy and connection with the old regime, once they had rejected the idea of a constitutional monarchy, or of any link with the Fourth Duma (which, in any case, was very unrepresentative, because it had been based on the electoral coup introduced by Stolypin in 1907). Moreover, the Government and soviets both owed their position to the anarchic moods of the masses, the workers, peasants and soldiers (the 'peasants in uniform'), whose support they needed to retain if they were not to be overwhelmed by them.

Solzhenitsyn's preconceptions about the Provisional Government receive graphic expression in his depiction of events on the first day that the Provisional Government was established.[30] While the seemingly victorious Military Commission of the Duma is meeting, its members are thrown into panic by the noise of a stray volley of gunshots, demonstrating that there is no one to defend the Provisional Government, the so-called 'chosen one of the people'. With savage irony, Solzhenitsyn suggests that anything could have happened, had not Kerensky, with his 'responsibility for the whole fate of the Revolution', taken the sudden decision to jump on a window sill and shout from a window of the Tauride Palace: 'To your places, everyone! All to their military posts! ... Defend the State Duma! ... It's Kerensky speaking! The State Duma is being shot at!' The author comments ironically: 'But not everyone knew his place, and not everyone had a weapon, and not everyone knew how to operate it. And in that chaotic panic, shouting, swearing, grousing and roaring nobody heard and nobody noticed that a man was shouting from a small window.' This scene is praised by the nationalist Palamarchuk as 'symbolic', but the liberal critic Aron Lur'e stated in 1991 that although it is humorous, it displays a certain 'lack of taste'. In the opinions of liberal critics,

Solzhenitsyn exaggerated in his portrayal of members of the Provisional Government; some of them were very intelligent men, not fools, as Solzhenitsyn suggests. Another liberal critic, Andrei Nemzer, has voiced the valid complaint that, although Solzhenitsyn portrays many historical figures in an interesting new way, Kerensky is depicted as a mere caricature, just as he always has been in Soviet historiography, thus arousing the suspicion of the intelligent reader.[31] As another perceptive Soviet commentator has remarked, at least Kerensky succeeded in organizing the Provisional Government.[32] A less biased historian than Solzhenitsyn might also give Kerensky credit for his genuine belief in consensus politics and his desire to safeguard democracy.

One issue raised by Solzhenitsyn in connection with the Provisional Government and singled out for special comment by the conservative critic Palamarchuk, is the role of Freemasons in the February Revolution – a subject which was just beginning to emerge in historical discussions in the USSR. Palamarchuk reports that *The Red Wheel* correctly shows that Milyukov was not a Mason, but that Guchkov (the head of the conservative Octobrist Party) lied when he claimed not to be a member, since the émigré writer Nina Berberova's research has allegedly proved that he was a member, and in 1916 planned a coup against the Tsar along with fellow Masons, including some of the military commanders.[33] However, other historians have suggested that Guchkov later left the Masons, which was one reason why he and Milyukov found it difficult to establish good relations with the other members of the First Provisional Government, many of whom were Masons. The role of Masons in the Provisional Government is a fascinating field for historical research if it is treated objectively,[34] but too often in contemporary Russia it leads to chauvinist references to the alleged 'Jewish–Masonic conspiracy' behind the Revolution.

Another controversial point was Solzhenitsyn's scorn of the cultural intelligentsia who welcomed the February Revolution. He is particularly scathing in his attitude to the theatre director Meyerhol'd, who directs a grandiose, luxurious production of Lermontov's play *Masquerade*, which was fated to become the last production in the Chief Imperial Theatre. (The images of a masquerade, and of blindness, are frequently used by Solzhenitsyn to evoke the general atmosphere of the February Revolution and its aftermath.) Solzhenitsyn's hostility to Meyerhol'd is aroused by the fact that he went on to serve the Provisional Government, and later to play an important part in the cultural politics of the Bolshevik regime; yet in view of the revelations which had appeared in the Soviet press about the torture and death of Meyerhol'd and his wife in the Stalin era,[35] Solzhenitsyn's excessive hatred for him might also appear in questionable taste.

Another interpretation uncongenial to liberal Soviet intellectuals in the 1990s was Solzhenitsyn's satirical presentation of three famous cultural figures of the Silver Age, Dmitrii Merezhkovskii, his wife Zinaida Gippius and their friend Dmitrii Filosofov, who are easily recognizable under the names 'the mistress of the house', 'the husband' and 'the friend'. Both Merezhkovskii and Gippius greet the February Revolution with rapture, and feel great sympathy for Kerensky.[36] Solzhenitsyn seems to be suggesting that since Gippius and Merezhkovskii (and other intellectuals of various political views who later emigrated, such as Berdyaev and Rozanov) were guilty of welcoming the February Revolution which set in motion the disintegration of Russia, they later had no right to complain about persecution of the intelligentsia by the Bolsheviks. Solzhenitsyn's judgement of the pre-revolutionary intelligentsia is very harsh, made in the light of hindsight, and unduly coloured by his hostility to the Soviet intelligentsia of his own time.

Solzhenitsyn is also eager to stress the accidental nature of the February Revolution, and to overturn the myth that the February Revolution was 'bloodless'. He relates a previously little known story about lieutenant Timofei Kirpichnikov, who triggered the first successful soldiers' rebellion in the Volynsk regiment by shooting the commanding officer of his company. Solzhenitsyn stresses that, although these were called 'guards regiments', they were in fact reserve detachments consisting of novices, while the true guards regiments were fighting at the front. It was this news about the 'revolt of the guards' that helped to draw the Petrograd garrison into anarchy. Solzhenitsyn also stresses that some of the commanders who were the most fervent adherents of the February Revolution, such as Admiral Nepenin, were subsequently murdered by their troops as alleged 'tsarist tyrants', paving the way for officers of a 'new type' such as Captain Voronovich, who felt at home among the rebellious soldiers who had murdered their fellow officers. The nationalist critic Palamarchuk highlights Voronovich's flawed character, relating that he later joined the 'Greens' during the Civil War, when he was prepared to betray Denikin and eventually to surrender to the Bolsheviks without a fight.[37]

In the chapter of press cuttings entitled 'February Mythology', Solzhenitsyn again points to the contrast between the intelligentsia's rapturous welcome of the 'bloodless revolution' and the actuality of the murders, robberies and pogroms which were occurring;[38] the implication is that the atrocities which began with the February Revolution simply developed to a greater degree in the Bolshevik 'Red Terror'. Yet although *The Red Wheel*, along with Pasternak's *Doctor Zhivago* and other fictional works and memoirs, has succeeded in proving that the February Revolution was not 'bloodless', Solzhenitsyn's work could be interpreted as a reminder that it is a rare revolution which sheds no blood. By no stretch of the imagination can the incidents which took place in the immediate aftermath of the February Revolution be compared with the widespread terror of the years of civil war.

Another myth which Solzhenitsyn is intent to undermine is the Soviet version of the right-wing 'Kornilov revolt' of August 1917, which, in his view, did not exist at all, but was invented by 'the falsehood and hysteria of Kerensky'. There is much truth in Solzhenitsyn's statement that Kerensky summoned the troops, then panicked, and strengthened the Bolsheviks by calling upon them to help 'save the revolution'; but he fails to mention that, possibly through some misunderstanding between Kerensky and his intermediary with Kornilov, V. N. Lvov, Kerensky came to believe that Kornilov's real intentions were to overturn the Provisional Government and establish a military dictatorship. Perhaps, with hindsight, even if Kerensky's fears were well founded, this would have posed a lesser threat to Russia than the Bolshevik Revolution, but in August 1917 the prospect of such an outcome would have provided a legitimate cause for concern.

One of the weaknesses of the semi-fictional genre chosen by Solzhenitsyn is that *The Red Wheel* concentrates on the personalities and political factors which influenced the events of the revolutionary period, to the exclusion of social and economic factors. Yet Solzhenitsyn's work is designed to diminish the importance of politics and politicians, indeed to emphasize that democratic politics proved to be a positive hindrance to Russia. He includes a shortened transcript of Duma debates in the last weeks of the Russian monarchy, suggesting that they present a record of noisy futility, and that the Duma itself was responsible for its own demise. Solzhenitsyn comments: 'What is terrifying is not that any demagogue can climb up on to the tribune at any moment and mumble all sorts of rubbish. What is terrifying is that there was not one shout of indignation, not a murmur from anywhere in the Duma chamber – everyone was so shocked and timid in front of the left wing. What is terrifying is that eleven years of four State Dumas were ending in such insignificant muttering.' His conclusion is: 'This Duma would never meet again. And today, as I read through the Duma transcripts from November 1916, and many, many others, I feel that I am not sorry.'[39]

Politicians who took a prominent part in the post-February period are subjected to even harsher criticism. As the critic Nemzer points out, the gallery of political figures portrayed in Solzhenitsyn's work can be roughly divided into three types: 'actors', 'theoreticians' and practical men.[40] The actors, of whom some prominent examples are Kerensky, Rodzianko, the chairman of the old Duma, and Prince Lvov, the sentimental Prime Minister of the First Provisional Government who believes he can reconcile the warring factions, attempt to seize the present moment and enjoy showing off against the contemporary political background, allowing the tide of events to carry them along or sweep them away. The two characters who fit into the category of 'theoretician' are the leader of the Kadet Party Milyukov and the non-party socialist Himmer, who does not feature prominently in the works of western historians, but in Solzhenitsyn's interpretation is presented as the chief organizer and the brains behind the First Provisional Government and the Petrograd Soviet. By equating these two men, Solzhenitsyn deliberately diminishes the role of Milyukov, who had been a prominent figure in the opposition to tsarism, and became Foreign Minister in the First Provisional Government. Himmer and Milyukov are, perhaps, the two political organizers of the events of February whom Solzhenitsyn hates the most. By presenting Milyukov as a doctrinaire, abstract thinker who has no concern for the true interests of Russia, Solzhenitsyn discredits the principal advocate of such western ideas as constitutional monarchy and parliamentary democracy. Solzhenitsyn suggests that, for all their iron will, obstinacy and capacity for work, both Milyukov and Himmer are alike in their inner uncertainty, indecisiveness and secret desire to share the responsibility thrust upon them. The two men appear to incarnate the principle of 'dual power', which played such a significant role in the first months after the Revolution. Solzhenitsyn implies that the intriguer from the Soviet initially needs the bourgeois Provisional Government, and the champion of liberalism needs a friendly Soviet. It is perhaps surprising that Solzhenitsyn, who dislikes political wrangling, is not sympathetic either to compromise and coalition, regarding them merely as signs of weakness. He regrets the fact that such 'theoreticians' manage to enlist the more talented 'practical men' on their side by encouraging them to join political parties.

As many of Solzhenitsyn's publicistic works have demonstrated, he is hostile to the concept of political parties, since a party means a part of the whole, and any party doctrine is by definition narrow. One of the more sympathetic characters in *The Red Wheel*, the Kadet V. Maklakov, states: 'Every party conflict teaches people not to be just.'

In Solzhenitsyn's opinion, it is Maklakov who in negotiations with tsarist ministers suggested the most sensible solution: a responsible ministry composed of intelligent, qualified professional bureaucrats, which aroused the ire of his party leader Milyukov. Solzhenitsyn's own bitter experience of a one-party state has led him to an excessively hostile view of the democratic political process and those who represent parties of a Western European type. Yet in the early 1990s Solzhenitsyn's theme proved highly relevant to the burgeoning democracy in Russia, as was attested by a critic who argued that members of the Congress of People's Deputies could learn useful lessons from *The Red Wheel*;[41] and by R. G. Abdulatipov, the President of the Soviet of Nationalities of the Russian Federation, who declared in 1991: 'I am close to the view of A. Solzhenitsyn (in his novels of the *Red Wheel* cycle) that inter-party conflict exhausts Russia.'[42]

The view which Solzhenitsyn saw as the fundamental 'myth' about the February Revolution was implied in a question which he was asked in the West: 'But, after all, isn't the whole of our understanding of Russian history – at least in the West – built on the premise that the February Revolution was a positive phenomenon, and, that if the October coup had not occurred, Russia would have gone along a path of peaceful development?'[43] The critic Palamarchuk reports Solzhenitsyn's decisive reply: 'There it is – one of the central legends. If you penetrate the daily flow of the February days, it immediately becomes clear that the revolution was leading to nothing but anarchy.' This is, of course, a debatable, unprovable point; perhaps alternative policies or better circumstances might have saved the Provisional Government. Moreover, even if it could be proved that, given the circumstances and personalities of 1917, the failure of the Provisional Government was inevitable, that would not necessarily invalidate any future democratic experiment in Russia. Solzhenitsyn goes on to draw a more valid conclusion: 'The striking history of 1917 is the history of how February fell of its own accord. The liberal and socialist rulers who then ruled Russia ruined it half a year before its complete collapse. And from the beginning of September 1917 the Bolsheviks could have taken the fallen power with their bare hands, without any difficulty.' He argues that it was only the excessive caution of Lenin and Trotsky that made the Bolsheviks wait for another month. (Here Solzhenitsyn perhaps underestimates the importance to the Bolsheviks of military preparedness, of securing a majority in the Petrograd Soviet and of making the seizure of power coincide with a vote in the All-Russian Congress of Soviets, due to meet on 25 October.) In Solzhenitsyn's view, the October Revolution represented not an active seizure of power by the Bolsheviks but a collapse of the Provisional Government.

Solzhenitsyn regards a thorough knowledge of the February Revolution as essential for all those who wish to discuss the future of Russia. He maintains: 'We need to know February and beware, because the repetition of February would be an irreparable catastrophe. And it is important that everyone understands this before any state changes occur.' However, Solzhenitsyn's warnings fell on deaf ears, and when the four volumes of *March 1917* were finally published in the West in 1986–8 he had to admit that they were already too late: 'And so it has happened that my historical work about February . . . has appeared so late that it has again become topical.'

Solzhenitsyn's views on the Provisional Government are shared by other Russian intellectuals of a conservative, Russian Orthodox persuasion. Maksimov, for example, has argued that the problems of the Russian democrats 'of the sadly notorious period of the Provisional Government' are inseparable from the fact that they themselves shook their own state to its very foundations';[44] and has warned of the danger of instant democracy after the fall of the Soviet regime, since '1917 showed where an unexpected turn to democracy can lead'.[45] However, not all Solzhenitsyn's compatriots accept his views uncritically. The émigré writer Vasilii Aksyonov has expressed disagreement with Solzhenitsyn's notion that the Provisional Government fell because of its excessive anarchy; in his opinion, its 'weakness, quantitative and qualitative inadequacy' were a major cause of its downfall.[46] V. Turbin contests Solzhenitsyn's view that Russia could have escaped a revolution, and his contrast between 'good' and 'bad' politics.[47] The liberal critic Aron Lur'e concedes that Solzhenitsyn's *The Red Wheel* is a monumental work, but does not regard it as a 'revelation'. He argues that Solzhenitsyn's political views are not original; for a hundred and fifty years Russian thinkers have been pitting Russia against the West and claiming that Russia has a special 'mission', a special path of development. In his view, the ideas of Sakharov, who believed in 'convergence' between the Russian and western systems, are more inspiring than Solzhenitsyn's mistrust of a multi-party system.

In 1990 Alla Latynina warned: 'Solzhenitsyn is not a political leader but an artist and thinker, and his books are not some new catechism from which quotations are to be drawn for use in assessing the political situation.' She appealed to her fellow Russians: 'Let us read Solzhenitsyn's works in this country. Unlike the West, which is tired of reading about Russian history, we will not be bored. They deal with our fate, and not just our past but our future.' Despite such exhortations, it is unlikely that many Russians, with the exception of professional critics and historians, will manage to read all the 'knots' of Solzhenitsyn's extremely long, complex epic from beginning to end. However, if there continues to be a shortage of objective studies of the Provisional Government by Russian historians, Solzhenitsyn's historical interpretations may gain popular currency, and the liberal and socialist politicians of 1917 may continue to receive a bad press in Russia.

By 1990 Solzhenitsyn himself had recognized the limitations of *The Red Wheel* if he wished to exert a direct influence on his fellow countrymen, since he broke his former self-imposed silence and issued the pamphlet *How Shall We Reorganize Russia?*,[48] in which he distilled the essence of his thinking on the February Revolution, and explained the relevance of the experience of 1917 for the contemporary USSR.[49] Solzhenitsyn argues that in searching for a new political form for the Soviet state, contemporary Soviet people need to be more careful and foresighted than 'our unfortunate grandfathers and fathers of the year 1917'. They must take pains 'not to repeat the chaos of historic February, not to turn out to be the toy of enticing slogans and enraptured orators, not to submit voluntarily, in order to be shamed once again'. Solzhenitsyn's description of the situation in 1917 reveals his distaste for political parties and chaotic democratic processes in general.

Solzhenitsyn argues that not all changes of power are necessarily beneficial, and that responsible reflection is necessary before any new and decisive step is taken. He emphasizes that the harshest critics of the tsarist government in 1916, such as the Kadet leader Milyukov, were completely unprepared for power, and that when they seized it only a few months later, 'they ruined everything'. He draws a direct comparison between these inexperienced statesmen of 1916–17 and the 'leaders who have newly come to power now'. In particular, he cites a 'victorious critic of the Base System' who as soon as he became elected to office in Moscow showed insensitivity in relation to the rest of the country, which had fed the capital, Moscow, for sixty years. (This is an allusion to Gavriil Popov, who was elected Mayor of Moscow in 1991, but resigned in 1992.[50]) Solzhenitsyn draws a parallel between the democratic ferment of the Gorbachev era and the situation in February 1917: 'Thus, in the ferment of meetings and the emergence of little parties[51] we do not notice how we have put on the farcical garb of February – those ill-fated eight months of 1917.' He criticizes those who are elated by this comparison with the February Revolution: 'But others have immediately noticed, and with ecstasy and lack of foresight exclaim: "A new February Revolution!"'

Solzhenitsyn also warns of the danger, after three-quarters of a century of centralized power, of moving too far in the other direction. He has inherited the traditional Russian belief, eloquently expressed by Dostoevskii, that moderate democracy within a framework of order is alien to the Russian people, and that for Russians the only alternative to dictatorial power is complete licence or anarchy. Solzhenitsyn warns that 'We should not hurry to rush headlong into chaos: anarchy is the first downfall, as the year 1917 taught us.'

Although some of Solzhenitsyn's criticisms of western democratic systems are valid, many people in the West would accept Churchill's famous dictum that 'Democracy is a very bad form of government, but all the others are so much worse.' The burden of Solzhenitsyn's remarks is that, although he grudgingly accepts the need for some democracy in the USSR, he is more concerned with safeguarding the stability of the Russian state and creating a new political system based on Russian traditions that would avoid the 'tyranny of the majority' and the excessive commercialism that he regards as typical of western democracies. However, in basing his model on that of Stolypin's Duma in the early twentieth century, suggesting an indirect form of elections and hedging the right to vote around with age and residence restrictions unpleasantly reminiscent of the property qualifications needed for voters in the Third Duma (after Stolypin's unconstitutional coup of 1907), Solzhenitsyn demonstrated that he was out of touch with the current situation in Russia. The events of August 1991 and its aftermath showed that Soviet people, once they had tasted western-style democracy, wished it to be extended, to encompass direct elections to the presidency and the Congress of People's Deputies and greater independence for the republics and autonomous regions. Solzhenitsyn's scheme was a restrictive, conservative programme which, though well-intentioned, did not answer the needs of the Soviet population in 1990.

The dubious conclusions drawn by Solzhenitsyn also cast doubt on his analysis of the events of February 1917.[52] It is true that the leaders of the Provisional Government were inexperienced, disunited, and perhaps tried to introduce a greater measure of freedom than their country could cope with after centuries of despotism. However, Solzhenitsyn does not place enough weight on the problems which confronted them, some of which were not of their making: the fact that they took power in the midst of a major war inherited from the tsarist regime; the opposition of the Allies to the efforts of the Provisional Government to enter into peace negotiations; and the difficulty of maintaining a moderate, liberal position in a period of war and anarchy, when they were beset by extremists from the right and the left.

Although Solzhenitsyn's interpretation of the February Revolution and his distrust of democracy lay at the basis of his political analysis, the main responses to Solzhenitsyn's scheme within the USSR were concerned not with these issues, or even with his government reforms, but with his controversial proposal for a union of the three Slav states, Russia, Belorussia and Ukraine, which managed to annoy Soviet imperialists, democrats, Great Russian chauvinists and Ukrainian nationalists alike. In September 1990 Gorbachev took time to discuss Solzhenitsyn's pamphlet in the Congress of People's Deputies.[53] While focusing mainly on Solzhenitsyn's secessionist views, Gorbachev also took issue with his attack on democracy and radical ideas in the name of prudence and stability, based on his analysis of the failure of the February Revolution and Provisional Government. Gorbachev declared: 'I feel myself to be a democrat and, moreover, one who is inclined to take radical views of the present day.... But this does not hinder me; on the contrary, it helps me to combine my views with the great responsibility and prudence that I believe I should show in the role that I am performing at your behest.'

What neither Gorbachev nor Solzhenitsyn's other critics in the Congress discussed in 1990 was the important premise behind Solzhenitsyn's pamphlet: 'The hour of Communism has struck. But concrete *perestroika* has not yet collapsed. And, instead of liberation, we may be flailing about under its ruins.' This was a prophetic utterance in 1990, when the demise of the Communist Party was still a year away;[54] the warning about 'flailing about under the ruins' has proved to be uncomfortably accurate in many parts of the ex-Soviet Union, still more so in former Yugoslavia. The reference to concrete recalls a passage in the revised (1978) version of *The First Circle*: 'Remember, in the beginning was the Word. Which means, the Word is stronger than concrete.' Concrete symbolizes the totalitarian nature of Soviet communism, which, in the author's view, can only be defeated by religious belief.[55] The image of the 'ruins' of communism recalls the collection by Solzhenitsyn and some of his colleagues, *From under the Rubble* (1974), which suggested a religious solution to the spiritual crisis facing Soviet people. As in *From under the Rubble*, in his new pamphlet too, Solzhenitsyn suggests the need to strive for 'self-limitation' rather than human rights.[56] This is not a recommendation likely to appeal to politicians, and has not been practised either by Yeltsin or his opponents in the post-communist period.

CONCLUSION

After the collapse of communism in 1991, more information about the Provisional Government continued to appear in Russia; and parallels were drawn between the Provisional Government, whose failures provoked the Kornilov revolt, and the flaws of contemporary Russian democracy, threatened by a right-wing backlash.[57] One perceptive analysis was that of Alexander Yakovlev, who claimed in 1992 that the victorious democrats did not wish to confront the reasons for the failure of the Provisional Government, since the current leaders were 'stubbornly repeating the mistakes of that February, which ended in a disaster for Russia'.[58] At the same time, Solzhenitsyn argued that his pamphlet of 1990 had still not been seriously discussed in Russia;[59] but he had another opportunity to speak directly to his countrymen in a documentary film portrait by Stanislav Govorukhin, shown on Russian television in September 1992. Solzhenitsyn argued that the Russian people had not been prepared for democracy in February 1917, and stated explicitly: 'The eight months back then and the past seven years today are very similar.' He denied charges that he is an enemy of democracy, declaring: 'What I am against is not democracy but the prospect of our all being crushed at once by the massive wreckage of communism, which is doomed to destruction.' Solzhenitsyn gave a perceptive analysis of the current political situation in Russia as 'a stage in the collapse of communism in which its upper floors have fallen in but the middle level is still alive and well and busy laying its hands on everything around it'. In particular, he lamented the continuing power of relabelled ex-communists, the KGB, and financial 'sharks', and deplored a situation in which 'the words "democrat" and "patriot" have become equally vituperative'.[60]

Ironically, by 1993 Yeltsin's more authoritarian rule had moved closer to the programme outlined in Solzhenitsyn's pamphlet of 1990, which was now being regarded more sympathetically by Russian critics.[61] Yeltsin's suppression of parliament in October 1993, which won Solzhenitsyn's support, suggested that the President had learnt the lesson that the main reason for the collapse of Russian democracy in 1917–18 was its failure to use force against its enemies;[62] and the centrist administration established in 1994 under Chernomyrdin could be interpreted as an example of Solzhenitsyn's concept of a 'responsible ministry'.

11 Tsarism Reconsidered

Before Gorbachev's accession, the official Soviet attitude to the last Tsar and the immediate pre-revolutionary period had been one of unalloyed hostility. Tsar Nicholas II and his Empress Alexandra Fyodorovna, if they were mentioned at all, were seen as parasites and oppressors, infatuated with the charlatan Rasputin, who had received their just deserts in 1917, when the people's wrath had forced the Tsar to abdicate. For most Soviet readers, the popular historical novels of Valentin Pikul' were the main source of information about the late tsarist period, particularly his novel about Rasputin, *At the End of the Line* (1979), with its nationalistic, anti-Semitic overtones, which cannot be taken seriously as history.[1] Little was known about the rapid development of Russia since the late nineteenth century, or about such statesmen of the late tsarist period as Witte and Stolypin. *Glasnost* allowed these subjects to be discussed in a more objective manner, although at times the earlier disparagement of the tsarist period has given way to a somewhat naïve enthusiasm for the culture and traditions of the pre-revolutionary era.[2] Such nostalgia for earlier times, a sentiment by no means confined to Russia, can be innocuous enough; but some Russians, disillusioned with Soviet history, have been attracted to a new and equally misleading myth about the past, ignoring the failings of the royal couple and the real political strains which led to popular discontent and the abdication of the Tsar in February 1917. Extreme Russian nationalists have deliberately fostered such nostalgia, suggesting that the 'Jewish–Masonic conspiracy' was responsible for toppling the Russian monarchy and destroying the Russian state.

In the early Gorbachev era, interest in the last Tsar was rekindled by Elem Klimov's film *Agony*, which had been finished in 1974, but not released until 1985 (under the title *Rasputin*), because its picture of Nicholas II and his family had formerly been considered too sympathetic.[3] In 1987 the text of Nicholas II's abdication statement was published by a special commission; but one of the first serious works by a historian to discuss the delicate issue of the Tsar's execution, G. Ioffe's *Great October and the Epilogue of Tsarism* (1987), still had to treat this issue with a certain degree of circumspection, and to operate on the basis of the only archives then available.[4] Ioffe attributes blame not to the Bolshevik leadership, but to the executive of the Ekaterinburg

Soviet, who allegedly blocked the attempts of Yakovlev, an emissary from Moscow acting on instructions from Sverdlov, the Secretary of the Orgburo of the Central Committee, to take Nicholas and his family to Moscow. In a review of this book published in 1988, the historian P. Cherkasov argued that the royal couple should have been tried in open court, and attacked the massacre of the Tsar's children and servants on humanitarian grounds: 'Four daughters and an incurably sick son. What was their guilt before the Russian people and the Revolution?'[5] Yet Cherkasov was by no means uncritical of Nicholas II, and deplored the attempts of White émigrés and western propagandists to turn the Tsar and his family into martyrs, forgetting many of the 'real crimes' the Tsar had committed against his people. He also claimed that there had been little interest in the news of the execution in 1918, when at the height of the Civil War 'the whole country was washed in blood'.

Once the subject of the Tsar's fate had been reopened, journals vied with each other in treating this sensational subject.[6] In 1988 it became known that since the 1970s the playwright Eduard Radzinskii had been investigating the archives and trying to find eye-witnesses to the Tsar's execution. In 1989 the press published a sensational report alleging that the Romanov burial site had been found,[7] and, pending the investigation of the bones by British scientists, even wilder rumours began to gain currency, such as the theory that Alexandra and her daughters had escaped execution and gone to live secretly in a European country. Although in 1993 DNA tests proved conclusively that the Tsar and Tsaritsa had died at Ekaterinburg, they still failed to solve the historical mystery of whether the Grand Duchess Anastasia (and her brother Aleksei) had been executed along with the Tsar's other children.

One startling revelation appeared in Radzinskii's book on the Tsar, which gained wide publicity in the press.[8] The reappraisal of Lenin had made it possible for Radzinskii to overturn a myth which had persisted in the USSR for seventy-two years: the assumption that Lenin and the government in Moscow had known only about the shooting of the Tsar and his family after the event. Radzinskii had discovered a telegram sent to Sverdlov and Lenin from Ekaterinburg on 16 July 1918: 'Inform Moscow that, due to military circumstances, the trial agreed upon with Filippov brooks no delay; we cannot wait. If you are opposed, inform us right away. Goloshchekin, Safarov. Contact Ekaterinburg yourselves regarding this matter.'[9] Evidently, the members of the Ekaterinburg Soviet were panicking; there was no time to hold a trial, because the town was about to fall to the Whites. Testimony from A. Akimov, one of Lenin's guards, confirmed that a telegram approving the execution of the Tsar and his family signed by Sverdlov and Lenin was sent to Ekaterinburg on the evening of 16 July. On the night of 16–17 July 1918, eleven people were shot to death without trial in the basement of the Ipat'ev House.

Apart from the debate which surfaced in the press, the huge interest which the Tsar's fate held for the Russian public is evident from Radzinskii's revelation that during the four years that he had been working on his book on the Tsar, he had received 'thousands of letters with testimony, accounts and documents', and became 'the commissioner of a unique people's investigation'. By 1990 the subject of the Tsar's murder had become so popular that a film entitled *Assassin of the Tsar* was planned, with the participation of foreign actors, based on a script by Alexander Borodyanskii. Clearly, the tragic pages of twentieth-century history were now seen as sensational subjects which could be exploited for commercial gain. Tsarist memorabilia became very popular in Russia; and although this can, to some extent, be dismissed as a fashion among young people designed to shock their elders, like the simultaneous fashion for swastikas and Nazi relics, such nostalgia also led to more serious political consequences which once would have seemed unthinkable: the formation in May 1990 of a monarchist party which wished to see the return of the Romanov family to its position of supreme power.[10] At one time there were eleven deputies of the Orthodox Constitutional Monarchy Party of Russia in the Congress of People's Deputies. A faction of reactionary Leningrad writers wished to see Grand Duke Vladimir Kirillovich, the heir of the Romanovs, on the Russian throne;[11] in 1991 he paid a visit to St Petersburg, amid considerable publicity, and when he died shortly afterwards was buried in the Peter and Paul Fortress Church with full Orthodox honours. Boris Yeltsin also suffered some adverse publicity when it was revealed that in 1977, as head of the local Communist Party in Ekaterinburg (formerly Sverdlovsk), he had been responsible for ordering the demolition of the Ipat'ev House, which might otherwise have become a place of pilgrimage. As late as 1993, an exhibition about the last Tsar and his family held in the Manège Gallery in Moscow still proved to be a revelation to many Russian people.[12]

Some literary works published in the 1990s have also treated the subject of the last Tsar, debunking the old Soviet myths, but sometimes creating in their place new myths about the late tsarist period. Vladimir Maksimov, for example, in his novel *Looking into the Abyss* (1990) depicts a visit to the Ipat'ev House by Admiral Kolchak in 1919.[13] Kolchak is distressed by the cramped cellar, feeling: 'It was real carnage', and 'They could at least have spared the women and children, for God's sake.' Maksimov suggests that Kolchak met N. Sokolov, the independent procurator who later investigated the Tsar's murder. Kolchak remembers his one meeting with the Tsar, which occurred in July 1916 in Mogilev, when the Admiral was conscious of Nicholas's weakness of will, indifference to everything around him and the sense of doom which enveloped him.

Maksimov's Russian patriotism is reflected in his evocation of Kolchak's distress at seeing the remains of the three-hundred-year history of the Romanov dynasty: 'ash, collapse, a handful of bones'. Kolchak feels that the monarchy should have had sufficient foresight to survive the Revolution and save the dynasty, 'to oppose the mortal concatenation of circumstances with all the wisdom and profundity of its divine knowledge'. He suggests that it was only because of such a single-minded desire to preserve the dynasty that Ivan the Terrible had permitted himself to kill his own son and 'infringe all divine and human laws', then to repent his sins. The author's own stance here is unclear: does Maksimov condone the behaviour of Ivan the Terrible on the grounds that he preserved the dynasty and the integrity of the Russian state, or is he merely conveying what he thinks a man of monarchist sympathies would have felt in 1919? If it is the author himself speaking (in view of the fact that the names of Ivan IV and Stalin were frequently linked) this appears a somewhat curious argument. However, Maksimov is correct in suggesting that the last Tsar was lacking in the single-minded sense of his autocratic power which characterized Ivan IV.

Maksimov's Kolchak analyses the virtues and weaknesses of Nicholas II, ackowledging that instead of strength of character, nature endowed Nicholas with many other virtues: 'simplicity, delicacy, rare generosity, but the first frequently turned out worse than robbery for those around him, the second inspired rogues, and the third was used by everyone who was not too lazy – from embezzlers to terrorists'. Maksimov implies that for Nicholas 'the state was his own family'; 'Everything outside this enclosed world seemed loud and a tedious fuss, with which he was doomed to have contact by his descent and the duty which followed from this parentage.' Because of this character flaw, the Tsar was found wanting when the Revolution broke out: 'At the fateful hour when strength of will was required of him to take upon himself the ultimate responsibility for the fate of the dynasty and the state, he preferred to run in a cowardly way into that little world, leaving the country to wholesale pillage by unbridled devilry. And then the inglorious abdication, vegetation in Tobolsk, and his swift, absurd death.' Here the views of author and character appear to co-incide: the reference to the Revolution as 'devils' work' recalls the frequent allusions to Dostoevskii in Maksimov's work. As a Russian patriot, Maksimov seems to be blaming the Tsar for betraying his country and the Romanov dynasty. This view corresponds to that of some western historians who interpret the Tsar's abdication as a form of 'suicide', emphasizing the indecent haste with which he allowed himself to be stampeded into giving up his throne.[14]

Maksimov's Kolchak regards the men responsible for the Tsar's trial and execution – Beloborodov, Goloshchekin, Yurovskii and Medvedev – as 'devils who have arisen from the darkness'. The author gloats at the fact that these men, after shedding much more innocent blood, were themselves dragged through 'all nine circles of the hell of tor-ture' in Stalin's Russia, with no one to pray to. He relates that when Beloborodov was being dragged to his execution, he hoped that his past service to the party might save him. He shouted: 'I am Beloborodov, tell the Central Committee I'm being tortured!', but Maksimov com-ments sarcastically: 'But the Central Committee is not the Lord God, shout as much as you like, it won't help!' Although Maksimov's hatred of the Tsar's murderers is understandable, his attitude is redolent of the excessive desire for vengeance which is too prevalent in contem-porary Russian society.

In 1990, when Maksimov's novel referred to the independent inves-tigator Sokolov (1882–1924), Sokolov's own book *The Murder of the Tsar's Family* was published in the USSR for the first time.[15] Sokolov's investigation corroborated Radzinskii's account, revealing that the as-sassination was planned by the top Bolshevik leaders, chiefly Sverdlov, who, according to the critic O. Platonov, 'by that time was a highly experienced organizer of many such murders and bloody mass crimes'.[16] (It is interesting that Platonov, writing in a nationalist newspaper which shared some values with hard-line Communists, did not offend his readers' sensibilities by referring directly to Lenin.) Platonov's review presents a very revealing nationalist interpretation of the Tsar's fate:

The murder of the Tsar's family was the most terrible and sinister crime of the twentieth century.... For Russians, the Tsar and his immediate family were not simply people but the highest expression of Russia's statehood, the expression of the exalted idea of Holy Rus'.... Russians view the villainous murder of the Tsar's family as the deliberate destruction of principles that were and always will be sacred, that are stored forever in the people's consciousness and psychology, perhaps are encoded in their genes.

A similar view was expressed in 1993 by the Russian Orthodox Patriarch Aleksii, who, at a memorial service for the Romanovs in Ekaterinburg, spoke of the Tsar's execution as a sin weighing heavily on the Russian soul.

It is such views, newly emerging with great force in the 1990s after seventy years of suppression, that help to explain certain objections to the critical picture of Tsar Nicholas II painted in Solzhenitsyn's *The Red Wheel*, which began to be published in Russia in 1990. This portrait, which presents Nicholas as a happy family man but an incompetent ruler, has been interpreted by some western critics as one of the most successful among the gallery of historical personages depicted in Solzhenitsyn's epic, but has engendered relatively little public debate within Russia. However, Solzhenitsyn's portrayal clearly aroused some private controversy, since the critic Pyotr Palamarchuk maintained that 'The "tsarist" chapters . . . aroused distress and disagreement in many readers.'[17] As Alla Latynina shrewdly pointed out, Solzhenitsyn's critical approach to the Russian past was likely to be unacceptable both to Communists and 'national Bolsheviks'. She cited Solzhenitsyn's own ironic characterization of the views of Chalmaev and other nationalists writing in *Molodaya gvardiya* in the years 1966–70: 'The Russian people is the noblest in the world in its qualities; neither its ancient nor its modern history has ever suffered any stains, and it is impermissible to reproach either tsarism or Bolshevism for anything; there have been no national mistakes or sins, either before 1917 or since.'[18] *The Red Wheel* was bound to antagonize Russians of many different political views, as it did not disguise what Solzhenitsyn considered to be the 'mistakes or sins' of many historical personages, including Tsar Nicholas II, whom by 1990 many Russians revered as a tragic martyr.

The nationalist critic Palamarchuk, who generally has sympathy for Solzhenitsyn's views and allows the author to speak for himself, finds the 'tsarist chapters' one of the most unacceptable parts of *The Red Wheel*.[19] He reproaches Solzhenitsyn for applying to Nicholas II his usual method of depicting characters 'from within', without making any exception 'even for the personage who has from time immemorial been honoured by the people's consciousness as an incarnation of the soul and will of the nation'. In Palamarchuk's view, the weakness of will and mental aberrations of the man who personified the supreme power of the Russian state are a matter for distress rather than for condemnation. Eventually there is nothing left for the Tsar but his 'sacrificial death', which, in the critic's opinion, he chose consciously, since he did not allow himself or his family to abandon his native land. (Unlike Maksimov, the critic omits to mention the Tsar's ill-fated attempt to secure an invitation from his cousin King George V to visit England.) Palamarchuk feels that 'From whatever point of view you look at the tragedy of the Tsar's family, this event still remains a tragedy, and far from a matter of indifference to his compatriots.' Palamarchuk seems to find it unacceptable that Solzhenitsyn should depict the last Tsar with irony, criticize him in any way or treat him with anything other than the total religious devotion that was expected of the Russian people in tsarist times. However, not all Russians felt like this: the democratic critic Vladimir Potapov agreed that Nicholas II was weak, and contested Palamarchuk's view that Solzhenitsyn's portrait of the Tsar was 'not sufficiently respectful'.[20] Nevertheless, Palamarchuk's old-fashioned nationalism certainly represented an important trend of thought in 1990, demonstrating the complete transformation which had occurred in public debate since 1987: it was now perfectly acceptable to treat the previously sacrosanct Lenin with scorn, and at the same time to demand that the previously reviled Tsar should be depicted with respect.

Palamarchuk also takes issue with certain specific aspects of Solzhenitsyn's portrait: he claims, for example, that the last Russian Tsar was an extremely cultured, well-educated man, as even his enemy Witte was prepared to admit. The critic is on less firm ground when he objects to Solzhenitsyn's use of extracts from the Tsar's diary to reveal that even at the most critical moments for the state, Nicholas was preoccupied with petty family matters. Palamarchuk defends Nicholas by saying: 'Nicholas II, who was so scrupulous about his duty, would never have allowed himself to entrust to paper important questions, and even less, the secrets of his rule.' This objection is unconvincing, since historians have also pointed out how out of touch Nicholas was with political events, even during the critical days leading up to the February Revolution, using not only the evidence of his diaries, but also public documents such as his telegrams to Rodzianko, the chairman of the Duma.[21] Palamarchuk finds it 'even more bitter' to read the critical chapters on the Empress in *October 1916*, reminding his readers that she sacrificed herself and her five children to 'the altar of her second homeland'. This is true, but tragic death does not absolve anyone of all responsibility for earlier mistakes and crimes (as Russian nationalists would be the first to admit in the case of Old Bolsheviks such as Zinoviev and Kamenev).

Palamarchuk is better pleased with the chapters in *March 1917* dealing with the Tsar's abdication, suggesting that the very 'material of the narrative' inevitably turns Solzhenitsyn's approach into a more sympathetic one. Solzhenitsyn implies that the abdication is wrung out of the Tsar by the Octobrists Guchkov and Shul'gin who visit him from Petrograd, with the help of another 'conspirator', the commander of the western front General Ruzskii. After a long inner struggle the Tsar does not sign their prepared text, but his own abdication statement, whereupon Guchkov patronizingly advises him to pray. (Alexander Guchkov, the Octobrist leader, is the target of Solzhenitsyn's particular scorn, because he was responsible for a treacherous, though abortive palace coup against the Tsar in 1916.) In his depiction of the events surrounding the abdication, Solzhenitsyn contrasts the malign glee of Guchkov and his fellow conspirators celebrating their Pyrrhic victory, with the calm dignity of the Tsar. Guchkov exclaims: 'What a wooden man, gentlemen! Such an act! Such a step! But did you see any serious emotion in him? I don't think he was even conscious of what he was doing. He has fatally skated over the surface all his life. That's the reason for all our misfortunes.' Solzhenitsyn contradicts Guchkov's superficial judgement by describing the solitary ex-monarch on his knees before an icon of Christ the Saviour, reflecting that he had been prepared to accept any sacrifice, so as not to bring division to his country: 'As long as Russia is saved.' Solzhenitsyn's Nicholas regards Guchkov as a 'vile man' who wanted to humiliate the Tsar, an apostate Old Believer who had no right to tell the Tsar to pray when he had forgotten how to pray himself. It is at this moment that Solzhenitsyn's Nicholas writes in his diary 'All around there is treachery and cowardice and deceit.'[22] The critic Palamarchuk regards this note as particularly significant, because he sees the Tsar's diary as one in which 'the Tsar has for long years been used to joke'. Evidently, contemporary Russian nationalists such as Palamarchuk could accept Solzhenitsyn's analysis of the Tsar's patriotic motives for abdication, but not his earlier criticisms of the Tsar's behaviour which had led to this crisis.

Democratic critics were more interested in countering charges that Solzhenitsyn was a monarchist, and enlisting him on their side in the contemporary political debate. The liberal critic Andrei Nemzer, for example, admits that Solzhenitsyn's attitude to the Tsar has aroused some controversy, referring to 'observations about Solzhenitsyn's monarchism, which have resounded in various different ways: either as a reproach, or as a statement of fact, or as a half-reproach (he's a monarchist, but he depicted the last emperor without due respect), or as praise'.[23] Nemzer takes issue with all these views, arguing convincingly that Solzhenitsyn himself is not a monarchist, since his publicistic writings have frequently shown him to be hostile to all parties, with their narrow ideologies; his aim in *The Red Wheel* is to analyse monarchism as 'just another ideology'. Nemzer, as a democrat, emphasizes that in his pamphlet *How Shall We Reorganize Russia?* Solzhenitsyn said: 'Out of all the contemporary stream we will undoubtedly choose democracy', and that his objections to democracy were more concerned with warnings about the unsatisfactory forms that democracy can take, and about the danger of elevating it into a supreme value, rather than with the essence of democracy itself.

Nemzer presents a more objective interpretation of Solzhenitsyn's portrait of Nicholas II than Palamarchuk, acknowledging that the Tsar, like Lenin and many other characters in *The Red Wheel*, has been 'seen and depicted in a new way'. He regards Solzhenitsyn's portrayal of the Tsar as harsh, but just, emphasizing that, contrary to the slanders on the royal family in Pikul''s 'cheap novel' (republished in 1992 under the title *Evil Force* with its former cuts restored[24]), the Tsar was a sincere believer and a model family man, a patriot, and a kind, tactful, decent human being, perhaps the most attractive private personality depicted in *March 1917*. However, Nemzer agrees with Solzhenitsyn's view that Nicholas's mistakes stem not only from his weakness of will, but are also the reverse side of his virtues. The Tsar's weakness springs partly from his mistaken identification of passivity with Christian humility; partly from his concern for Russia, which, Nicholas sometimes imagines, will be better off without him; from his wish to behave in a dignified manner; and from his nobility of spirit and faith in people, whom, even if they are his personal enemies, he cannot believe to be enemies of Russia. Solzhenitsyn's fair treatment of the Tsar is also evident from his eagerness to undermine the slander spread by many of the Tsar's enemies at the time (and, as Nemzer points out, by the Communist Party up to 1990), that the Tsar and Empress were pro-German and attempting to make a separate peace. In Nemzer's words, 'Unfortunately for himself and for Russia, Nicholas II wanted to fight to a victorious conclusion.' Yet Solzhenitsyn was also intent on pointing out the sad truth of the proverb 'If the people sins, the Tsar will pardon; if the Tsar sins, the people will not pardon.' By a tragic irony, the man who has put his family above his kingdom learns a minute before his death that his family will perish with him.

Nemzer adopts a tactful approach to the Russian people's sensibilities about the figure of the Tsar. He states: 'I think that it was very difficult for Solzhenitsyn to write the "tsarist chapters", and I understand the feelings of those who enter into an argument with the writer, contrary to both artistic and historical logic.' He feels that the problem of the 'sacredness' of the monarchy, on which the question of the Tsar's responsibility turns, is not one which can be resolved in the press. Yet Nemzer quite rightly points out that Solzhenitsyn does not interpret Nicholas II's abdication as a fateful accident (unlike the assassination of Alexander II), but an event which resulted from a long chain of interrelated incidents. The author does not by any means lay all the responsibility for the Tsar's fall on Nicholas himself; all the political forces of tsarist Russia bear some responsibility for the catastrophe, and their sins reflected the sins of the monarch and his age.

STOLYPIN

Glasnost allowed Russian historians and publicists to admit that considerable economic progress had taken place in the last fifty years before the Revolution, and to raise the question of whether Russia could have experienced an alternative path of development if some of the valuable pre-revolutionary initiatives had been allowed to continue. One of the most important points in this debate was the rediscovery of a major historical figure, Pyotr Stolypin (1862–1911), Prime Minister from 1906 to 1911, who had sought to break up the peasant commune and to prevent revolution by creating a class of efficient, independent peasant proprietors. Hitherto, the image of Stolypin propagated in official Soviet historiography had been that of a reactionary, the ruthless suppressor of the 1905 Revolution and instigator of an unconstitutional coup against the Duma on 3 June 1907. His agrarian reforms had been deemed 'progressive' in an economic sense, but too little, too late; and Stolypin had been seen as motivated entirely by the interests of the gentry class. The name of Stolypin had been familiar to the Soviet public only through such abusive expressions as 'Stolypin neckties' (*stolypinskie galstuki*), which alluded to the gallows used to execute terrorists, and 'Stolypin cars' (*stolypinskie vagony*), railway cars specially designed to transport peasants' households, including their cattle, to the new settlements in Siberia, and later extensively used for the transportation of prisoners under Lenin and Stalin. Thus in the popular mind the name of Stolypin had been synonymous with the brutal oppression of revolutionaries and peasant settlers.

The revision of attitudes to Stolypin was initiated in 1988 by the economist Vasilii Selyunin, who, in his widely-read article 'Sources', praised Stolypin as an 'outstanding statesman', and deplored the effect of the revolution, which had largely destroyed Stolypin's agrarian reforms and returned most of the land to 'communal' control.[25] Selyunin traced an explicit link between economic freedom and human freedom in general; his references to Stolypin and NEP are designed to suggest that an alternative, capitalist system might have developed in Russia. The contemporary significance of this theme was obvious: Selyunin was using historical examples to advocate the establishment of a market system in Russia, and the replacement of state ownership of the means of production which had created 'the temptation to expropriate the individual personality, its physical and mental powers, to organize work in accordance with a single plan'. Selyunin was not the only scholar to re-examine Stolypin's legacy in the light of *glasnost*: the agrarian historian Danilov said in 1988 that 'professional historians have discovered with astonishment that the notion has suddenly become widespread that there was a "Stolypin alternative" in the history of Russia, and that this would have spared it from revolutionary upheavals and sacrifices'.[26] Unfortunately, it was not only professional historians who rediscovered Stolypin; he also began to be adopted as a hero by the extremists of *Pamyat'*.

It was in this climate that Solzhenitsyn's definitive two-volume version of *August 1914*, with its extremely positive view of Stolypin, was published in Russia in 1990. Indeed, this work may have been partly responsible for stimulating the public debate about Stolypin from 1988, as many intellectuals would have been familiar with Solzhenitsyn's readings on Radio Liberty. Solzhenitsyn elevates Stolypin to a near-mythical status as one of the greatest Russian statesmen of all time, a pillar (*stolp*) of the state, and a new Peter the Great, whose policies, had he not met an untimely death at the hand of a terrorist in 1911, were the only ones capable of saving Russia from revolution. Since Solzhenitsyn's portrait of Stolypin has already received detailed consideration in the West,[27] the pages that follow will be confined to some of the discussions which have accompanied its reception in Russia.

The émigré critics Vail and Genis, in an article published in Russia in 1990, highlighted the hagiographic nature of Solzhenitsyn's portrait of Stolypin, which, like the depiction of the saintly Matryona in his story *Matryona's House*, they attributed to the author's search for a positive hero.[28] Yet, hagiographic or not, some Russian critics are in total agreement with Solzhenitsyn's image of Stolypin, enlisting Solzhenitsyn as an ally in their defence of the principle of free ownership, and economists' proposals to give the land back to the peasants.

Alla Latynina cites Solzhenitsyn's opinion that 'the basic concepts of private property and private economic initiative are innate in man and necessary for his personal liberty', and relates it to his close interest in Stolypin.[29] Latynina states: 'According to Solzhenitsyn, the peasants viewed Stolypin as their liberator from burdensome dependence on the peasant commune. In Solzhenitsyn's eyes, Stolypin was an intelligent reformer who acted purposefully to create an economically independent middle class – the bulwark of stability – to give all energetic and enterprising people room for action, and to create strong local government, the guarantee of the country's economic stability.' The implication is that a strong middle class and a property-owning democracy would also be of great benefit to contemporary Russia.

The most controversial aspect of Solzhenitsyn's portrait of Stolypin, both when it was originally published in the West, and when it eventually appeared in the USSR, was the allegation of anti-Semitism against Solzhenitsyn because of his hostile depiction of Bogrov, Stolypin's Jewish assassin.[30] Latynina, in an attempt to defend Solzhenitsyn from xenophobic nationalists who were trying to claim him, expresses the suspicion that, although 'articles charging Solzhenitsyn with betraying his homeland and labelling him an "anti-patriot", "Zionist" and "Vlasovite" are a thing of the past . . . the time is coming for articles of a different sort, accusing the present Solzhenitsyn of being a nationalist and anti-Semite'. Latynina attacks a recent interview on Radio Liberty with the critic Benedikt Sarnov, who said: 'When Bogrov assassinates Stolypin, he acts not as an agent of the secret police or a psychopath, but as a Jew stirred up by Jewish feelings.' Sarnov related this attitude to people in Russia who 'are looking for an enemy and finding him in the Jew'. Latynina goes over some of the ground covered by western critics who attempt to refute this allegation, pointing to the sympathetic portrait of the Jew Arkhangorodskii in the same novel,[31] and emphasizing Solzhenitsyn's own statement that 'a genuine writer cannot be an anti-Semite'.[32]

Latynina's arguments were not weighty enough, however, to prevent more conservative critics from devoting particular attention to the Jewish theme in *August 1914*. Palamarchuk stresses the factual accuracy of the fascinating chronicle of Stolypin's assassination, 'expounded by the writer from authentic documents for the first time', and suggests that Bogrov's activity as a double agent working both for the SRs and the Okhrana, disclosed in his interrogation, was so repellent that the author himself was moved to comment: 'Dostoevskii explored many spiritual abysses, unravelled many fantasies – but not all.'[33] Solzhenitsyn's research had led him to the conclusion that Bogrov was not a representative of any wider conspiracy, but was operating alone, motivated by the view that 'Stolypin did nothing directly against the Jews, and even introduced certain improvements, but it did not come from the heart. To decide whether or not a man is an enemy of the Jews, you must look beneath the surface.'

Bogrov feels that Stolypin 'too insistently, blatantly and challengingly promoted Russian national interests, Russian representation in the Duma, the Russianness of the state. He was trying to build not a country in which all would be free, but a nationalist monarchy. Thus the future of the Jews in Russia was not affected by his goodwill towards them. The development of the country along Stolypin's lines did not promise the Jews that they would flourish.'[34] Palamarchuk points out that this was the consideration that motivated Bogrov to murder Stolypin; and that Solzhenitsyn is simply reporting a historical fact when he relates Bogrov's confession to a rabbi before his execution: '"Tell the Jews that I did not wish to harm them. On the contrary, I was fighting for the good and happiness of the Jewish people." And that was the one and only part of his testimony to remain unchanged.'[35]

Palamarchuk can be assumed to agree with Solzhenitsyn's analysis of the dire consequences of Stolypin's assassination, since he simply repeats without any attempt at refutation the author's view that: 'Only two years had passed since Stolypin's death, but almost everything that appeared in print in Russia mocked his memory and ridiculed his absurd scheme for building a great Russian nation.'[36] Although Palamarchuk appears to accept Solzhenitsyn's opinion that only Stolypin could have saved the monarchy, other liberal critics have disputed this view. In a lecture in March 1991 Aron Lur'e claimed that this argument was impossible to prove: Stolypin was unable to achieve much because he was removed from power too soon, then murdered.[37] Similarly, V. Dyakin argued: 'Stolypin's reforms were the maximum of what only a part, and a minor part of the ruling authorities at that were prepared to give in order to save the regime.'[38] Lur'e also pointed out a certain inconsistency in Solzhenitsyn's position: on the one hand, Solzhenitsyn implies that he would have liked Stolypin to save the monarchy; on the other hand, he himself often attacks the monarchy (and his Stolypin finds it a tiresome hindrance to his plans). This contradictory attitude to the monarchy was also remarked upon by the more conservative critic Palamarchuk, who claimed that Solzhenitsyn allowed his 'sincere sympathy for Stolypin's case' to distort his presentation of Nicholas's relations with Stolypin.[39] Interestingly enough, this criticism of Palamarchuk's may possess some validity and not be simply a consequence of his excessive respect for the Tsar, since it has been corroborated by Stolypin's son. Arkadii Stolypin, while generally praising Solzhenitsyn for conveying 'the very depth of my father's personality', finds Solzhenitsyn's characterization of the relationship between the Tsar and Prime Minister somewhat inaccurate, in that the Tsar is presented as less friendly to Stolypin than he was in reality.[40]

By the 1990s anti-Jewish feelings were rife in Russia, and political meetings were held which openly combined support for the Tsar with anti-Zionism; at one such meeting the prominent Russian nationalist writers Rasputin and Soloukhin were present.[41] Another 'village prose' writer, Viktor Astaf'ev, was already on record as having accused 'the Jews' of murdering the Tsar.[42] By 1991 supporters of *Pamyat'* were openly selling on the streets of Leningrad copies of the nineteenth-century forgery *The Protocols of the Elders of Zion*, which proclaimed a world-wide Jewish conspiracy, and pamphlets claiming that the Jews had been responsible for the Revolution and the execution of the Tsar. Solzhenitsyn's *August 1914* was grist to the mill of such right-wing extremists; some Russians indeed confirmed Richard Pipes' opinion, which in 1985 had appeared unduly alarmist, that 'To a Russian audience it's very clear in the way he [Solzhenitsyn] dwells on Bogrov's Jewishness that he is blaming the revolution on the Jews.'[43] Although the émigré poet and critic Lev Loseff is correct to argue that Solzhenitsyn cannot be charged with anti-Semitism simply because some readers, due to their careless and selective reading, might feel encouraged in their anti-Jewish bigotry,[44] it is nevertheless unfortunate that some aspects of Solzhenitsyn's work do lend themselves to such an interpretation. Even if Solzhenitsyn has consciously attempted to avoid anti-Semitism in his work, his intense hatred of Communism, his traditional Russian Orthodox beliefs and his desire for the rebirth of the Slav lands have led him, perhaps subconsciously, to introduce certain elements typical of an anti-Semitic caricature into his depiction of Bogrov.[45] In particular, Solzhenitsyn's depiction of Bogrov as a 'snake', which evokes the figure of Satan in the Garden of Eden, and his emphasis on Bogrov's specifically Jewish motives for killing Stolypin, provide Jewish readers with legitimate cause for concern in a society where anti-Semitism and chauvinism have become widespread and virulent.[46] This issue was addressed by the liberal critic Vladimir Potapov, who emphasized the realistic nature of Solzhenitsyn's analysis of Bogrov's Jewish feelings, especially in view of the murder of Jewish Duma deputies – a sentiment which has been attested to in a contemporary memoir about Bogrov by the prominent SR E. Lazarev.[47] Potapov does, however, wonder if it was necessary to emphasize this point in contemporary Russia, at a time of rampant anti-Semitism and mass Jewish emigration from Russia.[48] He attempts to defuse the issue by suggesting that Solzhenitsyn places more emphasis on terrorism than Zionism in the actions of Bogrov and the revolutionary movement as a whole. Nevertheless, he also correctly points out that Solzhenitsyn ignores certain less palatable aspects of Stolypin's activity, such as his donations to the anti-Semitic Union of the Russian People and his encouragement of double agents, such as the SR Petrov.[49]

The most detailed and interesting attempt to contest the view of Stolypin promoted in Russia by the works of Solzhenitsyn and other more extreme Russian nationalists was an article of 1990 by the historian P. Zyryanov.[50] This article, published in the serious history journal *Questions of History*, demonstrates that by 1990–1 historians were beginning to emerge from their long silence and to provide a deeper analysis of topical historical subjects which had already been discussed by writers and publicists. Zyryanov's article also highlights some of the advantages enjoyed by historians over writers when tackling historical controversies. In the first place, they can – indeed, must – refer to their sources; and secondly, they are able to suggest alternative historical possibilities. Unlike Solzhenitsyn, Zyryanov has the freedom to allude to different possible interpretations of Bogrov's activities, and to discuss whether high officials or the Kiev Okhrana might have been implicated in Stolypin's murder. Works by historians also have an advantage over historical novels, even those of Solzhenitsyn which are based on research, in that they are able to analyse historical events in depth. Instead of the somewhat one-dimensional, uncritical approach to Stolypin's reforms adopted in Solzhenitsyn's *August 1914*, Zyryanov is able to explore the aims, achievements and limitations of Stolypin's agricultural and local government reforms from many points of view.

Zyryanov provides an objective analysis of Stolypin's life and work which differs considerably from that presented in Solzhenitsyn's novel. He warns against the dangers of 'hero-worship', stressing Stolypin's anti-Semitic contacts, his brutal methods of keeping order, and his anti-democratic tendencies. In particular, he emphasizes Stolypin's links with the fascist Black Hundreds, showing that when he was Governor of Saratov he enlisted their support to suppress the peasantry and the revolutionary movement. Zyryanov also highlights another well-known aspect of Stolypin's career: the introduction after the 1905 revolution of harsh courts-martial which completed legal proceedings within forty-eight hours and carried out sentences within twenty-four hours. Russia had never known such a cruel punitive law: from August 1906 to April 1907, 1102 death penalties were carried out, sometimes on innocent people, until the emergency powers, which would not have been ratified by the Second Duma, were naturally abrogated on 20 April 1907.

Solzhenitsyn hardly mentions this aspect of Stolypin's activity at all – although, by implication, his harsh attack on revolutionary terrorists and his depiction of Bogrov's execution assume that severe reprisals against them were justified. After examining all aspects of Stolypin's career, Zyryanov comes to the conclusion: 'All in all, Stolypin was an important statesman, but hardly a particularly outstanding one.' The historian's analysis suggests that, while Stolypin played an important role in the tsarist period, his legacy and achievements were more complex and problematic than Solzhenitsyn implies. It would seem that the Russians are mistaken if they surround Stolypin with a 'cult of personality' based on a limited understanding of his historical role. However, history has shown that the Russian nationalist aspect of Stolypin's activity may ultimately prove to be more influential than his political conservatism, since it continues to exert an appeal for contemporary Russians. Solzhenitsyn's *August 1914* has made a significant contribution to the contemporary idealization of Stolypin: as in his portraits of Stalin and Lenin, Solzhenitsyn proves himself to be a limited and biased historian, but a great creator of historical myths. Solzhenitsyn's fictional portrait of Stolypin may well prove to be more influential than any dispassionate historical assessment.

Ironically, by 1990 some points made in the journal *Molodaya gvardiya*, which gave the strongest support to the Communist Party, actually reflected the historical truth. A letter by a reader, V. Khorin, suggested that the great interest in pre-revolutionary Russian history had perhaps swung too far to the opposite extreme, leading people to interpret the reigns of the last two reactionary tsars in too positive a light.[51] He maintained that the idea of the League of Nations was now attributed to Alexander III, while everything good in contemporary agriculture was ascribed to Stolypin. Khorin commented: 'It turns out that there were no "Stolypin neckties", no "Stolypin cars" for the doomed'. Stolypin had received immoderate praise at the first Congress of People's Deputies, but Khorin wants to know why, if Stolypin was so irreproachable, he was removed from power. The writer, like many Russians by 1990, no longer seeks his answer in literary works, but hopes to find enlightenment in the historical journal *Questions of History*, although he doubts the validity of recent publications (perhaps he has Zyryanov's article in mind). This remark suggests that Russians with preconceived ideas find it difficult to accept dispassionate works by historians if they suspect them of holding political views of which they disapprove.

Although, as we have seen, the treatment of the pre-revolutionary period in recently published fiction sometimes comes close to political nostalgia, the ensuing debate about Stolypin and Tsar Nicholas II by historians such as Zyryanov has fulfilled the useful function of making the fall of tsarism more comprehensible to the Russian public. The works of Solzhenitsyn and other writers and historians have demonstrated that, if it had not been for the obstinacy and incompetence of Nicholas II and the strains caused by the First World War, Lenin and the Bolsheviks might not have been able to come to power in the first place.

12 The Rise and Fall of Literature and History in the 1990s

By the 1990s a genuine pluralism[1] had emerged in contemporary Russian historical fiction: writers were able to discuss such contentious issues as tsarism, the revolutions of 1917, Lenin and Stalin from different points of view. Yet it was precisely at this time, when the literary press and broadcast media had won the right to speak more freely, and historians to give a more accurate picture of the past, that interest in both history and literature appeared to decline sharply in Russia.

After the euphoria of the early years of *glasnost*,[2] by 1990–1 writers and critics began to imply that *glasnost* had not helped Soviet literature, but, paradoxically, had helped to destroy it.[3] The 'death of Soviet culture' was announced by writers of different political persuasions,[4] and critics engaged in heated debates about whether literature mattered any more.[5] Equally ironically, the historian R. W. Davies, who had chronicled the tremendous interest expressed by tens of millions of Soviet citizens in their country's past during the 1980s,[6] was obliged to admit that 'by the end of 1989 the intense interest in history had begun to fade'.[7]

LOSS OF MORAL AUTHORITY

One important reason for this development was that the increased information about the past made available to the Soviet public led to a growing disillusionment with both writers and historians. *Glasnost* brought to the forefront of cultural debate the question of the moral responsibility of writers, scholars and the intelligentsia in general for the past and present state of Russian literature and society.

By the 1990s, the Russian literary and historical establishment was perceived as having lost all claims to moral authority.[8] Writers were accused of having set themselves up as teachers and prophets advocating social utopias, while collaborating, actively or passively, with the

Soviet regime for over seventy years; and hence were deemed to bear a responsibility for the Revolution, the Gulag, and other crimes of twentieth-century Russia.[9] Similarly, as the dichotomy between the truth of Soviet history and the works of historians became increasingly evident, the public became aware of how historians and history teachers had conformed to the party and lied to them in the past.

In this debate the traditional Russian question 'Who is to blame?' came to take precedence over the more constructive 'What is to be done?',[10] and the theme of repentance was increasingly interpreted in a highly personal way. Individuals who held prominent positions in the Union of Writers were accused of persecuting fellow writers in the past;[11] some writers publicly repented of their own past blindness or misdeeds,[12] whereas conservative literary officials like Bondarev still tried to defend themselves. At the same time, radical historians such as Yurii Afanas'ev informed the public about the purges of historians carried out in the 1970s by Trapeznikov, with the full support of the party leaders Brezhnev and Suslov.[13]

The desire to single out scapegoats for the crimes and persecutions of the past is very understandable in a country which has never experienced the equivalent of the Nuremberg trials,[14] but in some respects the new freedom to criticize fellow writers and scholars has led to unsavoury consequences.[15] Liberals of the 1960s (the so-called *shestidesyatniki*) have been forced to defend themselves against more radical younger critics;[16] Jewish writers have been showered with anti-Semitic abuse,[17] and all the writers who published their works in the Brezhnev era have been disparaged by members of the former 'underground'.[18] Just as the acrimony of the televized Congress debates in 1989–90 rapidly disillusioned many Soviet viewers unaccustomed to parliamentary democracy, the increasing bitterness in debates on historical and literary questions and the 'bacchanalia of mutual recriminations' indulged in by rival camps of writers[19] may be one reason for the public's loss of interest in history and literature in the 1990s.[20]

By 1993 some Russians were arguing that the process of investigating the past had gone too far; others that it had not gone far enough. In the post-communist era writers are still only accepted by what has been called the 'liberal gendarmerie'[21] if they have resisted injustice in the past and not collaborated with the Soviet regime. Radical critics are still unhappy about the past misdemeanours of new literary officials, and writers continue to stand in judgement over their fellows.[22] The new Minister of Culture Evgenii Sidorov, previously known as a liberal critic, has been accused by Natal'ya Ivanova of 'sitting on the fence' during the Gorbachev era;[23] although a dispassionate spectator is inclined to protest: 'Let him who is without sin cast the first stone'. Some younger writers and critics have even gone as far as to denounce writers formerly considered to be twentieth-century classics, such as Gor'kii and Bulgakov,[24] and have taken iconoclasm to an extreme by attacking nineteenth-century classics like Pushkin and Turgenev as products of the Russian radical tradition which contributed to the fall of the tsarist regime.[25] Western literary theories about 'the death of the author' which emphasize the irrelevance of a writer's biography and the primacy of the text would still find little favour in contemporary Russia.[26]

The reappraisal of Soviet history and the publication of 'returned literature' since 1985 have given new authors and works a central place in the Russian literary canon and swept away the reputations of former 'Soviet classics'.[27] This reassessment had a major effect on writers of historical fiction, since it was one of the most widespread and popular literary genres in Russia in the years 1986–9.

In the first place, the vast majority of conformist Soviet writers who followed the dictates of 'socialist realism' have now been dismissed as *pisatelokratiya* ('the dictatorship of failed scribblers').[28] Other writers whose reputation is not as high as it once was include 'liberals' such as Rybakov and Shatrov, who had tried 'to tell as much truth as possible in opposition to the censorship';[29] former dissidents, who had been published in Russia too late to have much impact,[30] and whose entire work had been based on opposition to the Soviet regime;[31] and émigré writers, either because readers were disillusioned with their political views or the low artistic quality of their work, or because they were perceived as having abandoned their homeland for an easy life in the West.[32] The critic Mikhail Zolotonosov ironically highlighted this process in his article 'YaITsATUPER as a phenomenon of Soviet culture' (the strange word is *reputatsiya* (reputation) spelt backwards).[33] In March 1991 German Baluev, the editor of the Leningrad newspaper *Literator*, stated baldly: 'Ninety per cent of Russian writers are no longer necessary for the people.'[34] Most probably, former dissidents who now live in emigration would have more impact on the reassessment of Russian history and the current political situation in Russia if they were to return home.[35] It will be interesting to see if this is true of Solzhenitsyn, who went back to Russia in May 1994;[36] some critics, however, believe that he has left it too late to exert a significant influence.[37]

HISTORICAL FICTION AS A CASUALTY OF DEMOCRACY

It is probably no coincidence that the decline of interest in historical fiction coincided with the introduction of democracy in Russia and the transformation of the limited policy of *glasnost* into something resembling freedom of speech.[38] One reason why historical fiction enjoyed such a huge popularity in 1987–8 is because broad masses of the population were discovering what many members of the intelligentsia already knew. But as *glasnost* developed, television and mass-circulation newspapers took up many historical subjects and the issues they raised in a more immediate way. By 1990–1 the pace of political events in the USSR had become so rapid that writers and critics were more concerned with political debate than with writing fiction[39] – on historical or any other themes – while most Soviet people were riveted to their television sets watching the debates in Congress. If they read at all, they preferred the press and *publitsistika* to serious literature or history. This development was welcomed by one commentator, who felt that hitherto the discussions about 'returned literature' had prevented Russians from thinking for themselves.[40]

Historical fiction also began to decline in influence by the 1990s because, as historical and ideological taboos broke down and there were few good works of 'returned literature' left to publish, the focus of critical attention moved from individual works of fiction to an assessment of the general position of culture in Russia.[41] As Natal'ya Ivanova pointed out, it was actually necessary for public opinion to shift from historical analysis to the problems of the present, since the main question facing contemporary Russians in the 1990s was not Stalin or Lenin, but 'the orientation towards Utopia, which has entered into our blood'.[42] Russians would only be able to overcome their enslavement to totalitarianism if they were able to concentrate on the present and avoid the false utopias of the 'radiant future' or the 'radiant past'.[43]

Another less positive reason for Russians' concentration on the present in the 1990s is that, as *glasnost* gradually shed more light on the past, they became increasingly aware that the previously acclaimed accomplishments of Soviet socialism had steadily diminished, while the toll of crimes and errors had tremendously increased. Many felt demoralized by these historical revelations and did not wish to dwell on Russia's 'accursed past'.[44] Others may have felt that the rehabilitation of Stalin's victims in 1990 had precluded any need to delve deeper into Soviet history; while young people became bored with excessive concentration on the past,[45] or felt disaffected from their elders, wishing to distance themselves from their country's history. By the 1990s, for many Russians the problems of the present had become overwhelming; history must have seemed unimportant to many at a time of mounting economic crisis and ethnic tension.

There is evidence that historical fiction – indeed all fiction – was regarded as irrelevant by many Russians in the 1990s, because it was unable to respond to the current political situation. Many writers and cultural figures were undergoing a crisis of creativity, uncertain how to adapt to the new conditions of freedom or the troubled political climate.[46] People were turning to literature for help, but in vain, as literature was in crisis, like life itself.[47] The publication of so much high-quality 'returned literature' in Russia had intimidated new writers, and some of the established ones found it 'impossible to write after *Gulag*'.[48] Few works of fiction had depicted contemporary society;[49] writers were either too afraid,[50] or too confused[51] to analyse Gorbachev and *perestroika*, or Yeltsin and the post-communist era.[52]

By the 1990s, literature had come to face the dilemma of freedom and impotence. Since 1985 words had proved the easiest thing to licence in the USSR, but they had not cured the political or economic crisis. At one time it seemed unthinkable that the works of Pasternak, Grossman and Solzhenitsyn would be published in the USSR, but they *were* published, and nothing happened. The Soviet people expected a 'miracle' when Solzhenitsyn's *The Gulag Archipelago* was published in 1989,[53] as the author did himself;[54] but when *Gulag* eventually achieved publication in Russia the expected miracle failed to materialize, and Russians were saying in the spring of 1991: 'the government has not fallen'. Perhaps if Solzhenitsyn's works had been published in Russia earlier, in 1987 or 1988, they would have had an impact greater than the artistically inferior works of Rybakov and Shatrov; but by the 1990s the theme of Stalinism was no longer of such great interest to the Russian public, and democratic readers and critics may have been repelled by the attempt of conservative publicists to 'appropriate' Solzhenitsyn as a supporter of their cause.[55]

LITERATURE AND HISTORY IN THE NEW MARKET SYSTEM

Another reason for the decline of literature and history in the 1990s is that the new market system in publishing has had adverse effects on both creative literature and the writing of history.[56]

In 1991 the veteran literary critic Aron Lur'e claimed that the only themes in contemporary Russian literature were 'the camps, the Jews, the KGB and sex'.[57] For a fiction writer it may not be worth labouring for a long time in the hope of producing a masterpiece: Natal'ya Ivanova related in 1993 that one writer had earned only 50 dollars for a novel which took over ten years to write. Similarly, when some Russian historians were asked in March 1993 why there are more foreign researchers than Russians in the newly-opened archives, they complained that it is very difficult now for historians to find a publisher for their work, or to earn money for it if they do. The reassessment of history is still at the mercy of a lack of funds: in August 1993 a museum curator in Murmansk was quoted as saying that in the autumn a new lecturer would be appointed who would present a revised history of the Revolution and Civil War, but at present there was no money to change the exhibits.[58] In the meantime, the current vogue for selling copies of archival materials for foreign currency may mean that the Hoover Institution in California will possess better collections of Russian historical documents than libraries and archives within Russia itself.[59]

By the 1990s too, public taste had changed: whether because they were tired of the current political and economic crisis, or because they had no time to read on account of the endless queues, many Russians preferred undemanding television shows, such as low-quality Mexican soap operas or programmes by the right-wing faith healer Anatolii Kashpirovskii,[60] or escapist literature, such as romantic fiction, detective stories by Agatha Christie and Raymond Chandler, western best-sellers by Arthur Hailey or James Hadley Chase, science fiction, erotica or books on sensational subjects like oriental and martial arts, UFOs, alternative religions, folk medicine and psychic phenomena. The ambitious were reading books on business or marketing, while intellectuals were seeking solace in Russian and western classics, such as Dostoevskii, Joyce and Dante, or had returned to the works of Russian religious philosophers of the early twentieth century. Moreover, if literature was to be considered purely as entertainment, it now had to compete with videos, rock music, street theatre, western films and youth culture, which were already exerting more influence than literature over the minds of young Russian people.

Alla Latynina spoke for many members of the cultural intelligentsia when she defined the situation in Russia in the 1990s as 'this savage period of primitive accumulation'.[61] However, while conscious of the many drawbacks of a market system, she came to the conclusion that 'the *diktat* of the market is several orders of magnitude better than the *diktat* of ideology. In fact, it is incomparably better', even though she realizes that the market has no obligation to be concerned with culture at all.[62]

HAVE LITERATURE AND HISTORY SERVED THEIR PURPOSE?

Perhaps the main reason for the decline of historical fiction in the 1990s is that it has served its purpose. As we have seen, the debate about the past was a debate about the present, and the debate about literature was a debate about politics. With the introduction of democracy and freedom of speech, however limited, it was no longer necessary to conduct political debates indirectly, through the medium of history or literature. In 1990 the critic Natal'ya Ivanova admitted that 'the game was up'; literature had only been of paramount interest to Russians in the absence of a free press. She argued: 'We were all pretending when we discussed literature. We were deprived of the opportunity to talk about freedom – and pretended that the artistic features of some literary work were simply of vital importance.'[63] Another critic conceded that, in the absence of democratic freedoms, literary factions had to some extent been a substitute for political parties.[64]

Although it is hardly surprising that much 'returned literature', written in earlier periods of Soviet history, is concerned with historical themes, Ivanova is correct in pointing to the continuing need for 'Aesopian language' as the reason why in the early years of *glasnost* Russian fiction focused so firmly on the past when writers' and critics' main concern was the present. That is why by 1989–90, after the initial revelations about Soviet history had been assimilated, the chief focus of cultural debate shifted from an interest in historical truth to a more topical subject: the alternative interpretations of history by different groups within Russia who wished to promote their own socio-political conceptions of the present and future of their country.[65] Such debates suggest that it is not so much that Russians' interest in history is diminishing in the 1990s, but rather that Russia has been experiencing a time in which 'there is a great deal of history in *publitsistika*, and of *publitsistika* in history'.[66] The return of national self-awareness has led many Russians to continue investigating their history, which has proved so many-sided that writers and publicists have found in it arguments supporting diametrically opposed views on the development of Russian society.

Conclusion

Our study of some of the main works of historical fiction published in Russia since 1985 and the critical debates they have inspired raises a number of interesting questions· about the nature of history, literature and politics in contemporary Russia. Since the process of reassessing Russian history and literature and rebuilding a new society is still continuing, any conclusions offered here can only be tentative and provisional.

THE VALUE OF HISTORICAL FICTION

The publication of 'returned literature' on historical themes has been very important, for a number of reasons. The first and most fundamental point is that the liberation of Russian literature from censorship is in itself of inestimable value.[1] Now that Gorbachev has fallen from power and still receives a bad press in Russia, it is necessary to emphasize the vital significance of his policy of liberalizing literature and the media.[2] *Glasnost* – along with foreign policy – may well be regarded by historians as Gorbachev's greatest achievements (some would say: his *only* achievements). The publication of 'returned literature' under *glasnost* amounted to nothing less than the belated restoration of their own culture to the Russian people; moreover, literature and the press may have enjoyed more freedom under Gorbachev than in the new 'democratic' era under Yeltsin.

Secondly, since 1985 literature has played a vital role in opening up new historical questions for discussion.[3] Indeed, fiction *initiated* the whole process: whereas, for the most part, journalists, historians and economists only started to provide a frank treatment of formerly taboo historical subjects after Party policy had changed in the Gorbachev era, novelists and poets had been concerned with these questions since the Khrushchev 'thaw' and even earlier.[4]

Even if much information about Soviet history had previously been available in the West, or disseminated in Russia through the 'informal' or 'folk understanding of history', the publication of literary and publicistic works on Stalinism and the legacy of the Revolution in the years 1985–8 was still an important breakthrough, because it meant that the *public* process of confronting the past had begun. Fiction published in journals of mass circulation in the Gorbachev era became the first medium to introduce new historical topics to a wide public in the USSR, playing a particularly valuable role in educating and influencing people too young to remember the limited revelations of the Khrushchev 'thaw'.

Novels or literary memoirs sometimes provided factual information new even to a western audience, as in the case of Anatolii Zhigulin's memoir *Black Stones*, with its depiction of an anti-Stalinist conspiratorial organization in Voronezh.[5] Less exceptionally, literature proved to be a powerful means of illustrating the human cost of historical events, the impact of policies on individuals. Accounts of 'dekulakization' and famine in collectivization novels, and the recollections of life in Stalin's prisons and camps have a greater impact on the imagination than dry statistics published in the press or a history textbook.

'Returned literature' was also of great moral value to the Soviet population, because it demonstrated that an alternative tradition of resistance to tyranny and violence had existed since the inception of Bolshevik rule, and that the best writers had, as far as possible, remained loyal to historical truth and freedom of thought in different periods of Soviet history. The publication of truthful works of literature was of great therapeutic value to the Soviet population, encouraging people to relate their own personal tragedies, and to confront the social and psychological legacy of the past.

Some classic literary works newly published in Russia since 1985 have also played a huge, though incalculable part in undermining the whole utopian concept of 'remaking history' which inspired both Lenin and Stalin (not to mention Gorbachev's *perestroika*). In *Doctor Zhivago*, for example, Pasternak suggests that 'the remaking of the world' is insignificant in comparison with the individual's experience of nature, love or art. Other anti-utopian works like Zamyatin's *We*, Platonov's *The Foundation Pit* and *Chevengur*, as well as the newly-published works of émigré writers such as Bunin, Nabokov and Brodskii, also emphasize the importance of the individual's experience and undermine the social experiment attempted in the USSR since 1917. Such works venture beyond realistic novels and essays on historical subjects in their defence of the free human spirit and their advocacy of a spiritual dimension beyond both history and ideology. Another great, though indefinable influence has been exerted by Dostoevskii's *The Devils* and *The Brothers Karamazov*, which, along with works of Russian religious philosophy newly available in Russia such as Georgii Fedotov's *Russia and Freedom* and Nikolai Berdyaev's *The Sources and Meaning of Russian Communism*, exposed the limitations of a materialist utopia and advocated a distinctively Russian path of historical development.[6] The significance of such ideas for contemporary Russians found expression in the new popularity of the genre of the anti-utopia in the late Gorbachev era, when works by Alexander Kabakov, Vyacheslav Rybakov, Lyudmila Petrushevskaya and Vladimir Makanin depicted a hypothetical future society of food queues and general demoralization.[7]

THE RELATIONSHIP BETWEEN LITERATURE AND HISTORY

Although literature and historiography have long been intimately linked within Russian and Soviet society, this relationship was transformed under *glasnost*, leading to both beneficial and detrimental effects for literature and the understanding of history. Although it considerably increased the number of historical subjects treated in literature, fiction has frequently produced an inaccurate picture of Soviet history, and not all historical works have been of high artistic quality. Somewhat paradoxically, artistic quality and historical accuracy may sometimes come into conflict: for example, Rybakov's *Children of the Arbat*, much criticized on artistic grounds, does at least tell a compelling story, and is artistically superior to its sequels *1935 and Other Years* and *Fear*, which are arguably more historically accurate.

The greatest success achieved by *glasnost* in history and historical fiction was the Soviet authorities' recognition that the former official treatment of Soviet history, especially of Stalinism, had become so corrupted and debased as to become meaningless. This was conceded by the decision taken in 1988 to pulp school textbooks on the history of the USSR and to cancel the school history examinations for 1988.

The liberalization of literature and history went hand in hand. By November 1987 a special commission had restored some 6,000 books to public use which had previously been held in 'special access' shelves.[8] Evidently, if many former historical 'unpersons' could be put on the stage by Shatrov or discussed in novels by Rybakov, there was no reason to keep serious historians away from their writings. Although academic historians were initially slow to respond to the challenges of *glasnost*, by 1988 steps had been taken towards a renewal of the history profession.[9]

However, the new textbooks hurriedly produced in 1989 still propagated a Leninist line, and by the 1990s were again in need of revision.[10] As late as 1993, Otto Latsis admitted that many old Brezhnev-era textbooks were still in use, and that there was still a great deal of confusion about history in post-communist Russia: 'In an undefined society without any history, a generation is growing up with no idea about the past and the future, or about good and evil.'[11] By the 1990s, teachers at schools and universities had to transcend the available textbooks if they wished to retain their pupils' respect.[12] In 1993, new humanities textbooks for schools and higher educational institutions sponsored by the Soros Foundation were at last being published, although this initiative provoked some indignation among Russian nationalists.[13]

The effect of historical fiction on the understanding of history in the USSR since 1985 is more difficult to evaluate. 'Round table' discussions on 'history and literature' held in the years 1987–8 repeatedly emphasized the greater readiness of writers than historians to tackle controversial historical issues.[14] While historians' complaints about the unavailability of archives possessed some validity,[15] their initial reticence to reassess the past was also undoubtedly a result of the psychological inertia and timidity ingrained by years of repression.

The main danger involved in the understanding of history through literature is that fiction may propagate and perpetuate historical inaccuracies. It would hardly be surprising if Russian writers' knowledge of their own history were limited or flawed, since, until very recently, they had only a restricted access to historical information, and there was little knowledge of western historiography among Russian historians, still less among creative writers. In fairness to writers, they should not be blamed for the failings of historians: Rybakov and Shatrov have repeatedly asked for more information and help from historians, arguing that there need be no conflict between history and historical fiction.[16]

However, the historical fiction published under *glasnost* also raises the general question of the importance of historical accuracy in literature.[17] On the one hand, writers of historical fiction possess a certain leeway to invent, and in the West readers have long been accustomed to allowing writers full licence to make of historical characters and events what they will. Many western readers, concerned less with factual accuracy than with a writer's ability to convey the spirit of a historical period, might consider, for example, that Rybakov has skilfully exploited his freedom as a novelist when he posits an imaginary last meeting between Kirov and Ordzhonikidze in Moscow in November

1934 shortly before Kirov's assassination, or that Solzhenitsyn has a perfect right to invent a crucial meeting between Lenin and the demonic Parvus.[18]

On the other hand, it could be argued that historical accuracy is more important in a Russian literary context than in other cultures (even though its absence is more understandable). Because of the shortage of accurate works by historians, Soviet writers of the *glasnost* era possessed a great responsibility, and it was incumbent upon them to get their facts straight as far as possible, or to make it clear to their readers which parts of their work were fictional, and which were based on fact. Some authors of historical fiction such as Rybakov and Solzhenitsyn have, albeit with undoubted sincerity, made excessively sweeping claims for the historical accuracy of their work.[19] Many works of historical fiction published in the Gorbachev era to some extent succumb to the temptation of 'psycho-history' – the limited view that history is merely a result of the ideas and and actions of individuals, with no reference to political systems or wider economic, ideological and international factors.[20] However, this is partly an inevitable result of the demands of the novelistic or dramatic genre, which focuses on the thoughts and actions of individual characters.[21] Rather than blaming Russian authors of historical fiction for their inconsistencies and contradictions, it is perhaps more helpful to see them as creators of works which combine fiction, history and publicistic passion.

Certain fictional works published under *glasnost* contain controversial conclusions which have been rightly challenged by Russian historians, notably V. P. Danilov's criticism of the nationalistic, anti-Semitic interpretation of collectivization in the works of Mozhaev and Belov.[22] In Rybakov's *1935 and Other Years* it is suggested that ten million peasants were dekulakized, and the total number of deaths during collectivization and the famine is estimated as thirteen million. These are still extremely controversial issues in the West; such high figures have repeatedly been challenged by Stephen Wheatcroft and others,[23] and have also been called into question by information from Soviet archives which supports a much lower excess mortality rate of three to four million, or, at most, four to five million during the years 1929–34.[24]

Although the debate about deaths during collectivization and the purges of the 1930s is by no means over (especially since the discovery of numerous mass graves and the long-awaited publication of some of the data from the 1937 census have injected new evidence into the discussion),[25] Rybakov may have been guilty of contributing to the popularization of a new myth in the USSR at a time when the high estimates of Solzhenitsyn, Conquest and Medvedev had been questioned by western scholars. If so, he was merely following the lead of some Soviet historians and publicists, who, as they have privately explained, simply took their data without acknowledgement or any independent verification from western studies of Stalinism like Conquest's *The Great Terror*, or, like Bestuzhev-Lada, simply made guesses biased towards obtaining a maximum figure.[26]

Distortion of historical truth, perhaps inevitable in works of fiction, does not matter much as long as the issues raised by writers are investigated in greater detail by historians. Although historical inaccuracy in fiction may have been of some significance in 1987, when historians had few other sources of information about what was happening in the higher echelons of the party apart from that provided in Rybakov's *Children of the Arbat*, it matters far less in the 1990s, when many more archival materials are available. Literary investigations of Soviet history, whatever their degree of historical accuracy, are in the last resort only fictional, and afford no substitute for historical or biographical studies.

Another criticism levelled at many of the newly published works of historical fiction is that they have been very traditional in tone; their main difference from socialist realism has been in ideology rather than in tone or style.[27] Few influential works of historical fiction in the period since 1985 have attempted to adopt alternative, non-realistic approaches to history. One exception is Abuladze's film *Repentance*, one of the first important new works of the Gorbachev era to suggest that 'History is so fantastically absurd in many of its manifestations that it cannot be . . . authentically created by means of realistic art – it requires forms and a style that are more in keeping with its essence.'[28] Another is Andrei Bitov's novel *Pushkin House*, published in Russia in 1987, which does not mention Stalin directly, but uses intertextuality and interweaving historical planes to evoke a Russian intellectual's relationship with his country's past, implying that Stalinism has caused serious damage to the human psyche, distorting the consciousness of the Soviet people over several generations.[29] Boris Yampol'skii's *Moscow Street* uses fantasy to convey the atmosphere of terror and suspicion prevalent in the Stalin era; while other writers, mainly émigrés, have employed satire, fantasy and the grotesque to evoke the essence of Stalinism.[30] A more general meditation on history is implied in such fantastic tales as Bitov's *Pushkin's Photograph (1799–2099)*, which satirizes any remodelling of the past to suit present needs and standards,[31] and Kuraev's *Captain Dikshtein*, which emphasizes the accidental, disrupted nature of the historical process, suggesting that there is no historical 'truth' existing in isolation from the patterns imposed on it by historians.[32] Such aesthetic techniques are not the subject of this book, although they would repay further investigation. It could be argued that such works are more successful artistically than some of the works discussed in this book (for example, those of Shatrov and Rybakov), but they have been less influential politically, both because their relationship to history is more oblique than realistic works, and because they were published too late to do more than complement the information already made available to the public on the historical subjects to which they indirectly allude. Writers and directors were sometimes criticized for their allusive techniques:[33] by 1989, for example, in an age of 'open *publitsistika*', when Lenin and the revolutionary period had become the main focus of media attention, novels about the Stalin era published abroad in the Brezhnev era, such as Voinovich's *Chonkin* and Vladimov's *Faithful Ruslan*, which employ satire, allegory, humour and the grotesque, received some censure for their lack of a definite message, and their failure to suggest any reasons for the origins of the Russian 'troubles'.[34]

Many democratic critics have pointed out the great value of documentary prose works in contemporary Russian society, although they are, perhaps, guilty of the implicit assumption that such works manifest historical veracity, and that it is this veracity – rather than their artistic power – which gives the works their value.[35] It is, nevertheless, quite true that historical truth was what *mattered* to the Russian people at the time of their first publication. Perhaps in the post-communist era readers and critics will have greater leisure and inclination to distinguish between truth and fiction and come to appreciate the more subtle pleasures of textual analysis and literary theory, although this still seems highly doubtful in the troubled political circumstances of post-Soviet Russia.

Sophisticated western critics sometimes criticize the traditional tone of Russian historical fiction with insufficient appreciation of the historical and political context in which literary works first appeared in Russia. Although in the 1990s Russian critics and readers may be more appreciative of, perhaps even expect, the use of experimental literary techniques, this was certainly not the case in the years 1987–8, when, as the poet Andrei Voznesenskii said, 'the newspapers drip[ped] with the blood of Stalin's victims'.[36]

THE POLITICAL IMPACT OF HISTORICAL FICTION

The publication of historical fiction since the inception of *glasnost* has had important social and political implications for the former USSR and contemporary Russia. In the first place, the reappraisal of history contributed to the unfolding of a process which Richard Sakwa defines as 'information, discussion and participation',[37] and, since 'all reform begins with information',[38] it acted as part of the triggering mechanism leading to political reform.

Another political development was that, as during the Khrushchev 'thaw',[39] the cultural liberalization of the Gorbachev era once again fostered a blossoming of the intelligentsia, which was able to act relatively independently as a counterweight to the bureaucracy and administrative system.[40] However, by 1989–90 the intelligentsia began to decline as a special group.[41] Individual members of the cultural intelligentsia were still playing an important part in Congress or the media (although none reached the heights of Havel in former Czechoslovakia); but a 'normal', western-style pattern of class relationships was beginning to form with the decline of the communist system, the introduction of democratic elections, and marketizing economic reforms.

The decline of the democratic intelligentsia can also be attributed to people's growing disillusionment with the activities of the democrats in power. Some of the radicals active in the 1980s, such as Korotich, have now joined the new 'brain drain' of Russian talent trickling abroad.[42] Other intellectuals prominent during the age of *perestroika*, such as Gavriil Popov, have already risen and fallen in the post-communist era. Richard Sakwa is undoubtedly correct to argue that 'The prominent role of the intelligentsia during *perestroika* was only a transitional one'; indeed, it was such a short-lived triumph that some Russian intellectuals could be forgiven for having missed it altogether.[43] In 1992, for example, the critic Tat'yana Vol'tskaya argued that the intelligentsia has never possessed real power in Russia.[44] The rise and fall of literature and the cultural intelligentsia in the years since 1985 can be seen as just one aspect of this general pattern. Nevertheless, writers and intellectuals still have an influential part to play in commenting on political events, as was demonstrated after the coup attempts of 1991 and 1993.[45]

From the point of view of the political authorities, historical fiction had both positive and negative effects. Initially, in the years 1985–7, Gorbachev's policy of using *glasnost* in history and culture to promote his policies of economic and political reform achieved a moderate success, enabling him to defeat his conservative opponents and to analyse the

defects of the 'administrative-command economy'. Works by Rybakov
and Shatrov praising Lenin's NEP fostered a favourable attitude towards
a mixed economic system; while collectivization novels by Mozhaev,
Belov and Antonov promoted the concepts of private and co-operative
farming.[46] From 1988 onwards, newly published works attacking Stalinism
and Leninism implicitly warned against the dangers of a return to dictatorship, corruption, terror and an immutable bureaucracy, features
also characteristic of Brezhnev's 'era of stagnation'.

In practice, however, the reassessment of the past soon proved to be
not only a means of supporting the new party line, but also an end in
itself for the liberal Soviet intelligentsia. By 1987 many writers and
editors were escaping from official control and raising certain subjects
for moral, rather than political reasons.[47]

The rapid failure of the coup of August 1991 demonstrated not only
the democratic achievements of Gorbachev's years in power, but also
the positive results of unremitting propaganda against the Stalinist and
Brezhnevite dictatorships. By this time, neither the army, nor the KGB,
nor even the coup leaders, who were not Stalinists, but right-wing tra-
ditionalists, were prepared to use mass terror to impose their will on
the people.

However, in the Gorbachev era it also became clear that *glasnost*
had failed to cure the USSR's enormous economic problems, and that
mere half-measures had proved ineffective in promoting democratic
change. From 1987 onwards, the processes which Gorbachev had unleashed – *glasnost* and the re-examination of Soviet history – led to
much of the political ferment in the USSR which eventually caused
Gorbachev's own downfall and the disintegration of the Soviet Union.
If the Party originally hoped to limit the process of historical exploration, after 1987 the flood of works on historical themes and the plurality of voices became so powerful that the Party could no longer
control them all, unless it chose to resort to repressive measures. The
re-publication of many documents, memoirs and literary works about
Lenin, the Civil War and the Red Terror opened the eyes of many
Russians to the cruelties of their revolutionary past; while revelations
about the Nazi–Soviet Pact and the crimes of Stalinism led to the rise
of nationalist sentiment, particularly in the Baltic states. Other nationalities analysed the adverse effects of Soviet imperialism on their countries, which led to the flare-up of repressed ethnic tensions, and ultimately
to their decision to secede from the USSR.[48] The democratic intelligentsia began to adopt a nihilistic attitude to the Soviet regime, wishing to dismantle what it now perceived as the whole disastrous social

experiment initiated in 1917. At the same time, neo-Stalinists and Russian nationalists who wanted to return to the values of the past made common cause as the 'Red–Brown alliance', which attempted the unsuccessful coups of 1991 and 1993.

Another more general moral and spiritual consequence of the rapid reappraisal of Soviet history was constantly pointed out by conservatives, who warned, not without substance, that revelations about the past, far from being cathartic, would undermine people's faith in the Soviet system and their country as a whole, leading to negative consequences such as crime, corruption, drug-taking, drunkenness and despair. Eventually it was not only conservatives who came to feel that *glasnost*, coinciding with a time of falling living standards, had, if not actually caused the general crisis of morale and legitimacy, greatly accelerated the process of disillusionment. In 1989 one writer argued that it had created the feeling among ordinary Russians that 'the past is disgraceful, the present is monstrous and the future is uncertain and unpredictable'.[49] By the 1990s, many young people were completely alienated from the whole process of reappraisal and reform, wishing to follow their own completely separate agendas.[50]

It is unlikely that Gorbachev predicted all the consequences of his actions – in the cultural field, as in many others – and perhaps he later came to regret them, but once the floodgates had been opened, it proved impossible to control the tide of freedom. The experience of the Gorbachev era demonstrated that, unless terror is imposed, as in China, democracy cannot be stopped half way, and that intellectuals, once they have tasted partial freedom, will press on until they have achieved full freedom of speech and the press. So this process of historical reassessment, initially encouraged by the Party, eventually far surpassed the Party's original intentions, and unleashed forces which undermined the legitimacy of the regime and eventually swept it away.[51]

Although in the Gorbachev era Soviet people were initially disillusioned with what they regarded as the limited political impact of the publication of dissident and émigré literature, now that the Communist government *has* fallen, a strong case could be made for the view that the new climate of intellectual and spiritual freedom, created by the publication in their homeland of such writers as Pasternak, Grossman and Solzhenitsyn, contributed to the democratic revolution in Russia. This is the view taken by the British poet laureate Ted Hughes, when he said: 'Poetry has brought down the government [in Russia].' If the words 'prose' and *publitsistika* are substituted for 'poetry', or the term 'poetry' is used in its widest sense, there is some truth in this assertion.

THE POLITICIZATION OF HISTORY IN CONTEMPORARY ·RUSSIA

The reappraisal of history by writers and historians since 1985 has led to a more truthful, although not entirely accurate or objective history of twentieth-century Russia. Many problems besetting individual historians and writers are aspects of a wider problem: the intense politicization of history and literature in Russia since 1985.

Under *perestroika*, it was still necessary to approach the writings of Russian historians with caution, since historians and publicists were sometimes careless with their facts and hasty in their judgements.[52] Historical figures formerly treated with prejudice and hostility sometimes came to be regarded with uncritical admiration: in 1987–8 this was true of opponents of Stalinism, such as Bukharin, Larin and Kondrat'ev; since 1989 it has been increasingly true of Tsar Nicholas II and Stolypin. In the 1990s, strongly held anti-communist convictions have coloured the works of many Russian historians, writers and critics, whose conclusions are often diametrically opposed to those which they would have expressed in the past. The history with which many Russians have come into contact in the press and literary journals is closer to the straightforward, sometimes simplistic 'counter-communism' espoused by Russian émigrés and western historians of the Cold War period, than to the more complex views of contemporary 'revisionist' historians.[53]

From the late 1980s, Russian historians have had greater opportunities to meet western historians whose aim is to approach their source material as objectively as possible,[54] and it is to be hoped that in the future more of them will be influenced by this ethic. Although since 1987–8 the arguments of Russian historians have been far more closely related to evidence than they were in the Brezhnev era,[55] and there is now an interesting new generation of historians in the former USSR, in the early 1990s complaints could still be heard that historians were not 'restructuring themselves' quickly enough, although public interest in historical questions remained high.[56] It could, however, be argued that it is unreasonable to expect Russian historians to change their entrenched attitudes and methods in such a short time.

Since 1985, Russian historians and writers of historical fiction have not been able to stay aloof from the political debate, but, on the contrary, have been subject to all the twists and turns in the political situation and bedevilled by rapidly changing fashions. Russian writers and readers now reject out of hand all subjects previously favoured by the

Party, and subjects which were very popular, even daring, in 1987–8 – alternative paths to socialism, balanced views of NEP, a serious examination of the views of Bukharin, Trotsky and Stalin's other intra-party rivals – are now out of favour. If once they were expected to toe the party line and eschew all speculation, or to ignore all alternative possible paths of Russian development, perhaps Russian historians are now too ready to suggest that history has nothing but a 'subjunctive mood', and to dwell too fondly on alternatives to Bolshevism, even if the evidence does not warrant it.

There is now a new conformism on the part of some Russian historians, as on the part of the new breed of politicians. Former communist historians have simply declared themselves to be democrats or nationalists, and are busy rewriting (or simply ignoring) their former views. Some historians of the older generation readily accept fashionable new historical interpretations, such as the use of the word 'totalitarianism' to analyse the Stalin era.[57] Although this concept is now found less useful by western historians, to Russian historians it is a convenient means of claiming that Stalinism was not a uniquely Russian phenomenon, and did not differ markedly from other forms of twentieth-century totalitarianism, such as Italian fascism, German Nazism, Maoism in China, or communist regimes in Cambodia, Vietnam or North Korea. Such comparisons are used to shift specific responsibility from Russians for the horrors of their past.

Another obstacle preventing the development of a truthful history in Russia is the public's thirst for rapid, sensational exposés, not thorough, informed analysis, which has led to a trivialization of interest in the past, and inadvertently caused as much harm as good. Initially, in the years 1987–8, it was primarily conservative writers and historians who warned against the dangers of sensationalism and dwelling too much on the darker side of Soviet history, because their own positions and power were threatened;[58] but by 1988 Gorbachev too had come to warn against the 'thirst for sensations',[59] in an attempt to preserve his own position by confining the historical discussions to limited revelations about the Stalin era, based on a Marxist–Leninist viewpoint. Nevertheless, the fact that some liberal writers also complained of sensationalism and opportunism in the treatment of Soviet history suggests that this was a serious contemporary problem.[60] In the post-communist era some democrats have expressed a wish that the process of reassessing the past, which led to the traumatization of the population and the disintegration of the USSR, had occurred more slowly and rationally.[61] Such debates also illustrate the more general difficulty in Russia since

1985 of drawing a distinction between a serious critical approach to the past and a purely sensational one, since this has been largely a matter of timing and political judgement.

Symbols and drama are always characteristic of revolutions, and the period since 1985 has attested to the great importance of historical symbols in the consciousness of the Soviet people. In the years 1987–90, during the anti-Stalin and anti-Lenin revolutions, historical names were restored to many towns, streets and institutions,[62] and statues were toppled. During the 'second Russian revolution' of 1991 this process was also allowed to take its course, in order to symbolize the end of communist rule. However, in 1993–4 some Russians were arguing that the destruction of statues was 'barbaric',[63] or represented a mistaken attempt by Russians to deny their history.[64]

By 1993 the Russian public's appetite for historical revelations had to some extent become satiated, but it still evinced an interest in such exciting subjects as the fate of the Tsar and his family,[65] the discovery of Rasputin's diary,[66] the shooting of Lenin[67] or the activities of the KGB.[68] Russians were also fascinated by information gleaned from the newly-opened archives, such as the discovery of Hitler's skull and Goebbels's diaries.[69] One of the most fashionable books of 1992–3 was V. Suvorov's *The Ice-breaker*, which propagated the dubious opinion that the chief instigator of the war was not Hitler, but Stalin.[70] There was also a significant audience for 'Our Friend', an American television film about Stalin, but this may have been primarily due to the fact that it was an American interpretation of the subject.

Although the historical fiction and *publitsistika* published in the years 1987–9 exerted a tremendous impact on public opinion in the former Soviet Union,[71] in the volatile political circumstances of contemporary Russia a question mark now hangs over the permanence of the transformation wrought by the historical writings of the Gorbachev era. Although all Stalin's victims were officially rehabilitated by an amnesty of August 1990, in the post-communist era, humiliation at the loss of an empire and disillusionment with the democrats' record in power appears to have rekindled enthusiasm for Stalin – almost half of the Russians polled in the summer of 1992 still regarded him as 'a great leader';[72] while opinion polls of the 1990s continued to express an even more favourable view of Lenin.[73] Moreover, the propensity of Gorbachev and Yeltsin (not to mention the leaders of other post-Soviet republics) to favour authoritarian solutions suggests that wider lessons about the dangers of dictatorship have by no means been absorbed in the former USSR.

As we have seen throughout this book, *glasnost* increased not only the honesty of writers, editors and historians, but also intensified their factionalism and cliquishness, sanctioning not only liberal reformist views, but also the explicitly racist views of the conservatives, who objected to learning Russian history through the works of liberal Jewish writers such as Rybakov and Shatrov.[74] This conflict has worsened since 1989, when an unholy alliance has existed between neo-Stalinists and conservative nationalists, suppported by some elements in the KGB and the army, who have answered the question 'Who is to blame?' with the view that the 'Jewish–Masonic conspiracy' has been responsible for all the ills of modern Russian history, including the abdication of the Tsar, the Bolshevik Revolution and the introduction of collectivization.[75]

A wide variety of viewpoints on historical topics – as on all others – can now be openly expressed in Russia. Many new facts have now been revealed to the Russian public, but these have frequently been selectively presented, and have given rise to clashing interpretations and new conflicts. There is now no generally agreed interpretation of the revolutions of 1917, the role of Lenin and Stalin, the purges, the war – indeed, of any significant event in twentieth-century Russian history. An optimist would emphasize the pluralism now permitted in historical and literary debate; a pessimist would suspect that history may still be used as a political battleground in Russia for the foreseeable future. Such fears were borne out when the new prejudices and deliberately falsified approach to the past harboured by some extremist political groups in Russia created a climate of opinion that culminated in the armed rebellion of October 1993.

If in 1987–8 democratic writers and critics had regarded it as their main task to combat the ruling Communist Party, they gradually came to see their main enemies as the conservative, nationalist intelligentsia. In the post-communist era many writers and critics are extremely conscious of their duty to combat fascism, and still feel unable to devote themselves to 'art for art's sake' and apolitical literary criticism.[76] It is for the most part only some younger writers and critics who take a more detached viewpoint, feeling free to advocate a pure, apolitical art divested of didacticism and historical or socio-political significance.[77]

Although up to the end of 1993 groups advocating neo-fascist views appeared relatively weak, Zhirinovsky's success in the December 1993 elections renders it less inconceivable that an authoritarian nationalist regime, supported by the Russian Orthodox Church, could one day be established in Russia. Accordingly, democratic writers, historians, critics and publicists still feel that it is incumbent on them not to allow reactionary views to become dominant.

One positive aspect of the post-communist era is that historical issues are increasingly being subjected to serious analysis by historians rather than fiction writers, and in 1993 new journals have appeared devoted to the publication of documents from historical archives.[78] On the other hand, the 'folk' understanding of history in Russia has by far outstripped academic history, leading to the creation of new myths about the NEP period, the Provisional Government, the tsarist regime, the figure of Stolypin, and even of Hitler, whom neo-fascists revere as Stalin's most effective enemy. The popularity of Stanislav Govorukhin's film *The Russia We have Lost,* and appeals for the canonization of Nicholas II, attest more to a sentimental nostalgia for some 'radiant past' than to a real understanding of the complexities of Russian history.[79] It is to be hoped that academic historians will eventually put the record straight, but it will now be too late for them to have the enormous political impact that they would have had in the years 1987–8.

The success of historians and writers in communicating more profound interpretations of Soviet history has also been called into question by the superficial, distorted opinions of contemporary political leaders: Zhirinovsky's comparison of the different phases of Soviet history with various sexual practices,[80] and Rutskoi's interpretation of the Revolution as a Jewish, western plot.

The continuing unavailability of the presidential archives and other important sources, and the possible absence of any definitive information about what was happening between Stalin and his comrades at the top of the party except the fictional reconstructions of Rybakov, Solzhenitsyn and other writers, still raise the danger that, like the images of Richard III and Henry V in Shakespeare's history plays, portraits of Stalin, Lenin and other historical figures in literature and film may exert a more lasting influence on people's minds than the belated contributions of historians.

It has been one of the central arguments of this book that the debate about historical fiction has been a political debate. The ideologically charged atmosphere in Russia since 1985 has given rise to a number of distorted approaches to history among the Russian intelligentsia. In the first place, Russians have become judges in relation to their country's past, sometimes blaming historical figures and writers of earlier generations for not possessing the knowledge available in the late 1980s, and elevating a new mythology of resistance to Leninism and Stalinism. Secondly, they have misused writers or historical events for their own political purposes, as we have seen in the case of Solzhenitsyn's writings and the interpretation of Stolypin's policies. Thirdly, they have attempted to extrapolate past events to today's reality, irrespective of whether such parallels are appropriate, or, indeed, of whether people can ever learn lessons from history.[81]

Since 1985, Russian writers, critics and publicists have eagerly sought to draw historical parallels between contemporary reality and past events, such as NEP, the Civil War or the February Revolution. On the first day of the coup of August 1991, for example, Yurii Afanas'ev spoke of a tragedy as great as those which had affected Russia in 1917 and in 1941, the year of Hitler's invasion,[82] and other commentators drew a comparison between the coup against Gorbachev and the fate of Khrushchev in 1964, removed by a conspiracy of his former supporters in the Politburo while he was on holiday in the Crimea.[83] Even in 1994, respected young historians cannot resist the temptation to use historical research to shed light on the present: Gennadii Bordyugov has compared the use of emergency measures under Lenin and Stalin with Yeltsin's storming of the White House, and Boris Starkov has found that the archives of the 1930s illustrate the persistent struggle between totalitarianism and democracy in Russia.[84]

Such has been the political crisis facing Russia in the 1990s, both before and after the fall of communism, that one of the most commonly drawn historical parallels, in the press and in private conversations, has been not with episodes in Soviet history, but with 'the Time of Troubles' (1598–1613),[85] a period when Russia was leaderless, prey to perpetual strife, and countless coups and counter-coups, until the coronation of Mikhail Romanov in 1613 marked a return to stability with the foundation of the new Romanov dynasty. It remains to be seen whether Boris Yeltsin's presidency proves to be more akin to the reign of Tsar Mikhail, or of Boris Godunov, who died in 1605 after a short reign characterized by constant strife with rival boyar families.

The politicization of literature and history which characterized nineteenth-century Russian society and the entire Soviet period has continued unabated into the post-communist era. History has still been used by politicians to control the present, as was graphically demonstrated in 1992, when new archival materials were made available during the trial of the Communist Party; and only certain historians favoured by the Russian government, such as Dmitrii Volkogonov, have been allowed into secret archives.[86] In particular, Yeltsin favoured the selective publication of materials from the archives to discredit his rival Gorbachev, such as a document proving that Gorbachev had long known about the Katyn massacre, but had chosen to conceal it. Yeltsin's opponents also use history for political ends, as was evident in late 1994, when the Russian Communist Party leader Gennadii Zyuganov again brought up the issue of Yeltsin's destruction of the house where the Tsar and his family were murdered.[87]

The intense politicization of both history and literature in Russia since 1985 raises the suspicion that both have been used in a utilitarian way, and, now that they have served their short-term political purpose, will be cast aside. However, a more positive view of the current situation would be that literature and history will no longer be asked to accomplish more than they are capable of, and will eventually return to the 'normal' place they occupy in advanced western societies. Yet if history and politics continue to be so closely interrelated in Russia, the danger still persists that history could be misused by a new authoritarian regime. As Yurii Afanas'ev has said: 'History must be an autonomous discipline if is to cease being a handmaiden of propaganda and a means of legitimizing any regime in power.'[88]

In view of the chaos of the post-communist period in Russia and the ex-Soviet Union, commentators could be forgiven for wondering whether the 'new orthodoxy' of 1987, or the 'radical consensus' of 1988[89] were not preferable to the spiritual vacuum, resurgent nationalism and ethnic conflict of the 1990s. The revolutionary reappraisal of history and the disintegration of ideology in Russia have led to the loss of an empire and a society witnessing the breakdown of law and order, in which crime, corruption and speculation are rife. For many ordinary Russians, 'democracy' means widespread poverty, rampant inflation and growing unemployment; a prolonged conflict between president and parliament which culminated in the armed rebellion of October 1993 and a large neo-fascist vote in December 1993; a continuing 'civil war' among writers and other professional groups; and the penetration of the Russian market by western-style consumerism, mass culture and pornography. It is hardly surprising that many writers published since 1985 have recalled Dostoevskii's warning that in Russia liberty may lead to unbridled licence; recent events suggest that a tendency to go from the extreme of despotism to the extreme of anarchy is indeed a feature of Russian political life. Striking parallels can be drawn between the period of tsarist reform, the February Revolution and the Civil War, and the period of *perestroika*, the democratic revolution of 1991 and its chaotic aftermath.

The current disillusionment with history in Russia, particularly on the part of young people, could have harmful results. First Gorbachev, then Yeltsin have thrown Russia headlong into a rapid process of western-style democratization and 'transition to the market', although most Russians are woefully ignorant of the history of western democracy and capitalism, which many now desire to emulate. Russians often fail to acknowledge that the market economy and democratic political system developed over many centuries in the West, and that, without a gradual, sober assessment of their problems and opportunities, they are in danger of repeating its mistakes, of conducting yet another doomed historical experiment.[90] A countervailing danger is that, now that many Russians have become disillusioned with the horrors of Soviet history, but know far less about the problems of the late tsarist period, they have become an easy prey for demagogues such as Zhirinovsky whose views hark back to the policies of imperialism, russification and anti-Semitism espoused by Alexander III, Nicholas II and the Black Hundreds.

LITERATURE IN CONTEMPORARY RUSSIA

The publication of previously censored works in Russia since Gorbachev's accession has radically altered Russians' perception of their own literary history and has provided new information for western scholars;[91] but from the point of view of the Russian reader of the 'returned literature', *perestroika* caused considerable confusion and dislocation. Works of different literary periods were published at the same time, often without adequate commentary. For the literary historian, it is difficult to know how to date a work of literature: from the time of its writing, the time of its circulation in *samizdat* or its first publication in the West, or the time of its publication in Russia?[92] It has also been difficult for literature teachers in schools and universities to change their ideas, and curricula have been slow to change. Like historians, many literary scholars and teachers of the older generation have not been accustomed to originality and independent thinking, and may feel disoriented for a long time to come.

Elsewhere I have examined in more detail the discussions which raged in the literary press in the early 1990s about the 'death' of Soviet culture and the changing role of literature in Russia.[93] Here it will be useful to analyse the current state of historical fiction, and of Russian literature as a whole.

In the post-communist era we are witnessing a certain decline of interest in serious fiction about Soviet history,[94] reflecting the wider disillusionment with both literature and history in Russian society. The newly-published works by Russian and western historians to some extent obviate the need for novels and plays on historical themes; while younger writers and critics argue that it is no longer sufficient for writers to raise sensational historical issues, but that literature must be of high artistic quality. Nevertheless, good historical fiction is still being written and valued in Russia: the Booker Prize shortlist of 1992 still contained one work dealing with the Stalin period (Fridrikh Gorenshtein's *Place*); the list submitted for the 1993 prize included Sinyavskii's *Good Night* (1984), which provides a fantastic evocation of Stalinism, and the 1993 shortlist included novels about Stalinism and the Second World War (Astaf'ev's *The Accursed and the Dead*), and the Soviet army in Afghanistan (Oleg Ermakov's *The Sign of the Beast*).[95]

Some of the best novels of 1992–3, such as Mark Kharitonov's *Lines of Fate, or Milashevich's Trunk*, which won the Booker Prize in 1992,[96] have no ideological content, but are interesting works 'on the junctures of philosophy and literature . . . history (historiosophy) and literature'.[97] The winner of the 1993 Booker Prize, Makanin's *A Baize-Covered Table with a Decanter in the Middle*, evokes the ambience and rituals of a communist court in order to explore the relationship between the 'little man' and the oppressive political system, a theme common in Russian literature since Pushkin's *Bronze Horseman*.[98] Evgenii Popov's novel *On the Eve of the Eve* (1993) suggests that Russia keeps losing one chance after another in its historical development, and 'now, before our very eyes, has seemingly missed one more chance to get off the historical treadmill'.[99] Such writers do not treat history directly, like Shatrov and Rybakov, but are concerned with the fate of the individual in the global movement of history, and the moral responsibility of the intelligentsia for the past and future of Russia.[100]

Although in the future it is possible that historical fiction may become less important as a genre, the tradition of treating serious historical issues in fiction is so deep among Russian writers and so familiar to Russian readers (far more so than in the West) that it is unlikely to disappear altogether, notwithstanding the anti-ideological stance of many younger writers. Since the main purpose of recalling the past is to shed light on the present and attempt to avoid further mistakes in the future, a re-evaluation of history will probably continue to figure prominently in literature published in Russia.

Opinions are divided on the new literary and cultural climate in postcommunist Russia. Radical younger writers and critics argue that no catastrophe has occurred; the exaggerated emphasis formerly placed on literature in Russian society was a result of Russia's backwardness.[101] In their view, the cultural situation in Russia has simply been 'normalized', as in the West, and writers have now become craftsmen engaged in professional work aimed at a narrow intellectual élite. Similarly, some of Yeltsin's ministers, notably Egor Gaidar, have contended that it will not be a tragedy if the literary journals fail, since there will simply be a book market, as in Western Europe.[102] At the same time, other writers and critics, both westernizers and slavophiles, regard the writer's loss of influence and the possible demise of the 'thick journal' in Russia as tantamount to a loss of the country's cultural and spiritual identity.

Whereas in 1990–1 critics had lamented the lack of literary masterpieces,[103] by 1992 a more optimistic mood prevailed, even if some critics who take a positive view of the contemporary literary scene tend to focus on good contemporary émigré writers (*russkaya literatura*) rather than literature produced within Russia itself (*rossiiskaya literatura*).[104] While it is undeniably true that publishing houses are putting all their efforts into profitable junk, and that very few contemporary novels are being published in book form,[105] the 'thick journals' have managed to keep serious literature alive in the years 1992–4. Indeed, the journals now have no choice but to publish contemporary literature, because the store of previously banned or secreted works, written either in Russia or in emigration, has finally run out. A number of new journals and literary almanacs emerged[106] publishing works by young[107] and formerly neglected writers;[108] in 1991 one of the established journals, *Znamya*, published at least eight new writers in their twenties or thirties; and younger writers such as Valeriya Narbikova (born in 1958) and Oleg Ermakov (born in 1961) were included on the Booker Prize shortlist in 1993.[109] Younger writers seem to be more able to adapt to current conditions than their elders, and are more sanguine about the possibility of obtaining sponsorship to publish their work.[110]

Another positive aspect of the current situation is that 1992 was a very good year for literature. One critic has gone so far as to say: '1992 was one of the most significant years in the history of Russian literature in the second half of the twentieth century'.[111] The best works have been produced by writers who concentrated on their profession, refusing to become politicians or to get involved in literary disputes. The award of the 1992 Booker Prize to Kharitonov was seen as symbolic, since he had neither co-operated with the Soviet regime nor actively resisted it, but had simply devoted himself to his craft.[112] Unfortunately, however, his novel *Lines of Fate* could not be published in book form until 1994, since it was initially not considered commercially viable.

Kharitonov's experience graphically illustrates the major change affecting Russian literature in the post-communist era: it no longer possesses the great political significance or popular appeal that it had in the last years of Soviet power. As in the West, the press and electronic media have become the main arenas for political debate. Literature no longer consists of only two main ideologically opposed strands; the literary repertoire has become very eclectic, and the readership too has become highly differentiated. It is unlikely that in the future the whole country will read certain key works of literature at the same time, as it read *Children of the Arbat, Doctor Zhivago* and *Life and Fate* in the Gorbachev era. Individual readers will now make their own, separate discoveries, and literature will no longer be judged simply according to the political sensitivity of the subject it treats, unlike literature 'about Stalin' or 'about the camps' in the years 1987–8. It has been argued, for example, that the salient feature of Ermakov's novel *The Sign of the Beast* is not that 'it is a novel about *Afghanistan*, but that it is a *novel* about Afghanistan'.[113]

There are various possible directions in which Russian literature might develop in the post-communist period. By the 1990s some writers and critics began to express the hope that there might be a new kind of apolitical 'alternative literature' which aspires to 'create spiritual values' and 'a new literary language'.[114] However, recent evidence suggests that 'alternative literature' still has no more readers than it had before, in the underground.[115]

Another possibility is that the future may belong to a variant of traditional 'socialist realism' – a new kind of politically committed democratic or nationalist literature. The wheel has come full circle since 1985: Evtushenko, one of the first writers to test the new policy of *glasnost* after Gorbachev's accession with his poem *Fuku!*, made a claim to being considered the poet laureate of the post-communist era with his poem of 19 August 1991 eulogizing 'Yeltsin on a tank'.[106] Evtushenko's 'terrible poem' was condemned by the émigré *enfant terrible* Eduard Limonov, who saw it as an example of a new kind of opportunistic literature by 'democrats' intent on promoting a 'cult of Yeltsin'.[117] Although in 1992 Evtushenko fell victim to factional disputes in the Union of Writers,[118] in 1993 Yeltsin rewarded his support with congratulations on the occasion of his sixtieth birthday, and the award of the Order of the Friendship of the Peoples.[119] Limonov, on the other hand, was inside the White House with Yeltsin's opponents during the rebellion of October 1993, and stood for election in December 1993 as a member of Vladimir Zhirinovsky's neo-fascist Liberal Democratic Party.

The evidence of the post-communist period up to 1994 suggests that a third, and most likely scenario is that the best Russian literature will no longer be a mouthpiece for the government, but will revert to its traditional pre-revolutionary role as a forum for the discussion of important moral and social issues and the telling of unpalatable truths.[120] By 1993, some critics who had formerly argued that literature might lose its social and moral status as a form of resistance to the system were prepared to admit that they had been wrong.[121] The majority of Russian writers and critics do not wish literature to be reduced to the level of a mere entertainment or decoration,[122] rather than being a matter of life and death for Russian readers.[123] Russian literature's traditional role as conscience of the nation will be hard to overcome, and even in the post-communist period some writers still possess considerable moral and political influence. This became clear in June 1992 when Yeltsin telephoned Solzhenitsyn while in Washington on a state visit: they reportedly discussed such burning issues as world peace, land reform, the position of Russian minorities in the other independent states and 'the restoration of the spiritual foundations of the people's life'.[124] In July 1994 members of the new parliament voted, albeit reluctantly, to invite Solzhenitsyn to address the Duma.

It is to be hoped that, notwithstanding all the problems currently facing Russian writers, the last decade of the twentieth century will witness a resurgence of literature in Russia. While there are still Russian writers who believe in Dostoevskii's dictum 'Beauty will save the world',[125] there will still be a Russian literature, perhaps even a 'great literature', although we may have to wait until the twenty-first century to emerge from what Tat'yana Tolstaya describes as the 'fog' of the illogical Russian universe[126] into a genuine literary renaissance.

Notes and References

Notes to the Introduction

1. A. Nove, *Glasnost in Action: Cultural Renaissance in Russia* (London, 1989).
2. V. Shentalinskii, meeting at St Antony's College, Oxford, October 1990. For a similar view, see T. Ivanova, 'Kto chem riskuet?', *Ogonek*, no. 24 (11–18 June 1988), p. 12.
3. For Tolstoi's view, see I. Berlin, 'The Hedgehog and the Fox', in Berlin (ed.), *Russian Thinkers* (London, 1978), p. 30.
4. This phrase was used by the literary scholar A. Lur'e at a lecture at the Central Lecture Theatre, Leningrad, spring 1991.
5. Nove, op. cit.; R. W. Davies, *Soviet History in the Gorbachev Revolution* (London, 1989).
6. J. Graffy, 'The Literary Press', in J. Graffy and G. Hosking (eds), *Culture and the Media in the USSR Today* (Basingstoke and London, 1989), pp. 107–57; D. Brown, 'Literature and Perestroika', *Michigan Quarterly Review*, vol. 28, no. 4 (Fall 1989).
7. H. Goscilo, 'Introduction: A Nation in Search of its Authors', in H. Goscilo and B. Lindsey (eds), *Glasnost: An Anthology of Russian Literature under Gorbachev* (Ann Arbor, 1990), p. xv.
8. V. Erofeyev, 'Pominki po sovetskoi literature', *Aprel'*, no. 1 (1991), pp. 274–82.
9. R. Marsh, *Soviet Fiction since Stalin: Science, Politics and Literature* (London and Sydney, 1986).
10. Davies, *Soviet History*; S. Wheatcroft, 'Unleashing the Energy of History', *ASEES*, vol. 1, no. 1 (1987), pp. 85–132, and his 'Steadying the Energy of History', *ASEES*, vol. 1, no. 2 (1987), pp. 57–114.
11. P. Broué, 'Gorbachev and History', in S. White (ed.), *New Directions in Soviet History* (Cambridge, 1992), pp. 3–23; J. Shapiro, 'The Perestroika of Soviet History', *Slovo*, vol. 2, no. 1 (May 1989), pp. 5–13; Shapiro, 'The Prophet Returned?', *Revolutionary History*, vol. 2, no. 1 (summer 1989), pp. 54–6; J. Scherrer, 'History Reclaimed', in A. Brumberg (ed.), *Chronicle of a Revolution* (NY, 1990), pp. 90–107; R. W. Davies, 'History and Perestroika', in E. A. Rees (ed.), *The Soviet Communist Party in Disarray: The XXVIII Congress of the Communist Party of the Soviet Union* (London, 1991), pp. 119–147; the collection of essays in 'Perestroika, Current Trends and Soviet History', *Survey*, vol. 30, no. 4 (June 1990).
12. Nove, op. cit., pp. 15–102; W. Laqueur, *The Long Road to Freedom: Russia and Glasnost* (Boston and London, 1989), pp. 48–77.
13. Graffy, 'The Literary Press'; J. Graffy, 'The Arts', in M. McCauley (ed.), *Gorbachev and Perestroika* (London, 1990), pp. 70–102; R. Marsh, 'Glasnost and Russian Literature', *ASEES*, vol. 6, no. 2 (1992), pp. 21–39.
14. N. N. Shneidman, *Soviet Literature in the 1980s: Decade of Transition*

(Toronto, 1989); R. Pittman, '*Perestroika* and Soviet Cultural Politics: The Case of the Major Literary Journals', *Soviet Studies*, vol. 42, no. 1 (January 1990), pp. 111–132.

15. Goscilo and Lindsey, op. cit.
16. R. Marsh, *Images of Dictatorship: Stalin in Literature* (London and NY, 1989), pp. 70–102.
17. D. Brown, *The Last Years of Soviet Russian Literature: Prose Fiction 1975-91* (Cambridge, 1993).
18. On the lesser importance of poetry in relation to prose and *publitsistika*, see A. Shaitanov, 'Teper' tebe ne do stikhov...', in V. Okhotskii and E. Shklovskii (comp.), *Vzglyad: kritika, polemika, publikatsii* (M., 1991), pp. 127–140.
19. For a study of film in the Gorbachev era, see A. Lawton, *Kinoglasnost: Soviet Cinema in Our Time* (Cambridge, 1992).

Notes to Chapter 1   The Background: History and Literature in Contemporary Russia

1. Yu. Afanas'ev, 'Perestroika i istoricheskoe znanie', in Afanas'ev (ed.), *Inogo ne dano* (M., 1988), p. 498 (first published *LR*, 17 June 1988). On Soviet history before *perestroika,* see R. W. Davies, *Soviet History in the Gorbachev Revolution* (Basingstoke and London, 1989), pp. 1–6.
2. See, for example, Yu. Afanas'ev, *SK* (21 March 1987); P. Volobuev, *VI KPSS*, no. 7 (1987), pp. 137–52; E. Ambartsumov, *VI*, no. 6 (1988), pp. 82–4.
3. See A. Nekrich, 'Perestroika in History: the First Stage', *Survey*, vol. 30, no. 4 (June 1989), pp. 27–32; T. Zaslavskaya, 'O strategii sotsial'nogo upravleniya perestroiki', in *Inogo ne dano*, p. 29.
4. S. Wheatcroft, 'Unleashing the Energy of History', *ASEES*, vol. 1, no. 1 (1987), pp. 85–6.
5. G. Svirski, *A History of Post-war Soviet Writing: The Literature of Moral Opposition*, trans. and ed. R. Dessaix and M. Ulman (Ann Arbor, 1981); D. Spechler, *Permitted Dissent in the USSR: Novy Mir and the Soviet Regime* (NY, 1982); G. Hosking, *Beyond Socialist Realism: Soviet Fiction since Ivan Denisovich* (London, 1980). In the 1970s the second section of *LG* to some extent continued where Tvardovskii's *NM* broke off.
6. Yu. Trifonov, *Dom na naberezhnoi, DN*, no. 1 (1976).
7. M. Shatrov, *LG* (8 May 1988) relates that Academician A. Egorov, then Director of the Institute of Marxism–Leninism, wrote to Andropov on 27 January 1982 in his capacity as head of the KGB, recommending that the play should be removed from the repertoire of the Moscow Arts Theatre.
8. D. Doder and L. Branson, *Gorbachev: Heretic in the Kremlin* (NY, 1990), p. 17.
9. The image of the mankurt was frequently used by critics and publicists in the Gorbachev era as a symbol of the collective loss of memory of

the Soviet people: see, for example, G. Volkov, *SK* (4 July 1987). However, L. Heller, 'Restructuring literary memory', *Survey*, vol. 30, no. 4 (June 1989), p. 65 argues that this is an unsatisfactory image, as Soviet people themselves, rather than some external enemy, destroyed their own historical memory.

10. R. Marsh, *Soviet Fiction since Stalin* (London, 1986), pp. 15–16, 20.
11. R. Marsh, *Images of Dictatorship* (London and NY, 1989), pp. 108–134.
12. A. Sakharov, 'Progress, Coexistence and Intellectual Freedom' (1968), in H. Salisbury (ed.), *Sakharov Speaks* (NY, 1974).
13. A. Solzhenitsyn *et al.*, *From under the Rubble*, trans. by A. M. Brock, M. Haigh, M. Sapiets, H. Sternberg and H. Willetts (London, 1975).
14. R. Sakwa, *Gorbachev and his Reforms, 1985–1990* (London, 1990), pp. 8–11, 65–82. I am grateful to Archie Brown for an interpretation based on his article in A. Brown, M. Kaser and G. S. Smith (eds), *Cambridge Encyclopaedia of Russia and the Former Soviet Union* (Cambridge, 1994), pp. 127–43.
15. K. Chernenko, 'Utverzhdat' pravdu zhizni, vysokie idealy sotsializma', *Izvestiya*, 26 September 1984, pp. 1–2; discussed by J. and C. Garrard, *Inside the Soviet Writers' Union* (London and New York, 1990); J. Wishnevsky, 'Aleksandr Yakovlev and the Cultural "Thaw"', *Radio Free Europe/RL Research Bulletin*, 6 (5 February 1987), Article no. 51, p. 2; R. Pittman, 'Writers and Politics in the Gorbachev Era', *Soviet Studies*, vol. 44, no. 4 (1992), pp. 666–7.
16. *Sovershenstvovanie razvitogo sotsializma i ideologicheskaya rabota partii v svete reshenii iyun'skogo (1983 g.) plenuma TsK KPSS* (M., 1985), pp. 30–1.
17. *Pravda* (12 March 1985); see also Gorbachev's speech at the Central Committee Plenum, *Pravda* (24 April 1985).
18. For the origin of the term, see B. Orlov, 'Bespredel, ili chto zhe vy, muzhiki?', *LG* (12 February 1992), p. 11.
19. Wheatcroft, 'Unleashing . . .', p. 85; see below, p. 32.
20. Evtushenko made an important contribution to Khrushchev's de-Stalinization campaign with his poem *Nasledniki Stalina*, *Pravda* (21 October 1962), published with Khrushchev's personal permission. In the Brezhnev era, Evtushenko resorted to safer themes in order to regain his former privileges, a stance which earned him the scathing epithet of 'party poet' from Russian dissidents in the 1970s. This remark was made to me in 1974 by a religious dissident, Alexander Ogorodnikov, and was the general view in the dissident circle around the Russian nationalist journal *Veche*. Western critics also expressed a similar view: Ronald Hingley, in *Russian Writers and Soviet Society* (London, 1979), p. 233 calls Evtushenko a 'licensed liberal'.
21. On Karpov, see N. Condee and V. Padunov, 'The Outposts of Official Art: Recharting Soviet Cultural History', *Framework*, no. 34 (1937) p. 91; *NM*, no. 5 (1982).
22. For a detailed account, see M. Walker, *The Waking Giant: Gorbachev's Russia* (NY, 1986), p. 195.
23. E. Evtushenko, *Fuku!*, *NM*, no. 9 (1985). Evtushenko, who has always been acutely attuned to changes in official policy, made an outspoken

speech demanding intellectual freedom and an end to censorship at the RSFSR Writers' Union in December 1985: *LG*, no. 51 (1988), published only a partial account; a full version was published in *The New York Times* (18 December 1985).

24. J. and C. Garrard, op. cit., pp. 195–6.
25. M. Zakharov, 'Applodismenty ne delyatsya', *LG* (31 July 1985); see also a later article by Zakharov, 'Provodim eksperiment?', *LG* (11 June 1986), which states that several Moscow theatres would be operating an experimental programme in 1987.
26. *Pravda* (26 February 1986).
27. *Materialy samizdata, Arkhiv samizdata*, pp. 1–3.
28. For further discussion, see D. Gillespie, 'Art, Politics and *Glasnost'*: The Eighth Soviet Writers' Congress and Soviet Literature, 1986–7', in M. Scriven and D. Tate (eds), *European Socialist Realism* (Oxford, 1988), pp. 149–70.
29. On Yakovlev, see A. Yakovlev, 'Protiv antiistorizma', *LG* (15 November 1972); R. Pittman, '*Perestroika* and Soviet Cultural Politics: The Case of the Major Literary Journals', *Soviet Studies*, vol. 42, no. 1 (January 1990), pp. 113–14; for the events of 1970, see Marsh, *Soviet Fiction*, p. 16.
30. Pittman, '*Perestroika . . .*', pp. 113–14; Wishnevsky, 'Aleksandr Yakovlev . . .', pp. 1–4.
31. 'Soveshchanie v TsK KPSS', speech by A. Yakovlev, *SK* (23 October 1986), p. 2.
32. A. Brown, 'The Soviet Leadership and the Struggle for Political Reform', *Harriman Institute Forum*, vol. 1, no. 4 (1988), p. 2.
33. See below, p. 34.
34. See G. Lapidus, 'KAL 007 and Chernobyl: The Soviet management of crises', *Survival*, vol. 29, no. 3 (May–June 1987), pp. 215–23.
35. G. Hosking, *The Awakening of the Soviet Union* (London, 1991), pp. 140–1.
36. See Marsh, *Soviet Fiction*, p. 295. Yuri Gladilin, *The Making and Unmaking of a Soviet Writer* (Ann Arbor, 1979), p. 146 states: 'In the last forty years it has become a tradition in our country for executive positions in the field of literature to be sinecures for failures, for failures, naturally, from the ranks of party functionaries.'
37. For further information on Zakharov, see Condee and Padunov, 'Outposts of Official Art', pp. 87–8.
38. Svirski, *History of Post-War Soviet Writing*, pp. 217–18. On Bek, see below, pp. 30–3.
39. On Yakovlev's support for the appointment of Korotich and Zalygin, see Pittman, '*Perestroika . . .*', pp. 114, 119.
40. For further changes in the *NM* board in 1987, see Pittman, '*Perestroika . . .*, pp. 119–20.
41. Trifonov's *Short Stay in the Torture Chamber* (1986) was published in *Znamya* by his friend Grigorii Baklanov, who had been active alongside Trifonov in the campaign of 1970 to protect the journal *NM* and its famous editor Tvardovskii from persecution: see D. Gillespie, *Iurii Trifonov: Unity through Time* (Cambridge, 1992), p. 6. Oleg Chukhontsev's meeting with Brodskii at the International Congress on the Problems of

World Literature in April 1987 led to the publication of some of Brodskii's poems in *NM*: see Pittman, *'Perestroika . . .'*, p. 120.

42. N. Gumilev, 'Stikhi raznykh let', *Ogonek*, no. 17 (April 1986), pp. 26–8; *LR* (11 April 1986). See also a favourable article on Gumilev by V. Karpov, *Ogonek*, no. 36 (1987), pp. 18–24.

43. L. Miller, 'Mertvyi sezon prodolzhaetsya', unpublished article which the Soviet press refused to print, dated 25 October 1990.

44. N. Condee and V. Padunov, 'Spring cleaning in Moscow's House of Cinema', 41st Edinburgh International Film Festival, 8–23 August 1987: Official Programme, pp. 6–9; I. Christie, 'The Cinema', in J. Graffy and G. Hosking (eds), *Culture and the Media in the USSR Today* (Basingstoke and London, 1989), pp. 44–6.

45. Christie, op. cit., pp. 43–77.

46. The transcript of the Politburo meeting of 26 June 1986 was published in *LG* (14 October 1992), p. 11 under the title: 'What "Writers" Ruled the Union!'; it appears genuine enough, but is somewhat suspect, as it was clearly released in 1992 as a contribution to Yeltsin's campaign to discredit Gorbachev.

47. For further discussion, see Marsh, 'Glasnost and Russian Literature', *ASEES*, vol. 6, no. 2 (1992), pp. 21–39; J. Wishnevsky, 'Censorship in These Days of Glasnost', *RL* 595/88 (3 November 1988); Wishnevsky, 'A Rare Insight into Soviet Censorship', *RL*, 372/90 (3 August 1990); A. Rybakov, 'Vchera i segodnya', *LG* (22 May 1992), p. 9. In conversation with I. Zolotusskii, S. Zalygin revealed in *LG* (28 October 1992), p. 5 that 'civil censorship' affected the publication of Solzhenitsyn; the 'atomic censorship' was activated when five ministries protested against G. Medvedev's *Chenobyl'skaya tetrad'*, *NM*, no. 6 (1989); 'military censorship' affected the publication of S. Kaledin's *Stroibat*, *NM*, no. 4 (1989); and 'prison censorship' attacked L. Gabyshev's novel *Odlyan, ili Vozdukh svobody*, *NM*, nos 6–7 (1989).

48. Sakwa, op. cit., p. 9.

49. A. Trehub, 'Gorbachev meets Soviet Writers: a Samizdat Account', *RL Report* (23 October 1986); *Détente*, no. 8 (Winter 1987), p. 11.

50. Gorbachev's speech was delivered in Khabarovsk on 31 July 1986; for the Soviet newspaper report, see *Pravda* (2 August 1986).

51. *NS*, no. 7 (1988), p. 106.

52. M. S. Gorbachev, 'Ubezhdennost' – opora perestroiki. Vstrecha v TsK KPSS', *Pravda* (14 February 1987), p. 1.

53. A remarkable editorial in *Kommunist*, 1987, no. 15 (October 1987) which may well display the hand of Yakovlev, argued that 'Socialist society must learn to value and respect its artists who have the courage to speak the truth.'

54. For a more detailed consideration of the order in which these works were published, see Marsh, 'Glasnost and Russian Literature', pp. 23–9; Graffy, 'The Literary Press', in Graffy and Hosking, *Culture and the Media*, pp. 107–57.

55. A. Romanov, 'The Press We Choose', *Moscow News* (20 December 1987), p. 4; V. Lakshin, 'Aiming Higher: Readers Vote', *Moscow News* (20 December 1987), p. 4.

56. M. S. Gorbachev, 'Otvety M. S. Gorbacheva na voprosy redaktsii gazety "Unita"', *Pravda* (20 May 1987), pp. 1, 3–4.

57. On the use of the terms 'liberal' and 'conservative', see J. Woll, *'Glasnost'* and Soviet Culture', *Problems of Communism* (November–December 1989), pp. 43–4.

58. 'Chto takoe ob"edinenie "Pamyat"'', *RM* (31 July 1987), p. 1.

59. *Pravda* (3 November 1987).

60. N. Andreyeva, 'Ne mogu postupat'sya printsipami', *SR* (13 March 1988), p. 3.

61. A. Roxburgh, *The Second Russian Revolution* (London: BBC, 1991), pp. 83–7.

62. N. Andreyeva, 'Printsipy perestroiki: revolyutsionnost' myshleniya i deistvii', *Pravda* (5 April 1988), p. 2; for a selection of articles critical of Andreyeva, see *CDSP*, vol. XL, no. 15, pp. 7–9, 28.

63. On the rapid growth of informal associations (*neformaly*), from 30,000 by late 1987 to at least 60,000 by early 1989, see *Pravda* (27 December 1987), (10 February 1989).

64. Sakwa, p. 119.

65. See the speeches by Karpov and Bondarev, *XIX konfererentsiya*, vol. 1, pp. 140–5, 223–8.

66. Pittman, *'Perestroika . . .'*, p. 116.

67. For further discussion, see J. Dunlop, 'Solzhenitsyn Begins to Emerge from the Political Void', *RL Report on the USSR*, no. 36 (8 September 1989), pp. 1–6. An account of the meeting between Gorbachev and Zalygin taken from the *samizdat* journal *Referendum* was reported in *RM* (28 October 1989), p. 1.

68. *RM* (18 November 1988), p. 16.

69. Woll, *'Glasnost' . . .'*, p. 48.

70. V. Lakshin, *Solzhenitsyn, Tvardovsky and 'Novy Mir'*, trans. and ed. M. Glenny (Cambridge, MA, 1980).

71. V. Korolenko, 'Pis'ma k Lunacharskomu', *NM*, no. 10 (1988); discussed below, pp. 140–1.

72. A. Romanov, 'The press we can't get hold of', *Moscow News* (28 August 1988), pp. 4, 13.

73. Pittman, *'Perestroika . . .'*, p. 117.

74. *Pravda* (8 January 1989).

75. These were Zalygin's own words, cited in *Washington Post* (21 April 1989).

76. The text of Solzhenitsyn's 1967 'Open Letter to the Fourth Congress of Soviet Writers' was published in V. Konetskii, 'Parizh bez prazdnika', *Neva*, no. 1, (1989), pp. 109–11; Solzhenitsyn's 'Live not by lies' in *XX vek i mir*, no. 2 (1989).

77. N. Il'ina, 'Zdravstvui, plemya molodoe, neznakomoe', *Ogonek*, no. 2 (1988), pp. 23–6; Woll, p. 43.

78. *Pravda* (18 January 1989), p. 6.

79. *Ogonek* (11–18 February 1989), p. 5; *Soviet Analyst*, vol. 19, no. 12 (1990), p. 18.

80. See, for example, V. Chebrikov, *Pravda* (11 February 1989); *Pravda* (27 April 1989).

81. See Woll, p. 40.
82. See the survey in *Ogonek*, no. 44 (1989), p. 5.
83. *Argumenty i fakty*, no. 40 (1989), p. 1.
84. Pittman, 'Writers and Politics', pp. 679–81; no enquiry into this incident was held.
85. Another example was the court case of 1988–90 between the Leningrad writer Nina Katerli and the *Pamyat'* activist A. Romanenko, who contested her view that he was propagating Nazi ideology.
86. *Izvestiya* (20 June 1990).
87. Pittman, 'Writers and Politics', p. 674.
88. See, for example, K. Stepanyan, 'Nuzhna li nam literatura?', *Znamya*, no. 12 (1990), pp. 222–30; M. Kharitonov, 'Apologiya literatury', *LG* (19 June 1991), p. 11; V. Erofeyev, 'Pominki po sovetskoi literature', *Aprel'*, no. 1 (1991), pp. 274–82. See also below, pp. 226–31; and for more detailed discussion, see R. Marsh, 'The Death of Soviet Literature: Can Russian Literature Survive?', *Europe–Asia Studies*, vol. 45, no. 1 (1993), pp. 132–4.
89. The circulation of *Pravda* fell in the space of a year from 9.5 to 6.5 million, although it had a new liberal Marxist editor, Ivan Frolov. At the same time the circulation of most radical and non-party papers increased.
90. Issues 9–12 (1990) were published as numbers 5–8 (1991): see editorial note, *NM*, no. 5 (1991), p. 2.
91. M. Dejevsky, 'Gorbachev Threat to Glasnost', *The Times* (17 January 1991), p. 24.
92. See, for example, the statement of leading intellectuals attacking the Communist Party, 'Prestuplenie rezhima, kotoryi ne knochet skhodit' so stseny: zayavlenie chlenov uchreditel'nogo soveta "MN"', *MN* (20 January 1991), p. 1: signed by playwright A. Gel'man, satirist M. Zhvanetskii, critic Yurii Karyakin, publicists Igor' Klyamkin and Andrei Nuikin, the writer and guitar poet Bulat Okudzhava, the journalist Yurii Chernichenko and the economist and prose writer Nikolai Shmelev.
93. Channel 4 News (5 February 1991).
94. Kravchenko was replaced after the coup of 1991 by Egor Yakovlev, the liberal editor of *MN*.
95. These terms are used by V. Toporov, 'Dnevnik "Literatora"', *Literator* (Leningrad), no. 21 (May 1991), p. 7.
96. For further information, see R. Pittman, 'Writers and the Coup: the Chronology of Events in Summer 1991', *Rusistika*, no. 4 (December 1991), pp. 16–19; Marsh, 'The Death . . .', pp. 125–6.
97. I. Rishina and M. Kudimova, 'Oboidemsya bez raskola? Reportazh s zasedaniya sekretariata pravleniya SP SSSR, 23 avgusta 1991 g.', *LG* (28 August 1991).
98. 'Slovo k narodu', *SR* (23 July 1991), p. 1.
99. 'K pisatelyam Rossii', *LR* (30 August 1991), p. 2; see also Yurii Bondarev's statement, 'Moya pozitsiya', ibid., p. 3.
100. For further discussion, see Marsh, 'The Death . . .', pp. 126–7.
101. 'IX s"ezd pisatelei', *LG* (3 June 1992), p. 1; 'A byl li S"ezd?', *LG* (10 June 1992), p. 3. See *LG* (3 February 1993), p. 3 for Sergei Mikhalkov's

establishment of a 'Veterans' Union' of the MSPS.

102. 'Sodruzhestvo nezavisimykh pisatelei', *LG* (1 January 1992), p. 3.
103. R. Solntsev, 'Ne "alternativnyi", a drugoi', *LG* (6 November 1992), p. 9; M. Kudimova, 'Kak my vidim Soyuz Rossiiskikh Pisatelei', *LG* (30 October 1991), p. 9.
104. See, for example, V. Ognev, 'Tol'ko o zdravom smysle', *LG* (10 February 1993), p. 3.
105. A. Arkhangel'skii, 'Toshchii sokhnet, tolstyi sdokhnet', *LG* (26 June 1991), p. 25; M. Rubantseva, *RG* (18 November 1992), p. 4. For further discussion, see Marsh, 'The Death . . .', pp. 130–2.
106. *Novoe literaturnoe obozrenie* and *Novaya yunost'* respectively.
107. On government subsidies for some literary and youth magazines, see E. Yakovleva, *Izvestiya* (26 August 1993), p. 4.
108. On successful commercial activities organized by Vladimir Filimonov for *NM*, see E. Rybas, *NG* (12 May 1993), p. 2.
109. Alla Latynina, talk at St Antony's College, Oxford (19 October 1993).
110. D. Bykov, *RG* (8 December 1992), p. 7; A. Nemzer, *NG* (10 December 1992), p. 1; A. Latynina, *LG* (16 December 1992), p. 7.
111. V. Toporov, 'Dnevnik "Literatora"', *Literator*, no. 17 (1991), p. 1; no. 18 (1991), p. 5; A. Latynina, 'Chto vperedi?', *LG* (23 January 1991), p. 10; 'Smert' kul'turnoi knigi', *LG* (26 February 1992), p. 7.
112. G. Baluev, the editor of the Leningrad newspaper *Literator*, told me this in March 1991. The phrase 'economic censorship' was also used in an appeal to the Russian government by prominent members of the PEN Club, 'Dorozhaet vse, desheveet lish' tvorcheskii trud', *LG* (26 February 1992), p. 2.
113. For further discussion, see V. Tolz, 'The Soviet Media', *RFE/RL Research Report*, vol. 1, no. 1 (3 January 1992), pp. 30–1; J. Wishnevsky, 'Russia: Liberal Media Criticize Democrats in Power', *RFE/RL Research Report*, vol. 1, no. 2 (10 January 1992), pp. 10–11; D. Hearst, 'Planned Russian censorship "will be worse than under communists"', *Guardian* (16 July 1992), p. 6.
114. *Izvestiya* (12 January 1993), p. 1; *NG* (23 February 1993), p. 1.
115. *Pravda* reappeared a month later.
116. See the selection of articles in *CDPSP*, vol. XLV, no. 40 (1993), pp. 17–20.
117. I. Montgomery, 'Trial by Television', *Guardian* (27 December 1993), Section 2, p. 12.
118. For further discussion of the limitations on free speech, see D. Wedgwood Benn, *From Glasnost to Freedom of Speech: Soviet Openness and International Relations* (London, 1992); S. White, *After Gorbachev* (Cambridge, 1993), pp. 100–1.
119. See below, pp. 232–3. For further discussion, see Marsh, 'The Death . . .', pp. 128–34.

Notes to Chapter 2 The Years 1985–6: Reassessment of History Begins

1. For a detailed discussion, see R. Marsh, *Images of Dictatorship: Stalin in Literature* (London and NY, 1989); on changing Soviet views of Stalin, see S. Cohen, 'The Stalin Question since Stalin', in S. Cohen (ed.), *An End to Silence: Uncensored Opinion in the Soviet Union* (NY, 1982), pp. 42–50; R. Medvedev, 'The Stalin Question', in S. Cohen, A. Rabinowitch and R. Sharlet (eds), *The Soviet Union since Stalin* (Bloomington, 1980), pp. 32–49.

2. R. Marsh, *Soviet Fiction since Stalin* (London, 1986), pp. 21–2.

3. R. W. Davies, *Soviet History in the Gorbachev Revolution* (London, 1989), pp. 2–6.

4. Marsh, *Images of Dictatorship*, pp. 54–64; E. Burdzhalov, *VI*, no. 4 (1956).

5. Marsh, *Images of Dictatorship*, pp. 64–70; Cohen, op. cit., p. 47 cites one Muscovite as saying in 1978: 'Stalin today is less dead than he was twenty years ago.'

6. See the difference of opinion on the influence of *tamizdat* between Yu. Karabchievskii and V. Vozdvizhenskii, in *Vzglyad: kritika, polemika, publikatsii*, vol. 3 (M., 1991) pp. 173–4, 188.

7. Davies, op. cit., pp. 129–30; Marsh, *Images of Dictatorship*, pp. 70–2.

8. Zh. Medvedev, *Gorbachev* (Oxford, 1986), p. 210; Marsh, *Images of Dictatorship*, p. 71.

9. *Pravda* (9 May 1985). According to C. Schmidt-Hauer, *Gorbachev: The Path to Power* (London, 1986), p. 130, Gorbachev did not join in the applause.

10. One former Trotskyist, N. I. Muralov, was rehabilitated without publicity as early as April 1986.

11. See above, p. 11.

12. This subject was subsequently mentioned by the economist Gavriil Popov, in *Nauka i zhizn'*, no. 4 (1987): 'It has been confirmed . . . that Beria had his minions kidnap young girls for pleasure'; A. Antonov-Ovseenko, *Yunost'*, no. 12 (1988), p. 84 relates that during Beria's interrogation in 1953 a list was compiled of the women Beria had raped, including the wives of high government officials. See also F. Burlatskii, *LG* (24 February 1988); *Nedelya*, no. 8 (1988), pp. 11–12; *Izvestiya* (19 October 1988), p. 3. An alternative view of Beria as a potential reformer is being confirmed by archival sources in the 1990s.

13. D. Volkogonov, *Pravda* (9 September 1988); N. Vasetskii, *LG* (4 January 1989); see also below, p. 68.

14. See *The New York Times* (18 December 1985).

15. 'Otvety M. S. Gorbacheva na voprosy gazety "Yumanite"', *Pravda* (8 February 1986), p. 2.

16. 'Mr Gorbachev meets the Writers', trans. R. Sobel, *Détente*, no. 8 (Winter 1987), pp. 11–12.

17. B. Okudzhava, *Devushka moei mechty*, *DN*, no. 10 (1986), pp. 42–7. This simple tale was later amplified by Okudzhava in a moving cycle of poems about the terror, published in January 1988. For further discussion, see G. S. Smith, 'Okudzhava marches on', *SEER*, vol. 66, no. 4 (October 1988), pp. 553–63.

18. Yu. Trifonov, *Nedolgoe prebyvanie v kamere pytok, Znamya*, no. 12 (1986); omitted from Trifonov's cycle *Oprokinutyi dom* (M., 1981).
19. Yu. Trifonov, *Dom na naberezhnoi* (M., 1976); *Starik* (M., 1978).
20. For a fuller discussion, see D. Gillespie, *Iurii Trifonov: Unity through Time* (Cambridge, 1992); N. Kolesnikoff, *Yuri Trifonov: A Critical Study* (Ann Arbor, MI, 1991).
21. On Bubennov, see Marsh, *Images of Dictatorship*, p. 44. A third denouncer, Fyodor Panfyorov, had died in 1960 before the Innsbruck Olympics. Yet another, the veteran writer Marietta Shaginyan (1888–1982) had demanded that the Stalin Prize Trifonov had won for his novel *Studenty* should be rescinded. See *DN*, no. 10 (1987), pp. 255–62.
22. Trifonov was only able to join the Writers' Union in 1957: see *DN*, no. 10 (1989), p. 17.
23. S. Chuprinin, 'Situatsiya', in *Vzglyad*, p. 12.
24. See below, p. 228; M. Zolotonosov, *LG* (21 July 1993), p. 4 refers to Trifonov as 'the best of the permitted writers'; see also Yu. Karabchievskii, in *Vzglyad*, p. 170. For memoirs recalling Trifonov in the Stalin era, see S. Baruzdin, *DN*, no. 10 (1987), pp. 255–62; stories depicting the denunciation and 'working over' (*prorabotka*) of prominent writers and scholars which had taken place in academic institutions during Stalin's time include V. Tendryakov, *Okhota, Znamya*, no. 9 (1988).
25. A. Bek, *Novoe naznachenie, Znamya*, nos 10–11 (1986); for the original publication in the West, see A. Bek, *Novoe naznachenie* (Frankfurt, 1971). For the history of the novel's publication, and further discussion, see Marsh, *Soviet Fiction since Stalin*, pp. 33, 44–5, 72; *Images of Dictatorship*, pp. 76–7, 113–15.
26. G. Baklanov, *Znamya*, no. 10 (1986), pp. 3–4. F. Chapchakov, *LG* (4 February 1987), p. 5 pointed out that 'Certain phrases could have come out of today's newspapers.'
27. For a detailed discussion of the novel's artistic merits, see J. Woodhouse, 'Stalin's Soldier: Aleksandr Bek's *Novoe naznachenie*', *SEER*, vol. 69, no. 4 (October 1991), pp. 601–20.
28. See Marsh, *Images of Dictatorship*, pp. 113–15. Bek's abiding fascination with Stalin's character is reflected in his unfinished novel on the young Stalin: *Na drugoi den'*, *DN*, nos 7–8 (1989).
29. For the reaction of the widow of Tevosyan, Stalin's Minister of Ferrous Metallurgy, see R. Medvedev, *Problems in the Literary Biography of Mikhail Sholokhov*, trans. A. D. P. Briggs (Cambridge and London, 1977), pp. 122–3; G. Svirskii, *Na lobnom meste. Literatura nravstvennovo soprotivleniya (1946–1976 gg.)* (London, 1979), p. 307.
30. Paradoxically, it also corresponds to the view of some 'revisionist' western historians who claim that Stalin himself cannot be held entirely responsible for Stalinism: see J. Arch Getty, *Origins of the Great Purge* (NY, 1985); T. Dunmore, *Soviet Politics 1945–1953* (London, 1984).
31. 'Roman ob odnom romane', *MN* (31 May 1987), p. 16.
32. On Bek's investigative method of writing prose, see 'Kak my pishem', *VL*, no. 5 (1962), pp. 151–2.
33. See A. Bek, *Sob.soch.*, M., 1974–5, IV, p. 581. Metallurgy and engineering formed the subject of his earlier works *Kurako* (1934), *Talant* (1956),

first published as *Zhizn' Berezhkova*, *NM*, nos 1–5 (1956); for further discussion of this relatively conventional novel about an inventor, see Marsh, *Soviet Fiction*, pp. 36–7 *et passim*.

34. A. Bek, *Novoe naznachenie* (Frankfurt, 1971), p. 53.
35. V. Kozlov, *SK* (10 November 1987).
36. A. Egorov, *LG* (3 June 1987). On the contemporary debate about 'cogs' (*vintiki*), see Davies, op. cit., pp. 80–1.
37. F. Chapchakov, *LG*, (4 February 1987), p. 5. No doubt he is referring to Solzhenitsyn's *Odin den' Ivana Denisovicha* and Evtushenko's *Nasledniki Stalina*.
38. D. Volkogonov, *Triumf i tragediya*, *Oktyabr'*, nos 10–12 (1988). For a devastating critique of Volkogonov's work, see M. Heller, 'Mr Stalin, I Presume?', *Survey*, vol. 30, no. 4 (June 1989), pp. 155–63.
39. G. Popov, *Nauka i zhizn'*, no. 4 (1987), pp. 54–65; for further discussion, see Davies, op. cit., pp. 88–90.
40. *Sshibka* was, in fact, Bek's original title for the novel in 1964, rejected by the editors of *NM*, which he explained in a diary entry of 1964: '*Sshibka* – a heavy, unfortunate-sounding word. But it attracted me by its accuracy. *Sshibka* is a medical–scientific term introduced by I. P. Pavlov. And, apart from that, in its common meaning it is a skirmish, a collision, a fight, a battle': see *Novoe naznachenie* (M., 1987), pp. 3–4.
41. In real life Molotov was sent as ambassador to Mongolia after the 'Anti-Party Group Affair' of 1957.
42. See, for example, M. Gorbachev, *Pravda* (26 June 1987).
43. Baklanov, interview with *MN* (6 November 1988), p. 11. On Popov, see below, p. 170.
44. L. Lazarev, *Oktyabr'*, no. 11 (1989), pp. 182–8.
45. I am grateful to Riitta Pittman for her account of a talk by Yakovlev at St Antony's College, Oxford, January 1992. On Yakovlev's discussion with Elem Klimov, head of the Film-Makers' Union, see Roxburgh, *The Second Russian Revolution*, pp. 61–2.
46. J. Graffy, 'The Arts', in M. McCauley (ed.), *Gorbachev and Perestroika* (London, 1990), p. 200. Shevardnadze, then head of the Georgian Communist Party, had encouraged Abuladze to make the film in the National Georgia Film Studio from 1979 on the basis of a state commission. He may have been sympathetic to Abuladze's project because his wife's parents had been victims of Stalin's purges.
47. A. Wilson, 'Cinemas packed to see Stalin's ghost laid low', *Observer* (16 November 1986), p. 17.
48. Davies, op. cit., p. 8.
49. For a selection of critical articles, see *CDSP*, vol. XXXIX, no. 5 (4 March 1987), pp. 1–7, 23.
50. Davies, op. cit., p. 183.
51. Hosking, op. cit., p. 142–3.
52. T. Mamaladze, *Izvestiya* (31 January 1987), p. 3. For Abuladze's response to this last question, see *Novoe vremya*, no. 6 (1987), p. 29.
53. For young people's dislike of the scene in which Varlam's grandson Tornike Aravidze commits suicide, see Mamaladze, op. cit., p. 3.
54. 'Ya sdelal etot fil'm dlya molodykh . . .', Alla Gerber in conversation

with Tengiz Abuladze, *Yunost'*, no. 5 (1987), p. 82.

55. See L. Pol'skaya's interview with Abuladze, *LG* (25 February 1987), p. 8. The director may be referring obliquely to Solzhenitsyn's as yet unpublished article 'Live not by Lies'. Abuladze also points to another popular contemporary film on the subject of young people's hatred of falsehood, Juris Podnieks's *Is it Easy to be Young?* (1986).

56. See, for example, N. Izmailova, *Nedelya* (2–8 February 1987), p. 19.

57. T. Khlopyankina, *Moskovskaya pravda* (4 February 1987), p. 4. At this time only the year 1937, when party members were purged, could be mentioned.

58. T. Abuladze, *LG* (25 February 1987), p. 8: he refers to famous Georgians, such as the film director Sandro Akhmeteli and the Georgian Party leader Mamia Orakhelashveli, who met their deaths in 1938, but had subsequently had streets in Tbilisi named after them.

59. Later discussed by A. Antonov-Ovseyenko, *Neva*, no. 11 (1988); Nove, op. cit., p. 102.

60. Abuladze, *LG* (25 February 1987), p. 8. He also quotes Eisenstein: 'The truth always triumphs in our country, but often our lives aren't long enough.' Abuladze himself died in 1994.

61. *LG* (6 May 1987), p. 10.

62. Mamaladze, op. cit.; an almost identical phrase, 'the truth adopted by the 27th CPSU Congress' is used by Izmailova.

63. Abuladze, op. cit. See also the comments of Mamaladze, op. cit.; G. Kapralov, *Pravda* (7 February 1987), p. 3. Unfortunately, people like Avel' are still flourishing under the new capitalist system in post-communist Russia.

64. L. G. Ionin, '. . . i vozzovet proshedshee', *Sotsiologicheskie issledovaniya*, no. 3 (1987), pp. 62–72.

65. Ibid., pp. 64, 70.

66. The word used is *khram*, a Georgian Christian church.

67. Mamaladze, op. cit.

68. I. Klyamkin, 'Kakaya ulitsa vedet k khramu?', *NM*, no. 11 (1987), pp. 150–81; summarized and discussed by T. Shanin, *Détente*, no. 11 (1988).

69. On the expanding theatrical repertoire of 1986, see Yu. Gladil'shchikov, *SR* (23 February 1986), p. 1. Other plays depicting a trial included Aitmatov's *Farewell, Gulsary!* and Roman Solntsev's *The Article*, both at the Sphere Theatre Studio, and the Film Actors' Theatre's production of *I Demand a Trial*, adapted by the film director Evgenii Tashkov from Oleg Perekalin's play *Hot Spot*.

70. M. Shatrov, *Ogonek*, no. 45 (1988).

71. M. Shatrov, *SK* (5 May 1988); Shatrov's complaint is disputed by the conservative V. Bushin, 'Kogda somnenie umestno', *NS*, no. 4 (1989), p. 174. Shatrov's four films on Lenin, 'Shtrikhi k portretu Lenina', made years earlier and saved only by chance, were also shown on Soviet television in Gorbachev's time.

72. This happened in the case of some of the 'Lenin plays' of Nikolai Pogodin.

73. For a vivid account of the original production, see D. Joravsky, 'Glasnost theater', *New York Review of Books*, vol. 35, no. 17 (10 November 1988), pp. 34–9.

74. Discussed by Gladil'shchikov, SR (23 February 1986) p. 1.
75. Discussed in *LR* (21 March 1987), p. 9.
76. M. Shatrov, *Moskovskii komsomolets* (13 April 1988).
77. I am grateful to a student for providing me with the text of this discussion, although I have been unable to trace the exact reference. Another example of Shatrov's caution is his portrayal of the hard-line French Communist André Marty instead of Stalin himself. Because Marty was no longer a household name in 1986, the director chose to present him with a mane of black hair and a semi-military tunic which were reminiscent of Stalin.
78. In particular, it is sometimes argued that Lenin closely followed Nechaev's fanatical injunctions in 'Catechism of a Revolutionary'.
79. For a positive review emphasizing that 'life goes on', see Yu. Rybakov, *SK* (15 March 1987), p. 2.

Notes to Chapter 3   The Second Phase of *Glasnost*: the Year 1987

1. V. Rasputin, *Pozhar*, *NS*, no. 7 (1985); V. Astaf'ev, *Pechal'nyi detektiv*, *Otkyabr'*, no. 1 (1986); Ch. Aitmatov, *Plakha*, *NM*, nos 6–9 (1986).
2. This is also the view of M. Dejevsky, 'Glasnost and the Soviet Press', in J. Graffy and G. Hosking (eds), *Culture and the Media in the USSR Today* (London, 1989), pp. 129–30; G. Hosking, 'At Last an Exorcism', *TLS* (9–15 October 1987), pp. 1111–12.
3. E. Ligachev, *Pravda* (24 March 1987), p. 2; ibid. (17 September 1987), p. 2; *SK* (7 July 1987, p. 2); V. Chebrikov (11 September 1987), p. 3.
4. See, for example, M. S. Gorbachev, *Pravda* (28 January 1987), pp. 1–5; 'Ubezhdennost – opora perestroiki. Vstrecha v TsK KPSS', *Pravda* (14 February 1987), p. 1; 'Otvety M. S. Gorbacheva na voprosy redaktsii "Unita"', *Pravda* (20 May 1987), pp. 1, 3, 4. For further discussion of Gorbachev's policy, see R. Marsh, *Images of Dictatorship: Stalin in Literature* (London and NY, 1989), pp. 72–3, 79, 98–9.
5. A. Hewett and V. Winston (eds), *Milestones in Glasnost and Perestroyka* (Washington, 1991), p. 505.
6. A. Akhmatova, *Rekviem*, *Oktyabr'*, no. 3 (1987), pp. 103–5; *Oktyabr'* upstaged the journal *Neva*, which had announced the publication of *Rekviem*, by using a *samizdat* copy of Akhmatova's poem, released by the poet in 1963. *Rekviem* later also appeared in *Neva*, no. 6 (1987), pp. 74–9.
7. For another classic work on a similar theme, see L. Chukovskaya, *Sof'ya Petrovna*, *Neva*, no. 2 (1988).
8. A. Urban, 'I upalo kamennoe slovo', *LG* (22 April 1987), p. 4. The re-evaluation of Zhdanov's role in Russian culture in 1989 culminated in the renaming of Leningrad University, which had formerly borne Zhdanov's name: see *Pravda* (18 January 1989), p. 3.
9. Cited in V. Oskhotskii, *VI*, no. 6 (1988), p. 43; for an attack on other 'returned literature', see D. Urnov, *LO*, no. 1 (1989), p. 16.
10. A. Tvardovskii, 'Po pravu pamyati', *Znamya*, no. 2 (1987); *NM*, no. 3.
11. On the publishing history of Tvardovskii's poem, see E. Sidorov,

'Osvobozhdenie – o poeme Aleksandra Tvardovskogo "Po pravu pamyati"',
LG (4 March 1987), p. 4. See also the memoir of Tvardovskii's brother
Ivan, *Yunost'*, no. 3 (1988), pp. 10–32, with afterword by A. Tvardovskii's
colleague Yurii Burtin; discussed in R. W. Davies, *Soviet History in the
Gorbachev Revolution* (London, 1989), p. 51.

12. *NM*, no. 3 (1987), p. 198.
13. 'Iz pochty "Znameni": chitateli o poeme A. T. Tvardovskogo "Po pravu
    pamyati"', *Znamya*, no. 8 (1987), pp. 227–36. Note from the editors,
    p. 228.
14. Introductory letter by P. M. Chaplin, war veteran, member of CP since
    1944, ibid., p. 227.
15. See, for example, M. A. Kaitmanova, ibid., p. 230.
16. Mariya Stepanovna Dranga from the town of Makeevka, ibid., p. 235.
17. A. Sorokin from Irkutsk, ibid., p. 235.
18. *Izvestiya* (26 August 1988), p. 3; *MN* (4 September 1988); A. Nove,
    Glasnost in Action (London, 1989), p. 35.
19. The monument was constructed of stone taken from the Solovki islands
    prison camp.
20. For further discussion, see R. Wells, 'The Genetics Dispute and Soviet
    Literature', *Irish Slavonic Studies*, no. 1 (1980), pp. 20–42.
21. For full accounts, see Z. Medvedev, *The Rise and Fall of T. D. Lysenko*,
    trans. I. M. Lerner (NY, 1969); D. Joravsky, *The Lysenko Affair* (Cam-
    bridge, MA, 1970).
22. One of the official reasons for the imprisonment of the biologist Zhores
    Medvedev in a psychiatric hospital in 1970 was that he had written a
    samizdat history of the genetics dispute: see R. Medvedev and Z. Medvedev,
    A Question of Madness, trans. E. de Kadt (London, 1971), p. 44.
23. On L. A. Zil'ber, see 'Peredat' lyudyam', *Ogonek*, no. 21 (May 1988);
    S. Dyachenko, 'Podvig', *Ogonek*, no. 47 (1987), pp. 10–12; on N. P.
    Dubinin, see E. Leont'eva, *Sovetskaya industriya* (4 January 1987), p. 4.
24. See, for example, L. Sidorovskii, *LR* (20 November 1987) which con-
    tains quotations from Vavilov's letters to Beria after his arrest. For dis-
    cussion of Lysenkoism in the Soviet media, see Davies, *Soviet History*,
    pp. 70–2.
25. D. Granin, interview with I. Rishina, *LG* (27 May 1987), p. 4.
26. V. Amlinskii, *I opravdan budet kazhdyi chas*, *Yunost'*, nos 10–11 (1986).
27. This is noted by E. Sidorov, *LG* (28 January 1987), p. 4, who states that
    'Academician Lysenko was no Shakespearean villain.'
28. E. Sidorov, *LG* (28 January 1987), p. 4.
29. D. Granin, *Zubr*, *NM*, nos 1–2 (1987).
30. Interview with Granin by I. Rishina, *LG* (27 May 1987), p. 4.
31. D. Granin, *Zubr* (M., 1989), p. 123.
32. Zavenyagin is also presented in a positive light in Rybakov's *Deti Arbata*.
33. A. Solzhenitsyn, *V kruge pervom*, *NM*, nos 1–5 (1990).
34. See, for example, Yu. Andreyev, *Pravda* (14 June 1987), p. 3; A. Turkov,
    LG (11 March 1987), p. 4.
35. G. Popov, 'Sistema i zubry', *Nauka i zhizn'*, no. 3 (1988), pp. 56–64.
36. A. Kazintsev, 'Pod semeinym abazhurom', *SR* (17 June 1987), p. 4.
37. V. Kozhinov, *NS*, no. 7 (1988), p. 106. For other conservative attacks on

Granin, see V. Bondarenko, 'Ocherki literaturnykh nravov', *Moskva*, no. 12 (1987), pp. 189–90; D.Il'in, 'Neprikasaemaya literatura', *NS*, no. 6 (1989), pp. 140–9.

38. Granin, *Zubr*, p. 124.
39. S. Rassadin, 'Vse podelit'?', *Ogonek*, no. 20 (May 1988), pp. 14–16.
40. V. T., 'Pravda i polupravda v novoi knige o sovetskoi nauke', *RM*, no. 3677 (1987), pp. 11, 14.
41. The critic is mistaken in thinking that *The Buffalo* was the first work published in the USSR to refer to Beria's role, as it had already been mentioned in Granin's earlier work *Into the Storm*, published during the Khrushchev 'thaw': see D. Granin, *Idu na grozu* (M., L., 1964).
42. Z. Medvedev, *The Medvedev Papers: The Plight of Soviet Science Today*, trans. V. Rich (London, 1971), pp. 71–112; R. Berg, *Sukhovei: Vospominaniya genetika* (NY, 1983), pp. 221–7, 230, 231, 233.
43. V. I. Lenin, *Polnoe sob.soch.* (M., 1965), vol. 54, pp. 265–6.
44. D. Granin, 'Zubr v kholodil'nike', *LG* (21 July 1993), p. 3; for the lively post for and against Granin's *Zubr*, and the unsuccessful attempt to secure Timofeyev-Resovskii's rehabilitation in 1988, see note by I. Rishina, ibid.
45. D. Paul and C. Krimbas, 'Nikolai V. Timofeeff-Ressovsky, *Scientific American* (February 1992), pp. 64–70.
46. V. Dudintsev, *Belye odezhdy*, *Neva*, nos 1–4 (1987). Granin helped to secure the publication of Dudintsev's novel: see I. Rishina, *LG* (27 May 1987), p. 4.
47. Dudintsev was reportedly working on a novel about the Lysenko affair in 1964: see M. Mihajlov, *Moscow Summer* (London, 1966), p. 44.
48. Interview with Dudintsev by N. Zagal'skaya, *SK* (17 February 1987), p. 6; republished in *Belye odezhdy* (M., 1988), pp. 5–11.
49. Dudintsev, *Belye odezhdy*, pp. 408–9. Quoted in full in Davies, pp. 74–5.
50. Dudintsev, op. cit., p. 653.
51. Ibid., p. 88.
52. Pavlik Morozov was denounced as a 'symbol of legalized and romanticized treachery' in *Yunost'*, no. 3 (1988), p. 53; see also discussion in *Izvestiya* (15 July 1989), p. 3. The cult of Pavlik was also exposed in S. Govorukhin's influential film of 1990, *'This is no way to live'*.
53. Some of Stalin's interrogators did resist illegality, as in the case of T. Deribas, head of the NKVD in the Far East: see E. Al'bats, *MN* (8 May 1988). *KP* (21 August 1988) refers to the shooting of 74 military procurators for having 'sabotaged' the preparation of trials. The network of good people in Soviet society is evoked by the epigraph from *Revelation*, chap. 7, vv. 13–14; chap. 3, v. 3.
54. For a less sympathetic view of Simonov's opportunism, see the interview with V. Kaverin, *LG* (15 June 1988).
55. Interview with Dudintsev, *Belye odezhdy*, p. 9. For Dezhkin's explanation, see pp. 214–15.
56. Ibid., p. 11.
57. I. Zolotusskii, 'Vozvyshayushchee slovo', *LO*, no. 7 (1988).
58. V. Kamyanov, in *Vzglyad: kritika, polemika, publikatsii*, vol. 3 (M., 1991), p. 246.

59. See V. Shaposhnikov, *LG* (13 May 1987); L. Ionin, *Izvestiya* (2 June 1987), p. 3.
60. A similar debate took place in 1956–7 over Dudintsev's novel *Ne khlebom edinym*. In an interview with N. Kataeva, *Pravda* (10 May 1987), p. 3, Dudintsev refers to the numerous 'Ryadnos' who still exist in Soviet society.
61. This view is expressed through the mouth of the secret police colonel Sveshnikov (whose patronym is 'Porfir'evich', recalling Porfirii Petrovich in *Crime and Punishment*).
62. For polemics over Dudintsev's novel, see *MN* (4 October 1987), p. 8; *Znamya* no. 9 (1987), p. 203.
63. *MN* (15 May 1988).
64. V. Amlinskii, 'Daty, sroki, imena...', interview with Elena Yakovich, *LG* (4 May 1988), p. 5 after the publication of Amlinskii's new documentary work on the political fate of Nikolai Bukharin, *Na zabroshennykh grobnitsakh*, *Yunost'*, no. 3 (1988).
65. V. Soifer, 'Gor'kii plod. Iz istorii sovremennosti', *Ogonek*, nos 1–2 (1988); A. Nove, *Glasnost' in Action* (London, 1989) p. 131.
66. S. Antonov, *Vas'ka*, *Yunost'*, nos 3–4 (1987). Antonov's work was set in type by the journal *Yunost'* (which published it a decade later), but forbidden by the censorship in 1975.
67. Margarita figures as 'Rit'ka', the young daughter of a dispossessed 'kulak', in Antonov's novel *The Ravines*: see below, pp. 76–7.
68. Antonov, *LG* (17 June 1987).
69. Mitya also figures as the child hero in Antonov's novel *The Ravines*.
70. *LG* (17 June 1987).
71. In the book version of the novel Antonov made a slight revision to accentuate this parallel: 'he scratched his head, thought for a little and added ...'.
72. Yu. Trifonov, *Ischeznovenie*, *DN*, no. 1 (1987); for more detailed discussion, see D. Gillespie, *Iurii Trifonov: Unity through Time* (Cambridge, 1992), pp. 180–93.
73. Yu. Gladil'shchikov, *LR* (27 March 1987), p. 11.
74. A. Koestler, *Slepyashchaya t'ma*, first published in Russia, *Neva*, nos 7–8 (1988); the tragedy of his hero Rubashev is said to be based on that of Bukharin.
75. See, for example, V. Trifonov, *Vremya i mesto*, *Sob.soch. v chetyrekh tomakh*, vol. 4 (1987), p. 260 (first published *DN*, nos 9–10 (1981)).
76. A. Pristavkin, *Nochevala tuchka zolotaya*, *Znamya*, nos 3–4 (1987). Tvardovsky's *Po pravu pamyati* had earlier referred to the deportation of the Crimean Tartars, Kalmyk and Ingush. For an interesting review of Pristavkin's novel, see Hosking, *TLS* (9–15 October 1987), pp. 1111–12.
77. V. Gerasimov, *Stuk v dver'*, *Oktyabr'*, no. 2 (1987).
78. A. Latynina, *LG* (15 April 1987), p. 4.
79. D. Kugul'tinov, *LG* (7 September 1988); figures for the deportations in 1943–4 were given in *LG* (17 May 1989).
80. I. Prelovskaya, *Izvestiya* (12 March 1992), p. 3.
81. V. Vyzhutovich, *Izvestiya* (13 October 1992), p. 2. Yakovlev was obliged to appear because Gorbachev refused.

Notes to Chapter 4 Two Key Writers: Shatrov and Rybakov

1. A. Rybakov, *Deti Arbata*, *DN*, nos 4–6 (1987).
2. Part 1 was announced by *NM* in 1966; Part 2 by *Oktyabr'* in 1978.
3. For the history of the novel's writing and publication, see Rybakov's interview with I. Rishina, 'Zarubki na serdtse', *LG* (19 August 1987), p. 4; see also an earlier interview with Rybakov, *LG* (20 August 1969).
4. On Rybakov's decision not to circulate his work in *samizdat*, see F. Barringer, 'Soviets to read of mass terror', *International Herald Tribune*, Paris (16 March 1987), p. 2.
5. For further discussion, see Marsh, *Images of Dictatorship*, pp. 80–97; R. Marsh, 'Stalin and Stalinism in Contemporary Literature: the Case of Anatolii Rybakov', in Robert Lewis (ed.), *Stalin and Stalinism: Forty Years On* (Exeter, forthcoming).
6. Letter from A. Brandt, *LG* (19 August 1987), p. 4.
7. *LO*, no. 1 (1988).
8. For the topicality of this issue, see M. Gorbachev, *Pravda* (26 February 1986); for discussions about NEP which culminated in the introduction of the New Economic Mechanism in July 1987, see R. W. Davies, *Soviet History in the Gorbachev Revolution* (London, 1989), pp. 27–46.
9. A. Latsis, *S raznykh tochek zreniya: 'Deti Arbata' Anatoliya Rybakova* (M., 1990), p. 87.
10. A. Latynina, *LG* (14 December 1988), p. 4.
11. A. Latsis, *Izvestiya* (17 August 1987), p. 4; J. Barber, 'Children of the Arbat', *Détente*, no. 11 (1988), p. 9; Davies, op. cit., p. 187; Marsh, op. cit., pp. 94, 96; N. Kuznetsova, 'Pokayanie ili preklonenie? O romane Anatolya Rybakova "Deti Arbata"', *RM* (30 October 1987), p. 12; E. Gessen, 'Kommentarii k kommentariyam', *Strana i mir*, no. 6 (1987), pp. 133–8; B. Vail, 'Stalynskoi ulybkoyu sogreta . . .', *RM* (15 January 1988), pp. 10–11.
12. A. Latsis, *Izvestiya* (17 August 1987), p. 4.
13. N. Kuznetsova, *RM* (30 October 1987), p. 12.
14. Cf R. Conquest, *The Great Terror: A Reassessment* (London, 1992), pp. 37–52 with A. Getty, *Origins of the Great Purges* (Cambridge, 1985), pp. 207–10.
15. See Rybakov's interview with I. Rishina, 'Zarubki na serdtse', *LG* (19 August 1987), p. 4.
16. Barber; on the XVII Congress, see S. Mikoyan, *Ogonek* no. 50 (1987), p. 6. On the problem of psycho-history, see below, pp. 239–40.
17. Interviews with Vyacheslav Ogryzko, in *S raznykh tochek*, pp. 48–9. Rybakov rejected Rasputin's criticism in *MN* (17 July 1988), p. 11. B. Okudzhava, in *Ogonek*, no. 27 (July 1987), p. 5 took de-Stalinization further than Rybakov himself, referring to the widespread nature of the civilian purges in the 1930s.
18. A. Rybakov, interview with I. Rishina, *LG* (19 August 1987), p. 4; A. Latsis, 'S tochki zreniya sovremennika', *Izvestiya* (17 August 1987), p. 4.
19. Letters from K. Sidorova, L. Strizhakova, *LG* (19 August 1987), p. 4; see also angry letter from R. Magomedov, Dagestan, *LG* (19 August 1987).
20. A. Malyugin, *S raznykh tochek*, p. 259.

21. A. Turkov, *LG* (8 July 1987), p. 4; L. Anninskii, *S raznykh tochek*, p. 32 praised Rybakov's recreation of Stalin's style of speaking and writing.
22. N. Kuznetsova, *RM* (30 October 1987), pp. 12–14.
23. See V. Kozhinov, 'Pravda i istina', *NS* no. 4 (1988), pp. 160–75; for further discussion, see Davies, op. cit., p. 187; Marsh, op. cit., p. 94; Barber, op. cit.
24. *LG* (14 December 1988), p. 4.
25. S. Kunyaev, 'Razmyshleniya na starom Arbate', *NS* no. 7 (1988), pp. 26–7; see also Kozhinov, *S raznykh tochek*, p. 153; a similar point is made about Soviet interpretations by Solzhenitsyn in *The Gulag Archipelago 1918–1956*, vol. 1, transl. T. P. Whitney (Fontana, London, 1974), pp. 24–5.
26. A. Latynina, 'Dogovorit' do kontsa', *S raznykh tochek*, p. 256.
27. See Davies, op. cit., pp. 59–99 *et passim*; Nove, op. cit., pp. 15–36, 73–102. In May 1988 an influential television film, *Protsess (The Trial)*, provided a frank discussion of Stalinism and the purge trials.
28. Three of the most influential articles were V. Kozhinov, 'Pravda i istina'; V. Selyunin, 'Istoki', *NM*, no. 5 (1988), pp. 162–89; V. Klyamkin, 'Kakaya ulitsa vedet k khramu?', *NM* no. 11 (1987), pp. 150–88. For a collection of comments on Stalin both by his contemporaries, and by Soviet and émigré writers and historians of the Gorbachev era, see Kh.Kobo (ed. and comp.), *Osmyslit' kul't Stalina* (M., 1989).
29. These included D.Volkogonov, *Triumf i tragediya, Oktyabr'*, nos 10–12 (1988); (Volkogonov later became Yeltsin's military adviser); R. Medvedev, *O Staline i stalinizme, Znamya*, nos 1–4 (1989); S. Cohen, *Bukharin: politicheskaya biografiya* (M., 1989); R. Conquest, *Bol'shoi terror, Neva*, nos 9–12 (1989); nos 1–8 (1990). Roy Medvedev's *On Stalin and Stalinism* (1989), articles in the revitalized historical journal *Voprosy istorii*, and translations of works by foreign historians, such as S. Cohen, *Bukharin: politicheskaya biografiya* (M., 1989); R. Conquest, *Bol'shoi terror, Neva*, nos 9–12 (1989); nos 1–8 (1990).
30. M. Shatrov, *Brestskii mir, NM*, no. 4 (1987). For further discussion, see D. Joravsky, *New York Review of Books* (10 November 1988), pp. 34–9; Marsh, *Images of Dictatorship* (London and NY, 1989), pp. 78–9; A. Nove, *Glasnost in Action* (London, 1989), pp. 37–9.
31. See the description of the play's denouement in G. Volkov, *SK* (31 December 1987), p. 4.
32. For a cautious review by a Communist, see V. Maksimova, *Pravda* (28 January 1988), p. 6.; Volkov takes a more positive view. Lenin's *Letter to the Congress*, part of his *Testament*, was published in *MN*, (18 January 1987).
33. Joravsky, op. cit., p. 35.
34. Maksimova, for example, sees Trotsky as 'an actor, a hypocrite, a conjuror'; for a more balanced view, see *Izvestiya*, (26 December 1987).
35. See Shatrov's discussion with the American historian Stephen Cohen, *MN* (14 June 1987).
36. M. Shatrov, *Dal'she ... dal'she ... dal'she!*, *Znamya*, no. 1 (1988). For further discussion, see Marsh, *Images of Dictatorship*, pp. 99–102; Davies, op. cit., pp. 139–41; Joravsky, op. cit.; J. Shapiro, 'Shatrov and his critics:

on the debate about "Dal'she . . . dal'she . . . dal'she"', unpublished paper presented to Soviet Industrialization Project Seminar, CREES, Birmingham, May 1988; D. Spring, 'Stalin Exits Stage Left', *THES* (12 February 1988), p. 14; J. Burbank, 'The Shatrov Controversy', *Michigan Quarterly Review*, vol. 28, no. 4 (Fall 1989), pp. 580–8.

37. For further discussion, see below, pp. 158–9, 182–3.
38. F. Lastochkin, 'Premiere: better to go further than nowhere', *Moscow News*, no. 15 (1988).
39. Later published in an interview with Bukharin's widow Anna Larina: see F. Medvedev, 'Pravda vsegda sovremenna', *Ogonek*, no. 17 (1988), p. 31.
40. Stalin's role in the murder of Trotsky was later admitted in N. Vasetskii, 'Likvidatsiya', *LG* (4 January 1989).
41. Franker discussions of the purge trials were later contained in Rybakov's *1935-yi i drugie gody*, Arthur Koestler's *Darkness at Noon*, Shalamov's *Kolymskie rasskazy* and Solzhenitsyn's *The Gulag Archipelago*.
42. Yu. Afanas'ev and M. Shatrov, 'The Chime of History', *Moscow News*, no. 45 (1987).
43. V. V. Gorbunov and V. V. Zhuravlev, 'Chto my khotim uvidet' v zerkale revolyutsii?', *SR* (28 January 1988); G. Gerasimenko, O. Obichkin, B. Popov, all listed as 'doktor istoricheskikh nauk, professor', 'Nepodsudna tol'ko pravda: o p'ese M. Shatrova', *Pravda* (15 February 1988).
44. For a cautious Soviet view, see Pavel Volubuev's press conference of 4 November 1987; reproduced in 'Novosti' pamphlet *The October Revolution and Perestroika* (1988), p. 25; for further discussion, see A. Rabinowitch, *The Bolsheviks Come to Power* (London, 1979), p. 267.
45. For Shatrov's view of Trotsky as a 'petty bourgeois revolutionary', see *Suddeutsche Zeitung* (4 February 1988); Igor' Klyamkin, in *NM*, no. 11 (1987) argues that the industrialization proposals of the Left Opposition were not intended to overstep the bounds of NEP.
46. *Znamya*, no. 1 (1988), p. 41.
47. D. Volkogonov, 'Fenomen Stalina', *LG* (9 December 1987).
48. For further discussion, see Burbank, op. cit., p. 588, n. 5. For the negative responses, see *Znamya*, no. 5 (1988), pp. 219–36; for editorial comment, see p. 219.
49. Burbank, op. cit., p. 585.
50. Davies, op. cit., p. 140; V. Glagolev, *Pravda* (10 January 1988); Profs G. Gerasimenko and O. Obichkin, *Pravda* (15 February 1988).
51. Discussed in Davies, op. cit., p. 140.
52. Editorial comment, *Pravda* (15 February 1988).
53. Dr V. V. Gorbunov and Prof. V. V. Zhuravlev, *SR* (28 January 1988).
54. V. I. Lenin, *Polnoe sob.soch.*, 5th edn, vol. 45, p. 356; see also E. Yakovlev, *MN*, no. 4 (1989).
55. D. Kazutin, 'Istorii podsudny vse', *MN*, no. 2 (1988).
56. *SK* (4 February 1988), p. 3.
57. N. Andreyeva, 'Ne mogu postupat'sya printsipami', *Sovetskaya Rossiya* (13 March 1988): see above, pp. 19–20.
58. H. Pearson, *The Smith of Smiths* (1934), chapter 3, p. 54.
59. She also adds that 'even Rybakov, the author of *Children of the Arbat*, has frankly admitted that he borrowed certain plot elements from *émigré*

publications'. For the response to Andreyeva, which does not mention Shatrov, see *Pravda* (5 April 1988).
60. See the letter signed by Zakharov, Tovstonogov, Gel'man and Rozov, *Pravda* (29 February 1988), p. 2.
61. A. Turkov, 'Chtoby plyt' v revolyutsiyu dal'she', *LG* (8 August 1987), p. 4.
62. *LG*, (29 July 1987), p. 1.
63. A. Latynina, *LG* (14 December 1988), p. 4.
64. *Pravda* (6 February 1988); *Nedelya*, no. 7 (1987), pp. 16–17.
65. Yu. Feofanov, *Izvestiya* (14 June 1988).
66. See Gorbachev's attack on the 'essentially anti-Soviet' nature of Trotskyism, *Pravda* (3 November 1987). By 1989 Trotsky had still not been rehabilitated, although his works began to be published in the USSR: see P. Broué, 'Gorbachev and History', in S. White (ed.), *New Directions in Soviet History* (Cambridge, 1992), pp. 8–10; J. Shapiro, 'The prophet returned?', *Revolutionary History*, vol. 2, no. 1 (summer 1989), pp. 54–6.
67. For criticism of Rybakov, see A. Latynina, *LG* (14 December 1988), p. 4; M. Chudakova, *LO* no. 1 (1990); M. Zolotonosov, *Oktyabr'*, no. 4 (1991); L. Bakhnov, *DN*, no. 12 (1990).
68. Conversations with historians from Yaroslavl' attending the conference: 'Stalin: Forty Years On', Exeter, March 1993.
69. M. Zolotonosov, '"Deti Arbata". Nostal'gicheskie zametki o pozdnesotsialisticheskoi literature', *MN* (10 October 1993), p. 5B.

Notes to Chapter 5   Collectivization and the Repression of the Peasantry

1. For discussion in the press and historical journals, see A. Nove, *Glasnost in Action: Cultural Renaissance in Russia* (London, 1989), pp. 73–81; R. W. Davies, *Soviet History in the Gorbachev Revolution* (London, 1989), pp. 1–2, 47–58.
2. M. Alekseyev, *Drachuny* (M., 1982); for earlier, cautious references, see I. Stadnyuk, *Lyudi ne angely* (M., 1962); V. Tendryakov, *Konchina, Moskva*, no. 3 (1968). Articles on collectivization by historians such as V. P. Danilov had also appeared before Gorbachev's accession.
3. B. Mozhaev, *Muzhiki i baby, Don*, nos 1–3 (1987); see also A. Tvardovskii's *Po pravu pamyati, Znamya*, no. 2 (1987); *NM*, no. 3; discussed by E. Sidorov, *LG* (4 March 1987), p. 4; see above, pp. 43–4.
4. B. Mozhaev, 'Ot avtora', *Don*, no. 3 (1987), p. 106. The first part of the novel depicted the villages in the NEP period; see B. Mozhaev, *Muzhiki i baby* (M., 1976). For further discussion of Part I, see D. Gillespie, 'History, Politics and the Russian Peasant: Boris Mozhaev and the Collectivization of Agriculture', *SEER*, vol. 67, no. 2 (April 1989), pp. 183–210.
5. For its publishing history, see *KO* (20 November 1987), p. 3; B. Mozhaev, 'Lyudi soprotivleniya', *MN* (31 July 1988), p. 10. The novel was approved by Glavlit, but rejected or delayed by almost all the leading journals, including *NS, DN* and *NM* (under its then editor Vladimir Karpov).

6. It aroused so much interest that three publishing houses – Sovetskii pisatel', Sovremennik and Kniga – published it in book form in 1988.

7. On Tikhonov's views, see Davies, op. cit., p. 49.

8. A. Yakovlev, cited in *Vestnik Akademii Nauk*, no. 6 (1987), p. 69; M. S. Gorbachev, *Pravda* (3 November 1987).

9. See, for example, M. Alekseyev, *LG* (25 November 1987); Yu. Chernichenko, *LG* (13 April 1988); extracts from a previously unpublished novel by V. Sosnyura, *LG* (11 May 1988); V. Astaf'ev, *KP*, (12 May 1988); I. Tvardovskii, *Yunost'*, no. 3 (1988), pp. 10–32.

10. *MN* (12 July 1987); Z. Maslennikova, *Neva*, nos 9–10 (1988).

11. A. Platonov, *Kotlovan*, *NM*, no. 6 (1987); for another classic work on this theme, see Nikolai Klyuev's poem *Pogorel'shchina*, *NM*, no. 7 (1987).

12. J. Brodsky, 'Catastrophes in the Air', in *Less than One* (London: Penguin, 1987).

13. A similar technique is used effectively by V. Voinovich in *Zhizn' i neobychainye priklyucheniya soldata Ivana Chonkina* (Paris, 1976), p. 168, to satirize Stalin's speech on the outbreak of war.

14. I. Klyamkin, *NM*, no. 11 (1987); he nevertheless concludes that collectivization was necessary.

15. This parallel is made explicit in Mozhaev's *Muzhiki i baby*.

16. *VI KPSS*, no. 5 (1988), p. 81.

17. *VI*, no. 6 (1988), pp. 71–4 (Conference on History and Literature, April 27–8, 1988).

18. N. Ivanova, *DN*, no. 4 (1988).

19. V. Belov, *Kanuny*, part 3, *NM*, no. 8 (1987); S. Antonov, *Ovragi*, *DN*, nos 1–2 (1988).

20. See Davies, op. cit., p. 58.

21. Even in the boldest earlier works, such as Zalygin's *Na Irtyshe* (1964), dekulakization had sometimes been seen as unjust, but the basic correctness of the policy had not been explicitly questioned.

22. On this issue, see I. Klyamkin, *NM*, no. 11 (1987); R. Medvedev, *Sobesednik*, no. 18 (1988).

23. M. Sholokhov's *Podnyataya tselina*, Book 1, was finished in 1930, but not published until 1932. With Stalin's agreement, Sholokhov was allowed to keep in the cruel scenes of dekulakization in the village Gremyachii Log.

24. An exception was B. Mozhaev, *Iz zhizni Fedora Kuz'kina*, *NM*, no. 7 (1966); republished under its original title in *Zhivoi. Povest' i rasskazy* (M., 1979); for further discussion, see G. Svirski, *A History of Post-war Soviet-Writing* (Ann Arbor, 1981), p. 272; Gillespie, op. cit., pp. 185–7. Mozhaev cites the eminent physicist Pyotr Kapitsa as remarking: 'I also am a Kuz'kin': *MN* (31 July 1988). The radical critic Yurii Karabchievskii maintained that, although he did not like 'village prose', he made an exception for *Kuz'kin*: *Vzglyad*, vol. 3 (M., 1991), p. 167.

25. Antonov's *The Ravines* also contains an interesting depiction of a short-lived peasant rebellion against collectivization, but does not present it in such a positive light as Mozhaev.

26. For a similar analysis, see the interview with Antonov by O. Martynenko, 'Across the Ravines', *Moscow News Weekly*, no. 51 (1987), p. 11; V.

Selyunin, 'Istoki', *NM*, no. 5 (1988), pp. 162–89.

27. *Don*, no. 1 (1987), p. 25.
28. Ibid., no. 2 (1987), p. 12. E. Sidorov makes a similar point in relation to Tvardovskii's depiction in *For the Right of Memory* of his father's pride in being recognized as a proprietor of the land: see *LG* (4 March 1987), p. 4.
29. 'Ot avtora', ibid., no. 3 (1987), p. 106; see also the discussion of Mozhaev's work by members of the 'Rassvet' kolkhoz in Rostovskaya oblast': *LG* (6 April 1988).
30. For fuller discussion of Mozhaev's political stance, see D. Holohan, 'Collectivization and the Utopian Ideal in the Work of Boris Mozhaev', unpublished PhD thesis, University of Bath, 1994.
31. In 1988 only V. Selyunin, 'Istoki', *NM*, no. 5 (1988) hinted that Lenin had supported collective farms in the early 1920s.
32. See, for example, *Don*, no. 2 (1987), p. 12. A similar view is expressed by Mozhaev in his 'Afterword'.
33. N. Bukharin, 'Politicheskii testament Lenina', prepared on the occasion of the fifth anniversary of Lenin's death (21 January 1929), had recently been republished in *Kommunist*, no. 2 (1988).
34. *LG* (6 April 1988).
35. *Don*, no. 2 (1987), pp. 75–84. For fuller discussion of Mozhaev's Russian nationalist, Orthodox interpretation of history, see Holohan, op. cit.; Gillespie, op. cit., pp. 201–6. Mozhaev compares the collectivizers with Dostoevskii's 'devils' Stavrogin and Pyotr Verkhovenskii, and also refers to Ivan Karamazov's desire to 'return his ticket' to paradise if one child suffers. Mozhaev again referred to Dostoevskii's *The Devils* to reject materialist and rationalist notions of progress at a symposium in Palermo on 'Civilization and Literature'. See 'Vysshii sud', *Don*, no. 7 (1987), pp. 138–40, and Lyudmila Saraskina's discussion of the novel in relation to Dostoevskii's *The Devils*, *Oktyabr'*, no. 7 (1988), pp. 181–99.
36. See, in particular, *Don*, no. 2 (1987), pp. 21, 81.
37. V. Danilov, 'Tret'ya volna', *VI*, no. 3 (1988), p. 22. See also Danilov's article in *VI KPSS*, no. 7 (1987), pp. 144–5 which condemns Mozhaev's 'completely stupid conception' of the mistakes made in the first collectivization drive of 1930, and takes issue with Tikhonov's introduction.
38. Gillespie, op. cit., p. 203, n. 29.
39. V. Danilov, *VI*, no. 3 (1988), pp. 22–4.
40. R. Medvedev, *Let History Judge* (Oxford, 1989), p. 99.
41. For the plethora of interpretations of Belov's work, see V. Pankov (ed.), *'Kanuny' Vasiliya Belova. S raznykh tochek zreniya* (M., 1991).
42. Belov, op. cit., p. 51.
43. Belov's criticism of Trotsky's responsibility is refuted in I. Klyamkin, *NM*, no. 11 (1987).
44. *Pravda*, (15 April 1988), p. 3.
45. A. Turkov, 'Davnie grozy', *DN*, no. 4 (1988).
46. V. Belov, *Vse vperedi*, *NS*, nos 7–8 (1986).
47. V. Belov, Part 1 of *God velikogo pereloma*, *NM*, no. 3 (1989); translated by D. Gillespie in *Soviet Literature*, pp. 3–68 (1990); Part 2 was published in *NM*, nos 3–4 (1991); Part 3 was announced in *NS*, no. 4 (1993)

for publication in the second half of the year. For Belov's nationalistic statements, see above, p. 23.

48. I. Shafarevich, 'Russofobiya', *NS*, nos 6, 11 (1989).
49. For earlier literary references to the famine, see M. Alekseyev, *Drachuny* (1982); A. Stadnyuk, *Lyudi ne angely* (1962). For further discussion, see R. Conquest, *The Harvest of Sorrow: Soviet Collectivization and the Terror-famine* (London, 1986); extracts published as R. Conkvest, *Zhatva skorbi*, in *NM*, no. 10 (1989); *VI*, nos 1, 4 (1990).
50. V. Tendryakov, *Konchina, Moskva*, no. 3 (1968).
51. Yu. Afanas'ev, *LR* (17 June 1988); countered by P. Kuznetsov, *Pravda*, (25 June 1988).
52. V. Tendryakov, *Khleb dlya sobaki*, *NM*, no. 3 (1988), p. 19.
53. Ibid., p. 22.
54. V. Tendryakov, *Para gnedykh*, *NM*, no. 3 (1988), p. 18, had already cited Roy Medvedev's figures in *Let History Judge*, and Stalin's own statement, reported in Winston Churchill's *The Second World War*, that the casualties attendant on collectivization possibly amounted to 10 million people. By 1988 Medvedev's book had not been published in the USSR, and only parts of Churchill's memoirs had been translated.
55. Ibid., p. 30. The total amount of grain exported in 1933 amounted to 10 million centners (a centner equals 100 kilogrammes).
56. See below, pp. 101–3.
57. For more discussion of Tendryakov's changing reputation, see N. Ivanova, 'Potaennyi Tendryakov', *Yunost'*, no. 9 (1989), pp. 84–7; for discussion of his earlier works, see G. Hosking, *Beyond Socialist Realism* (London, 1980), pp. 84–100; R. Marsh, *Soviet Fiction since Stalin* (London and NY, 1989), *passim*.
58. V. Grossman, *Vse idet . . .*, *Oktyabr'*, no. 6 (1989), chapter 14; see below, pp. 120–2.
59. See, in particular, the posthumously published story by Fyodor Abramov: *Poezdka v proshloe*, *NM*, no. 5 (1989), pp. 5–39; discussed in D. Gillespie, 'Ironies and Legacies: Village Prose and Glasnost', *Forum for Modern Language Studies*, vol. XXVII, no. 1 (1991), pp. 77–81. See also Abramov's stories *SOE*, *Za zemlyakov*, and *A u papy byli druz'ya?*, *Ogonek*, no. 9 (1989), pp. 9–11.
60. For further discussion, see N. Ivanova, *NM*, no. 8 (1988), p. 259.
61. O. Martynenko, *Moscow News* (20 December 1987), p. 11.
62. See, for example, the interviews with B. Mozhaev, 'Lyudi soprotivleniya', *MN* (31 July 1988), p. 10; with Belov, 'Vozrodit' v krest'yanstve krest'yanskoe', *Pravda* (15 April 1988), p. 3; with Antonov, 'Across the Ravines', *Moscow News*, no. 51 (1987), p. 11.
63. Davies op. cit., p. 195.
64. See discussion of Shatrov above, pp. 68, 69; Davies, op. cit., pp. 36–8.
65. Yu. Prokushev, *LG* (9 March 1988); Yu. Maksimov, *LG* (6 April 1988); K. Myalo, 'Oborvannaya nit'. Krest'yanskaya kul'tura i kul'turnaya revolyutsiya', *NM*, no. 8 (1988), pp. 249; V. Kozhinov, 'Samaya bol'shaya opasnost',' *NS* no. 1 (1989), pp. 141–75.

Notes to Chapter 6   The Stalin Terror: Prisons and Camps

1. For further discussion, see R. W. Davies, *Soviet History in the Gorbachev Revolution* (London, 1989), pp. 74–87; A. Nove, *Glasnost in Action* (London, 1989), pp. 73–102. For contemporary reactions, see A. Vasilevskii, 'Stradanie pamyati', in V. D. Oskotskii and E. A. Shklovskii (eds), *Vzglyad: kritika, polemika, publikatsii*, vol. 3 (M., 1991), pp. 75–95; N. Ivanova, 'Ot "vragov naroda" k "vragam natsii"', in *Ogonek: luchshie publikatsii 1988 goda*, p. 44.

2. See the speech of the student D. G. Yurasov in March 1987, *RM* (29 May 1987); for further discussion, see Davies, op. cit., pp. 168–70.

3. A. Vaksberg, *LG* (4 May 1988); discussed by Nove, op. cit., pp. 89–91.

4. Solzhenitsyn himself admits in *The Gulag Archipelago*, vol. 2, (London: Fontana, 1976), p. 200, that 'Shalamov's camp experience was more bitter and longer then mine'. Solzhenitsyn asked Shalamov to co-author *Gulag* with him, but Shalamov, who was already old and sick, had to decline.

5. J. Glad, 'Introduction' to V. Shalamov, *Kolyma Tales* (Harmondsworth: Penguin, 1990), p. 15.

6. Shalamov's *Kolymskie rasskazy* were published in many different journals from July 1987, which to some extent diminished their impact. Zalygin published a selection in *NM*, no. 6 (1988); but it was not until 1989 that they were gathered together in one book. See also the brief autobiographical information given on the eightieth anniversary of Shalamov's birth: V. Shalamov, 'Literaturnaya nit' moei sud'by', *LG* (8 July 1987), p. 6.

7. See, for example, I. Kon, *Argumenty i fakty*, no. 18 (1988).

8. N. Mandel'stam, *Vospominaniya*, extracts in *Yunost'*, no. 8 (1988); further publication in *Yunost'*, nos 7–9 (1989); E. Ginzburg, *Krutoi marshrut*, extracts in *Yunost'*, no. 9 (1988); published in full in *Daugava*, nos 7–12 (1988); ibid. nos 1–6 (1989). Other important memoirs include A. Larina, *Nezabyvaemoe*, nos 10–12 (1988); K. Simonov, *Glazami cheloveka moego pokoleniya Znamya*, nos 3–5 (1988); E. Gnedin, *Sebya ne poteryat'*, *NM*, no. 7 (1988); L. Chukovskaya, *Spusk pod vodu*, in *Povesti* (M., 1988); O. Volkov, *Gorstka prakha*, *Yunost'*, no. 3 (1989).

9. L. Razgon, *Nepridumannoe*, *Yunost'*, no. 5 (1988); ibid. nos 1–2 (1989); A. Zhigulin, *Chernye kamni*, *Znamya*, nos 7–8 (1988).

10. See, for example, D. Danin, 'Perezhitoe i ponyatoe. Vmesto predisloviya', in L. Razgon, *Nepridumannoe* (M., 1989), p. 5. In *MN* (31 July 1988), p. 12, Zhigulin claims to have received hundreds of thousands of letters in response to his Kolyma poems, either in printed form or circulating in *samizdat*. Apparently it was difficult to secure the publication of his poems in the Brezhnev era after Tvardovskii's protection had been removed.

11. For further discussion, see M. Geller, *La Littérature Soviétique et le Monde Concentrationnaire* (Lausanne, 1974).

12. See, for example, the German Communist quoted in S. Shved, *Vospominaniya*, *Ural*, no. 2 (1988).

13. E. Ginzburg, *Krutoi marshrut*, *Yunost'*, no. 9 (1988), p. 35.

14. A. Vasilevskii, 'Stradanie pamyati', in *Vzglyad*, vol. 3 (M., 1991), p. 77.

15. I. Taratin, *Poteryannye gody zhizni*, *Volga*, no. 5 (1988).

16. Shved, *Vospominaniya*; Ginzburg, *Krutoi marshrut*.

244 Notes and References

17. The few memoirs by peasants that did apear were all the more valuable: see, for example, N. Murzin, *Ural*, nos 9–11 (1988).
18. Vasilevskii, op. cit., p. 86; for examples of revenge, see the tsarist general Roshchakovskii, depicted in Razgon, *Nepridumannoe*, pp. 69–107; the memoirs of Bulgakov by E. Bulgakova, *Sovremennaya dramaturgiya*, no. 5 (1988), which suggests that Bulgakov had a feeling of revenge when he heard of the arrest of his enemies, including writers who were former members of RAPP, such as Kirshon and Averbakh. These memoirs, which also justify the arrest of Mandel'shtam and contain other revelations about Bulgakov, have led to a controversy about whether Bulgakov was anti-Semitic: see M. Zolotonosov, *LO*, no. 5 (1991); *LG* (21 July 1993), p. 4; attacked by V. Vozdvizhenskii, *LG* (29 September 1993), p. 4.
19. M. Kapustin, *KO*, no. 38 (1988); Ya. Kaplinskii, *Raduga* (Tallinn), no. 7 (1988); see also discussion of Grossman, below, pp. 103–5. By contrast, Vasilevskii, op. cit., p. 92 quotes Christa Wolf as saying that Nazism was incapable of internal evolution towards democratic reform, such as the 20th Congress or *perestroika*.
20. See, for example, B. D'yakov, *Povest' o perezhitom, Oktyabr'*, no. 7 (1964).
21. For Zhigulin's vivid account, see *Chernye kamni, Znamya*, no. 8 (1988), pp. 89–99; he was not put on trial because Stalin had died. Criticized in G. Gorchakov, 'Trudnyi khleb Pravdy', *VL*, no. 9 (1989), pp. 105–17; see also M. Korallov, 'Iz Voronezha i Berlaga', *VL*, no. 9 (1989), p. 125.
22. T. Rikhter, *Dolgaya noch' stalinskikh lagerei, Za rubezhom*, no. 35 (1988).
23. *Volga*, no. 5 (1988).
24. See Solzhenitsyn, *Gulag*, vol. 1, pp. 15–18; for counter-examples, see Zhigulin, *Znamya*, no. 7 (1988), pp. 38–42; Boris Mazurin, 'Rasskaz i razdum'ya ob istorii odnoi tolstovskoi kommuny "Zhizn' i trud"', *NM*, no. 9 (1988) tells of a Tolstoyan commune completely destroyed in 1937 whose members courageously refused to submit voluntarily to arrest.
25. Razgon, *Nepridumannoe*, p. 46 refers to the one attempt to escape by Gai.
26. B. Yampol'skii, *Moskovskaya ulitsa, Znamya*, nos 2–3 (1988).
27. N. Mandel'shtam, *Yunost'*, no. 8 (1988); for another perceptive analysis of popular reactions to Stalin's terror, see L. Ginzburg, *Chelovek za pis'mennym stolom* (M., 1989).
28. See, for example, S. Kelina, *Moskovskii komsomolets* (25 September 1988).
29. Shalamov, *Kolyma Tales*, p. 90.
30. Vasilevskii, op. cit., p. 82.
31. For further discussion, see Davies, op. cit., pp. 82–7. On the opposition of Martemyan Ryutin, see L. Razgon, *MN* (26 June 1988); A. Vaksberg, *LG* (4 May 1988).
32. D. Andreyeva, *Moskovskii komsomolets*, (30 November 1988).
33. V. Shalamov, *Poslednii boi mayora Pugacheva, NM*, no. 6 (1988), pp. 116; for a more systematic discussion of resistance in the camps before and after Stalin's death, see *Gulag*, vol. 3 (London: Fontana, 1978), pp. 193–280.
34. A. Zhigulin, *Chernye kamni, Znamya*, no. 7 (1988).
35. See also the revelation about the independent behaviour of A. Kuznetsov, executed in connection with the obscure 'Leningrad affair' in 1949: A. Afanas'ev, *KP* (15 January 1988).
36. Zhigulin, *Znamya*, no. 7 (1988), p. 21.

37. This conflicts with the view of D. Brown, *The Last Years of Soviet Russian Literature* (Cambridge, 1993), p. 72, that Zhigulin was 'falsely convicted of anti-Soviet conspiracy' by the Stalinist secret police.
38. A. Tvardovskii, *Za dal'yu – dal'* (M., 1961), p. 171 (first published *NM*, no. 5 (1960).
39. *Znamya*, no. 8 (1988), pp. 65, 83; discussed in S. Lominadze,'"Prestuplenie" i nakazanie', *VL*, no. 9 (1989), no. 9, p. 157, n. 5.
40. This issue was raised by the historian Boris Starkov at the 1994 BASEES Conference, and in the subsequent discussion.
41. Zhigulin, *Znamya*, no. 7 (1988), p. 28ff.
42. A. Zhigulin, 'Vina! Ona byla, konechno . . .', interview with A. Shatalov, *MN* (31 July 1988), p. 12.
43. Korallov, *VL*, no. 9 (1989), pp. 118–49.
44. See, for example, T. Marshall, 'Stasi files reveal secret tales of heroism and betrayal', *Guardian* (29 December 1993), p. 8. Many NKVD files are still kept secret in Russia, in order to avoid widespread demoralization.
45. See *KP* (31 August 1988) on the founders of the KPM; discussed in Korallov, op. cit., pp. 118–19.
46. *Molodoi kommunar'* (20–4 September 1988).
47. E. Yakovlev and D. Muratov, cited by Korallov, op. cit., p. 119.
48. Korallov, op. cit., p. 131.
49. Yu. Dombrovskii, *Fakul'tet nenuzhnykh veshchei*, *NM*, nos 9–11 (1988).
50. Dombrovskii's novel is a sequel to *Khranitel' drevnostei*, *NM*, nos 7–8 (1964).
51. Galina Belaya, professor of literature at Moscow State University, paper at World Congress of Slavists, Harrogate, 1990.
52. Yu. Dombrovskii, *Fakul'tet nenuzhnykh veshchei* (M., 1989), p. 256.
53. Ibid., pp. 575–6.
54. See, for example, Vasilevskii, op. cit.; I. Vinogradov, 'Mir bez nenuzhnykh veshchei', *MN* (11 September 1988), p. 11.
55. S. Lominadze, ' "Prestuplenie" i nakazanie', *VL* no. 9 (1989), p. 155.
56. 'Varlam Shalamov: proza, stikhi'', *NM*, no. 6 (1988), p. 106; from an unpublished fragment 'O proze', held in the Central State Archives of Literature and Art. For a more detailed comparison between Solzhenitsyn and Shalamov, see G. Hosking, 'The Ultimate Circle of the Stalinist Inferno', *New Universities Quarterly*, vol. 34 (Spring 1980). For the lowest depths to which the human spirit can be reduced, see V. Shalamov, *Sententsiya*, *NM*, no. 6 (1988), pp. 145–9.
57. 'Varlam Shalamov: proza, stikhi'', *NM*, no. 6 (1988), p. 106.
58. Razgon, *Nepridumannoe*, pp. 72–3.
59. See Davies, op. cit., p. 78 for Razgon's account of the monstrous Colonel Tarasyuk, commandant of a camp in the Far North, who was later praised as a great organizer of production. A similar type, Antonov, director of the Enisei camp, had been described in A. Pobozhii, *Mertvaya doroga*, *NM*, no. 8 (1964).
60. Razgon, *Nepridumannoe*, pp. 263–74.
61. See, for example, *MN* (21 August 1988); *Daugava*, no. 9 (1988); A. Adamovich, *Ogonek* (25 September 1988) reported that the mass grave at Kuropaty outside Minsk contained some 50,000 victims of the purges;

LG (27 April 1989) refers to mass graves at Bykova, near Kiev, where up to 240,000 bodies have been found; *Pravda* (8 July 1989) mentions a mass grave at Donetsk in Ukraine; *Independent* (6 September 1989) reports the discovery of a mass grave of 80,000 near Cheliabinsk. In the 1990s further graves and crematoria were discovered in the Altai, Kirgizia, outside Leningrad and in Moscow itself: see Stephen White, *After Gorbachev* (Cambridge, 1993), pp. 83, 304, n. 56.

62. Other prominent examples of literary works on this theme, published in Russia after Dombrovskii's novel, are A. Rybakov, *Tridtsat' pyatyi i drugie gody*, *DN*, nos 9–10 (1988); M. Kuraev, *Nochnoi dozor*, *NM*, no. 12 (1988); I. Metter, *Pyatyi ugol*, *Neva*, no. 1 (1989); G. Vladimov, *Vernyi Ruslan*, *Znamya*, no. 2 (1989); Solzhenitsyn, *V kruge pervom*, *NM*, nos 1–4 (1990).

63. See, for example, I. Bestuzhev-Lada, *Nedelya*, no. 15 (1988); E. Albats, *MN* (8 May 1988).

64. A. Nemzer, in *Vzglyad*, p. 223.

65. *Daugava*, no. 9 (1988).

66. N. Ivanova, 'Vozvrashchenie k nastoyashchemu', *Znamya*, no. 8 (1990), pp. 235–6.

67. For the religious themes in Dombrovskii's novel, particularly the parallels between interrogators and Pilate, and informers and Judas, see M. Ziolkovski, 'Pilate and Pilatism in Recent Russian Literature', in S. D. Graham (ed.), *New Directions in Soviet Literature*, pp. 173–9. A moral for contemporary Russian readers is drawn in I. Vinogradov, 'Mir bez nenuzhnykh veshchei', *MN* (11 September 1988), p. 11.

68. N. Ivanova, 'Ot "vragov naroda" k "vragam natsii"', in *Ogonek: luchshie publikatsii 1988 goda*, p. 44.

69. 'Varlam Shalamov: proza, stikhi', *NM*, no. 6 (1988) pp. 106–7. Shalamov advocates a new form of 'documentary prose' and a new role for the artist as 'not an Orpheus descending into hell, but a Pluto ascending from hell'. See also V. Shalamov, 'Novaya proza: iz chernykh zapisei 70-kh godov, *NM*, no. 12 (1989) pp. 1–58; 'O moei proze', *NM*, no. 12 (1989), pp. 58–71.

70. Vasilevskii, op. cit., pp. 94–5.

71. L. Kopelev and R. Orlova, 'Evgeniya Ginzburg v kontse krutogo marshruta', *Daugava*, no. 6 (1989) speaks of the profound development of Ginzburg's ideas; she is quoted as saying 'I hate left-wing people. All of them' and 'All revolutions are criminal'.

72. V. Soloukhin, 'Pochemu ya ne podpisalsya pod tem pis'mom', *NS*, no. 12 (1988), pp. 186–9; for an effective reply, see B. Sarnov, *Ogonek*, no. 12 (1988).

73. V. Kozhinov, 'Pravda i istina', *NS*, no. 4 (1988), pp. 160–75; see above, p. 75; V. Kozhinov, 'Samaya bol'shaya opasnost'', *NS*, no. 1 (1989), pp. 141–75.

74. A. Latynina, cited in Vasilevskii, op. cit., p. 93; the reference is to the discussion between Medvedev and Shafarevich, *Moscow News*, no. 24 (1988), pp. 12–13.

75. See, for example, Vasilevskii, op. cit., p. 94.

76. N. Ivanova, 'Proiti cherez otchayanie', *Yunost'*, no. 1 (1990), p. 86.

77. Vasilevskii, op. cit., p. 95; see also I. Vinogradov, *MN*, no. 45 (1989),

p. 12. *Gulag* had considerable impact in 1989 and was still the second 'best-seller' in 1990: see A. Bulykh, 'Samyi, samyi, samyi . . .', *Sem'ya*, no. 52 (1990), p. 3. For responses to *Gulag* in Russia, see '"Arkhipelag GULAG" chitayut na rodine', comp. V. Borisov, N. Levitskaya; notes by D. Yurasov, *NM*, no. 9 (1991).

78. The percentage of anti-Stalin letters in Anatolii Rybakov's postbag, which in 1987 had amounted to 15 per cent, by 1989 had diminished to a mere 3–4 per cent: see A. Rybakov, 'U menya net drugogo vykhoda . . .', *DN*, no. 9 (1989), p. 264.

79. See, for example, V. Selyunin, 'Istoki', *NM*, no. 5 (1988), pp. 163–70; L. Bat'kin, 'Vozobnovlenie istorii', in Yu. Afanas'ev (ed.), *Inogo ne dano* (M., 1988), pp. 154–91.

80. T. Khlopyankina, 'Stalin s nami, Stalin sredi nas', *MN* (7 May 1989), p. 11; the same demand had been made by the lawyer Valerii Savitskii on the television programme *Vzglyad* (11 November 1988). For a well-argued contrary view, see Rybakov, *DN*, no. 9 (1989), p. 263. This issue is still a live one in other countries too; similar issues have been raised by the trials of Ivan Demyanyuk in Israel, Erich Honecker in Germany and Paul Touvier in France, and the possible prosecution of war criminals in Britain.

Notes to Chapter 7 The Second World War

1. R. W. Davies, *Soviet History in the Gorbachev Revolution* (London, 1989), pp. 61–2, 100–14; A. Nove, *Glasnost in Action* (London, 1989), pp. 47–52; Frank Ellis, *Vasiliy Grossman: the Genesis and Evolution of a Russian Heretic* (Oxford and Providence, RI, 1994); G. Gibian, 'World War Two in Russian National Consciousness', in J. and C. Garrard (eds), *World War Two and the Soviet People* (London, 1993), pp. 147–59. On earlier war prose, see D. Piper, in H. Klein, with J. Flower and E. Homberger, in *The Second World War in Fiction* (London, 1984); Marsh, *Soviet Fiction since Stalin* (London, 1986), pp. 195–207.

2. *SK* (3 September 1988); due to the fall of the birthrate, an additional 22–3 million births did not occur.

3. For varying estimates of the number of prisoners of war who died, see *MN* (30 August 1987) (5.7 million, of whom 4 million are known to have died); B. Sokolov, *VI*, no. 9 (1988) (5.8 million, of whom 3.3 million died in captivity).

4. Literature of the Afghan war is a huge subject in itself, which is beyond the scope of this study: see H. Swartz, 'The Soviet-Afghan War in Russian Literature', unpublished D. Phil. thesis, University of Oxford, 1992. For Soviet views, see Lt-Col. I. Tkachenko, *LG* (18 October 1989); *NM*, no. 10 (1989).

5. See, for example, V. Bykau, *Mertvym ne bol'no* (1966); G. Baklanov, *Iyul' 41 goda* (1965); B. Okudzhava, *Bud' zdorov, shkolyar!* (1961).

6. Lt-Col. I. P. Repin, 'V stroyu pobeditelei – literatura', *VL*, no. 5 (1985), pp. 7–19.

7. See the account of a lecture by Professor Yurii Borisov in March 1987, at which someone in the audience shouted out that Stalin had 'murdered most of the officer corps': cited in S. Wheatcroft, 'Unleashing the Energy of History', *ASEES*, vol. 1, no. 1 (1987), p. 111. See also the account of Borisov's April lecture in *RM* (29 May 1987), p. 4.

8. Reported in *Voenno-istoricheskii zhurnal*, no. 6 (1987), p. 64. The journal also published the first instalment of the memoirs; but it was not until 1989 that some previously unpublished excerpts were published: see *Pravda* (20 January 1989).

9. N. Pavlenko, *Kommunist*, no. 9 (1988), p. 93. This subject had previously been mentioned in A. Nekrich *(22 June 1941)*, published in 1965, then withdrawn; Nekrich had been expelled from the Party in 1967.

10. Pavlenko op. cit.; A. Samsonov, *Sotsialisticheskaya industriya* (24 May 1987); *SK* (21 June 1988); A. Vaksberg, *LG* (20 April 1988); see also I. Bestuzhev-Lada, *Nedelya*, no. 5 (1988); V. Shmidt, *Nedelya*, no. 13 (1988).

11. *Moscow News* (14 June 1987); *Ogonek*, no. 26 (June 1987); B. Viktorov, *Pravda* (29 April 1988); D. Volkogonov, *Pravda* (20 June 1988).

12. D. Volkogonov, 'Triumf i tragediya', *Pravda* (20 June 1988).

13. E. Maksimova, 'Za zhivykh i mertvykh', *Izvestiya* (21 August 1987); correspondence in *Izvestiya*, (29 August, 5, 11 September 1987); *LG* (25 June 1986); E. A. Brodskii, *Oni ne propali bez vesti* (1987), reviewed in *LG* (11 November 1987).

14. V. Shaposhnikov, 'Tsena pobedy', *LG* (22 June 1988), p. 4.

15. For posthumous contributions to this debate, see Simonov's long-delayed interviews with senior military men in *Znamya*, no. 5 (1988); discussed in Nove, op. cit., pp. 50–3; see also Lakshin's account of Tvardovskii's interview with General Gorbatov: *Ogonek*, no. 20 (1988).

16. See the articles by Evgenii Dolmatovskii, *LG* (25 June 1986); and Chingiz Aitmatov, *Yunost'*, no. 5 (1988).

17. L. Razgon, *Yunost'*, no. 5 (1988); on this theme, see also Shaposhnikov, *LG* (22 June 1988), p. 4.

18. V. Astaf'ev, *Pravda* (25 November 1985); *LG* (7 October 1987).

19. Lt-General M. Manakin, Hero of the Soviet Union, *LG* (25 November 1987).

20. The conference, organized under the auspices of the Academy of Sciences, Union of Writers and Academy of Social Sciences, was reported in *LG* (18 May 1988).

21. V. Shaposhnikov, 'Tsena pobedy', *LG* (22 June 1988), p. 4.

22. Davies, op. cit., p. 193; R. Marsh, *Images of Dictatorship* (London, 1989), p. 70. For attacks on Stadnyuk, see I. Bestuzhev-Lada, *Nedelya*, no. 15 (1988); A. Samsonov, *Sotsialisticheskaya industriya* (24 May 1987).

23. *VI*, no. 6 (1988), p. 55.

24. See, for example, T. Vasil'eva, *Slezy nevoli*, *Zvezda*, no. 5 (1988); A. Genatulin, *Tyunel'*, *Znamya*, no. 12 (1987); Ya. Panovko, *U kazhdogo svoya voina*, *Zvezda*, no. 5 (1988).

25. D. Gusarov, *Propavshii otryad*, *Znamya*, no. 5 (1988).

26. V. Shaposhnikov, *LG* (22 June 1988), p. 4.

27. V. Tendryakov, *Donna Anna*, *NM*, no. 3 (1988), pp. 43–6.

28. A. Blok, *Selected Poems*, ed. A. Pyman (Oxford, 1972), p. 241.
29. For further discussion, see M. Ziolkowski, 'Glasnost in Soviet Literature: An Introduction to Two Stories', *Michigan Quarterly Review*, vol. 28, no. 4 (Fall 1989), p. 645–6.
30. For a similar realistic analysis, see the sociologist V. Shubkin, *LG* (23 September 1987), who recognizes that 'It was the pre-war country which entered the war'.
31. *NM*, no. 3 (1988), pp. 58–9.
32. *Moscow News* (7 February 1988).
33. N. Ivanova, 'Potaennyi Tendryakov', *Yunost'*, no. 9 (1989), pp. 84–7 [p. 86]. She cites the conversation between S. Yakovlev and I. Klyamkin, 'Ispytaniya i nadezhdy', *LO*, no. 4 (1989); and Anatolii Yakobson's recently published article 'O romanticheskoi ideologii', *NM*, no. 4 (1989), which studied the role of poetry of the 1920s in forming 'a superman of a new type, a superman of the revolution, a truly strong personality'.
34. Ivanova, p. 87, citing I. Rodnyanskaya's afterword to Yakobson's article, *LO*, no. 4 (1989), p. 231.
35. V. Tendryakov, *Lyudi ili nelyudi, DN*, no. 2 (1989).
36. *Ogonek*, no. 40 (1987), p. 17; V. Grossman, *Zhizn' i sud'ba, Oktyabr'*, nos 1–4 (1988). In the West extracts had first been published in *Kontinent*, nos 4–5 (1975); nos 6–7 (1976); the first full publication in the West, *Zhizn i sud'ba* (Lausanne, 1980); V. Grossman, *Life and Fate*, transl. R. Chandler (London, 1985). For more detailed discussion, see Ellis, op. cit.; S. Lipkin, *Stalingrad Vasiliya Grossmana* (Ann Arbor, MI, 1986); S. Markish, 'Primer Vasilya Grossmana', in *Vasilii Grossman. Na evreiskie temy*, vol. 2 (Israel: Biblioteka-Aliya, 1985); on the representation of Stalin, see Marsh, *Images of Dictatorship*, pp. 116–19.
37. Interview with A. Anan'ev, *LG* (27 July 1988), p. 7.
38. S. Lipkin, 'Pravoe delo pobezhdaet. Sud'ba romana Vasiliya Grossmana', *MN* (18 October 1987), p. 11.
39. See, in particular, V. Voinovich, *Antisovetskii Sovetskii Soyuz* (Ann Arbor, MI, 1985), pp. 201–4. For other Soviet accounts of Grossman's difficulties, see *Ogonek*, no. 40 (1987), p. 19; *LG* (6 June 1988) p. 4; there is a rather sanitized account in A. Bocharov, *Oktyabr'*, no. 1 (1988), p. 128.
40. See the interpretations by V. Kardin, 'Zhizn' – eto svoboda . . .', *Ogonek*, no. 23 (1988), p. 22; A. Bocharov, *Oktyabr'*, no. 2 (1988), p. 107.
41. A. Bocharov, *Vasilii Grossman* (M., 1970); see also his *Chelovek i voina* (M., 1973) for another conventional commentary on the war.
42. *Oktyabr'*, no. 2 (1988), p. 107.
43. When this omission was pointed out, these pages were published in *Oktyabr'*, no. 9 (1988), with a specious excuse for the original omission.
44. I. Zolotusskii, 'Voina i svoboda', *LG* (6 June 1988), p. 4.
45. M. Gareyev, 'Velikii Oktyabr' i zashchita Otechestva', *Oktyabr'*, no. 2 (1988), pp. 175–83.
46. For outspoken criticism of Stalin's role as a war leader, see A. Adamovich, 'Voinu vyigral narod', *MN* (28 February 1988), p. 2; extracts from Marshal Zhukov's memoirs, *Pravda* (20 January 1989); see also the volume *Uroki istorii* (M., 1989), published to commemorate the fiftieth anniversary of the outbreak of the war, in which historians, military men and political

figures discussed the origins and lessons of the Second World War.
47. On references to Vlasov in Marshal Zhukov's memoirs, see A. Mirkina, 'Marshal pishet knigu', *Ogonek*, no. 18 (April 1988), p. 18; V. Kondrat'ev and A. Samsonov, discussion of K. Simonov's memoirs 'Glazami cheloveka moego pokoleniya', *LG* (18 May 1988), p. 6 (Simonov's memoir of military commanders published in *Znamya*, no. 5 (1988)). The first Soviet article in which Vlasov was not presented as a villain was A. Frenkin, *LG* (13 September 1989); discussed more fully in A. Solzhenitsyn, *The Gulag Archipelago*, vol. 1 (London: Fontana, 1974), pp. 251–3.
48. A. Rybakov, *Strakh*, *DN*, nos 9–10 (1990): discussed further in R. Marsh, 'Stalin and Stalinism in Contemporary Literature: the case of Anatolii Rybakov', forthcoming. Further frank articles on the military purges had included: V. Chalikova, *Neva*, no. 10 (1988); Yu. Geller, 'Nevernoe ekho bylogo', *DN*, no. 9 (1989), pp. 237–8.
49. V. Voinovich, *Zhizn' i neobychainye priklyucheniya soldata Ivana Chonkina*, *Yunost'*, no. 12 (1988) and nos 1–2 (1989), (first published, Paris, 1976).
50. See, for example, V. Iverni, 'Komediya ncsovmestimosti', *Kontinent*, no. 5 (1975), pp. 427–54; Marsh, *Images of Dictatorship*, pp. 125–6.
51. A. Vasilevskii, 'Na perelome', *LO*, no. 1 (1990), p. 17. A similar view was expressed to me in conversation by the *Ogonek* writer V. Shentalinskii.
52. See, for example, A. Nemzer, 'V poiskakh utrachennoi chelovechnosti', in *Vzglyad*, vol. 3, pp. 215–236.
53. G. Gordeeva, *LO*, no. 1 (1990), pp. 17–18.
54. A. Arkhangel'skii, *LO*, no. 1 (1990), p. 18; quotation from C. S. Lewis, introduced to Soviet readers by N. L. Trauberg, 'Neskol'ko slov o Klaive S. L'yuise', *VF*, no. 8 (1989), pp. 104–6.
55. A. Nemzer, *LO*, no. 1 (1990), p. 18.
56. See, for example, V. Karpov, E. Nosov and V. Kondrat'ev, 'Sorokovye rokovye', *LG* (9 May 1990).
57. D. Granin, 'Daty, kotorye vsegda s nami', *LG* (23 June 1993), p. 1. On the beginning of the war, see extracts from Voinovich's new novel *Maiiyun' 1941*, published in *LG* (17 February 1993), p. 5.
58. V. Astaf'ev, *Proklyaty i ubity*, *NM*, nos 10–12 (1992); planned as the first part of a trilogy.
59. See P. Broué, 'Gorbachev and History', in S. White (ed.), *New Directions in Soviet History* (Cambridge, 1992), pp. 18–19.
60. I myself witnessed such speeches by war veterans at a pro-Lenin demonstration in April 1991 in Smolny Square, Leningrad.

Notes to Chapter 8　Lenin and Leninism

1. R. W. Davies, *Soviet History in the Gorbachev Revolution* (London, 1989), pp. 115–25.
2. M. Gorbachev, *Perestroika. New Thinking for Our Country and the World* (London, 1987), p. 26.
3. See, for example, A. Egorov, *LG* (28 October 1987).
4. G. Popov, *Znamya*, no. 1 (1988), p. 199; V. Mau and I. Starodubrovskaya,

Kommunist, no. 5 (1988), pp. 69–80.

5. A. Gel'man, *Kommunist*, no. 9 (1988), pp. 17–18.
6. D. Joravsky, 'Glasnost Theater', *New York Review of Books* (10 November 1988), p. 36. For contrasting interpretations of the relationship between Inessa and Lenin, see B. Wolfe, 'Lenin and Inessa Armand', *Slavic Review*, vol. 22 (1963), pp. 96–114; A. Ulam, *Lenin and the Bolsheviks* (NY, 1968), pp. 284–5.
7. Lenin's *Testament* had been published in *MN* (18 January 1987).
8. Rosa Luxemburg's statement had already been published in *LG* (28 October 1987).
9. For attempts to link Lenin and Gorbachev, see Davies, op. cit., pp. 121–3. See also above, p. 78, for discussion of Lenin's article 'On Co-operation' in collectivization novels.
10. R. Marsh, *Images of Dictatorship* (London, 1989), p. 100.
11. For a similar view, see Joravsky, op. cit., p. 39.
12. See the discussion between Afanas'ev and Shatrov, *MN* (8 November 1987).
13. L. A. Gordon, *Ogonek*, no. 12 (1988), p. 4; M. Stepanchenko, *KP* (24 February 1988).
14. D. Urnov, *LG* (17 January 1988).
15. Davies, op. cit., pp. 123–5.
16. *MN* (15 November 1987).
17. B. Oleinik and M. Novikova, *LG* (4 May 1988).
18. P. Rodionov, *SK* (14 June 1988).
19. *Labour Focus on Eastern Europe*, no. 2 (1989), p. 27.
20. V. Selyunin, 'Istoki', *NM*, no. 5 (1988), pp. 163–70; for further discussion, see A. Nove, *Glasnost' in Action* (London, 1989), pp. 21–2.
21. A. Burganov, *DN*, no. 6 (1988), pp. 148–9; G. Popov, *SK* (21 July 1988).
22. I. Brodskii, *Nobelevskaya lektsiya*, *KO*, no. 24 (1988), pp. 8–9.
23. *MN*, no. 25 (1988), p. 2.
24. M. Dewhirst, 'The Second Rehabilitation of Alexander Solzhenitsyn?', *Soviet Analyst*, no. 23 (1988), p. 7; D. Smith, 'Reappraisal of Solzhenitsyn in the USSR', *RL Report on the USSR*, vol. 1, no. 36 (1989), p. 7. For Solzhenitsyn's polite refusal on the grounds that he lived outside the USSR, see *RM* (6 September 1988), p. 1.
25. *Sovetskaya molodezh* (3 December 1988), p. 3.
26. M. Shatrov, *Ogonek*, no. 45 (1988), p. 15.
27. *RM* (18 November 1988), p. 16.
28. J. Dunlop, 'Solzhenitsyn Begins to Emerge from the Political Void', *RL Report on the USSR*, vol. 1, no. 36 (1989), p. 1.
29. *RM* (28 October 1989), p. 1; on Zalygin's subsequent discussions with Gorbachev and his change of mind by April 1989, see Dunlop, op. cit., pp. 3–4.
30. A. Tsipko, *Nauka i zhizn'*, nos 11–12 (1988) and nos 1–2 (1989). Tsipko was reportedly protected by Yakovlev, because of his belief in free speech.
31. E. Anisimov, personal conversation.
32. J. Eisen (ed. and comp.), *The Glasnost Reader* (NY, 1990), p. 443.
33. *Pravda* (27 April 1989), p. 6; *CDSP*, vol. XLI, no. 18 (1989), p. 9. Aksyonov was removed from his post, and this incident was one reason

why the programme was taken off in the winter of 1990–1, to the discomfiture of many democrats.

34. R. Sakwa, *Gorbachev and his Reforms* (London, 1990), p. 101; J. Scherrer, 'History Reclaimed', in A. Brumberg (ed.), *Chronicle of a Revolution* (NY, 1990), pp. 90–107. Anatolii Sobchak later called for Lenin's reburial, but his view of the family's wishes was challenged: *Pravda* (24 September 1991), p. 4.
35. *Pravda* (27 October 1989).
36. *NM*, nos 8–11 (1989). See above, pp. 18–19.
37. *Pravda* (18, 29 December 1989).
38. V. Grossman, *Vse techet.*., *Oktyabr'*, no. 6 (1989); first published Frankfurt, 1970. For further discussion, see Frank Ellis, *Vasiliy Grossman: The Genesis and Evolution of a Russian Heretic* (Oxford and Providence, RI, 1994), pp. 205–11.
39. E. Anisimov, personal conversation.
40. *Oktyabr'*, no. 6 (1989).
41. N. Ivanova, 'Proiti cherez otchayanie', *Yunost'*, no. 2 (1990), p. 90.
42. G. Hosking, *The Awakening of the Soviet Union* (London, 1990), p. 143.
43. M. Zolotonosov, *Neva*, no. 1 (1990), p. 186.
44. M. Antonov, V. Klykov and I. Shafarevich, *LR* (4 August 1989); answered by A. Anan'ev, *LR* (1 September 1989); discussed in N. Ivanova, *Yunost'*, no. 1 (1990), p. 87. Anan'ev had earlier been attacked for publishing A. Sinyavskii's *Conversations with Pushkin*, which had been interpreted by conservatives as a sacrilegious attack on a great Russian writer in a journal edited by a Jew.
45. The reference is to A. Shafarevich's anti-Semitic essay 'Russofobiya', *NS*, nos 6, 11 (1989).
46. *NS*, no. 4 (1989) bears a photograph of Lenin as its frontispiece.
47. V. Soloukhin, 'Chitaya Lenina', *Rodina*, no. 10 (1989).
48. G. Bordyugov, V. Kozlov and V. Loginov, 'Kuda idet sud', *Rodina*, no. 10 (1989).
49. G. Bordyugov, V. Kozlov and V. Loginov, *Kommunist*, no. 14 (1989); reply to critics in ibid., no. 5 (1990); R. Medvedev, *Let History Judge*, 2nd edn (London, 1989). The defence of Lenin is sympathetically discussed in R. W. Davies, 'History and Perestroika', in E. A. Rees (ed.), *The Soviet Communist Party in Disarray* (London, 1991), p. 123; R. Service, *Lenin: a Political Life*, 2nd edn (London, 1991), p. 81.
50. *Izvestiya TsK KPSS*, no. 4 (1990).
51. For further discussion, see A. Lawton, *Kinoglasnost* (Cambridge, 1992), pp. 72–3. G. Melikhyants, *Izvestiya* (31 August 1992), p. 1 relates that Solzhenitsyn liked Govorukhin's film.
52. A. Latynina, 'Krushenie ideokratii: ot "Odnogo dnya Ivana Denisovicha" k "Arkhipelagu GULAG"', *LO*, no. 4 (1990), p. 7–8.
53. A. Latynina, 'Solzhenitsyn i my', *NM*, no. 1 (1990), pp. 241–58.
54. D. Smith, 'Reappraisal of Solzhenitsyn in the USSR', pp. 6–7; V. Potapov, 'Seyatel' slovo seet', *Znamya*, no. 3 (1990), pp. 204–9. For a survey of responses to Solzhenitsyn in the USSR, see N. Levitskaya, *Aleksandr Solzhenitsyn: Bibliograf}cheskii ukazatel' Avgust 1988–1990* (M., 1991).
55. See, for example, Marsh, *Images of Dictatorship*, p. 209; G. Hosking,

Beyond Socialist Realism (London, 1980), pp. 134–5.

56. A. Solzhenitsyn, *Avgust chetyrnadtsatogo*, *Zvezda*, nos 1–12 (1990); *Oktyabr' shestnadtsatogo*, *NS*, nos 1–12 (1990); *Mart semnadtsatogo*, *Neva*, nos 1–12 (1990); *Aprel' semnadtsatogo* was announced for publication in *NM* in 1992, but failed to appear because of the journal's difficulties with paper and funding.

57. Charles Trueheart, 'The Perimeter of the Prodigious Solzhenitsyn', *International Herald Tribune* (30 November 1987), p. 14; A. Solzhenitsyn, *Lenin v Tsiurikhe: glavy* (Paris, 1975).

58. N. Struve, 'Solzhenitsyn o Lenine',*VRKhD*, no. 116 (1975); M. Friedberg,'Solzhenitsyn's and other literary Lenins', *Canadian Slavonic Papers*, no. 2 (1977), pp. 12–37; B. Souvarine, 'Otvet Solzhenitsynu', *VRKhD*, no. 132 (1980), p. 265.

59. A. Solzhenitsyn, *Lenin v Tsiurikhe*, p. 225.

60. Discussed below, pp. 185–8.

61. Chapter 22 in *August 1914*; chapters 37, 43, 44 and 47–50 in *October 1916*.

62. V. Medvedev and A. Belyaev, 'Leninizm i perestroika', *Pravda* (8 February 1990), p. 3.

63. See, in particular, V. Loginov, 'Lenin bez legend', *Rabochaya tribuna* (14 April 1990), pp. 1–2; for other critical assessments, see A. Solovkin, 'Ob"ektivno sudit' ob istorii', *Za rubezhom*, no. 31 (1989); E. Savshak, 'Lenin s nami: Zavtra – 120 let so dnya rozhdeniya Il'icha', *Kirovskii rabochii* (21 April 1990).

64. See, for example, extract from Georges Nivat's book *Solzhenitsyn* (London, 1984) in *DN*, no. 4 (1990); *Russkaya rech'*, no. 5 (1990).

65. Personal interview with German Baluev, editor of Leningrad newspaper *Literator*.

66. M. Zlotonosov, 'Otdykhayushchii fontan. Malen'kaya monografiya o postsotsialistichekom realizme', *Oktyabr'*, no. 4 (1991), p. 174.

67. P. Palamarchuk, 'Aleksandr Solzhenitsyn: putevoditel'', *Moskva*, no. 10 (1990), pp. 184–20; citing Solzhenitsyn, *Sob. soch.* (Vermont and Paris, 1978–), vol. X, p. 522.

68. See Struve, op. cit., p. 190.

69. Solzhenitsyn, *Sob. soch.*, vol. X, p. 534; cited in Palamarchuk, op. cit., p. 192.

70. Palamarchuk, op. cit., p. 193.

71. A. Latynina, 'Solzhenitsyn i my', *NM*, no. 1 (1990), pp. 241–58.

72. See 'An Exchange with Boris Souvarine', in J. Dunlop, R. Haugh and M. Nicholson (eds), *Solzhenitsyn in Exile: Critical Essays and Documentary Materials* (Stanford, 1985), pp. 329–38.

73. E. Anisimov and R. Service, personal conversations.

74. Service, *Lenin*, p. 81.

75. M. Aldanov, *Samoubiistvo*, *Oktyabr'*, nos 3–4 (1991).

76. M. Aldanov, *Samoubiistvo: roman* (NY, 1958), pp. 16, 228.

77. Aldanov, op. cit., pp. 389, 409, 502, 308–9.

78. G. Adamovich, 'Introduction' to Aldanov (1958), pp. 5–6.

79. Cited by L. Anninskii, 'Za chto proklyaty?', *LG* (3 March 1993), p. 4. On Astaf'ev's novel, see above, p. 108.

80. V. Mezherskaya, *Sovetskaya Kirgiziya* (22 April 1990), p. 2; *Znamya*, no. 1 (1990), pp. 235–6.
81. 'V. I. Lenin: chelovek i istoriya', *Kommunist*, no. 5 (1991), pp. 3–5.
82. G. Z. Ioffe, 'The night of missed opportunities. What did not occur at the 2nd Congress of Soviets', *Moscow News*, no. 5 (1990).
83. V. I. Startsev, 'My s Leninym', *Pravda* (3 April 1990).
84. Gorbachev, *Pravda* (3 July 1990).
85. *Pravda* (4 July 1990).
86. *Pravda* (11, 16 August 1990).
87. *Pravda* (14 October 1990), p. 2.
88. R. Gul', 'Lenin', *Ogonek*, no. 7 (1992), pp. 10–12.
89. D. Hearst, 'On the revolution's anniversary, Russia pickles cabbages', *Guardian* (9 November 1992), p. 7; D. Volkogonov, *Lenin: Politicheskii portret v dvukh knigakh*, vol. 1 (M., 1994).
90. See V. Belykh, *Izvestiya* (21 October 1993), p. 1; V. Kuznetsova, *NG* (21 October 1993), p. 1. It is still not clear if Lenin will be moved: see *Guardian* (8 October 1993), p. 12; *Guardian* (21 October 1993), p. 11 cites Yeltsin's chief of staff Sergei Filatov as saying that the priority was to re-bury the remains of the last tsar and his family.
91. O. Latsis, *Izvestiya*, (20 October 1993), p. 2.

Notes to Chapter 9   The Civil War and the Revolutionary Period 1917–22

1. M. S. Gorbachev, 'Oktyabr' i perestroika: revolyutsiya prodolzhaetsya', *Pravda* (3 November 1987).
2. R. Service, *Lenin: a Political Life*, 2nd edn (London, 1991), p. 78; see also R. Service, 'Mikhail Gorbachev as a Political Reformer', in R. J. Hill and J. A. Dellebrant, *Gorbachev and Perestroika* (London, 1989).
3. E. Acton, *Rethinking the Russian Revolution* (London, 1990), p. 33.
4. E. Meshcherskaya, *Ogonek*, no. 43 (1987), pp. 26–30; *NM*, no. 4 (1988), pp. 198–242.
5. A. Vasinskii, *Izvestiya* (6 September 1987).
6. E. Losev, *SR* (10 July 1988); V. Kozhinov, *NS*, no. 4 (1988), p. 169 discussing Yurii Trifonov's *Otblesk kostra* (M., 1966).
7. M. Kuraev, *Kapitan Dikshtein*, *NM*, no. 9 (1987), cf. E. Drabkina's memoir *Kronshtadt, god 1921*, *Yunost'*, no. 10 (1987), which is written from the point of view of a participant in the force which crushed the rebels. The Kronstadt Revolt does not often figure in serious studies by historians; an exception is the summary by R. Medvedev, *Yunost'*, no. 11 (1988). The participants in the Kronstadt Revolt were not rehabilitated until January 1994; see *Izvestiya* (11 January 1994), p. 1.
8. For further discussion of Gumilev's rehabilitation, see R. Marsh, 'Glasnost and Literature', *ASEES*, vol. 6, no. 2 (1992), pp. 23–5. Compare G. Terekhov, *NM*, no. 12 (1987), pp. 257–8. *NM* 1987; M. Meilakh, 'Ne proshlo i semidesyati let', *LO*, no. 1 (1990), p. 70; *LG* (7 August 1991), p. 11.

9. See the discussion between Prof. F. Kuznetsov, Doctor of Philology, and Yurii Polyakov, Corresponding member of the USSR Academy of Sciences, in *LG* (30 September 1987), p. 3. Kuznetsov was notorious for his persecution of Vasilii Aksyonov, among others.

10. V. Baranov, *LG* (25 March 1987).

11. See, for example, Evtushenko's introduction to Nabokov's poems in *Ogonek*. Kuznetsov cites V. Nabokov, *Drugie berega, DN*, nos 5–6 (1988); published in English as *Conclusive Evidence* (1951), and in a revised form as *Speak, Memory* (1966).

12. An overall discussion of Nabokov's work by the scholar A. Mulyarchik entitled 'The Nabokov Phenomenon: Light and Shadows', appeared in *LG* (20 May 1987), p. 5.

13. *LG* (30 September 1987), p. 3; this was a response to an article in *Argumenty i fakty* suggesting that only the revolutionaries among the intelligentsia, those who had 'participated directly in the events of October', were prepared for the Revolution.

14. O. Chaikovskaya, *NM*, no. 8 (1987), pp. 241–2.

15. V. E. Mel'nichenko, *VI KPSS*, no. 5 (1988), pp. 73–4.

16. I. Klyamkin, 'Kakaya doroga vedet k khramu?', *NM*, no. 11 (1987), p. 170. For further discussion of Klyamkin, see Davies, op. cit., pp. 24–6, 32–4; Nove, op. cit., pp. 40–3, 73–6.

17. *Smena vekh* (M., 1921).

18. N. Berdyaev *et al.*, *Vekhi: sbornik stat'ei o russkoi intelligentsii* (M., 1909); republished in *LO*, nos 7–12 (1990).

19. A chapter from Bulgakov's *The White Guard* was published in *NM*, no. 2 (1987); see also M. Chudakova's biography of Bulgakov, *Moskva*, nos 6–8 (1987) and nos 11–12 (1988); M. Kaganskaya, 'Beloe i krasnoe', *LO*, no. 5 (1991), pp. 93–9.

20. See below, pp. 145–9.

21. B. Pasternak, *Doktor Zhivago, NM*, nos 1–4 (1988).

22. V. Gusev, in *'Doktor Zhivago' Borisa Pasternaka: s raznykh tochek zreniya* (M., 1990), p. 233.

23. For evidence of such bewilderment, see A. Voznesenskii, ibid., p. 227.

24. Cited in E. Rich, 'Russian writers, critics and publishers on perestroika and its influence on Soviet literature', *Soviet Literature*, no. 1 (1990), p. 150.

25. Rich, op. cit., p. 151.

26. For further discussion, see N. Cornwell, 'Soviet Responses to "Doktor Zhivago"', in A. McMillin (ed.), *From Pushkin to 'Palisandriia'* (London, 1990), pp. 201–15.

27. D. Likhachev, *NM*, no. 1 (1988), pp. 5–10; for the original letter, see 'Pis'mo redkollegii zhurnala "Novyi mir" B. Pasternaku', signed by B. Agapov, B. Lavrenev, K. Fedin, K. Simonov, A. Krivitskii, originally published in *LG* (25 October 1958); *NM*, no. 11 (1958); reprinted in *S raznykh tochek*, pp. 12–41.

28. A similar acceptance of the Revolution was expressed by Patriarch Aleksii in *Izvestiya* (5 November 1990), p. 1.

29. D. Urnov, '"Bezumnoe prevyshenie svoikh sil": o romane B. Pasternaka "Doktor Zhivago"', *Pravda* (27 April 1988), p. 3. The *Novyi mir* editors

referred to Zhivago's 'hypertrophic individualism'.
30. *LG* (22 June 1988). An influential article by Daniil Granin had, earlier, advocated the primacy of morality over ideology: see D. Granin, 'O miloserdii', *LG* (18 March 1987).
31. A. Turkov and N. Ivanova, *S raznykh tochek*, pp. 275–6; 196–7.
32. M. Voloshin, 'Iz tsikla "Usobitsa". Podgotovka teksta, publikatsiya i predislovie A. V. Lavrova', *NM*, no. 2 (1988), pp. 158–63. Other poems by Voloshin were published in *Rodnik*, no. 6 (1988); *DN*, no. 9 (1988); *Yunost'*, no. 10 (1988); the cycle was printed in full in *Yunost'*, no. 10 (1990). For further information on Voloshin, see C. Marsh, *M. A. Voloshin, Artist–Poet: A Study of the Synaesthetic Aspects of his Poetry* (Birmingham, 1983).
33. M. Voloshin 'Grazhdanskaya voina', *NM*, no. 2 (1988). reprinted in *Yunost'*, no. 10 (1990), p. 31.
34. M. Voloshin, *Rossiya raspyataya*, *Yunost'*, no. 10 (1990), pp. 24–31.
35. Parts of the novel were published in the edition *Rossiya, krov'yu umytaya* (1932); of the twenty-four planned chapters, only ten were printed; of forty-nine sketches, only twelve appeared. The phrase 'Russia washed in blood' was used by the hard-line writer Prokhanov to describe the 'terrible days of the coup' in October 1993: *Zavtra*, no. 1, (November 1993), p. 1.
36. A. Veselyi, *NM*, no. 5 (1988), pp. 135–61; the selection also includes his story *Bosaya pravda*.
37. The introduction is by Veselyi's daughter, not, as Alec Nove mistakenly says, his son (Nove, *Glasnost in Action*, p. 136).
38. *NM*, no. 5 (1988), p. 142; In *Yunost'*, no. 10 (1990), p. 11 it is explicitly stated: 'He was shot in 1938.'
39. R. Shpunt, 'Klevetnicheskaya kniga. O romane A. Veselogo "Rossiya, krov'yu umytaya"', *KP* (17 May 1937).
40. *NM*, no. 5 (1988), p. 140.
41. Ibid., p. 135.
42. Ibid. p. 140.
43. Veselyi's account bears a strong resemblance to Lev Razgon's description of the executioner Niyazov in Stalin's time: see above, pp. 110–11.
44. Solzhenitsyn, *The Gulag Archipelago*, vol. 1 (London: Fontana, 1974), p. 33.
45. *NM*, no. 10 (1988); reprinted from V. Korolenko, *Pis'ma k Lunacharskomu*, (Paris, 1922).
46. A similar view of the leniency of tsarist justice is expressed in Solzhenitsyn's *The Gulag Archipelago*, vol. 1, pp. 301, 432–4.
47. S. Zalygin, *NM*, no. 10 (1988), p. 198.
48. A. Tsipko, *Nauka i zhizn'*, nos. 11–12 (1988) and nos 1–2 (1989).
49. M. Gor'kii, *Nesvoevremennye mysli*, *LO*, nos 9, 10, 12 (1988).
50. Gorky, *Untimely Thoughts. Essays on Revolution, Culture and the Bolsheviks, 1917–1918*, trans. E. Ermolaev (London, 1968), p. 62.
51. I. Bunin, *Okayannye dni*, *LO*, nos 4, 6 (1989).
52. I. Bunin, *Okayannye dni*, 2nd edn (London, 1974), pp. 163.
53. I. Bunin, *Vospominaniya* (Paris, 1950), pp. 13–14.
54. Ibid., p. 79.

55. See, for example, E. Mawdsley, *The Russian Civil War* (Boston, 1987); W. B. Lincoln, *Red Victory: a History of the Russian Civil War* (NY, 1989).

56. S. P. Mel'gunov, *Krasnyi terror v Rossii*, 2nd edn (1924); republished by 'Sovetskii pisatel'' (1990); also published in journal *Rodnik*, nos 7–10 (1990).

57. V. I. Startsev, 'My s Leninym', *Pravda* (3 April 1990).

58. V. P. Buldakov and V. V. Kabanov, '"Voennyi kommunizm": ideologiya i obshchestvennoe razvitie', *VI*, no. 3 (1990).

59. Service, *Lenin*, p. 82.

60. V. Khodasevich, 'Stat'i. Zapisnaya knizhka', introduced by S. Bocharov, 'No vse zhe ya prochnoe zveno', *NM*, no. 3 (1990), pp. 160–7; on the previous censorship of Khodasevich's work, see J. Graffy, 'The Literary Press', in J. Graffy and G. Hosking (eds), *Culture and the Media in the USSR Today* (London, 1989), p. 145, n. 72; Z. Gippius, *Peterburgskie dnevniki 1919 goda, Gorizont*, no. 11 (1990), pp. 28–46.

61. A. Avtorkhanov, 'X S"ezd i osadnoe polozhenie v partii', *NM*, no. 3 (1990), pp. 193–205; extract from his book *Partokratiya*; see also the powerful attack on utopian thinking in Russia by A. Kiva, *Izvestiya* (5 November 1990), p. 3 (English translation in *CDSP*, vol. XLII, no. 44, pp. 1–3 under the title: 'Was October Worth it? The Dream Fades').

62. *Yunost'*, no. 10 (1990) includes: P. Lur'e, 'Dnevnik Pavla Abramovicha Lur'e, s 25 avgusta 1917 g. do 31 maya 1918 g.', pp. 6–10; extracts from L. Trotskii, 'Moya zhizn'', pp. 11–14; V. Korsak, 'U belykh', pp. 62–73; G. Gazdanov, 'Vecher u Kler', pp. 36–47; I. Shmelev, 'Rasskazy', pp. 48–61; A. Veselyi, 'Vol'nitsa. Bui. Krylo izstokryl'ya prazdnichek', pp. 11–14; M. Voloshin, 'Rossiya raspyataya', pp. 24–31; 'Usobitsa', pp. 31–4.

63. Wilfred Owen, *Collected Poems*, ed. C. Day Lewis (London, 1964), p. 31.

64. R. Rakhmatullin, 'Za chto pogibli shestnatsat' millionov rossiyan?', *Yunost'*, no. 10 (1990), p. 19.

65. By 1990 there was already severe conflict in the Baltic states and Nagorny-Karabakh. On the 'civil war' in literature, see N. Fed', 'Grazhdanskaya voina v literature?', *MG*, no. 3 (1990), pp. 231–68; M. Epstein, *Znamya*, no. 1 (1991), p. 220.

66. 'Triumf okayannykh dnei', ed. E. Atyakina and I. Khurgina, *Yunost'*, no. 10 (1990), pp. 2–3.

67. A. I. Denikin, 'Ocherki russkoi smuty', *Oktyabr'*, nos 10–12 (1990); published with abbreviations, cutting out some of the military material. Published in full in *VI*, nos 3–12 (1990), nos 1–12 (1991) and nos 1–9 and 11–12 (1992), (original publication: vol. 1, Paris, 1921; vol. 2, Berlin, 1926).

68. See, for example, S. Burin, 'RBR', *Yunost'*, no. 10 (1990), pp. 86–92.

69. M. Denikina, 'Kak sozdavalis' "Ocherki russkoi smuty"', *Oktyabr'*, no. 10 (1990), p. 57.

70. This is a reference to Voloshin's poem *Rossiya raspyataya*.

71. See Solzhenitsyn, *Gulag*, vol. 1, p. 263.

72. V. Maksimov, *Zaglyanut' v bezdnu* (New York, 1986), first published in

the USSR in 1990; extracts published in *Yunost'*, no. 10 (1990), pp. 18–39; published in full in *Znamya*, nos 9–10 (1990).

73. I. Vinogradov, 'Sem' dnei tvoreniya', *Oktyabr'*, no. 6 (1990), pp. 17–18.
74. V. Maksimov, 'Odisseya rossiiskogo kazachestva', introduction to 'I az vozdam . . . Glava iz knigi', *LG* (25 September 1990), p. 6. Maksimov's novel, first published Paris, 1986, was announced for publication in *Novyi mir* (1992), but has so far failed to appear.
75. J. Glad (ed.), *Conversations in Exile: Russian Writers Abroad* (Durham and London, 1993), p. 252.
76. Solzhenitsyn, vol. X, pp. 355–8; cited in P. Palamarchuk, *Moskva*, no. 10 (1990), p. 195.
77. See Solzhenitsyn's portrayal of the Maklakov brothers, the Kadet Vasilii and the tsarist minister Nikolai.
78. A. Nemzer, *LO*, no. 12 (1990).
79. See A. Nemzer, in *Vzglyad*, vol. 3 (M., 1991), p. 217.
80. For a hard-liner's unflattering comparison between Yeltsin and Kerensky, see V. Bushin, *SR* (6 March 1993), p. 3.

Notes to Chapter 10   The February Revolution and the Provisional Government

1. E. Anisimov, 'Glubokii ekskurs', *Nauka i zhizn'*, no. 1 (1988), p. 83 states that the Provisional Government had formerly been known in the USSR largely through Kukryniksov's cartoons.
2. *Moscow News* (8 February 1987).
3. *SK* (22 March 1988).
4. *Moscow News* (16 August 1987).
5. R. W. Davies, *Soviet History in the Gorbachev Revolution* (London, 1989), p. 134.
6. On Lenin's cordial relations with the Anarchist Kropotkin, see Yu. Gal'perin, 'Pervyi glavkom', *Ogonek*, no. 44 (1987), p. 11; E. Starostin, *Yunost'*, no. 5 (1988), p. 65; see also B. Oleinik, *LG* (4 May 1988).
7. Yu. V. Aksyutin, *Vestnik vysshei shkoly*, no. 4 (1988), p. 65; Lenin's note in *Polnoe sobranie sochinenii*, vol. XLIV, pp. 205, 396–7.
8. For a refutation, see V. Rozov, A. Gel'man in *Pravda* (29 February 1988).
9. N. Andreyeva, *SR* (13 March 1988); the reference is to B. Souvarine, *Stalin: A Critical Survey of Bolshevism*, trans. C. L. R. James (London, 1939).
10. B. Pasternak, *Doktor Zhivago*, chapter 5, section 8.
11. B. Pasternak, *Russkaya revolyutsiya. Neizvestnye stikhi Borisa Pasternaka*, *NM*, no. 4 (1989).
12. *Doktor Zhivago*, chapter 5, section 10.
13. See, for example, V. Kostikov, 'Sapogi iz shagrenovoi kozhi', *Ogonek*, no. 32 (August 1989), pp. 12–16.
14. A. I. Denikin, 'Ocherki russkoi smuty', *Oktyabr'*, nos 10–12 (1990).
15. V. Maksimov, *Zaglyanut' v bezdnu* (New York, 1986); extracts published in *Yunost'*, no. 10 (1990), pp. 18–39; published in full in *Znamya*, nos 9–10 (1990).

16. German Baluev, the editor of the Leningrad newspaper *Literator*, said of *The Red Wheel* in March 1991: 'I don't know of anyone who has read it'. V. Toporov, 'Dnevnik "Literatora"', *Literator*, no. 8 (February 1991), pp. 1–2 speaks of 'the lack of success, failure even' of *Krasnoe koleso*. For further criticism, see V. Vozdvizhenskii, 'Metamorfozy kul'tury', in *Vzglyad*, p. 191; but for an alternative view, see D. Shturman, 'Ostanovimo li krasnoe koleso?', *NM*, no. 2 (1993), pp. 144–71.

17. S. V. Tyutyukin and V. V. Shelokhaev, 'Revolyutsiya i nravstvennost'', *VI*, no. 6 (1990), pp. 3–20.

18. A. Kerenskii, *Rossiya na istoricheskom povorote*, *VI*, nos 6–12 (1990) and nos 1–11 (1991); for Guchkov's memoirs, see *VI*, nos 7–12 (1991); for the émigré Vladimir Chuguev's reminiscences of Kerensky, see V. Reshetnikov, 'Aleksandr Kerenskii. Pravda i vymysel', *Izvestiya* (4 July 1991).

19. A. Latynina, 'Solzhenitsyn i my', *NM*, no. 1 (1990), pp. 241–58. The 96-chapter version of *V kruge pervom*, not available in English, first published in A. *Solzhenitsyn*, vols I, II (Vermont and Paris, 1978); published in *NM*, nos 1–5 (1990).

20. 'Istoricheskaya epopeya A. I. Solzhenitsyna "Krasnoe koleso"', *Neva*, no. 2 (1990), pp. 7–8 (p. 8); quoted from A. Solzhenitsyn, 'Interv'yu zhurnalu Taim', *Za rubezhom*, no. 31 (1989), pp. 21–3.

21. A. Solzhenitsyn, 'Nashi pluralisty', quoted in Palamarchuk, *Moskva*, no. 10 (1990), p. 194. V. Bondarenko also published extracts in *Slovo*, no. 9 (1990), pp. 8–17, despite Solzhenitsyn's desire that his *publitsistika* should not be published in Russia. 'Nashi plyuralisty' was eventually published in *NM*, no. 4 (1992).

22. See, for example, A. Ulam, *A History of Soviet Russia* (NY, 1976), pp. 1–24; E. Acton, *Rethinking the Russian Revolution* (London, 1990).

23. *VRKhD*, no. 139 (1983), pp. 138–40.

24. Palamarchuk also quotes Solzhenitsyn, *Sob.soch.* (Vermont and Paris, 1978–) vol. X, pp. 355–8.

25. See the speeches made during an evening held in Solzhenitsyn's honour in the Bauman factory club in December 1988, eventually published as: 'Slovo o Solzhenitsyne', *NS*, no. 1 (1990), pp. 58–67 (pp. 64, 67).

26. See Chapter 1 above.

27. Solzhenitsyn, vol. X, pp. 355–8, cited in Palamarchuk, pp. 194–5.

28. H. Seton-Watson, *The Russian Empire, 1901–1917* (Oxford, 1967), pp. 696–7.

29. Palamarchuk, op. cit., p. 195.

30. Solzhenitsyn, vol. XVI, pp. 139–40.

31. A. Nemzer, 'Prozrevaya Rossiyu', *LO*, no. 12 (1990), p. 20, n. 5.

32. A. Lur'e, lecture, March 1991.

33. N. Berberova, *Liudi i lozhi: russkie masony XX stoletiya* (NY, 1986); published in *VL*, nos 1–5 (1990). For an attack on the unreliability of Berberova's work, see E. Beshenkovsky, 'Masonic Conspiracy? Again?', *Survey*, vol. 30, no. 41 (June 1989), pp. 167–74. See also G. Katkov, *Russia 1917: The February Revolution* (London, 1967), pp. 163–77.

34. See, for example, L. Khass, 'Eshche raz o masonstve v Rossii nachala XX veka', *VI*, no. 1 (1990).

35. A. Vaksberg, *LG* (4 May 1988).

36. *Mart 1917–go*, chapter 634. See also Solzhenitsyn, *Gulag*, vol. 1, p. 263, which condemns Gippius and Merezhkovskii for supporting Hitler during the war.
37. Solzhenitsyn, vol. XVI, p. 688; on Voronovich, see *Revolyutsiya i grazhdanskaya voina v opisaniyakh belogvardeitsev* (M., 1931), vol. 5, pp. 159–207.
38. *Mart 1917-go*, chapter 547.
39. On the Duma, see, in particular, chapters 62′, 65′ and 71′ of *Oktyabr′ 1916-go*.
40. A. Nemzer, 'Prozrevaya Rossiyu', *LO*, no. 12 (1990), pp. 19–27.
41. I. Zaslavskii, 'Chto chitayut nashi parlamentarii', LG (24 January 1990).
42. R. G. Abdulatipov, 'Mozhno byt′ levym, no ne levee serdtsa', *Rabochaya tribuna* (13 February 1991).
43. Solzhenitsyn, vol. X, 355–8.
44. V. Maksimov, *LG* (25 September 1990), p. 6.
45. J. Glad (ed.), *Conversations in Exile: Russian Writers Abroad* (Durham and London, 1993), p. 254.
46. V. Aksyonov, in *Materialy konferentsii: A. I. Solzhenitsyn i ego tvorchestvo* (Paris and New York, 1988), p. 13.
47. V. Turbin, *Novoe vremya*, no. 19 (1990). For other views on Solzhenitsyn, see Maksimov, *LG* (20 March 1990); answers from many writers and critics to a questionnaire on Solzhenitsyn in *LG*, nos 8, 11, 14, 16, 18, 20, 22, 24 (1991); Lakshin, *Argumenty i fakty*, no. 52 (1989).
48. A. Solzhenitsyn, *Kak nam obustroit′ Rossiyu?* (Leningrad, 1990); published in *KP* (18 September 1990); *LG* (18 September 1990), pp. 3–6. Solzhenitsyn insisted that the title should end in a question mark, demonstrating that he did not wish to instruct Russians, but to encourage them to work together to develop a suitable political structure.
49. For a historian's view on the relevance of 1917 for the contemporary scene, see V. Loginov, 'Vse eto uzhe bylo', *LG* (22 May 1991) p. 3.
50. See G. Popov's book *Nesostoyavshiisya mer (A Mayor who Didn't Succeed)* (M., 1993). For his criticism of the Stalinist 'Administrative System', see above, pp. 32–3.
51. Solzhenitsyn uses the diminutive form '*partiika*' to demonstrate his scorn for democratic political parties.
52. For an interesting discussion of contemporary western views, see Acton, op. cit., pp. 129–154.
53. V. Dolganov and A. Stepovoi, *Izvestiya* (26 September 1990), pp. 1–2; A. Vasilevskii, 'No my zhivem v Rossii', *LG* (29 May 1991), p. 11 suggests that this democratic procedure contradicts the idea of the writer as prophet; but the discussion of a writer's ideas in parliament, almost unthinkable in the West, suggests that writers were still taken very seriously in Russia.
54. For subsequent recognition of the correctness of Solzhenitsyn's prophecy, see B. Lyubimov, 'Chto poka ne sbylos′ – sbudetsya', *LG* (16 September 1992), p. 6.
55. Solzhenitsyn, vol. II, p. 323.
56. Solzhenitsyn's articles 'Na vozvrate dykhaniya i soznaniya', 'Raskayanie i samoogranichenie' and 'Obrazovanshchina' were eventually published in *NM*, no. 5 (1991).

57. L. Radzhikhovskii, 'Revolyutsiya – szadi', *Ogonek*, no. 9 (1992), p. 4. D. Shturman, 'U kraya bezdny. Kornilovskii myatezh glazami istorika i sovremennikov', *NM*, no. 7 (1993), pp. 213–32; V. Clark, 'When 1917 Lives, History is Dangerous', *Observer* (5 September 1993), p. 18.

58. A. Yakovlev, 'Wake up, brother Russia', *Guardian* (6 May 1992) cites the democrats' failure to introduce land reform and develop a responsible attitude towards democracy among the Russian people.

59. A. Solzhenitsyn, 'Revolyutsii ne vypriyamlyayut khod Istorii, a tol'ko delayayut ego ukhabistym', *LG* (22 September 1992), pp. 1, 3.

60. G. Melikyants, *Izvestiya* (31 August 1992), pp. 1, 3. For different responses to the film, see Lyubimov op. cit.; G. Orekhanova, *SR* (3 September 1992), p. 2; D. Kazennov, *LR* (4 September 1992), p. 6.

61. See, for example, P. Basinskii, 'Normal'naya russkaya literatura', *LG*, no. 1–2 (1993), pp. 4–5.

62. *MN* (10 October 1993), p. 7A; Roy Medvedev characterizes Yeltsin's methods as a novel experiment in '"democracy" without freedom'. 'Out with the old, and in with what?', *Guardian* (9 October 1993), section 2, p. 25.

Notes to Chapter 11   Tsarism Reconsidered

1. V. Pikul', *U poslednei cherty* (M., 1979); on its content and popularity, see K. Mehnert, *The Russians and their Favorite Books* (Stanford, 1983), pp. 157–9.

2. For further discussion of the reassessment of pre-revolutionary history, see R. W. Davies, *Soviet History in the Gorbachev Revolution* (Basingstoke and London, 1989), pp. 11–26.

3. J. Graffy, 'The Arts', in M. McCauley (ed.), *Gorbachev and Perestroika* (London, 1990), p. 199; S. Lawton, *Kinoglasnost* (Cambridge, 1992), p. 29.

4. G. Ioffe, *Velikii Oktyabr' i epilog tsarizma* (Moscow, 1987).

5. P. Cherkasov, 'Konets Romanovykh', *NM*, no. 7 (1988), pp. 259–62.

6. See, for example, E. Radzinskii, 'Rasstrel v Ekaterinburge', *Ogonek*, no. 21 (1989) and no. 2 (1990); V. Soloukhin, *NS*, no. 12 (1989).

7. *CDSP*, vol. XLI no. 16 (1989), pp. 25–6.

8. E. Radzinskii, *Tsarskie dnevniki: Nikolai II – Zhizn', smert'* (M, 1990); English translation: E. Radzinsky, *The Last Tsar*, trans. M. Schwartz (London, 1992).

9. Interview with E. Radzinskii by D. Grantsev, *Argumenty i fakty* (17–23 November 1990), pp. 6–7. Safarov was a member of the Presidium of the Urals Soviet, Isai Goloshchekin was head of the Urals Bolsheviks; his party alias was 'Filipp'.

10. *Vozrozhdenie Rossii*, no. 1 (1990).

11. R. Pittman, 'Leningrad, Loyalties and Literature', *Soviet Analyst*, vol. 19, no. 19 (26 September 1990), p. 5.

12. M. Frankland, 'Return of Tsar spurs nostalgia for bad old days', *Observer* (30 May 1993), p. 20.

13. V. Maksimov, *Zaglyanut' v bezdnu, Yunost'*, no. 10 (1990), pp. 18–39;

published in full in *Znamya*, nos 9, 10 (1990).

14. See for example, G. Katkov, *Russia 1917: The February Revolution* (London, 1967); R. Pearson, *Revolution in Russia* (London, 1973), pp. 31–2.
15. N. A. Sokolov, *Ubiistvo tsarskoi sem'i* (Moscow, 1990); first published 1920.
16. See O. Platonov, 'The heroic feat of investigator Sokolov. On the first Soviet publication of N. A. Sokolov's book "The Murder of the Tsar's Family"', *LR*, (1 February 1991), p. 12.
17. P. Palamarchuk, 'Aleksandr Solzhenitsyn: putevoditel'', *Moskva*, no. 10 (1990), p. 190.
18. A. Latynina, 'Solzhenitsyn i my', *NM*, no. 1 (1990).
19. Palamarchuk, op. cit. pp. 190–1.
20. V. Potapov, 'Zvezda, reka, zagadka . . . Zametki ob "Avguste Chetyrnadtsatogo"', *LO*, no. 11 (1990), pp. 18–22.
21. See, for example, L. Kochan, *Russia in Revolution, 1890–1918* (St Albans, 1974), pp. 193–4.
22. Solzhenitsyn, *Mart 1917-ogo*, vol. XVI, pp. 741–9.
23. A. Nemzer, 'Prozrevaya Rossiyu: Zametki o "Marte Semnadtsatogo"', *LO*, no. 12 (1990), pp. 19–27; p. 23.
24. V. Pikul', *Nechistaya sila* (M. , 1992).
25. V. Selyunin, 'Istoki', *NM*, no. 5 (1988), pp. 162–89. Gavriil Popov also praised the 'unforgettable Stolypin' and his support for small family farms: see *Pozitsiya* (Tartu), no. 1 (1989).
26. V. P. Danilov, *VI*, no. 3 (1988), p. 22.
27. V. Krasnov, 'Solzhenitsyn's New "Avgust chetyrnadtsatogo": A Novel Attempt to Revise History', in A. McMillin (ed.), *Aspects of Modern Russian and Czech Literature* (Columbus, OH, 1989); G. Tokmakoff, 'P. A. Stolypin in Solzhenitsyn's *Krasnoe koleso*: A Historian's View', in ibid., pp. 150–8; M. Geller, *Aleksandr Solzhenitsyn* (London, 1989), pp. 101–4, 111– 13.
28. P. Vail, A. Genis, 'Poiski zhanra. Aleksandr Solzhenitsyn', *Oktyabr'*, no. 6 (1990), pp. 197–202, especially p. 198. On this, see also Krasnov, op. cit., p. 136.
29. A. Latynina, *NM*, no. 1 (1990), pp. 241–58.
30. See, for example, R. Pipes, interview reported by J. Omang, *Washington Post* (4 February 1985); L. Navrozov, 'Solzhenitsyn's World History: August 1914 as a New Protocol of the Elders of Zion', *Midstream*, vol. XXXI, no. 6 (June/July 1985), pp. 46–53; L. Losev, 'Velikolepnoe budushchee Rossii: Zametki pri chtenii Avgusta chetyrnadtsatogo A. Solzhenitsyna', *Kontinent*, no. 42 (1984), pp. 289–320.
31. See, for example, Krasnov, op. cit., pp. 140–1; L. Losev, 'Solzhenitsynskie evrei', *Strelets*, no. 2 (1989), pp. 294–311; M. Perakh, 'Solzhenitsyn and the Jews', *Midstream*, vol. XXII, no. 6 (June/July 1977), pp. 3–17, esp. p. 13; R. Rutman, 'Solzhenitsyn and the Jewish Question', *Soviet Jewish Affairs*, vol. IV, no. 2 (1974), pp. 3–16, esp. p. 7; E. Frankel, 'Russians, Jews and Solzhenitsyn', ibid. , vol. V, no. 2 (1976), pp. 48–68, esp. p. 64.
32. This view was also quoted in a public lecture by Aron Lur'e, March 1991.
33. Solzhenitsyn, *Sob. soch.*, vol. XII, p. 320.
34. Ibid., vol. XII, p. 126.

35. Vol. XII, p. 320.
36. Vol. XII, p. 344.
37. A. Lur'e, lecture, March 1991.
38. V. S. Dyakin, 'Byl li shans u Stolypina?', *Zvezda*, no. 12 (1990), p. 124.
39. See, in particular, *Avgust 1914*, chapter 72. Palamarchuk quotes S. S. Ol'denburg, *Tsarstvovanie imperatora Nikolaya II* (Munich, 1949); reprinted Washington, 1981, as a less biased account.
40. A. Stolypin, 'Stolypin i Nikolai II v *Avguste chetyrnadtsatogo*', *Posev*, no. 3 (March 1984), pp. 58–60. Solzhenitsyn lays great store by the fact that the Tsar did not visit Stolypin in the clinic after the shooting; but P. N. Zyryanov, 'Pyotr Arkad'evich Stolypin', *VI*, no. 6 (1990), pp. 54–75 suggests that he did in fact go to the clinic, but was unable to see Stolypin.
41. *CDSP*, vol. XLII no. 8 (1990), p. 8.
42. See the exchange between Astaf'ev and the critic N. Eidelman, *Détente*, no. 8; this accusation was repeated in A. Shafarevich, *Russofobiya*, *NS*, no. 11 (1990). Astaf'ev also suggested that Russian literature should be off-limits to Jews.
43. Pipes, *Washington Post* (4 February 1985).
44. Losev, op. cit., p. 313.
45. Such subconscious anti-Semitism can also be detected in some of his other works: even the objective historian Alec Nove has pointed out that in *Gulag*, Solzhenitsyn places disproportionate emphasis on the role of evil Jews in the secret police under Lenin and Stalin: see Nove, *Glasnost in Action* (London, 1989), pp. 112–3.
46. See, for example, *LG* (27 August 1988); *Izvestiya* (14 August 1988).
47. E. Lazarev, 'Dmitrii Bogrov i ubiistvo Stolypina', *Volya Rossii*, no. 5, 1926, pp. 53–98; nos 8–9, pp. 28–65; reprinted in *Ubiistvo Stolypina*, compiled by A. Serebrennikov (New York, 1989). For an illuminating analysis of how Solzhenitsyn has altered this memoir for his own purposes, see Tokmakoff, op. cit., pp. 151–2.
48. V. Potapov, op. cit., p. 21.
49. Solzhenitsyn also, somewhat curiously, attempts to refute the widely documented view that the SR Evno Azeff was a double agent. It is also legitimate to wonder why Solzhenitsyn omitted any reference to the Tsar's adherence to anti-Semitic organizations.
50. P. N. Zyryanov, 'Pyotr Arkad'evich Stolypin', *VI*, no. 6 (1990), pp. 54–75.
51. V. Khorin, 'Uchit li istoriya? Iz pisem v redaktsiyu', *MG*, no. 7 (1990), p. 233 (letters, pp. 233–47).

Notes to Chapter 12   The Rise and Fall of Literature and History in the 1990s

1. I used this phrase in 'Reassessing the Past: Images of Stalin and Stalinism in Contemporary Russian Literature', in S. Duffin Graham (ed.), *New Directions in Soviet Literature* (Basingstoke and London, 1992), p. 96; formerly, when the word 'pluralism' had been used by Yakovlev, it meant 'socialist pluralism'.

2. J. Graffy, 'The Literary Press', pp. 107–57; J. Graffy, 'The Arts', in M. McCauley (ed.), *Gorbachev and Perestroika* (London, 1990), pp. 189–207; R. Marsh, *Images of Dictatorship* (London, 1989), pp. 70–207; D. Brown, 'Literature and *Perestroika*', *Michigan Quarterly Review*, vol. 28, no. 4 (Fall 1989).

3. A. Latynina, 'Chto vperedi?', *LG* (23 January 1991), p. 10. For much fuller discussion, see R. Marsh, 'The Death of Soviet Literature: Can Russian Literature Survive?', *Europe-Asia Studies*, vol. 45, no. 1 (1993), pp. 115–39.

4. The most famous was V. Erofeyev, 'Pominki po sovetskoi literature', *Aprel'*, no. 1 (1991), pp. 274–82; see also Yu. Bondarev, *LR* (14 December 1990), pp. 2–4; M. Kharitonov, 'Apologiya literatury', *LG*, (19 June 1991) p. 11.

5. This question was asked by many Soviet intellectuals in the early 1990s: see, for example, K. Stepanyan, 'Nuzhna li nam literatura?', *Znamya*, no. 12 (1990), pp. 222–30; Kharitonov, op. cit.

6. R. W. Davies, *Soviet History in the Gorbachev Revolution* (London, 1989), p. vii and *passim*.

7. R. W. Davies, 'History and Perestroika', in E. A. Rees (ed.), *The Soviet Communist Party in Disarray* (London, 1991), p. 121; Davies repeated this view in a paper at the annual BASEES conference, University of Birmingham, April 1993. For an alternative view, see *LO*, no. 12 (1990), p. 28.

8. See, for example, E. Shklovskii, 'U razbitogo koryta', *LG* (19 February 1992), p. 4.

9. 'One article of was entitled: 'The Blood of the Twentieth Century: is Literature Guilty?', *LG* (19 June 1991), p. 11.

10. The references are to A. Herzen, *Kto vinovat?* (1845), N. Chernyshevsky, *Chto delat'?* (1863) and V. I. Lenin, *Chto delat'?* (1903). For a similar view, see 'From the Editors', in H. Goscilo and B. Lindsey (eds), *Glasnost': An Anthology of Russian Literature under Gorbachev* (Ann Arbor, MI, 1990), p. xxv.

11. On the 'Pasternak affair', see V. Kaverin, 'Literator', *Znamya*, no. 8 (1987), pp. 80–121; on persecution of Sinyavskii and Daniel, see V. Simonov, *MN*, no. 8 (1987), p. 23; on Tvardovsky's loss of *Novyi mir* in 1970, see, among many other articles, Yu. Karyakin, 'Stoit li nastupat' na grabli? Otkrytoe pis'mo odnomu inkognito', *Znamya*, no. 9 (1987), pp. 200–24; A. Bocharov, 'Pokushenie na mirazhi', *VL*, no. 1 (1988), pp. 72–3; Yu. Burtin, '"Vam, iz drugogo pokoleniya...", k publikatsii poemy A. Tvardovskogo "Po pravu pamyati"', *Oktyabr'*, no. 8 (1987), pp. 191–202; N. Il'ina, 'Zdravstvui, plemya mladoe, neznakomoe', *Ogonek*, no. 2 (1988), pp. 23–6; A. Ivanov, 'Vysoka tsena istiny', *LR*, no. 18 (1988), p. 9; V. Lakshin, 'Ne vpast' v bespamyatstvo (iz khroniki 'Novogo mira' vremeni Tvardovskogo', *Znamya*, no. 8 (1988), pp. 210–17.

12. See, for example, Yu. Idashkin, 'Pravo na pokayanie', *Ogonek*, no. 25 (1989).

13. Yu. Afanas'ev, *SK*, (21 March 1987); P. Rodionov, *SK* (14 June 1988); E. Ambartsumov, *VI*, no. 6 (1988), pp. 2–3. On the party's suppression of all discussion of Stalinism after Khrushchev's fall, see F. Burlatskii, *LG* (14 September 1988).

14. In 1992 some Russian intellectuals suggested that vague appeals for 'mass repentance' are a poor substitute for actual trials of individuals associated with the old regime, since 'Guilt is personal': M. Berg, personal interview, April 1991; V. Kamyanov, 'Zabyt' tak skoro? Ob "okhote na ved'm"i printsipe kollektivnoi viny', *LG* (12 February 1992), p. 3. Some members of the Russian political leadership hoped to turn the Constitutional Court hearings into a 'Nuremberg trial' of the Communist Party: see V. Tolz and J. Wishnevsky, 'The Russian Government Declassifies CPSU Documents', *RFE/RL Research Report*, vol. 1, no. 26 (26 June 1992), pp. 8–11.

15. Scourges of past collaborators have also been criticized for their former silence: see attack on Bondarenko and Toporov, in A. Rubashkin, 'Sprosit' s sebya', *LG* (3 July 1991), p. 10.

16. Erofeyev, op. cit.; V. Toporov, 'Dnevnik "Literatora"', *Literator*, no. 17 (May 1991), p. 1; A. Kushner, 'Pozhiznennost' zadachi', *LG* (26 June 1991), p. 10.

17. For an anti-Semitic attack on Rybakov and Shatrov, see V. Kozhinov, 'Pravda i istina', *NS*, no. 4 (1988), pp. 160–75. Lev Kopelev and Alexander Yanov have expressed concern about this negative aspect of *glasnost:* see 'Vopros bez otveta', *Ogonek*, no. 46 (1989), pp. 13–14.

18. M. Berg, interview, 1991. By 1992–3, according to the literary editors Natal'ya Perova and Alla Latynina, there was also a younger 'underground' of writers hostile to the older 'underground'.

19. S. Chuprinin, 'Situatsiya (bor'ba idei v sovremennoi literature)', *Znamya*, no. 1 (1990), p. 202.

20. On Russian readers' disillusionment with literary disputes, see S. Chuprinin, 'Zadanie na dom. Chto proiskhodit s sovremennoi russkoi literaturoi', *Ogonek*, no. 4 (January 1992), p. 16.

21. S. Chuprinin, in *Vzglyad*, vol. 3 (M. , 1991), p. 19, citing Alla Latynina's jibe against her former ally Natal'ya Ivanova.

22. See, for example, M. Zolotusskii's attack on Aitmatov and Anan'ev, the liberal editor of *Oktyabr'*, for signing a letter attacking Solzhenitsyn and Sakharov: *LG* (21 July 1993), p. 4.

23. N. Ivanova, talk at St Antony's College, Oxford, June 1993.

24. M. Zolotonosov, 'Satana v nesterpimom bleske', *LO*, no. 5 (1991), pp. 93–9; this tendency attacked in B. Sarnov, 'The Empty Font', *Frankfurter Allgemeine Zeitung* (30 January 1993).

25. Discussed in L. Anninskii, 'Shestidesyatniki, semidesyatniki, vos'midesyatniki: k dialektike pokolenii v russkoi kul'ture', *LO*, no. 4 (1991), pp. 10–14; attacks on Russian classics were disputed by A. Latynina, in a talk at St Antony's College, Oxford, October 1993; A. Solzhenitsyn, *NM*, no. 4 (1993), p. 5.

26. The question of whether a writer's work can be separated from his or her biography has again become a hotly debated topic in the West because of revelations about Philip Larkin's racism and Heidegger's Nazi sympathies.

27. For fuller discussion, see Marsh, 'The Death of Soviet Literature'; Marsh, 'Glasnost and Russian Literature', *ASEES*, vol. 6, no. 2, (1992), pp. 21–39.

28. A. Nuikin, 'Kamo gryadeshi?', *LG* (19 June 1991), p. 11; V. Toporov,

'Dnevnik "Literatora"', *Literator*, no. 21, (May 1991), p. 11; V. Erofeyev, op. cit., p. 277; Rubashkin, *LG* (3 July 1991), p. 10.

29. Erofeyev, op. cit., pp. 280–1.
30. See Yu. Karabchievskii, 'Vozvrashchenie smysla', in *Vzglyad*, vol. 3 (M., 1991), p. 170; E. Rich, 'Russian Writers, Critics and Publishers on Perestroika and its Influence on Soviet Literature', *Soviet Literature*, no. 1 (1990), p. 151. Even Solzhenitsyn, who has the greatest claim to being the teacher and prophet of his nation, has had surprisingly little influence in Russia, although 1990 was heralded as 'the year of Solzhenitsyn'. See S. Zalygin, 'God Solzhenitsyna', *NM*, no. 1 (1990), pp. 233–40; for a contrary view, see K. Stepanyan, *Znamya*, no. 12 (1990), p. 225. The phrase 'the year of Solzhenitsyn' was also used as the title of a series in which critics and writers answered a questionnaire about Solzhenitsyn: see *LG*, nos 8 (1991), 11, 14, 16, 18, 20, 22, 24.
31. For a similar point in relation to Russian film makers, see D. Dondurei, *NG* (10 April 1993), p. 7.
32. For the debate on émigré writers, see, for example, A. Latynina, 'Kogda podnyalsya zheleznyi zanaves', *LG* (24 July 1991), pp. 9, 11; the interview with the émigré writer A. Kustarev, who lives in London: S. Taroshchina, 'Pominki po emigrantskoi literature', *LG* (3 July 1991), p. 11. For further discussion, see the interview with A. Sinyavsky and M. Rozanova, *MN*, no. 2 (1989); A. Miloslavskii, 'Ivan Aleksandrovich ne vinovat', *LG* (7 August 1991), p. 10; V. Maksimov, 'Kto tam – za kordonom?', *LG*, (16 October 1991), p. 11; E. Limonov, 'Da, ya vrag vashei perestroiki', *LG*, (7 August 1991), p. 11; V. Voinovich, 'So vsemi dolgami davno rasplatemshis'', ibid. ; M. Rozanova, 'Zvezda nad skhvatkoi', ibid.; *LG* (24 July 1991), p. 9; V. Aksenov, 'Krylatoe vymyrayushchee', *LG* (27 November 1991), p. 1; D. Granin, 'Unynie – velikii grekh', *LG* (1 January 1992), p. 3.
33. *Vzglyad*, vol. 3 (M. , 1991), pp. 274–91.
34. G. Baluev, interview, March 1991.
35. See the interview with Voinovich, I. Zolotusskii, 'Grustnye razgovory v pustoi kvartire', *LG* (22 April 1992), p. 5.
36. For his intention to return, see A. Solzhenitsyn, 'Revolyutsii ne vypryamlyayut khod Istorii, a tol'ko delayut ego ukhabistym', *LG*, (22 September 1993), pp. 1, 3.
37. N. Ivanova, speech at St Antony's College, Oxford, June 1993. For a variety of responses to Solzhenitsyn's return, see *CDPSP*, vol. 56, no. 22, pp. 1–6.
38. For the limited nature of this freedom, see S. White, *After Gorbachev* (Cambridge, 1993), p. 101.
39. On the politicization of literature, see Marsh, 'The Death'. Many writers and historians became Congress deputies: for example, V. Rasputin, Ch. Aitmatov, E. Evtushenko and Yu. Afanas'ev.
40. V. Kamyanov, in *Vzglyad*, vol. 3, p. 248.
41. One important article on this subject by G. Chuprinin was simply called 'The Situation': see *Znamya*, no. 1 (1990).
42. N. Ivanova, 'Vozvrashchenie k nastoyashchemu', *Znamya*, no. 8 (1990), pp. 235–6.

43. For another hard-hitting attack on utopian thinking in Russia, see A. Kiva, *Izvestiya* (5 November 1990), p. 3.
44. For this, and similar phrases, see the conversation between I. Shaitanov and G. Smith, *LG* (17 March 1993), p. 5; L. Anninskii, 'Za chto proklyaty?', *LG* (3 March 1993), p. 4.
45. By 1991 young people were apparently moaning: 'Oh no, not more about the camps!': A. Lur'e, lecture, March 1991.
46. A. Nuikin, 'Kamo gryadeshi?', *LG* (19 June 1991), p. 11; A. German, 'Pochemu ya ne snimayu kino posle 1985 goda', *LG* (1 May 1991), p. 14. Tat'yana Tolstaya has been quoted as saying: 'I know I can write, but I can't seem to find anything to write *about*': see I. Maryniak, 'Writing as the Clock Runs Wild', *Independent* (24 August 1991), p. 26.
47. V. Kardin, 'Skvoz' ternii . . .', *LG* (7 August 1991), p. 9.
48. A. Ageev, 'Posle shoka', *LG* (3 June 1992), p. 4. This is a variation of Teodoro Adorno's view that 'it is impossible to write after Auschwitz'.
49. There were some interesting works on contemporary society: see, for example, Yu. Polyakov, 'Sto dnei do prikaza', *Yunost'*, no. 11 (1987); S. Kaledin, *Smirennoe kladbishche*, *NM*, no. 5 (1987); M. Palei, *Evgesha i Annushka*, *Znamya*, no. 7 (1990).
50. Suggested by O. Trifonova, 'Pisat' do predela vozmozhnogo', *Yunost'*, no. 10 (1990), pp. 4–6.
51. Suggested by V. Kardin, 'Skvoz' ternii . . .', *LG* (7 August 1991), p. 9; T. Tolstaya, *Guardian* (19 March 1992), p. 25.
52. In the post-communist era some works are beginning to fill this gap: see A. Zinoviev, *Katastroika*, *Neva*, no. 3 (1993); A. Kurchatkin, *Strazhnitsa*, *Znamya*, nos 5–6 (1993).
53. A. Latynina, 'Solzhenitsyn i my', *NM*, no. 11 (1990), pp. 241–51. A similar view was expressed by A. Lur'e in a lecture in Leningrad, March 1991. See also P. Vail and A. Genis, 'Poiski zhanra. Aleksandr Solzhenitsyn', *Oktyabr'*, no. 6 (1990), pp. 197–202.
54. A. Solzhenitsyn, *The Gulag Archipelago*, vol. 1 (London: Fontana, 1974), p. 298.
55. See, for example, V. Bondarenko, 'Nazad puti net', *MG*, no. 5 (1989).
56. See A. Latynina, 'Chto vperedi?', *LG* (23 January 1991), p. 10; V. Toporov, *Literator*, no. 17 (May 1991), pp. 1, 5; no. 18 (May 1991), p. 5; no. 19 (May 1991), p. 5; N. Iovlev, E. Slavkin, 'My – za privilegii svobodnykh lyudei', *LG* (30 October 1991), p. 9; E. Etkind, 'Brein-drein', *LG* (6 November 1991), p. 9; 'Smert' kul'turnoi knigi', *LG* (26 February 1992), p. 7.
57. A. Lur'e, lecture, March 1991. A similar view emerges from the article by M. Zolotonosov, 'Otdykhayushchii fontan. Malen'kaya monografiya o postsotsialisticheskom realizme', *Oktyabr'*, no. 4 (1991), pp. 166–79.
58. A. Higgins, 'Selective memories of futile intervention', *Independent* (6 August 1993), p. 10.
59. *Slavic Review*, vol. 52, no. 2 (Summer 1993), p. 342. On the commercialization of the archives, see also the discussion: 'Research, Ethics and the Marketplace: the Case of the Russian Archives', *Slavic Review*, vol. 52, no. 1 (Spring 1993), pp. 87–104.
60. 'The Rich also Cry' , 'My Two Mothers' and 'Maria', which are well

below the standard of 'Dallas' and 'Dynasty', enjoyed great success on Russian television in the years 1991–4. Kashpirovskii became deputy leader of the Liberal Democratic Party, but subsequently dissociated himself from Zhirinovsky.

61. Latynina, *LG* (23 January 1991), p. 10.
62. Ibid. Some younger writers seem to be more enthusiastic about the market system, claiming that their elders are complaining because they have lost their privileges and cannot adapt to the new society: see, for example, O. Pavlov, 'Mezhdu volkom i sobakoi', *LG* (27 May 1992), p. 4.
63. N. Ivanova, 'Igra zakonchena', *KO*, no. 35 (1990), cited and discussed in K. Stepanyan, 'Nuzhna li nam literatura?', *Znamya*, no. 12 (1990), pp. 222–30.
64. S. Chuprinin, 'Situatsiya', in *Vzglyad*, vol. 3, p. 15.
65. See, in particular, the dispute over Solzhenitsyn's writings: J. Dunlop, 'Solzhenitsyn Begins to Emerge from the Political Void', *RL Report on the USSR*, vol. 1, no. 36 (1989), pp. 4–6.
66. *LO*, no. 12 (1990), p. 28.

Notes to Chapter 13 Conclusion

1. For an eloquent defence of free art see A. Sinyavskii, 'V tupikakh svobody', *LG* (1 April 1992), p. 3.
2. This is rarely recognized in Russia: an exception is A. Galkin and A. Chernyaev, *NG* (17 August 1993) who felt it necessary to remind their readers of Gorbachev's achievements, asking: 'Where is the public's memory?'.
3. For an overview of the breaking of historical taboos in fiction, see R. Marsh, 'Reassessing the Past: Images of Stalin and Stalinism in Contemporary Russian Literature', in S. Duffin Graham (ed.), *New Directions in Soviet Literature* (Basingstoke and London, 1992), pp. 93–6; on the general lifting of taboos in Soviet fiction under *glasnost*, see J. Graffy, 'The Literary Press', in J. Graffy and G. Hosking (eds), *Culture and the Media in the USSR Today* (Basingstoke and London, 1989), pp. 107–57; R. Marsh, 'Glasnost and Russian literature', *ASEES*, vol. 6, no. 2 (1992), pp. 21–9.
4. See, for example, R. Marsh, *Images of Dictatorship* (London, 1989); G. Svirski, *A History of Post-war Soviet Writing: The Literature of Moral Opposition*, trans. and ed. R. Dessaix, M. Ulman (Ann Arbor, MI, 1981); D. Spechler, *Permitted Dissent in the USSR: Novy Mir and the Soviet Regime* (NY, 1982).
5. See also the memoirs of K. Simonov, *Glazami cheloveka moego pokoleniya*, *Znamya*, nos 3–5 (1988); Dudintsev's *Belye odezhdy* (M., 1988), pp. 408–9.
6. G. Fedotov, *Rossiya i svoboda*, *Znamya*, no. 12 (1989); N. Berdyaev, *Istoki i smysl russkogo kommunizma* (M., 1990); for their influence on the Russian intelligentsia, see M. Zolotonosov, *MN* (10 October 1993), p. 5B. The influence of nineteenth-century Russian literature and Rus-

sian religious philosophy on contemporary Russian society are two important themes which deserve much fuller treatment.

7. A. Kabakov, *Nevozvrashchenets, Iskusstvo kino*, no. 6 (1989); V. Rybakov, *Hassle, Glas: New Russian Writing*, no. 1 (1991); L. Petrushevskaya, *Novye Robinzony, NM*, no. 8 (1989). By a remarkable coincidence, the film of A. Kabakov's *Nevozvrashchenets* depicting a military coup was shown on Soviet television on 20–1 August 1991. Another anti-utopian work was Vladimir Makanin, *Laz, NM*, no. 5 (1991), which made the Booker Prize shortlist in 1992.

8. *Izvestiya*, (3 April 1988).

9. See R. W. Davies, *Soviet History in the Gorbachev Revolution* (London, 1989), pp. 167–84.

10. See, for example, Yu. Korablev, I. Fedosov and Yu. Borisov, *Istoriya SSSR: uchebnik dlya desyatogo klassa srednei shkoly* (M., 1989), published in 3,110,000 copies.

11. O. Latsis, *Izvestiya* (5 August 1993), p. 5.

12. For an account of history lessons in Moscow in 1989, see H. Shukman, *THES* (2 March 1990).

13. Latsis, op cit.; attacked in *SR* (24 December 1992).

14. See, for example, *VI*, no. 3 (1988), pp. 3–57 and no. 6 (1988), pp. 3–114.

15. See Yurii Polyakov, cited in *Observer* (8 November 1987), p. 11.

16. See, for example, 'An Image of Greatness (interview with Mikhail Shatrov)', *Soviet Literature*, no. 1 (1988), p. 125; A. Rybakov, *DN*, no. 9 (1989), p. 266.

17. For fuller discussion of the relationship between history and fiction, see Marsh, *Images of Dictatorship*, pp. 1–10, 142–3, 207–10 and *passim*; Joseph W. Turner, 'The Kinds of Historical fiction: An Essay in Definition and Methodology', *Genre* (Oklahoma), vol. xii (Fall 1979), pp. 337, 342.

18. For criticism of this episode, see A. Latsis, 'S tochki zreniya sovremennika: zametki o romane "Deti Arbata"', *Izvestiya* (17 August 1987); J. Barber, 'Children of the Arbat', *Détente*, no. 11 (1988), pp. 9–11.

19. See A. Rybakov, *LG*, (19 August 1987), p. 6; disputed by Davies, op. cit., p. 187; J. Dunlop, R. Haugh and M. Nicholson (eds), *Solzhenitsyn in Exile* (Stanford, 1985), pp. 338, 330. On Solzhenitsyn's attitude to history, see Marsh, *Images of Dictatorship*, pp. 9, 141–7, 208–10, 212; on the historical accuracy of Solzhenitsyn's portrait of Stalin in the 96-chapter version of *The First Circle* published in Russia in 1990, see ibid., pp. 135–73.

20. This fallacy is discussed by E. H. Carr in *What is History?* (Penguin, Harmondsworth, 1987), pp. 44–55, 169–70.

21. For a plausible defence of his position, particularly the impossibility of waiting, see A. Rybakov, *DN*, no. 9 (1989), p. 266. The second and third parts of his trilogy demonstrate a willingness to learn from his mistakes.

22. V. Danilov, 'Tret'ya volna', *VI*, no. 3 (1988), pp. 21–4. For a different view, see D. Gillespie, 'History, politics and the Russian Peasant: Boris Mozhaev and the collectivization of agriculture', *SEER*, vol. 67, no. 2 (April 1989), p. 203, n. 29.

23. See, for example, S. Wheatcroft, 'More light on the scale of repression and excess mortality in the Soviet Union in the 1930s', *Soviet Studies*, vol. 42, no. 2 (April 1990), pp. 355–67 (p. 367); A. Nove, 'How many victims in the 1930s?', ibid. , p. 370; for a review of the western literature by a Russian scholar, see V. Danilov, *VI*, no. 3 (1988), pp. 116–21.
24. V. P. Danilov, *Pravda*, (16 September 1988).
25. See above, p. 305, n. 61; V. Tsaplin, 'Statistika zhertv stalinizma v 30-e gody', *VI*, no. 4 (1989), p. 176; discussed in E. Bacon, 'Glasnost and the Gulag: New Information on Soviet Forced Labour around World War II', *Soviet Studies*, vol. 44, no. 6 (1992), pp. 1075–7.
26. Davies, op. cit. p. 188. Soviet critics and publicists usually just accept these faulty conclusions: see, for example, N. Ivanova, citing O. Latsis, 'Problema tempov v sotsialisticheskom stroitel'stve: razmyshleniya ekonomista', *Kommunist*, no. 18 (1987), pp. 79–90.
27. On dissident literature, see A. Besançon, 'Solzhenitsyn at Harvard', *Survey*, vol. 24, no. 1 (Winter 1979), pp. 134–5; on Maksimov, see Hosking, *Beyond Socialist Realism*, p. 123.
28. T. Abuladze, cited in *LG* (25 February 1987), p. 8; for a similar view, see M. Lipovetskii, 'Zabudem slovo "realizm"?', *LG* (4 December 1991), p. 10.
29. A. Bitov, *Pushkinskii dom*, *NM*, nos 10–12 (1987); for further discussion, see E. Chances, *Andrei Bitov: Ecology of Inspiration* (Cambridge, 1993), pp. 202–45.
30. These include Voinovich, Vladimov, Aksyonov, Sinyavskii, Iskander and Sokolov. On fantastic and grotesque images of Stalin, see Marsh, *Images of Dictatorship*, pp. 120–33.
31. A. Bitov, *Fotografiya Pushkina (1799–2099)*, *Znamya*, no. 1 (1987).
32. For further discussion, see H. Goscilo, 'Introduction', in H. Goscilo and B. Lindsey (eds), *Glasnost: an Anthology of Russian Literature under Gorbachev* (Ann Arbor, MI, 1990), pp. xxxv–vi.
33. For criticism of Abuladze's Aesopian techniques, see T. Khlopyankina, 'Pod zvuki nabatnogo kolokola', *Sovetskii ekran*, no. 15 (1987), pp. 4–5.
34. *Vzglyad*, vol. 3, pp. 234–5.
35. See, for example, T. Ivanova, 'Zvezda zheny soseda Mitrofana', *Ogonek*, no. 34 (1988), p. 28; 'O popushchennom, opushchennom i nyne dopushchennom', *Ogonek*, no. 49 (1988), p. 10.
36. A. Voznesensky, review of V. S. Pritchett, *Chekhov: A Spirit Set Free*, in *The New York Times Book Review* (27 November 1988), p. 35. For the irrelevance of poetry in the contemporary political crisis, see I. Shaitanov and G. Smith, *LG* (17 March 1993), p. 5.
37. Discussed in R. Sakwa, *Gorbachev and his Reforms* (London, 1990), p. 66.
38. Quotation attributed to Ralph Nader.
39. E. Etkind, *Notes of a Non-Conspirator*, trans. P. France (Oxford, 1978), p. 52.
40. Sakwa, op. cit., p. 81; see also V. Korotich, quoted in *Independent* (9 February 1989).
41. S. Rassadin, 'Dzyk, dzyk!', *LG* (17 February 1993), p. 3 acknowledges that the intelligentsia has played its part and is no longer important in post-Soviet Russia.

42. E. Etkind, 'Brein-drein', *LG* (6 November 1991), p. 9. Other prominent democratic figures, such as Abuladze and Sakharov, have died.
43. Only 13 per cent of the deputies elected to the Congress in 1990 came from the intelligentsia.
44. *LG* (9 December 1992), p. 4.
45. See, for example, G. Vladimov, 'Tri oshibki zagovorshchikov', *MN* (24 August 1991), p. 1; broadcast appeal by B. Okudzhava during the rebellion of October 1993; G. Vladimov, 'Utro sleduyushchego dnya', *MN* (10 October 1993), p. 9A; comments by A. Yakovlev, Yu. Afanas'ev, D. Prigov, A. Gel'man, V. Bykov and A. German in ibid., pp. 5A, 7A.
46. By 1994 Mozhaev had come to warn against the chaotic policy of over-rapid privatization of land: see B. Mozhaev, *Ulichnye razgovory*, *Don*, nos 3–4 (1994).
47. *LG*, (6 May 1987), p. 10.
48. See, for example, the Supreme Soviet debate of July 1988, when the President of the Armenian Republic presented evidence indicating that in 1921 Stalin had been responsible for the reversal of the decision of the Caucasian bureau of the Communist Party that Nagorny-Karabakh should remain part of Armenia: *Izvestiya* (20 July 1988).
49. A. Migranyan, *NM*, no. 7 (1989), p. 183.
50. J. Riordan, *Soviet Youth Culture* (Basingstoke and London, 1989).
51. In an article written in 1990 I argued that glasnost in history 'threatened to sweep away' the Soviet regime, and that 'it will be difficult to control the tide of freedom'. See Marsh, 'Reassessing the past', p. 102. The process occurred more rapidly than most commentators could have predicted.
52. Davies, op. cit., pp. 188–91.
53. On 'counter-communism', see S. Cohen, *Rethinking the Soviet Experience: Politics and History since 1917* (NY and Oxford, 1985), pp. 14–15; on the danger posed by this philosophy in Russia, see P. Broué, 'Gorbachev and History', p. 5. For the controversy caused by Conquest's *The Great Terror* among revisionist historians, see the review by L. McReynolds, *Russian History*, vol. 21, no. 1, pp. 95–6.
54. This is, of course, an ideal; whether objectivity or complete evidence are really possible is another matter. See Carr, *What is History?*; C. N. L. Brooke, *Time, the Archsatirist* (London, 1968); R. Collingwood, *The Idea of History* (Oxford, 1946); B. Croce, *Philosophy, Poetry, History: An Anthology of Essays*. trans. C. Spriggs (London, 1966) for a selection of views on the role of interpretation in history and the degree to which history is similar or different from fiction.
55. Davies, op. cit., p. 192.
56. Discussions at World Congress of Slavists, Harrogate, 1990, and BASEES, 1993.
57. Discussions at the conference on 'Stalinism: 40 years on', Exeter, 1993.
58. See, for example, Yu. Bondarev at 19th Party Conference, cited in Davies, op. cit., p. 154; V. Falin, head of the Central Committee's International Department, *MN*, no. 36 (1988), pp. 8–9. Perhaps the most striking example was the lawsuit brought against the writer Ales' Adamovich and the newspaper *SK* by Ivan Shekhovtsov, an investigator in the Ukrainian prosecutor's office in the early 1950s, for allegedly 'blackening and

spurning' post-1930 history and everything patriotic Soviet citizens hold dear.

59. M. S. Gorbachev, *Pravda* (13 January 1988); *Pravda* (19 February 1988).
60. See, for example, A. Rybakov, 'S proshlym nado rasstavat'sya dostoino', *MN* (17 July 1988), p. 11; A. Zhigulin, *MN* (31 July 1988), p. 12.
61. See, for example, O. Chaikovskaya, 'Dostoinstvo vyshe politiki', *LG* (21 October 1992), p. 11.
62. This process took place under the aegis of the Committee of Toponyms, established in 1987 under Academician Likhachev. By 1993 it seemed to have gone too far: in the mania to change all names given by the Bolsheviks, Chekhov Street in Moscow was also renamed.
63. Responses to a questionnaire about Lenin circulated by James Montgomery, a student at the University of Essex, 1992.
64. *Independent* (11 February 1994), p. 12.
65. In July 1993, on the anniversary of the Tsar's death, after a memorial service at which the heir to the Romanov throne, Prince Georgii Romanov, was present, Cossacks and monarchists tried to fell a statue of Sverdlov in Ekaterinburg, but were foiled by the police.
66. *SWB*, SU/1687 (31 May 1993), p. i. A television serial about Rasputin is to be filmed in Moscow: *SWB*, SU /1718 (18 June 1993), p. ii.
67. V. Topolyanskii, 'Kto strelyal v Lenina?', *LG* (10 November 1993), p. 12.
68. A new book on sale in Moscow in December 1992 was C. Andrew and O. Gordievskii, *KGB* (first published London, 1990).
69. E. Rzhevskaya, 'Goebbels. Portret na fone dnevnika', *NM*, (1993) nos 2–3.
70. V. Shoklina, *NG* (8 May 1993), p. 2.
71. See, for example, T. Ivanova, 'Kto chem riskuet', *Ogonek*, no. 24 (1988), p. 12; A. Rybakov, 'U menya net drugogo vykhoda...', *DN*, no. 9, (1989), p. 264.
72. *Mir mnenii i mneniya o mire*, no. 3 (1993), p. 1.
73. *Glasnost'*, 1990, no. 22, p. 4; *Dialog*, no. 5 (1990), pp. 4–7. *Argumenty i fakty*, no. 39 (1991), p. 1. For demonstrations to mark Lenin's birthday in 1994, see *Independent* (22 January 1994), p. 10.
74. See, for example, V. Bushin, 'Kogda somnenie umestno', *NS*, no. 4 (1989), pp. 171–86.
75. For a distorted view of the role of the Jews in Russian history, see V. Belov, *Vse vperedi* (M., 1987); *God velikogo pereloma, NM*, no. 3 (1989); nos 3, 4 (1991); for the 'Jewish–Masonic conspiracy', see V. Shafarevich, *Russofobiya, NS*, nos 6, 11 (1989).
76. Yu. Nagibin, *LG* (9 December 1992), p. 4; Natal'ya Ivanova, talk at St Antony's College, June 1993; discussions in 1992–3 with Petersburg writer and anti-fascist campaigner Nina Katerli.
77. See R. Marsh, '"Alternative literature" in Russia: an interview with Mikhail Berg', *Rusistika*, no. 4 (December 1991), pp. 16–18; discussions with Petersburg poet Elena Chizhova.
78. *Istoricheskii archiv* and *Arkhivy Kremlya i Staroi Ploshchadi*; discussed in V. Rudnev, *Izvestiya* (26 January 1993), p. 6; 22 May 1993, p. 5.
79. Democrats attempted to counter Govorukhin's views, exploring the relevance of the 'Russian idea' for contemporary Russian politics: see the